AMERICAN INTERGOVERNMENTAL RELATIONS

AMERICAN INTERGOVERNMENTAL RELATIONS
FOUNDATIONS, PERSPECTIVES, AND ISSUES

Laurence J. O'Toole, Jr., editor
Auburn University

A division of Congressional Quarterly Inc.
1414 22nd Street N.W., Washington, D.C. 20037

Printed in the United States of America

Library of Congress, Cataloging in Publication Data

Main entry under title:

American intergovernmental relations.

Includes index.
1. Federal government—United States—Addresses, essays, lectures. 2. Intergovernmental fiscal relations—United States—Addresses, essays, lectures. 3. Federal-city relations—United States—Addresses, essays, lectures. I. O'Toole, Laurence J., 1948-

JK310.A48 1985	321.02'3'0973	85-12803

ISBN 0-87187-376-1

For Mary

CONTENTS

Part Three
Fiscal Aspects of Intergovernmental Relations   135

PREFACE

During the past generation, important developments in the practice of intergovernmental relations have been legion. These have included:
- the virtual explosion of the federal grant system—in terms of dollar amounts, number of programs, and complexity;
- the increase in participation and influence by bureaucrats in intergovernmental networks;
- the multiple efforts to manage and reform the system, especially by executives at the federal level, from Lyndon Johnson to Richard Nixon (for example, through direct federal-local ties, revenue sharing, block grants, federal administrative decentralization, and new varieties of intergovernmental regulation);
- the increased interdependence faced by officials at all levels of government;
- the difficulties governments have had to grapple with in the last decade—recession, inflation, taxpayer revolts, and retrenchment—when the fiscal condition of governments, and thus their political viability, has been threatened;
- the increasing perception on the part of political executives and some scholars that the American intergovernmental network is "overloaded," coupled with the growing recognition by many state and local officials, as well as interest groups and citizens, that they are being asked to bear the brunt of any efforts to simplify and rationalize the arrangement (by absorbing cutbacks, reorganizing programs, and weathering the ensuing political controversy).

Today, the American intergovernmental system is under challenge. Yet the contemporary debates have not been unanticipated. In fact, part of the idea behind the experiment with a federal system that the founders introduced two centuries ago was to establish an adaptable structure within which issue-specific disputes could occur and competing values could be engaged. Since then the framework has indeed dramatically altered, under forces of political, economic, and social modernization. These pressures have resulted in tremendously increased complexity and interdependence for all participants, whose multiple interconnections have made bargaining a fact of life.

With the importance attached to intergovernmental issues by President Reagan, especially during his first term in office, the field has now acquired unprecedented prominence, ferment, and vitality. Many analyses have been performed, and much has been written about the issues; however, there is currently in print no general collection of readings on the subject. *American Intergovernmental Relations* is intended to fill this gap.

The book is designed for use as either a main or a supplementary text in up-

per-division undergraduate and graduate courses on federalism and intergovernmental relations. Students of state and local government and politics should also
find the collection useful.

The readings themselves have been chosen to blend classic expositions with
discussions of contemporary findings and issues. To provide a broad survey of the
American intergovernmental system's foundations, perspectives, and issues—and
in so doing to document the themes of complexity and interdependence—this book
contains selections from many of the most important, enduring, and often
controversial documents on intergovernmental relations. Criteria for selection of
the individual articles have been their importance to the field, their fit with other
pieces and with the themes of the book, and their contrasting perspectives.

Part One explores the roots of today's American intergovernmental system.
Readings cover the ideas behind the original federal bargain, the classic
interpretations of how the system has developed (with an emphasis on cooperation
and conflict between governments), and some important theoretical perspectives
on the modern system.

Parts Two through Four explore the operations of contemporary American
intergovernmental relations along the related dimensions of politics, finance, and
administration. Each part highlights, explicitly or implicitly, the importance of
complexity and interdependence, and the predictable tensions within and across
governmental units. Readings include both analyses of the system as a whole (for
example, its fiscal aspects) and explorations of the perspectives and activities of
specific participants (such as mayors or governors).

Part Two opens with readings on the ambivalence Americans express about
the workings of their intergovernmental system and then considers the ways
political influence is distributed and utilized in the network. Additional readings
explore the strategies, tactics, and behaviors of some of the participants as they
engage in intergovernmental politics.

Part Three covers the primary resource used to forge links and exert
pressure—money. Readings explore the scale and types of intergovernmental
fiscal interdependence, the federal government's use of various types of grants, the
effects—fiscal and otherwise—of Washington's use of grants for cities and general
revenue sharing as a mechanism to attack problems in a complex system.

Part Four examines administrative aspects of the system. Readings emphasize the importance of administrative behavior for explaining the operations of a
system this complex and interdependent and also illustrate the consequences each
participant in intergovernmental bargaining seeks, and seeks to avoid, in
administration. Administrative disputes (for example, during the implementation
phase of a program) are shown actually to reflect political disagreements.

Part Five contains readings on a selection of current issues. Each issue is explained from the various perspectives important in the contemporary intergovernmental debate and linked to the themes of complexity and interdependence which
are developed throughout the book.

Each part opens with some introductory explanations and concludes with a
set of discussion and study questions. These review questions are designed to help
readers test their understanding of the basic information contained in the
articles, and expand their knowledge by encouraging them to integrate different
readings.

The overall goal has been to give readers the opportunity to grapple with intergovernmental issues and to think coherently and independently about the subject of American intergovernmental relations.

Many people have helped during the preparation of this book. First, I thank the authors and publishers of the works excerpted or reprinted here for granting permission to include the fruits of their own labors. My colleague Gerard S. Gryski offered many useful suggestions and critiques from the earliest stages of the book's germination. Two other colleagues, John Heilman and Gerald W. Johnson, located a great deal of material on the privatization phenomenon reported in the last section of the book and helped educate me about its importance. Joanne Daniels, director of CQ Press, encouraged me to pursue this idea and facilitated the production of the manuscript; Carolyn McGovern at CQ Press edited the book with just the right blend of grace, nuance, and good humor. It has been a pleasure to work with such dedicated professionals. My secretary Virginia Prickett assisted with a great deal of the massive quantity of correspondence necessitated by such a project, while my graduate assistant, John D. Miller, Jr., helped with the editorial work and some of the permissions. I thank as well the reviewers for CQ Press, Arnold M. Howitt, who read the entire manuscript; Donald F. Kettl; and Jeremy F. Plant. Their suggestions were especially valuable in strengthening the set of readings selected. Finally, I offer heartfelt appreciation to my wife, Mary, and son, Conor, who not only endured but abetted yet another preoccupation.

L. J. O'T.
Auburn, Alabama
May 1985

AMERICAN INTERGOVERNMENTAL RELATIONS

AMERICAN INTERGOVERNMENTAL RELATIONS: AN OVERVIEW

Should the federal government assume the burdens of the nation's most costly social welfare programs? Who (if anyone) should take on the responsibility for America's financially troubled central cities? Should state governments be able to force localities to initiate new activities without providing the wherewithal to cover expenses? What happens when federal judges become involved in the operations of state or local programs, as with the administration of state hospitals or the busing of schoolchildren? Should policy makers be encouraging people and industry to move to the still-developing but economically vital regions of the South and West? Or should we be concerned that portions of the Snowbelt, with high taxes and high incidence of poverty, are losing jobs and capital to other nations and other regions of this country?

Should the federal government be heavily involved in the uniform and systematic enforcement of such important policies as ensuring citizens' civil rights? Alternatively, should Washington have *any* role in the operations of local police and fire departments? What about the supposedly massive quantity of regulation—on matters as diverse as environmental protection, financial procedures, and equal access for the handicapped—imposed by the federal government on state and local governments and by the states on their own cities and counties? Is it excessive? Necessary? Or perhaps even insufficient, given the national interest in ensuring that a number of worthy goals be achieved?

How should we handle problems that confront one region of the United States but surpass that locale's ability to cope? When a volcano wreaks havoc on the state of Washington, how should the rest of us respond? When a city like Miami or Los Angeles finds itself deluged with newly arrived Hispanics, many of them poor and illegal immigrants with language, medical, educational, economic, cultural, and other problems, who should have to face the issues and the difficult decisions that arise? All these and many more are topics of intergovernmental relations.

Intergovernmental relations is the subject of how our many and varied American governments deal with each other; and what their relative roles, responsibilities, and levels of influence are and should be. The subject is no flash-in-the-pan concern; it has generated longstanding interest throughout American political and administrative history.

In fact, the establishment of the United States was itself a sort of experiment in intergovernmental relations, since an effort to create a federal system like this one had never before been attempted. Nearly every major matter of domestic policy debated and decided throughout the nation's 200 years has been imbued with important intergovernmental aspects. Intergovernmental issues have contributed to such significant events in American history as the Civil War, the establishment of the social welfare state during the New Deal era, the attack on poverty in the 1960s, and the shifts of responsibilities to the states during the Reagan years.

But the subject is more than a collection of isolated issues. In fact, it would be difficult to make systematic sense of policy disputes like those mentioned above without first understanding the intergovernmental system per se—its historical development as well as its current structure. To prepare for an exploration of current issues and disputes and to provide a context for the readings that follow, this chapter offers a brief overview of the intergovernmental system in the United States, emphasizing the federal government's role in the system's development.

Federalism, as we understand the term today, means a system of authority constitutionally apportioned between central and regional governments.[1] In the American system, the central or national government is often called the federal government; the regional governments are the states. The federal-state relationship is interdependent: neither can abolish the other and each must deal with the other. *Intergovernmental relations* is the more comprehensive term, including the full range of federal-state-local relations.

In the 1980s there are approximately 80,000 American governments—one national, 50 state, and the rest local. The latter consist of several distinct types. *Counties,* numbering some 3,000 units, are general-purpose governments originally created throughout most of the country to administer state services at the local level. Today, counties are genuine local governments providing an array of services to their citizens, and many—especially the larger, more urban ones—are increasingly involved in complex intergovernmental arrangements with other local jurisdictions, states, and the national government. *Municipalities,* numbering about 18,000, are local governments established to serve people within an area of concentrated population. The nation's largest cities and small villages alike are municipalities, although the types of powers they have and the services they offer may vary considerably. Municipalities are created to serve explicitly the interests of the local community. Through much of American history, municipalities have had extensive and often highly conflicting relationships with their "parent" states. Since the period of the New Deal in the 1930s and the rapid expansion of the intergovernmental system in the 1960s, municipalities—especially large cities—have dealt with Washington, as well, on many matters.

Other local governments include:

- *townships* (approximately 17,000), which are usually subdivisions of rural counties and are relatively unimportant except in some parts of New England and the mid-Atlantic states;
- *school districts* (15,000), which are separate governments established in many parts of the country to direct public school systems; and
- *special districts* (numbering 28,588 in a recent count), which are limited-purpose governments set up to handle one or perhaps a few public functions over a specially designated area.[2]

Special districts currently have responsibility for such activities as managing public housing; building and maintaining bridges, tunnels, and roads; supplying water and sewerage services to residents; assessing and regulating air quality in a region; and caring for the mass transportation needs of a metropolitan area. The creation of many of these districts over the years has been directly or indirectly encouraged by other governments—such as the states and Washington—which sought "coordinated" local action on one or another policy problem.

If given a chance to view their handiwork today, it is likely that the founders of this nation would find much to surprise them in the operations of American politics and government, especially in the intergovernmental aspects of the system. Yet intergovernmental developments over the past two centuries have been affected greatly by some fundamental choices consciously made by those early Americans.

The Founding and the Framework

The framers of the Constitution sought a way to combine the several states into a structure that would minimize "instability, injustice, and confusion," in the words of James Madison.[3] The founders were familiar with the arguments of political thinkers from earlier years, who claimed that government protective of individual rights had to be small-scale and had to cover a geographically limited jurisdiction. Yet their own experience suggested problems with such an arrangement. Under the Articles of Confederation, enacted after the Revolution, the 13 American states had agreed upon a formal arrangement that we now call a *confederation*.[4] The states were loosely joined for certain purposes, but their association fell far short of a real nation. The states retained almost all power, and the "united states" under the Articles found it virtually impossible to act with dispatch on matters of importance.

To solve this problem, the "federalists" of that period proposed to organize a nation able to act in a unified and central fashion for certain purposes. They argued that large republics, not small ones, were more likely to be able to prevent internal tyranny. However, they also suggested that the states themselves remain as independent governments with independent jurisdictions. In the absence of any such arrangement in the past, the new experiment in intergovernmental relations would have to develop out of the American experience.

The founders' construction of the new system virtually ensured continuing controversy about the respective roles of the national and state governments by creating sufficient ambiguity to leave many of the most important questions unresolved. As a result, later years were to see major changes in the nature of American intergovernmental relations under the influence of various political, economic, and social forces, while the basic framework remained constant.[5]

What does that framework actually stipulate? The Constitution seems to divide responsibilities between the two levels of government according to subject. Certain functions (for example, interstate commerce and national defense) are assigned to the national authorities, while many others (such as selection of presidential electors) are left to the states. Furthermore, and significantly, the states seem to have been given the advantage, since the Tenth Amendment in the Bill of Rights asserts that "the powers not delegated to the United States by the

Constitution, nor prohibited by it to the States, are reserved to the States respectively, or to the people."

Yet the explanation cannot end here, for the same Constitution provides contrasting cues. For instance, it also authorizes the national Congress to "provide for the . . . general Welfare" and to "make all Laws which shall be necessary and proper" for executing this and the other powers given to the legislature. What constitutes the general welfare, and which laws are necessary and proper, are inherently political questions. Thus, it should be no surprise that the answers adopted by different people and at different times have not been consistent. The founders established a framework in which American governments would have separate but not completely independent spheres. The different levels would find it both useful and necessary to engage in conflict and cooperation; neither would be willing or able to ignore the other.

The Idea of Dual Federalism

Even in the earliest decades of the nation's existence, this tension between the idea of *dual federalism* (that is, each of the two levels of government operating within its separate sphere without relying on the other for assistance or authorization), on the one hand, and ambiguous overlap, on the other, was evident.

The notion of dual federalism influenced the decisions of the nation's Supreme Court at least until the early decades of the twentieth century. Furthermore, during the 1800s various presidents sometimes vetoed legislation that would have created a federal presence in policy fields such as public works construction, on the grounds that the Constitution simply did not permit such national involvement in arenas reserved for the states.[6] In fact, in a number of fields, like education and social policy, dual federalism was the predominant view of federal-state intergovernmental relations.

Conflict and Cooperation in Earlier Times

Yet neither sphere was completely independent, even in the early years. Throughout the nineteenth century, for instance, the national government and the states often disagreed about the limits of their own authority. The Civil War is perhaps the prime example, but conflict occurred on other matters as well, such as policy on labor, social welfare, and economic regulation. Through the necessity of resolving jurisdictional disputes, therefore, the federal and state governments found it necessary to recognize their interdependence.

Conflict, however, was not the only stimulus for interaction. As various policy problems captured the attention of the nation's officials and citizenry, federal and state governments were sometimes able to piece together intergovernmental mechanisms to allow for pragmatic adaptation to immediate concerns. For instance, if some early national and state leaders viewed direct federal aid for internal improvements (for example, road and canal construction) as a violation of constitutional restrictions on intergovernmental arrangements, the governments *were* able to agree to cooperate in the formation of *joint stock companies,* part public and part private entities created to surmount the restrictions on direct participation by the national government. (Governments and private businesses could buy stock in a company and appoint members to its board of directors, thus indirectly supporting and influencing its operations.)[7]

Another mechanism for cooperation during the previous century, before the dramatically increased intergovernmental interdependence of recent years, was the *land grant*. Through this device, the federal government would offer some of its land (it owned plenty) to the states for specified purposes. The recipient government would be obliged to abide by certain federal requirements, but direct involvement by the national government was minimal. Land grants were intended to help achieve goals in the fields of education, economic development, and (on a very limited scale) social welfare.

Other forms of intergovernmental cooperation—for instance, technical assistance from federal to state governments and informal exchanges and loans of expert personnel during peak or crisis periods—were relatively common occurrences even during the nation's first century. Nevertheless, it was not until the twentieth century that the dual federal perspective declined appreciably in significance and American intergovernmental relations developed into a system with sustained high levels of *complexity* and *interdependence*. Several political, economic, and social events and trends fueled these developments.

Developments in the Early Twentieth Century

From early in the present century until recent years, federal involvement, especially of a financial nature, in intergovernmental relations escalated. The Progressive Era near the turn of the century saw a political impetus for an expanded role for government in general, as reformers argued that the society and the economy could not tolerate laissez faire. The concentration of power in large corporations, the reluctance of some state governments to enact regulatory and other social welfare legislation (although other states were leaders in enacting farsighted and sometimes tough policy on such subjects), and the dawning recognition that the nation's natural resources were limited and would have to be conserved—all these encouraged an expanded domestic policy role for Washington. This shift was also encouraged in many cases by the newly developing and professionalizing state bureaucracies, which saw in federal involvement opportunities for upgrading and for expanded funding; and by some interest groups that had been pushing at the state level for public attention to one problem or another. (Then, as now, organized interests—whether concerned with expanded highway construction or social services—have recognized that it is usually easier and more effective to deal with one central government on such matters than with scores of divergent ones throughout the states.)

The growing national will to attempt action in new arenas was followed by the central government's acquiring the practical wherewithal for action. The resources needed were money and clear authority; by the 1920s both had been generated.

Federal Financial Aid

In 1913 the U.S. Constitution was amended to permit the enactment of a federal income tax. Previously the national government had provided some limited financial support to the states, but the intergovernmental fiscal ties were few and far between. However, from the passage of the Sixteenth Amendment until very recently, the national government has been able to raise revenue more easily than have other American governments. The income tax, which was "elastic" (that is, its receipts increased faster than the economy during periods of growth), has been a more politically palatable revenue source than other sources typically emphasized by the states and local governments. (This situation has altered in two respects in recent years. First, the income tax increased its bite from individuals' paychecks during the periods of rapid inflation in the 1970s, resulting in a decline in its popularity and the enactment of an indexing provision to control the effects of inflation. Second, most states and even some local governments enacted income taxes of their own.) Thus, with the income tax the federal government created a source of money that could be tapped repeatedly to fill needs that had not yet received the wholehearted attention of the states.

The obvious mechanism of intergovernmental cooperation in many such cases was the *grant-in-aid*. By 1920 there were 11 grants-in-aid operating in the United States. Land grants and other varieties of intergovernmental assistance were never again to outstrip cash grants in importance. Because of the significance of grants-in-aid and because of their sustained use in the early twentieth century, it is useful to explain at this point some of the basic implications of this kind of federal program.

A grant-in-aid is a transfer of funds from one government to another for some specified purpose. Typically the recipient government is asked by the donor to abide by certain terms as conditions of the assistance.[8] These usually include a requirement that the recipient unit match the donor's financial contribution with one of its own, as well as a series of "strings," or stipulations as to how the funds will be utilized, how the program created by the grant will be managed, and how the recipient government will report to the donor.

Starting on a small scale early in this century, and then expanding rapidly during certain periods—especially the New Deal and Great Society eras—grants-in-aid from the federal government to the states and eventually local governments became extremely important features of the intergovernmental system in the United States. States too have provided financial support to their local governments. (In 1982 total state aid amounted to $97 billion. This total includes some federal aid passed to the local units through the states.)[9] But federal aid, because of its size, relative newness, and capacity to produce large-scale alterations in the intergovernmental system, may be considered an especially significant feature of America's fiscal federalism. Table 1 displays the quantity of federal aid disbursed through grants-in-aid to state and local governments since 1900.

Validation of Grants-in-Aid

As the national government began to exercise influence through the use of grants-in-aid in the early 1900s, some observers questioned whether the grant mechanism really amounted to an unconstitutional intrusion by federal authorities into the affairs of the states. Armed with the doctrine of dual federalism, critics of federal grants argued that Washington's offers were actually coercive inducements and violated the notion of separate spheres for these two levels of government. In a pair of landmark decisions in 1923 the Supreme Court ruled on the issues involved, thus paving the way for major expansions in the grant system—and for tremendously increased complexity and interdependence among

Table 1   Federal Aid to State and Local Government, Selected Years

Year	Amount (Billions)[a]	Number of Grants
1902	$ .028	5
1912	—	7
1913	.039	—
1920	—	11
1922	.242	—
1932	.593	12
1934	2.4	—
1937	—	26
1940	2.1	—
1946	—	28
1952	3.1	38
1960	7.0	—
1964	10.1	51
1967	15.2	379
1971	28.1	530
1974	43.4	550
1977	68.4	—
1980	91.5	—
1981	—	539
1982	—	441
1983	—	409
1984	97.8 (est.)	—

[a] 1961 dollars through 1952; otherwise, current dollars.

SOURCE: Advisory Commission on Intergovernmental Relations, *The Federal Role in the Federal System: The Dynamics of Growth—A Crisis of Confidence and Competence* (Washington, D.C.: ACIR, July 1980), pp. 120-121; and *Significant Features of Fiscal Federalism, 1982-83 Edition* (Washington, D.C.: ACIR, January 1984), p. 120.

levels of government—in succeeding years. The Court asserted that grants were voluntary arrangements and thus the federal government was not violating the constitutionally established separation of functions in the federal system.[10] As the years elapsed, the grant system became a dominant feature of the American intergovernmental system, as it tied thousands of governments intricately together.

Basic Types of Assistance

Grants have offered the opportunity for substantially expanded federal influence over state and local governments, and a number of important political and administrative consequences flow from this fact. Yet it is essential to recognize that while grants create chances for national involvement, they do not vitiate the intergovernmental system—or at least not necessarily. Grants have developed as the prime instruments used to promote bargaining and jockeying for advantage among governments; they are tools that have frequently stimulated simultaneous cooperation and conflict among such governments, and thus it should be no surprise that the system of intergovernmental aid employed in this country has elicited ambivalent evaluations from participants and citizens alike.

Grants may come in many shapes and sizes. The donor government may structure the purpose quite narrowly, for example, offering aid for construction of a sewage treatment plant. Such *categorical grants* were typical in the early part of this century. The donor may also design an intergovernmental program for a variety of purposes within a broad field such as education, community development, or social services. This type of aid, called a *block grant,* has gained some prominence more recently. In the early 1970s a new form of aid, *revenue sharing*, was created to enable one government to offer financial aid to another with virtually no restrictions as to its use.

All of these types of intergovernmental assistance require some rules and regulations regarding the method of distributing the aid. How is a unit selected to receive assistance and how much is it entitled to? Some grants, including all federal block grants, specify a precise formula in the legislation creating the program. Such *formula grants* include quantifiable elements, such as population, tax effort, proportion of population unemployed or below poverty level, housing density, or infant mortality rate. The specified formula is a rule that tells potential recipient governments precisely how they can calculate the quantity of aid to which they are entitled under the provisions of the law, so long as the recipient qualifies for such assistance under the other stipulations of the program. Usually, although not always, the elements in a formula are chosen to reflect characteristics related to the purpose of the aid (for example, number of school-age children for an education grant, age and/or density of residential housing for housing assistance). The factors included are also likely to have political significance, since there is no such thing as a "neutral" formula; all formulas reward some states or localities more than others, depending upon their relative standing given the formula specified.

However, another method of distributing aid is possible. *Project grants* allocate funding on a competitive basis, with potential recipients lacking advance knowledge about the size of the grant. Instead, the authorizing legislation typically indicates the sorts of jurisdictions that are eligible to apply for aid and the criteria that will be employed to judge the merit of a government's application. Whether or not a government then receives funding depends upon how strong a case it can make in its own behalf. Bureaucrats in the federal departments that supply aid determine the relative worthiness of different proposals and different jurisdictions, often by means of a detailed decision-making and evaluation system.

Why bother to make these distinctions among types of aid? The answer is that different types of grants have tended to produce different types of relationships between and among the participating governments. Much of the intergovernmental system during this century can be rendered intelligible by analyzing the consequences of different types of aid, the subject of the remainder of this chapter.

The Legacy of the New Deal

Most of the grant-in-aid programs developed by the national government in the early decades of the 1900s were restricted to relatively limited purposes. They assisted primarily in fields that commanded strong political support, such as agriculture and road construction. Federal assistance, and thus national influence, was directed almost entirely toward the states, rather than local governments. During this period, and in fact until the 1960s, the system of intergovernmental aid was dominated by categorical formula grants. For the first part of the century, these were accompanied by relatively few strings, required considerable matching on the part of the recipients, and were few enough in number that they did not seem to impose much of an administrative or political burden on the states.

With the New Deal in the 1930s the federal government under the leadership of President Franklin D. Roosevelt tackled the challenging economic and social problems of the depression era. Although it would have been technically possible to establish new national-level programs to cope with the difficulties of the period, the more politically palatable method of the grant-in-aid was used repeatedly instead. Thus, while the national government's role expanded, the states and local governments retained significant leverage. Within a two-year period, categorical grants were established in such a variety of fields that they became the foundation for the social welfare state in America. The first real forms of assistance to some of the nation's local governments, the cities, were initiated during this period as well. For the states and some of their local governments, then, national authorities were no longer distant or sporadically communicating entities. Instead, in many areas of domestic policy, two or three levels of government were tied together in intricate patterns of intergovernmental relations—much like a "marble cake," rather than a "layer cake" of dual federalism.[11]

Thus, the New Deal period witnessed a permanent increase in the density and importance of intergovernmental relationships in the United States, and indeed during the next couple of decades—even during the administration of Republican president Dwight Eisenhower—the number of federal programs and quantity of federal aid continued to grow. Eisenhower himself was uncomfortable with the apparently prominent role of the national government in domestic policy matters, and he established the Commission on Intergovernmental Relations with the explicit charge to identify areas of federal involvement that could feasibly be "returned" to the states. But even the very modest suggestions of this commission went unimplemented. It seemed during the 1950s, as it has often seemed since then, that the idea of separating functions by level of government was supported in the abstract, but was exceedingly difficult to execute. Concerted efforts to reduce the levels of complexity and interdependence in the intergovernmental system have, until very recently, been singularly unsuccessful.

The difficulty American governments experience when they attempt to find ways to reduce their reliance on one another is not surprising. Since the New Deal period, citizens and public officials have tried to harness the national government's tremendous resources in order to attack pressing problems and redress inequities. They have at the same time attempted to retain diversity and experimentalism through vital state and local governments wherever possible. Shifting to some form of dual federalism, with a much less intense pattern of relationships and dependencies among our governmental units, could affect federal commitments in a multitude of important policy areas—for instance, environmental protection, civil rights, income security, and education. Furthermore, such a change might entail radical shifts in the nation's tax system. And even the most carefully considered plans would have to face bewildering dilemmas about how to reduce intergovernmental interdependence without inflicting serious inequities on some states and localities.

These days, when, as in the 1950s, one hears so much about the need to limit the federal role in the intergovernmental system and simplify the pattern of American governments, such caveats are useful to keep in mind. It may even be asserted that creating a radically simplified intergovernmental arrangement by moving the national government out of a direct role in many important policy arenas is not a practical or responsible option. Why, then, are there so many suggestions for reform of the system? Why do so many policy makers and intergovernmental experts complain about the "overloaded" pattern?[12] Later in this book, the considerable legitimacy of a number of the criticisms will become clear. Focusing on the major developments affecting the intergovernmental system since the 1960s will be useful in understanding this controversy.

From Creative Federalism to the Reagan Era

With Lyndon Johnson's presidency and the election of a heavily Democratic and activist Congress in 1964, a several-year period of tremendously expanded intergovernmental activities and initiatives began. Johnson proposed a "creative federalism" that would signify multiple new national commitments to assist states, localities, and private individuals and organizations in their efforts to solve many of the domestic difficulties afflicting the society. These efforts of the Johnson era were directed primarily at problems of racial discrimination, poverty, and urban and rural development. The president and the Congress responded not just with rhetoric but with hundreds of intergovernmental programs.

One count placed the number of federal programs of grant-in-aid at 51 in 1964. In 1967 there were 379 (see Table 1). Almost all of the new programs from Washington were categorical grants, and—unlike earlier times—most of them were project grants. By the late 1960s most of the grants available were project grants, although many of these were relatively small in size and in toto the project grants constituted a minority of the aid dollars. In addition to these departures, the amount of support aimed directly at local governments rose sharply. Many localities (especially the nation's older, larger, more fiscally strapped cities) came to consider the federal government more of an ally than their own state governments and found themselves increasingly reliant on federal largesse.

The results of these and other massive changes in the intergovernmental system enacted in such a compressed period were, as might be expected, mixed.

Some Consequences of an Expanded System

In many respects the consequences of this major increase in intergovernmental activity were impressive. Although hampered by fiscal constraints, especially as the war in Southeast Asia drained its resources, the nation made measurable progress in attacking a number of troubling problems.[13] The dramatic increase in federal support was especially welcome to many state and local governments, which had difficulty obtaining the resources to fund programs demanded by their citizenry; also, the emphasis on a variety of project grants meant that potential recipients could find appropriately targeted programs.

The explosion in the grants system had the further effect of encouraging or mandating the professionalization of personnel and the use of up-to-date financial procedures in the administrative agencies handling the programs in the recipient units. Intergovernmental programs became increasingly influenced by functional specialists at all levels of government. The requirements attached to many of the new grants also forced states and localities to devote renewed attention to public problems they may have overlooked in the past.

Another trend that was fueled by creative federalism was the growing presence and influence in the nation's capital of interest groups, especially intergovernmental groups. Those concerned with specific intergovernmental programs, whether on environmental pollution or juvenile delinquency, increasingly looked to Washington as they tried to influence legislation and implementing regulations, to monitor the actions of the federal agency involved, and to maintain contact with other interested parties. The tremendous expansion of the grants system in the 1960s was both a result of and a stimulus for an increase in the number of such interest groups operating at the national level in intergovernmental politics. These changes, too, contributed to the growing complexity of intergovernmental policy making.

These sorts of interest groups were not the only ones to achieve a heightened national presence. As the grants process became ever more important and the system increasingly more complex, officials of state and local governments found it crucial to acquire information about the process in Washington and the decisions being made. Furthermore, state and local officials began to realize that their own interests might deserve representation in the national-level policy process. Accordingly, several groups of state or local general-purpose officials organized for the first time, moved the center of their operations to Washington, or upgraded their staff and expanded their activities on a national scale. These groups, including entities like the National Governors' Association, the Council of State Governments, and the U.S. Conference of Mayors, refer to themselves as public interest groups or *PIGs*. By the 1960s they became increasingly recognized as leaders in the representation of state and local interests in national policy making. In addition to the governments that began to locate offices and representatives in Washington, other more functionally specialized groups of state and local officials, such as highway officials, budget officers, and social workers, have organized into national groups and participate in the policy process. Nowadays, any discussion of an intergovernmental issue in Congress or an administrative agency is likely to elicit concern, participation, lobbying, and debate involving many such organizations.

Thus the major activities of the Johnson era encouraged several salutary developments and the further elaboration of other interesting trends. Yet, as might be expected when such massive changes are effected, there were also difficulties and tensions.

Frustrations and Tensions in the Modern System

The almost limitless choices made available to state and local officials by the tremendous increase in the number of intergovernmental programs also meant that the potential recipients could afford to "shop around" among programs and federal agencies to bargain for the most favorable deal. As a result of the interagency competition for clients, federal policy in a program would sometimes be loosely enforced. Recipients were more and more able to evade federal intent while absorbing federal dollars.

Conversely, the system with huge numbers of partially overlapping (and often project-duplicating) grants created vexing difficulties for officials at state and local levels. With several related programs available to assist a city in such tasks as rebuilding its sewers, a great deal of time, effort, and information went into deciding which program(s) to pursue. Grants established ostensibly for the same purpose might be housed in different federal agencies, require entirely different application and approval processes, stipulate very different matching requirements, and be implemented with conflicting schedules. Furthermore, as potential recipients of project grants scrambled to complete detailed applications for scores of grant requests on short notice, the winners were not necessarily the most competent or the most needy jurisdictions. Instead, "grantsmanship" (the ability to package proposals in the most salable fashion) was often rewarded.

Another set of tensions was generated for state and local governments by the systemic changes. Because there were now so many programs and because, in contrast to earlier periods, many of the newer grants were constructed with high matching ratios (that is, Washington would pay for most of the total expenses incurred under the program), it became increasingly difficult for state and local governments either to abstain from commitments to federal aid or to make such commitments wholeheartedly. The effect of a donor government's offering a grant is to lower the cost of the good or service provided for the potential recipient and thus to render it more attractive. However, when the number of individually appealing programs multiplies greatly, the consequence may be significant distortion in the recipient's own budget choices. Instead of spending its locally generated revenue on the public services judged most important by its own officials and citizens, then, a city may be encouraged to utilize a substantial portion as matching funds for programs that are, in essence, national priorities. The expansion of the aid system in the 1960s prompted complaints on this score from uneasy mayors, governors, and others who were concerned about their apparently declining ability to maintain some independence.

Such general-purpose officials had other concerns as well. Many of them believed the expanded system of categorical grants was composed of unduly narrow programs that were not easily adaptable to the needs in their own jurisdictions. Furthermore, the pattern, taken as a whole, had become so complex that it was all but impenetrable to generalists. In fact, these officials had a difficult time even discovering just how much aid was being received from federal sources. And many of the important, detailed decisions that are made as part of an intergovernmental grant bargain—for instance, determining the eligibility of clients for programs or establishing goals—were made far from the presence of the general-purpose officials. Increasingly important in the intergovernmental policy process was a great number of specialists across governmental levels—especially in administrative agencies charged with executing the program, legislative committees with responsibility for the substantive area, and pressure groups with a strong interest in the program. Intergovernmental experts, particularly those concerned about the decreasing ability of general officials to oversee and direct activities across this maze, dubbed these policy networks *vertical functional autocracies*.

In these chains of influence, it became increasingly difficult for anyone, even major officials like governors or mayors or presidents, to decipher just *who* was causing *what* to happen intergovernmentally. When responsibility is so diffused, the mechanisms of democratic government cannot readily ensure that policy reflects the will of the people or the people's representatives. In other words, another possible cost of such an arrangement is a decline in political responsiveness.

If one considers further the consequences of the development of such a dense intergovernmental pattern, additional questions emerge; and these, too, have plagued officials from the 1960s to the present day. In the pattern described here, it is difficult for actors in the system to make rational decisions to benefit the individuals or activities for which they have responsibility. It is also difficult to design any coherent change in the system itself. These problems stem directly from the dominant characteristics of the intergovernmental system: its complexity and its interdependence. This exploration of the range and difficulty of the issues prepares for more precise definitions of these two concepts.

Complexity means that the intergovernmental network is large and differentiated; no one participant can possibly possess enough information about its components and dynamics to operate in a consistently rational fashion. *Interdependence* means that intergovernmental relations exhibit an amalgamated pluralism: power is shared among branches and layers of government, even within functions, so that—rather than one level's consistently exercising dominant influence—nearly any action requires support from others. No one is in control of the system itself, and unanticipated consequences are a normal fact of life.

Especially since the era of creative federalism, but also as a consequence of the general framework established by the founders, many participants in the intergovernmental system have plenty of opportunities to exercise influence, particularly to delay or frustrate action to which they are opposed. However, it is much the more difficult to generate and systematically execute *positive* action in a rational fashion.

There are, in addition, less abstract implications of the present intergovernmental system. Tremendous increases in red tape have been a natural corollary. The federal government has usually viewed the requirements it imposes as essential to ensure a program's integrity. Yet recipient units claim that the burdens have become excessive. (Localities also blame the states in part for their red tape burden.) The number of federally created intergovernmental mandates has escalated sharply within the last 10 years and has become, perhaps, the bête noire of state and local officials.

Two general points emerge. First, the problems and tensions in the system are not primarily the product of ill will or ignorance, nor can they be traced primarily to one level of government. Rather, the American intergovernmental system was founded on ambivalent principles and built to establish arenas for conflict and controversy. A second and related point is that changing the particular pattern of intergovernmental relationships or reforming certain aspects of the system—for example, through the enactment of shifts such as Ronald Reagan proposed in the early 1980s—would have important consequences but could hardly put to rest the value conflicts of a complex and interdependent system.

At this point, it will be helpful to touch upon some of the developments in the American intergovernmental system since the period of creative federalism. Many of these are made comprehensible by an awareness of the difficulties just surveyed, and many, in turn, presage some of the topics of current interest and controversy.

Nixon's New Federalism

A number of the difficulties outlined above were obvious by the close of the Johnson administration. Richard Nixon reacted to the tensions in the changing system by proposing reforms ostensibly aimed at increasing the influence of general-purpose (especially elected) officials at all levels, shifting power away from Washington and toward federal field offices and state and local governments, reducing the control exercised by functional specialists, and trimming intergovernmental red tape. (This direction was maintained, though with somewhat diminished effort and effectiveness, by his successor, Gerald Ford.) Nixon's efforts were undoubtedly fueled also by a desire to shift policy away from the social activism of the Johnson years.

Of what, exactly, did Nixon's "new federalism" consist? He proposed a series of initiatives: revenue sharing, block grants, and administrative proposals.

1. *Revenue sharing.* One of Nixon's most ambitious suggestions was the establishment of a program of revenue sharing from the federal level to state and local governments. Revenue sharing (also called "general revenue sharing") had acquired a certain currency for several reasons: it seemed to meet the demands of state and local governments for more discretion, it was attractive to the most financially hard-pressed jurisdictions, it could shift some influence to the general-purpose elected officials and away from the functional specialists in state and local governments, and (for those, like Nixon, who were looking for politically acceptable mechanisms of reducing categorical support) it might permit the simultaneous trimming of more narrowly targeted programs. In 1972 the State and Local Fiscal Assistance Act was passed with the support of much of the Democratic leadership in Congress and of the major PIGs of state and local officials. This law established a revenue sharing program of approximately $6 billion per year for five years. All state governments and all general-purpose local governments were eligible for aid, which was to be allocated on the basis of complicated formulas. The program was extended, with modifications, in 1976; in 1980, and again later in 1984, the U.S. revenue sharing program was reenacted, although the states were eliminated from participation as the federal budget tightened in the later years. Revenue sharing has provided help to many governments (too many, in the view of observers who thought aid should be targeted more carefully to needy jurisdictions) but has remained, at most, only a small fraction of total federal assistance for the larger recipient governments.

2. *Block grants.* Another major proposal that would have a significant effect on the intergovernmental system did not originate with Nixon, although the idea is most closely identified with him. Block grants began during the Johnson administration, as intergovernmental analysts searched for mechanisms to alleviate some of the problems discussed above. Before the Nixon era, two block grants (one in health care, one in law enforcement) were created. Each was formed by combining a series of closely related categorical grants into a broader, formula-

based package. Nixon then suggested a series of enactments in six policy sectors. These stimulated considerably more antagonism than did the general revenue sharing proposal. Defenders of the categoricals, including members of the vertical functional autocracies, resisted; their concerns would have no statutory protection once a block grant was put into place. Although the general-purpose officials at the state and local levels were favorably inclined toward the *idea* of block grants, they were skeptical of some of the Nixon proposals, which would have reduced the overall level of intergovernmental funding. Ultimately, only three additional block grants emerged from this period: in employment, social services, and community development. Yet some of these programs have had a major impact on intergovernmental affairs, and they have been followed by additional block grants enacted during the Reagan years.

3. *Administrative initiatives.* Nixon encouraged the implementation of administrative reforms. The President supported a series of efforts to alter the grant application and review process. For instance, by both legislation and executive order, potential recipient governments were allowed to expedite their applications by combining several related requests, chief executives in certain cities were granted increased discretion over the uses for some categorical funds, and a number of donor agencies reduced their decision-making time. The emphasis on block grants was also designed in part to relieve administrative burdens. However, some of these alterations were temporary palliatives. The strength of the political forces responsible for the development of categorical programs has meant that block grants established with few restrictions tend over time to acquire more.

Despite all the changes mentioned here, the intergovernmental system was not radically altered. For one thing, the more traditional mechanism of the categorical grant was by no means disused. In fact, the number of such programs and amount of aid increased even through the Nixon years (see Table 1). For another, the return to a reliance upon formula-based grants reduced certain difficulties (for example, year-to-year funding uncertainties at the recipient level) but exacerbated others (such as interregional and interjurisdictional tensions, since the nature of a formula would fix in legislation a set of clear winners and losers). Also, administrative and regulatory difficulties in the system proved to be more tenacious than many had anticipated.

In short, despite the many changes, at the end of the Nixon-Ford period the intergovernmental system was larger than ever, remained impressively complex and interdependent, and continued to face criticism from nearly all perspectives.

The Carter Period

President Jimmy Carter was not the activist in intergovernmental matters that Nixon was—or, for that matter, that Carter's successor was. But, as a former governor familiar with the concerns of general political executives and of state and local units, Carter worked at developing communication links with the PIGs and with state and local governments, tried to advance some of the administrative reforms from the Nixon-Ford years, and paid special attention to economic problems facing the nation's urban areas. For instance, he stimulated passage of the Urban Development Action Grant (UDAG) program during a severe economic recession in the late 1970s.

Yet Carter proposed no overall plan for reform of the system, nor did he recommend any major changes in the pattern of intergovernmental aid. Two developments in the late 1970s, in fact, exacerbated some of the difficulties faced by policy makers and managers. First, a combination of sour economic conditions, increasing federal budget difficulties, and Carter's fundamentally conservative fiscal instincts placed stringent limits on any efforts to increase federal aid. Federal spending increases slowed and then in 1980 reversed direction. Yet the tensions that had come to mark the modern period of intergovernmental relations were, if anything, increased; for federal aid was being limited at a time when many units of government had come to depend on it. Second, during this period of strained resources, the federal government, especially Congress, did not easily loosen its hold on other units of government; instead, Washington sought to accomplish its intergovernmental goals via direct requirements, frequently including some that were mandated across many different programs. Carter was not the prime advocate of this form of intergovernmental regulation—in fact, he typically sought deregulation—but he did consent to the addition of significant new requirements in a number of programs.

Reagan's Attempted Revolution

The first part of Ronald Reagan's term in office saw perhaps the most systematic, if not the most sustained, effort to remake the American intergovernmental system since the New Deal period. Reagan, like Carter, had served as a governor and understood some of the consequences of complexity and interdependence for many participants in the intergovernmental network. However, unlike Carter, he believed that the United States had been created as a system in which national powers and jurisdiction would be severely limited, and in which the strongest, most vital governments, those with the broadest jurisdiction over domestic matters, were to be the states.

As a major part of his program early in the first term, Reagan offered several ideas for a massive restructuring of the intergovernmental system. In brief, Reagan's proposals, for which he adopted Nixon's term, the "new federalism," were as follows:

1. *An additional series of block grants.* In his first year in office, Reagan proposed that more than 100 categoricals be combined into a handful of broadly based block grants with very few regulations. Congress complied with several of these initiatives.

2. *A dramatic simplification of the system of intergovernmental aid.* Program responsibilities were to be shifted to single levels of government and away from the "marble cake" intergovernmental configurations. Despite Reagan's backing, the plan attracted only spotty support among the PIGs and virtually none among the program advocates in the nation's vertical functional autocracies. Congress made no real move to approve the plan, and Reagan's attention was diverted from this contentious issue.

3. *A devolution of responsibilities for many policies from the national level to the states.* Reagan suggested that scores of intergovernmental programs involving federal participation, including most of the remaining expensive ones, be turned over to the states in their entirety and that an appropriate quantity of revenue be shifted to the states as well. No action was taken on this proposal.

4. *Administrative simplification.* The president worked to trim red tape and lighten the putative burden of federal mandates. In this regard, Reagan scored his "successes," as did his predecessors. Yet many complained about the abdication of federal responsibility for important national goals, and others felt the reforms did not go nearly far enough.

Reagan's efforts to fundamentally restructure the intergovernmental system were challenged not only by proponents of increased national authority and advocates of strong categorical initiatives. While the nation's governors and mayors were often delighted with the idea of reducing the red tape and mandate requirements, they could hardly have been expected to rejoice in other features of the Reagan program. For instance, the fact that Reagan accompanied his suggestions with significant budget reductions in many of the most important programs meant that he was presenting these officials with increased discretion at the time that the pie was shrinking. (The cutbacks in federal aid in the Reagan years were far more severe than what had been experienced under Carter.) Also, the president's proposals to trade responsibilities and devolve many programs created quite a stir. Urban leaders were concerned that the federal assistance they had been receiving would not continue if funding decisions were moved to state capitals. And many states and localities were convinced that they would ultimately be the financial and political losers following the sorting-out of governmental responsibilities. By the second half of Reagan's first term, the most ambitious proposals had been set aside in favor of further grouping of categorical programs into block grants. Even these suggestions encountered hostility or indifference in Congress.

Thus, despite some major alterations during the last several years, especially during the Reagan administration, the fundamental aspects of American intergovernmental relations, including the strengths, weaknesses, frustrations, and dilemmas of the pattern, have remained prominent.

There is no denying that the form of the system has changed considerably since the nation's founding. Political, economic, and social forces have stimulated major changes in the overall scope of governmental activity, in the mix of values that intergovernmental arrangements are meant to serve, in the relative influence of the different governments, and in their degree of reliance on one another. Far from preserving a simple, stratified pattern, the choices made centuries ago created opportunities for dramatic shifts toward complexity and interdependence in the intergovernmental network.

Notes

1. Thus the term *federal* has two meanings in contemporary usage. One refers to a system of governance that employs a constitutional partitioning of authority between central and regional units. The other use of the term is as a synonym for the national government. Both notions are employed in this chapter and in various readings throughout the book. The meaning should be clear from the context.

2. U.S. Bureau of the Census, *1982 Census of Governments*, vol. 1, *Governmental Organization* (Washington, D.C.: U.S. Government Printing Office, August 1983), p. vi.

3. Clinton Rossiter, ed., Federalist No. 10, *The Federalist Papers* (New York: New American Library, 1961), p. 77.

4. At the time, the term *federation* had a meaning close to that of *confederation* today. See Martin Diamond's essay in this volume. The meaning changed after the initiation of the American experiment in federated government.

5. The concepts of federalism (in the first sense mentioned in note 1) and intergovernmental relations are linked but not identical. The former refers to certain aspects of the dealings between national and regional governments, while the latter is meant to encompass relations among all governments within a nation. Intergovernmental relations are considerably affected but not completely determined by federalism. This book examines federalism but focuses broadly upon intergovernmental relations. Nevertheless, judicial aspects of intergovernmental relations, and interstate, interlocal, and state-local relations receive relatively less attention because of space limitations.

6. One example is Madison's veto of a bill to authorize construction of roads and canals in the states. See Daniel Elazar, *The American Partnership: Intergovernmental Co-operation in the Nineteenth Century* (Chicago: University of Chicago Press, 1962), p. 15.

7. Ibid.

8. The terms *recipient* and *donor* are borrowed from Jeffrey L. Pressman, *Federal Programs and City Politics* (Berkeley: University of California Press, 1975).

9. Advisory Commission on Intergovernmental Relations, *Significant Features of Fiscal Federalism, 1982-83 Edition* (Washington, D.C.: ACIR, January 1984), pp. 122-123.

10. The cases were *Massachusetts v. Mellon* and *Frothingham v. Mellon* 262 U.S. 447 (1923).

11. See Morton Grodzins's classic essay in Part One of this volume.

12. For example, David B. Walker, *Toward a Functioning Federalism* (Cambridge, Mass.: Winthrop, 1981).

13. See Norman Furniss and Timothy Tilton, *The Case for the Welfare State: From Social Security to Social Equality* (Bloomington: Indiana University Press, 1977).

Part One

HISTORICAL AND THEORETICAL PERSPECTIVES

The enormous number of American governments exhibit an impressive variety and complexity. A solid understanding of this rich intergovernmental world is best gained by learning something of the American historical context. Also helpful is an assimilation of some of the theoretical perspectives that have been used by experts in the field to analyze, explain, and predict intergovernmental events.

History and theory are not, of course, identical. Yet in the field of intergovernmental relations, the two have typically been closely linked. To clarify this point, it will be helpful first to define what is meant by *theory*. A theory is a coherent set of statements describing and explaining the relationships and underlying principles of some aspect of the world. A useful (although somewhat oversimplified) distinction may be made between two kinds of theory: normative theory, which seeks to explain and justify how the world *ought* to be, and empirical theory, which offers explanations and predictions for how some part of the world actually *is* or *will be*.

These two types of theory are directed at quite different goals. However, in the field of intergovernmental relations (and, typically, in analyses of the related topic of American federalism), efforts to explain an intergovernmental system are often simultaneously bound up with attempts to persuade others that certain forms of intergovernmental relations are preferable. One obvious and understandable example was the attempt of the founders of the nation to design a basic framework and then persuade the public to accept it. Madison, Hamilton, and the others tried to construct powerful normative arguments in support of certain goals (such as the preservation of freedom), yet they also had to use empirical theories to help determine which governmental—and intergovernmental—structures were likely to result in the preferred outcomes. In other words, many intergovernmental theories have been both normative and empirical.

As was noted in the introductory chapter, there have been dramatic changes in intergovernmental relations—despite stability in the overall framework—during the course of American history. A clear understanding of these developments is essential for the following reasons: first, knowing the nature and significance of such changes can alert one to some of the most important features of the current system; second, history can suggest explanations for apparently haphazard or irrational intergovernmental patterns today; and third, because of the high normative content in many discussions of intergovernmental relations, modern debates and proposals often use historical justifications for courses of action. Thus, Lyndon Johnson and his advisers invoked intergovernmental history to explain and bolster some of their innovative notions of cooperation between and among governments; and, in contrary fashion, the administration of Ronald Reagan used historical events to explain and defend its efforts to move the nation closer to a dual federal structure.

The selections in Part One describe the historical evolution of intergovernmental relations and further explain its twofold theoretical aspects. The readings include a number of classic expositions with which any serious student of the subject should be familiar. As the reader will see, however, the experts are hardly in complete agreement on either history or theory.

The first selection is *The Federalist*, Number 39. *The Federalist* was actually a series of political tracts published as newspaper letters near the time that the Constitution was being considered for adoption. The papers, signed "Publius," were written by James Madison, Alexander Hamilton, and John Jay, three well-known supporters of the new Constitution, and were intended to persuade citizens to support the proposal. In the paper included here, Madison characterizes the American structure as one that combines national *and* federal characteristics. Despite the stilted eighteenth-century style of the language, the essay remains one of the most explicit discussions of what the founders had in mind. Pay particular attention to Madison's use of key terms, as well as to the nature of his argument in defense of the new American experiment in intergovernmental relations.

In the second selection, Martin Diamond explains what the founders were attempting to build and how they sought to justify the governmental structure. In this piece, he emphasizes the link between the founding and certain important values, such as liberty and the preservation of representative government.

Whereas the first two readings concentrate on the period of the founding and on the basic structure within which American intergovernmental relations would have to develop, the next three cover some important aspects of historical and modern intergovernmental relations in practice.

In a selection from his book *The American Partnership*, a study of intergovernmental relations in the nineteenth century, Daniel Elazar presents what is probably the most well known case that cooperation rather than conflict has marked intergovernmental affairs in this country throughout its history. Elazar points to the many pragmatic, cooperative arrangements from an earlier era, thus suggesting that theories based upon notions of dualism and conflict have never had empirical support. His essay also offers some explanation for how intergovernmental dynamics has stimulated the professionalization and development of bureaucracy in American government.

Elazar was a student of Morton Grodzins, whose essay excerpted here is perhaps the most widely quoted argument in intergovernmental relations. Employing the now-famous images of layer cakes and marble cakes, Grodzins provides apt descriptions of the intergovernmental complexity and interdependence that were beginning to attract attention in the mid-1960s. Grodzins's essay is worth reading for a number of other reasons as well. For instance, he explains the ties so often developed on intergovernmental matters among administrators, legislators, and interest groups, and he analyzes the link between intergovernmental relations and the structure of American political parties. Grodzins's overall goal, as he explains in a part of the essay not included here, is to describe the American system as one which has "decentralization by mild chaos," which he labels "an important goal for the American federal system."

Harry Scheiber, on the other hand, critiques and rejects the historically based claims of both Elazar and Grodzins that sharing and cooperation have been more prevalent than conflict in American intergovernmental relations. He also explains why such interpretations of intergovernmental history may have an important effect on the course of contemporary intergovernmental policy making.

Deil Wright is one of the most prominent experts on intergovernmental matters in the United States today. His interest is explicitly American intergovernmental relations rather than federalism, since he regards the former as a more satisfactory and inclusive concept in contemporary times. For him, the "hallmarks of the more complex and interdependent system" of intergovernmental relations are: "the number and growth of governmental units; the number and variety of public officials involved in intergovernmental relations; the intensity and regularity of contacts among those officials; the importance of officials' actions and attitudes; and the preoccupation with financial policy issues."[1] In the reading taken from his major text, Wright sketches three models of intergovernmental relations, surveys the evidence available to support each, and chooses one model as particularly appropriate to explain and describe contemporary intergovernmental activity.

The last selection in Part One offers an implicit contrast to much of the other material. William Riker, a leading empirically oriented political scientist and student of federalism as it has developed around the world, critiques the "moral evaluation" and "ideology" frequently employed to defend federalism as a basic element of intergovernmental structure. Riker argues that while policy consequences do derive from the choice to maintain a federal structure, many of the usual virtues claimed on behalf of federal (especially American federal) government are spurious. Riker's analysis suggests that intergovernmental experts should inject more empiricism and less ideology into their historical and theoretical work.

Note

1. *Understanding Intergovernmental Relations,* 2d ed. (Monterey, Calif.: Brooks/Cole Publishing Company, 1982), p. 8.

1. FEDERALIST NO. 39

James Madison

The last paper having concluded the observations which were meant to introduce a candid survey of the plan of government reported by the convention, we now proceed to the execution of that part of the undertaking.

The first question that offers itself is whether the general form and aspect of the government be strictly republican. It is evident that no other form would be reconcilable with the genius of the people of America; with the fundamental principles of the Revolution; or with that honorable determination which animates every votary of freedom to rest all our political experiments on the capacity of mankind for self-government. If the plan of the convention, therefore, be found to depart from the republican character, its advocates must abandon it as no longer defensible.

What, then, are the distinctive characters of the republican form? Were an answer to this question to be sought, not by recurring to principles but in the application of the term by political writers to the constitutions of different States, no satisfactory one would ever be found. Holland, in which no particle of the supreme authority is derived from the people, has passed almost universally under the denomination of a republic. The same title has been bestowed on Venice, where absolute power over the great body of the people is exercised in the most absolute manner by a small body of hereditary nobles. Poland, which is a mixture of aristocracy and of monarchy in their worst forms, has been dignified with the same appellation. The government of England, which has one republican branch only, combined with an hereditary aristocracy and monarchy, has with equal impropriety been frequently placed on the list of republics. These examples, which are nearly as dissimilar to each other as to a genuine republic, show the extreme inaccuracy with which the term has been used in political disquisitions.

If we resort for a criterion to the different principles on which different forms of government are established, we may define a republic to be, or at least may bestow that name on, a government which derives all its powers directly or indirectly from the great body of the people, and is administered by persons holding their offices during pleasure for a limited period, or during good behavior. It is *essential* to such a government that it be derived from the great body of the society, not from an inconsiderable proportion or a favored class of it; otherwise a

From Clinton Rossiter, ed., *The Federalist Papers* (New York: The New American Library, 1961), pp. 240-246.

handful of tyrannical nobles, exercising their oppressions by a delegation of their powers, might aspire to the rank of republicans and claim for their government the honorable title of republic. It is *sufficient* for such a government that the persons administering it be appointed, either directly or indirectly, by the people; and that they hold their appointments by either of the tenures just specified; otherwise every government in the United States, as well as every other popular government that has been or can be well organized or well executed, would be degraded from the republican character. According to the constitution of every State in the Union, some or other of the officers of government are appointed indirectly only by the people. According to most of them, the chief magistrate himself is so appointed. And according to one, this mode of appointment is extended to one of the co-ordinate branches of the legislature. According to all the constitutions, also, the tenure of the highest offices is extended to a definite period, and in many instances, both within the legislative and executive departments, to a period of years. According to the provisions of most of the constitutions, again, as well as according to the most respectable and received opinions on the subject, the members of the judiciary department are to retain their offices by the firm tenure of good behavior.

On comparing the Constitution planned by the convention with the standard here fixed, we perceived at once that it is, in the most rigid sense, conformable to it. The House of Representatives, like that of one branch at least of all the State legislatures, is elected immediately by the great body of the people. The Senate, like the present Congress and the Senate of Maryland, derives its appointment indirectly from the people. The President is indirectly derived from the choice of the people, according to the example in most of the States. Even the judges, with all other officers of the Union, will, as in the several States, be the choice, though a remote choice, of the people themselves. The duration of the appointments is equally conformable to the republican standard and to the model of State constitutions. The House of Representatives is periodically elective, as in all the States; and for the period of two years, as in the State of South Carolina. The Senate is elective for the period of six years, which is but one year more than the period of the Senate of Maryland, and but two more than that of the Senates of New York and Virginia. The President is to continue in office for the period of four years; as in New York and Delaware the chief magistrate is elected for three years, and in South Carolina for two years. In the other States the election is annual. In several of the States, however, no explicit provision is made for the impeachment of the chief magistrate. And in Delaware and Virginia he is not impeachable till out of office. The President of the United States is impeachable at any time during his continuance in office. The tenure by which the judges are to hold their places is, as it unquestionably ought to be, that of good behavior. The tenure of the ministerial offices generally will be a subject of legal regulation, conformably to the reason of the case and the example of the State constitutions.

Could any further proof be required of the republican complexion of this system, the most decisive one might be found in its absolute prohibition of titles of nobility, both under the federal and the State governments; and in its express guaranty of the republican form to each of the latter.

"But it was not sufficient," say the adversaries of the proposed Constitution, "for the convention to adhere to the republican form. They ought with equal care to have preserved the *federal* form, which regards the Union as a *Confederacy* of sovereign states; instead of which they have framed a *national* government, which regards the Union as a *consolidation* of the States." And it is asked by what authority this bold and radical innovation was undertaken? The handle which has been made of this objection requires that it should be examined with some precision.

Without inquiring into the accuracy of the distinction on which the objection is founded, it will be necessary to a just estimate of its force, first, to ascertain the real character of the government in question; secondly, to inquire how far the convention were authorized to propose such a government; and thirdly, how far the duty they owed to their country could supply any defect of regular authority.

First.—In order to ascertain the real character of the government, it may be considered in relation to the foundation on which it is to be established; to the sources from which its ordinary powers are to be drawn; to the operation of those powers; to the extent of them; and to the authority by which future changes in the government are to be introduced.

On examining the first relation, it appears, on one hand, that the Constitution is to be founded on the assent and ratification of the people of America, given by deputies elected for the special purpose; but, on the other, that this assent and ratification is to be given by the people, not as individuals composing one entire nation, but as composing the distinct and independent States to which they respectively belong. It is to be the assent and ratification of the several States, derived from the supreme authority in each State—the authority of the people themselves. The act, therefore, establishing the Constitution will not be a *national* but a *federal* act.

That it will be a federal and not a national act, as these terms are understood by the objectors—the act of the people, as forming so many independent States, not as forming one aggregate nation—is obvious from this single consideration: that it is to result neither from the decision of a *majority* of the people of the Union, nor from that of a *majority* of the States. It must result from the *unanimous* assent of the several States that are parties to it, differing no otherwise from their ordinary assent than in its being expressed, not by the legislative authority, but by that of the people themselves. Were the people regarded in this transaction as forming one nation, the will of the majority of the whole people of the United States would bind the minority, in the same manner as the majority in each State must bind the minority; and the will of the majority must be determined either by a comparison of the individual votes, or by considering the will of the majority of the States as evidence of the will of a majority of the people of the United States. Neither of these rules has been adopted. Each State, in ratifying the Constitution, is considered as a sovereign body independent of all others, and only to be bound by its own voluntary act. In this relation, then, the new Constitution will, if established, be a *federal* and not a *national* constitution.

The next relation is to the sources from which the ordinary powers of government are to be derived. The House of Representatives will derive its powers from the people of America; and the people will be represented in the same proportion and on the same principle as they are in the legislature of a particular State. So far the government is *national*, not *federal*. The Senate, on the other hand, will derive its powers from the States as political and coequal societies; and these will be represented on the principle of equality in the Senate, as they now are in the existing Congress. So far the government is *federal*, not *national*. The executive power will be derived from a very compound source. The immediate election of the President is to be made by the States in their political characters. The votes allotted to them are in a compound ratio, which considers them partly as distinct and coequal societies, partly as unequal members of the same society. The eventual election, again, is to be made by that branch of the legislature which consists of the national representatives; but in this particular act they are to be thrown into the form of individual delegations from so many distinct and coequal bodies politic. From this aspect of the government it appears to be of a mixed character, presenting at least as many *federal* as *national* features.

The difference between a federal and national government, as it relates to the *operation of the government*, is by the adversaries of the plan of the convention supposed to consist in this, that in the former the powers operate on the political bodies composing the Confederacy in their political capacities; in the latter, on the individual citizens composing the nation in their individual capacities. On trying the Constitution by this criterion, it falls under the *national* not the *federal* character; though perhaps not so completely as has been understood. In several cases, and particularly in the trial of controversies to which States may be parties, they must be viewed and proceeded against in their collective and political capacities only. But the operation of the government on the people in their individual capacities, in its ordinary and most essential proceedings, will, in the sense of its opponents, on the whole, designate it, in this relation, a *national* government.

But if the government be national with regard to the *operation* of its powers, it changes its aspect again when we contemplate it in relation to the extent of its powers. The idea of a national government involves in it not only an authority over the individual citizens, but an indefinite supremacy over all persons and things, so far as they are objects of lawful government. Among a people consolidated into one nation, this supremacy is completely vested in the national legislature. Among communities united for particular purposes, it is vested partly in the general and partly in the municipal legislatures. In the former case, all local authorities are subordinate to the supreme; and may be controlled, directed, or abolished by it at pleasure. In the latter, the local or municipal authorities form distinct and independent portions of the supremacy, no more subject, within their respective spheres, to the general authority than the general authority is subject to them, within its own sphere. In this relation, then, the proposed government cannot be deemed a *national* one; since its jurisdiction extends to certain enumerated objects only, and leaves to the several States a residuary and inviolable sovereignty over all other objects. It is true that in controversies relating to the boundary between the two jurisdictions, the tribunal which is ultimately to decide is to be established under the general government. But this does not change the principle of the case. The decision is to be impartially made, according to the rules of the Constitution; and all the usual and most effectual precautions are taken to secure this impartiality. Some such tribunal is clearly essential to prevent an appeal to the sword and a dissolution of the compact; and that it ought to be established under the general rather than under the local governments, or, to speak more properly, that it could be safely established under the first alone, is a position not likely to be combated.

If we try the Constitution by its last relation to the authority by which amendments are to be made, we find it neither wholly *national* nor wholly *federal*. Were it wholly national, the supreme and ultimate authority would reside in the *majority* of the people of the Union; and this authority would be competent at all times, like that of a majority of every national society to alter or abolish its established government. Were it wholly federal, on the other hand, the concurrence of each State in the Union would be essential to every alteration that would be binding on all. The mode provided by the plan of the convention is not founded on either of these principles. In requiring more than a majority, and particularly in computing the proportion by *States*, not by *citizens*, it departs from the national and advances toward the *federal* character; in rendering the concurrence of less than the whole number of States sufficient, it loses again the *federal* and partakes of the *national* character.

The proposed Constitution, therefore, even when tested by the rules laid down by its antagonists, is, in strictness, neither a national nor a federal Constitution, but a composition of both. In its foundation it is federal, not national; in the sources from which the ordinary powers of government are drawn, it is partly federal and partly national; in the operation of these powers, it is national, not federal; in the extent of them, again, it is federal, not national; and, finally in the authoritative mode of introducing amendments, it is neither wholly federal nor wholly national.   PUBLIUS

2.   WHAT THE FRAMERS MEANT BY FEDERALISM

Martin Diamond

... Relatively little serious attention has been given to the Framers' own view of federalism, because something confidently called "modern federalism" has been understood to have superseded the original version. It is the contention of this essay that the recovery of the Framers' view of federalism is necessary to the understanding of American federalism. In what follows, an attempt is made to indicate what the Framers meant by federalism, as that is revealed in the proceedings of the Federal Convention.

I

The American Republic has been regarded by nearly all modern observers as *the* example of a federal government. Indeed the various modern definitions of federalism are little more than slightly generalized descriptions of the American way of governing. . . .

According to these typical definitions, the essential federal characteristic is the "division of political power," a division of supremacy (sovereignty, as used to be said) between member states and a central government, each having the final say regarding matters belonging to its sphere. There is a corollary to this sort of definition which has also come to be generally accepted. All college students are now taught that, in this respect, there are three kinds of government—confederal, federal, and unitary (national)—and that the United States exemplifies the middle term. This familiar distinction illuminates the definitions of federalism. In this view, a confederacy and a nation are seen as the extremes. The defining characteristic of a confederacy is that the associated states retain all the sovereign power, with the central body entirely dependent legally upon their will; the defining characteristic of a nation is that the central body has all the sovereign power, with the localities entirely dependent legally upon the will of the nation. In this view, then, federalism is truly the middle term, for its defining characteristic is that it modifies and then combines the best characteristics of the other two forms. A *federal* system combines states which *confederally* retain sovereignty within a certain sphere, with a central body that *nationally* possesses

Author's Note: This paper was written while the author was enjoying a fellowship year at the Center for Advanced Study in the Behavioral Sciences.

From Robert A. Goldwin, ed., *A Nation of States* (Chicago: Rand McNally, 1974), pp. 25–41. Reprinted by permission, Kenyon Public Affairs Conference Center.

sovereignty within another sphere; the combination is thought to create a new and better thing to which is given the name federalism.

Now what is strange is this. The leading Framers viewed their handiwork in an entirely different light. For example, *The Federalist*, the great contemporary exposition of the Constitution, emphatically does not regard the Constitution as establishing a typically federal, perhaps not even a primarily federal system of government. *The Federalist* regards the new American Union as departing significantly from the essentially federal character. The decisive statement is: "The proposed Constitution, therefore, is, in strictness, neither a national nor a federal Constitution, but a composition of both." [1] As will become clear, our now familiar tripartite distinction was completely unknown to the men who made the Constitution. They had a very different understanding than we do of what federalism is. For them, there were but two possible modes: confederal or federal as opposed to unitary or national. They had, therefore, in strictness, to regard their Constitution as a composition of federal and national features. We now give the single word federal to the systems the Framers regarded as possessing both federal and national features. This means we now regard as a unique principle what they considered as a mere compound.

Consider Tocqueville's opinion: "Evidently this is no longer a federal government, but an incomplete national government, which is neither exactly national nor exactly federal; but the new word which ought to express this novel thing does not yet exist." [2] For good or ill, the word which came to express the novel thing turned out to be the old word federal. It is no fussy antiquarianism to assert the necessity to understand the Constitution the way its creators did, as possessing both federal and national features. In order to understand the system they created for us and how they expected it to work, we must be able to distinguish the parts that make up the whole, and see the peculiar place of each in the working of the whole. Now they regarded certain parts as federal and certain parts as national, and had different expectations regarding each. To use the word federal, as we do now, to describe both the "federal" and "national" features of their plan is to lump under one obscuring term things they regarded as radically different. It becomes thus difficult if not impossible to understand their precise intentions. This is a sufficient reason to do the job of recovering precisely what they meant by federalism.

Federalism meant then exactly what we mean now by confederalism: "a sort of association or league of sovereign states.". . . A brief consideration of the Articles of Confederation will further reveal what men meant then by a federal arrangement, especially when comparison is made to the Constitution.

In recent years we have come to think of the Articles as having created too weak a central government. This is not precise enough. Strictly speaking, neither the friends nor the enemies of the Confederation regarded the Articles as having created any kind of *government* at all, weak or otherwise. Article III declared that "the said states hereby enter into a firm *league of friendship* with each other.". . . Men referred then to the Articles as a kind of treaty, and, no more than any other treaty organization is thought to create a government, was it thought that the Articles had created one. The language of the Articles makes this clear. The word government never appears in that document, whereas the Constitution speaks repeatedly of the Government, the Treasury, the Authority, the Offices, the Laws of the United States. There are no such terms in the Articles; there could be none because it was fatally a federal arrangement, a league not a government.

Article I declared that "the stile of this confederacy shall be 'The United States of America.' " Twice more at the outset that capitalized expression occurs. But on every subsequent occasion (about forty times) the term is given in lower case letters as the "united states." That is, as a mere league, the Confederacy was not a governmental being to which a proper name could be strictly applied. In the Constitution, on the contrary, the term United States is invariably capitalized. Indeed, the formal language of the Articles makes clear that the Confederacy had no real existence save when the states were formally assembled. When speaking of its duties or functions, the Articles invariably refer to the Confederacy as "the united states *in Congress assembled.*" All men seem to have referred to the Confederacy in this exact phrase. It must be remembered also that the word "Congress" did not then mean an institution of government. As an ordinary word it meant then simply a "meeting," especially "an assembly of envoys, comissioners, deputies, etc. from different courts, meeting to agree on terms of political accommodation." [3] Under the Articles the United States had no being; its existence consisted solely in the congregation of envoys from the separate states for the accommodation of certain specified matters under terms prescribed by the federal treaty. The slightest glance at the Constitution, of course, shows that it refers to the duties and powers of the government of a country.

The Founding Fathers, like all other men at the time and perhaps all other men up to that time, regarded federalism, not as a kind of government, but as a voluntary association of states who sought certain advantages from that association. For example, at the very outset of the Convention, it became necessary for the delegates to state openly their understanding of the nature of the federal form. Gouverneur Morris "explained the distinction between a *federal* and *national, supreme* government; the former being a mere compact resting on the good faith of the parties; the latter having a complete and *compulsive* operation." [4] The entire Convention, with the single exception of Hamilton, in one remark, concurred in this view of the nature of federalism.[5]

From this view it followed that any federal arrangement would be characterized by certain ways of doing things. As one delegate put it, "a confederacy supposes sovereignty in the members composing it and sovereignty supposes equality." [6] That is, when forming a league, the member states retain their political character, i.e., sovereignty; and, each being equally a political entity, each state participates in the league as an equal member. That is, each state has one equal vote in making the league's decisions; moreover, because the league is a voluntary association of sovereign states and rests upon the "good faith" of the members, extraordinary or even unanimous majorities are to be preferred. Compare the Articles which called for at least a majority of nine of the thirteen states in all important cases. From this view of federalism it further followed that a league had no business with the individual citizens of the member states, the governing of them remaining the business of the states. In its limited activities, the central body was to deal only with *its* "citizens," i.e., the sovereign states.

According to the Framers, then, a federal system was federal in three main ways. First, the member states were equals in the making of the central decisions.

Second, these central agreements were to be carried out by the member states themselves. Third, the confederal body was not to deal with the vast bulk of political matters; governing, for all practical purposes, remained with the member states. Given this view of the meaning of federalism, we can readily see why the Framers could not possibly regard the new Constitution as merely a federal system, but rather regarded it as a "composition" of both federal and national elements.

II

The Federal Convention began its work by considering the detailed plan carefully prepared in advance and presented to it by the Virginia delegation. The Virginia plan proposed the creation of a powerful government which it throughout described by the shocking term *national*. It clearly went far beyond the common understanding that the Convention was only to propose amendments to the existing Confederacy. The great issue so abruptly placed before the Convention was made perfectly explicit when Governor Randolph, at the suggestion of Gouverneur Morris, proposed a substitution for the initial clause of the Virginia Plan. The original formulation was: "Resolved that the articles of Confederation ought to be so corrected and enlarged, as to accomplish the objects proposed by their institution; namely, common defense, security of liberty and general welfare." [7] The substitute formulation left no possible doubt about how far the Virginia Plan went. Resolved "that a Union of the States merely federal will not accomplish the objects proposed by the articles of Confederation, namely common defense, security of liberty, and general welfare"; and resolved further "that a *national* Government ought to be established consisting of a *supreme* Legislative, Executive and Judiciary." [8]

Randolph said, in short: by the Articles we meant to insure our defense, liberty and general welfare; they failed; no system of the merely federal kind will secure these things for us; we must create a supreme, that is, national government.

Discussion centered on the resolution proposing a national and supreme government. Oddly enough, the resolution was almost immediately adopted, six states to one. At this moment the Convention was pointed to a simply national government, and not the "composition" which finally resulted. But the matter was not to be so easily settled, not least because several small state delegations, which happened to be federally minded, subsequently arrived. Despite the favorable vote on the Randolph resolution, the Convention had not yet truly made up their mind. Too many delegates remained convinced federalists. They would have to be persuaded to change their minds or the final plan would have to be compromised so as to accommodate the wishes of those who would not go so far as a straightforwardly national plan. Therefore, as specific portions of the Virginia Plan were discussed in the ensuing weeks, the fundamental issue—a federal versus a national plan—came up again and again.

The most important feature of the discussions is the following. The Convention had originally squared off on the issue of federalism *versus* nationalism, the true federalists regarding nationalism as fatal to liberty, the nationalists regarding confederalism as "imbecilically" incompetent. Compromise would have been impossible across the gulf of two such opposed views. One or the other of the two original views had to be modified so that the distance between the two could be bridged by compromise. And that is precisely what happened. After three weeks of discussion, the issue had subtly changed. The opponents of a purely national government found themselves unable to defend the pure federal principle. The simple nationalists remained such in principle, while the pure federalists implicitly found themselves forced to acknowledge the inadequacy of the federal principle. Now the question was between those still advocating a purely national plan and those who, having abandoned a purely federal scheme, were determined only to work some federal features into the final outcome. Thus the famous compromise, the "composition" which finally resulted, was a compromise between the simple nationalists and half-hearted federalists, i.e., federalists who were themselves moving toward the national principle. Only because of this underlying victory of the simple nationalists was the issue finally made capable of compromise.

This does not mean that the pure federalists yielded easily or completely. The ideas which led them to their federalist position had a powerful hold over their minds. A fundamental theoretical issue, as we shall see, had to be raised before they could be made substantially to retreat from their federalist position. And, even then, important concessions had finally to be made to the unconvinced and only partially convinced. Moreover, the ideas supporting that federalist position have long retained their vitality in American politics; and the federal elements which finally found their way into the Constitution have always supplied historical and legal support to recurring expressions of the traditional federalist view. It is necessary to acknowledge the survival of this view and the grounds for its survival. But it is impossible to understand the work of the Convention without seeing that the view survived only after having first been shaken to its very root, and hence that it survived only in a permanently weakened condition.

How this happened is perfectly revealed in a notable exchange between Madison, straightforwardly for the national plan at that point, and Sherman of Connecticut, one of the intelligent defenders of the federal principle.

> The objects of Union [Sherman] thought were *few*. 1. defence against foreign danger. 2. against internal disputes & a resort to force. 3. Treaties with foreign nations. 4. regulating foreign commerce, & drawing revenue from it. These & perhaps a few lesser objects *alone rendered a confederation of the States necessary*. All other matters civil & criminal would be much better in the hands of the States. *The people are more happy in small than in large States.*[9]

Whereas Madison

> differed from the member from Connecticut in thinking the objects mentioned to be all the principal ones that required a National Government. Those were certainly important and necessary objects; but he combined with them the necessity of providing more effectually for the security of private rights, and the steady dispensation of Justice. Interferences with these were evils which had more perhaps than anything else, produced this convention. Was it to be supposed that republican liberty could long exist under the abuses of it practised in some of the States.[10]

Madison was skillfully pressing a sensitive nerve. Not only were the delegates concerned with the inadequacy of the Confederacy for "general" purposes, but nearly all were also unhappy with the way things had been going in the states themselves since the Revolution. Above all, the delegates agreed in fearing the tendency in many of the states to agrarian and debtors' measures that seemed to threaten the security of property. The Shays' Rebellion, for example, had terrified many of the delegates. Sherman had himself, after the passage quoted above, adverted to this dangerous tendency, and had, moreover, admitted that "too small" states were by virtue of their smallness peculiarly "subject to faction." Madison seized upon this.

> The gentleman had admitted that in a very small State, faction & oppression would prevail. It was to be inferred then that wherever these prevailed the State was too small. Had they not prevailed in the largest as well as the smallest tho' less than in the smallest; and were we not thence admonished to enlarge the sphere as far as the nature of the Government would admit. This was the only defence against the inconveniencies of democracy consistent with the democratic form of Government.[11]

Sherman, the defender of the federal principle, considered the ends of union to be few. Madison, the defender of the national principle, considered the ends of union to be many. Sherman would leave the most important matters of government to the individual states. Madison would place the most important matters—e.g., "security of private rights, and the steady dispensation of justice"— under a national government. Sherman believed that the people would be happiest when governed by their individual states, these being the natural dwelling place of republicanism. Madison believed that republican liberty would perish under the states and that therefore the people would be happiest when under a national government; only such a government made possible the very large republic which in turn supplied the democratic remedy for the inconveniences of democracy.

Madison, then, argued with Sherman and the other defenders of the federal principle in two ways. First, he appealed to the delegates to acknowledge that they really wanted very much more from union than Sherman admitted. . . . the Convention's decisive action turned on just this issue. The fact that nearly all the delegates, themselves included, wanted a very great deal from union became *the* stumbling block to the defenders of a federal plan. . . . the explicit endorsement of a national plan dramatically followed the most powerful showing of how much was wanted from union and how little could be supplied by the federal principle. But it would not have sufficed merely to demonstrate the incompatibility of federalism and a union from which much was desired. The delegates could still have done what any man can do who has two equal and contradictory desires. They could have abandoned their preference for the federal principle in favor of firm union, as Madison wished, or they could have abandoned a firm union in favor of the federal principle, as Madison emphatically did not wish. Madison therefore had also to give the delegates a reason to choose only one of the two incompatible alternatives, namely, a firm union under a national government. This meant persuading the delegates to renounce their attachment to federalism. And that is precisely what Madison attempted. He sought to undermine that attachment by supplying a new solution to the problem for which federalism had been the traditional answer.

The best men, like Sherman, who defended the federal principle at the Convention, and those, like R. H. Lee, who subsequently opposed adoption of the Constitution, did not defend federalism for its own sake. Who could? They defended the federal principle against the plan of a national or primarily national government because they thought they were thereby defending a precious thing, namely, republican liberty. They saw a connection between republicanism and federalism. They regarded federalism as the sole way in which some of the advantages of great size could be obtained by those who wanted to enjoy the blessings of republicanism. . . .

The true federalists rested their case on the proposition that only the state governments, and not some huge national government, could be made or kept truly free and republican. In this they were following the very old belief, popularized anew in the way men understood Montesquieu, that only small countries could enjoy republican government. The reasoning that supported the belief ran something as follows. Large countries necessarily turn to despotic rule. For one thing, large countries need despotic rule; political authority breaks down if the central government does not govern more forcefully than the republican form admits. Further, large countries, usually wealthy and populous, are warlike by nature or are made warlike by envious neighbors; such belligerency nurtures despotic rule. Moreover, not even the best intentions suffice to preserve the republicanism of a large country. To preserve their rule, the people must be patriotic, vigilant, and informed. This requires that the people give loving attention to public things, and that the affairs of the country be on a scale commensurate with the people's understanding. But in large countries the people, baffled and rendered apathetic by the complexity of public affairs, at last become absorbed in their own pursuits. Finally, even were the citizens of a large republic able to remain alert, they must allow a few men actually to conduct the public business. Far removed from the localities and possessed of the instruments of coercion, the necessarily trusted representatives would inevitably subvert the republican rule to their own passions and interests. Such was the traditional and strongly held view of the necessity that republics be small. . . .

It is clear, then, that Madison had to persuade the delegates, as it were, that they could have their cake and eat it, too. That is, they could have the firm union that would supply the blessings they wanted, *without* sacrificing the republicanism for which they had hitherto thought federalism was indispensable. Federalism was indispensable only so long as men held to the small-republic theory. And that is the theory Madison tried to demolish. Nothing is more important to an understanding of both the theoretical and practical issues in the founding of the American Republic than a full appreciation of Madison's stand on behalf of the very large republic. . . .

Madison turned the small-republic argument upside down. On the contrary, he argued, *smallness* was fatal to republicanism. The small republics of antiquity were wretched nurseries of internal warfare, and the Convention itself had been "produced" by the fear for liberty in the "small" American states. "Was it to be supposed that republican liberty could long exist under the abuses of it practised in some of the States. . . . Were we not then admonished to enlarge the sphere as far as the nature of the Government would admit." Smallness is fatal to republican liberty. Only a country as large as the whole thirteen states and more could provide a safe dwelling-place for republican liberty. Republicanism not only permits but requires taking away from the states responsibility for "the security of private rights, and the steady dispensation of Justice," else rights and justice will perish under the state governments.

This was the great and novel idea which came from the Convention: a large, powerful republic with a competent national government regulated under a wise Constitution. . . .

Notes

1. *Federalist* 39, p. 250. All references are to the edition of Henry Cabot Lodge, introduction by Edward Mead Earle (New York: Modern Library, 1941).
2. *Democracy in America*, ed. Phillips Bradley (New York: Alfred A. Knopf, 1945), I, 159.
3. Samuel Johnson, *Dictionary of the English Language* (2 vols.; Heidelberg: Joseph Englemann, 1828).
4. *Documents Illustrative of the Formation of the Union of the American States*, ed. C. C. Tansill (Washington: U.S. Government Printing Office, 1927), p. 121. Italics supplied.
5. *Ibid.*, p. 216.
6. *Ibid.*, p. 182.
7. *Ibid.*, p. 116.
8. *Ibid.*, p. 120.
9. *Ibid.*, pp. 160-61. Italics supplied.
10. *Ibid.*, pp. 161-62.
11. *Ibid.*, p. 162.

3. THE SCOPE OF COOPERATION

Daniel J. Elazar

... The American federal system has been fundamentally a co-operative partnership of federal, state, and local governments since the early days of the Republic. Within a dualistic structural pattern, the governments of the United States have developed a broadly institutionalized system of collaboration, based on the implicit premise that virtually all functions of government must be shared by virtually all governments in order to fulfill the demands of American democracy for both public service and private access. More specifically, the evidence presented [earlier in Elazar's book] indicates that the relative balance between the federal government and the states has not significantly shifted over the past one hundred seventy-five years. The two levels of government have played the same respective roles in the system from the first, and these roles have not been significantly altered, despite the great changes that have taken place within the United States and in the world. Consequently, the pattern of American federalism in practice, in so far as it differs from the classic theory of American federalism, has certain fundamental implications in the context of American history and in the context of democratic theory.

Programs and Policies: A Review

From the first days of American independence, the controversy as to the scope of national vis-à-vis state powers has been part and parcel of the American political scene. While the controversy has continued to rage unabated, the American people have by and large endeavored to use both federal and state governments as means to achieve specific ends, rather than as ends in themselves. When problems arose, solutions were sought that would harmonize with the reality of the times, involving government whenever and wherever necessary, generally at every level. Out of these attempts to solve actual problems, there evolved a series of co-operative relationships between all levels of government.

As the new nation began to expand under the Constitution, expansion came to center primarily around movement westward, the conquest of the continent. Out of this expansion arose a number of major problems that required governmental consideration. Among them, three major categories stand out:

From *The American Partnership: Intergovernmental Co-operation in the Nineteenth-Century United States* (Chicago: University of Chicago Press, 1962), pp. 297-305. Reprinted by permission of the author.

internal improvements, education, and disposition of the public domain. A fourth major category centering around the slavery issue reached national prominence and forced the ultimate conflict as a result of problems arising from territorial expansion westward and the attempt to spread slavery to the land frontier. It should be noted that each of these major categories has its counterpart in the twentieth century, which has required governmental action just as its forerunner did.

The term "internal improvement" covered a multitude of specific problems, all basically concerned with facilitating the geographic and material expansion of the American people, while at the same time binding the various sections of the country more closely together as one political and economic system. Roads, canals, railroads, harbors, public buildings and institutions, river improvements, land reclamation, mineral production and extraction, agricultural development, and the creation of a banking system to finance all these projects, constituted the internal improvement programs of the day. All demanded a share of the interest, energy, and money, both public and private, of the expanding nation. Internal improvements provided a major portion of the intergovernmental programs that emerged during the century, simply because they provided a major portion of all governmental activity.

While much attention was directed toward material progress, no less was given to the development of a responsible and capable citizenry, particularly in the newly settled areas of the Midwest and Far West. The dominant educational problems were to provide a basic foundation for productive citizenship through the common schools and to advance intellectual, agricultural, and mechanical training of young men and women in colleges and universities. As the frontier advanced, so did the desire for education. Population groups demanded government programs to fill needs that the struggling pioneers could not meet alone. Once again, the use of co-operative government programs provided the vehicle whereby such aid could be rendered within the framework of the federal system.

Since our nation is dedicated to the task of providing opportunity for each individual to engage in the pursuit of happiness in a manner as nearly approaching his own definition of that goal as socially possible, the disposition of the major national resource, the public domain, in a manner consistent with that high purpose continued to be a leading problem. As the nation evolved a policy for the solution of the problem, the tension between public and private interests brought forth increasingly greater efforts on the part of all levels of government. From these efforts emerged the federal land grants to the various states for a multitude of purposes, ranging from veterans' benefits to railroad construction; the direct federal land grants for transportation and development companies; and finally, the land grants to individual settlers under the various homestead and pre-emption acts. Even before the adoption of the Constitution, it was determined that the disposition of the public domain would provide the means whereby the other problems were to be attacked, with land serving in place of cash as the substance of federal grants-in-aid.

Several basic patterns for the actual implementation of co-operative federalism developed in the nineteenth century. Informal relationships developed, primarily in the field, where officials of the federal government, the states, and the localities exchanged information or co-operated to solve specific problems. Examples of this informal co-operation cover the range of governmental activities.

In relations with the Indians, the federal government theoretically held exclusive jurisdiction. Actually, federal authorities in any specific situation consulted with officials of the state and locality concerned and often relied upon their co-operation to implement a policy or subdue hostiles.[1] The co-operative relations between the second Bank of the United States and the various states in the development of a national monetary system were semiformal, based on national needs. Co-operation between the United States Army Corps of Engineers and state and local authorities in the construction and maintenance of river and harbor improvements made that program a shared one *de facto* long before such sharing was officially recognized in law. The localities contributed financial, material, and technical aid amounting to at least one-fifth of the cost of any Corps of Engineers project.[2] Problems of law enforcement also led to a number of informal co-operative relationships, both in routine law enforcement matters in which local police and United States marshals worked together and in more specialized fields such as control of smuggling and immigration.[3] Wherever the military was stationed, a series of informal co-operative relationships grew up, which covered a number of governmental functions; some were temporary reactions to emergency situations, and others ongoing relationships that continued for many years.

Other co-operative relationships that were never formalized grew up around federal programs designed to dispose of the public domain, which officially made no reference to the states and localities. These included the various homestead and reclamation programs, such as the homestead and pre-emption acts, the tree-culture acts, the town-site selection acts, and some parts of the desert lands and reclamation acts. As a general rule, whenever a federal program affected the citizens of a state, the state governments concerned became unofficial parties to, and even agents in, its administration.

For various reasons that were dealt with in previous chapters, a number of internal improvement programs were initiated through the federal government only. Certain western roads and railroads were constructed by the federal government or with direct federal aid generally because the regions they traversed were predominantly in the territorial stage of government. Little time elapsed before even these programs were incorporated into the co-operative system, originally with territorial and local authorities and ultimately with the state governments once they had been formed.[4] Collaboration in these programs was almost always quasi-formal even from the outset, since any portion of the road or railroad that was to be built within an existing state forced the builders to obtain the approval of the state legislature, as required by the terms of the Congressional grant, and the legislature would often demand tailoring of the planned improvement to meet the needs of the state. In almost every case, co-operation had to evolve because every program involved some issues of interest to each level of government. The choices that confronted the political leaders were such that the alternatives to co-operation would have produced at best unmanageable chaos and at worst disunion.

Another by no means separate form of intergovernmental co-operation involved formally co-ordinated relationships. Programs in this category did not involve the exchange of money, land, or personnel, but instead action was co-ordinated pursuant to statutory provisions enacted by Congress and the partici-pating state legislatures. Under such programs, the federal government and each participating state undertook to implement parts of a jointly produced nationwide or state-federal plan without sharing the costs for individual projects. This is the type of co-operation which the United States Constitution provides for the administration of national elections.

The master plan for an internal transportation and communications system designed by the United States Army Corps of Engineers in co-operation with the boards of public works in the various states in the early nineteenth century was of this nature. The public works that emerged from that joint endeavor still form part of the pattern of the twentieth-century American highway and railroad system. The sequence of national banking programs, which were designed to establish a national banking system with a stable nationwide currency, frequently provided examples of this form of intergovernmental co-operation.

Many times, a co-operative program would be initiated as a co-ordinated activity only to be expanded as a formal federal-aid program at a later date. The inland waterways system designed by Albert Gallatin and others in Jefferson's administration fits into this category. The history of the Dismal Swamp Canal is illustrative of the tenuous line that often existed between co-ordinated and formal federal-aid programs. Intergovernmental co-operation in the field of education was exceptional in that it moved in the other direction, beginning as a federal-aid program in most states and later becoming almost entirely transformed into a co-ordinated activity until the mid-twentieth century.

Midway in scope between co-ordinated and formal grant-in-aid programs were some quasi-grant programs, which developed particularly in cases in which the federal government had to reimburse various states for money spent on its behalf for "national defense." While the reimbursement could not be earmarked for specific purposes under federal law, it was almost universally used by the state leadership as an opportune way to establish or supplement funds for the promotion of education. This general use of reimbursement funds for educational purposes was instrumental in obtaining Congressional and executive approval for many reimbursements that would otherwise not have been granted. The administration entailed in the transfer of funds for such reimbursements was of necessity co-operative. Other illustrative quasi-grant programs included the exchange of documents and scientific specimens, which were not grants so much as they were attempts to facilitate academic, legal, and cultural interchanges within the Union.

The most significant formal co-operative programs were generally those which involved federal grants of land, money, and services to the states. These programs can be divided into two categories: those that included both financial aid and the contacts with federal personnel necessary to implement the federal aspects of the program (grants-in-aid), and those that made only personnel available (services-in-aid). . . .

Grants-in-aid in the nineteenth century took the form of land grants, grants of materials, cash grants based upon land sales, and direct cash grants, with land grants the most prevalent. Land grants were made to the states for education (common schools, colleges, and special educational institutions), internal improvements (roads, canals, river and harbor improvements, railroads), public purposes (public buildings, salt springs), reclamation (desert lands, swamp lands), veterans (bounty lands), and welfare (public institutions). Cash grants based on land sales were made for internal improvements and conservation. Direct cash grants were made for defense (the militia grants),[5] internal improvements (transportation and banking), veterans (soldiers' homes), education (land-grant-college supplementary aid), and agriculture (agricultural experiment stations). Materials grants included construction materials on public lands, plants, seeds, fish, publications, scientific specimens, and weights and measures. Services-in-aid included the sending of federal personnel to co-operate with state officials (road and canal construction, waterway improvements, agriculture); the sending of federal officials to prepare the groundwork for state programs (road, canal, and railroad surveying); and the lending of federal experts to the states for specific projects (road, railroad, and canal construction).

All these forms of intergovernmental co-operation involved considerable administrative interaction between federal, state, and local officials. This interaction was carried on through established departments and bureaus on the federal level and, usually, through boards and commissions generally comprised of ex officio elected officials on the state and local levels. The forms of this administrative interaction were quite fluid, since the entire system of co-operative relationships had to be developed through trial and error for each program.

While day-to-day operations rested largely with the various administrative bodies in the executive branches of several levels of government, the members of the legislative assemblies—and particularly the representatives of the states and localities in Congress—were alert and active in overseeing the numerous programs. The role of these politicians was an interstitial one. In a real sense, they provided the cement that held the bricks together and enabled the programs to function with a maximum of local control. Although this study could not deal with their activities in proper depth, in every program that involved federal action, they were continuously present and involved, always prepared to question an administrator's action, enlarge or decrease an appropriation, and contact the appropriate bureau on behalf of a public or private constituent. All this was in addition to the fundamental authority of Congress to establish the programs in the first place.

In addition to the formal administrative arrangements and the traditional role of the legislature, a spirit of professionalism arose among the officials implementing a particular program. Although it varied in intensity from program to program, where the spirit of professionalism was strong, it was strong at all levels of government. This spirit led to the development of a professional interest in the implementation and expansion of each program, which meant that the professionals involved in it would strive to increase the amount of federal-state co-operation as an effective vehicle for the expansion of their own functions. Often, when political pressures formally lessened the amount of intergovernmental action in a given program, the professionals involved would find ways to continue the program in a manner closely approximating its previous level. There were times when existing programs were expanded and even new programs initiated by devoted professionals after Congress had hesitated to grant formal authorization. Often the federal professionals were abetted in this by the cabinet secretary under whom they served.

It might be said that the evolution of a co-operative system was the result of a considerable effort on the part of a number of men who, along with the founding fathers, may justly be termed the architects of the American federal system. These men could be found at all three levels of government (they usually served at more than one level during their public careers) and in all three branches of government. Some of them were prominent figures as well in their day, others were hardly known outside of their immediate circles.... All were indispensable in the evolution of the American partnership.

Co-operative Federalism: The Alternate Hypothesis

On the basis of the evidence presented in the previous chapters, and summarized in this one, it would seem necessary to develop a different theory to explain the nature of the American federal system and its character over time. Any new theory must take into account the continuous existence of an amount of intergovernmental collaboration equal to, and in fact greater than, the amount of separation (as traditionally defined) in the federal system. More precisely, the amount of intergovernmental collaboration in the nineteenth century in relation to the total amount of governmental activity in American life (what may be termed the velocity of government) was no less than, nor substantially different from, the amount of intergovernmental collaboration that exists in the mid-twentieth century in relation to the total velocity of government. Co-operative—not dual—federalism has been the mode since the establishment of the Republic, in the nineteenth century as well as in the twentieth....

In a sense, a substantial share of the history of American government has been the search for methods to provide for the necessary collaboration of the various units of the federal system while at the same time preserving and strengthening those units as separate bases for such collaboration. It has been shown that much of what historians have mistaken for the rejection of intergovernmental co-operation in the nineteenth century was, in reality, the rejection of certain methods of interaction as failing to meet one or both of the above criteria.

Notes

1. For a few of the many examples of this, see records in the Thomas Gilcrease Institute of American History and Art, Tulsa, Oklahoma; the Indian Archives in the Oklahoma Historical Society Library, Oklahoma City, Oklahoma (these archives are themselves a grant from the federal government to the state of Oklahoma); the National Archives, Washington, D.C.; and "Miscellaneous Papers and Documents Relating to the Ute Uprising, 8/16/1887-5/28/1889" (microfilm) in the Colorado State Archives, Denver, Colorado.
2. This figure is based on calculations made for specific projects selected at random from materials in the U.S. Army Corps of Engineers records, National Archives.
3. William E. Burke, *Federal Finances* (Chicago: F. J. Schultze and Co., 1891). The enforcement of the federal fugitive slave laws provides an excellent example of both the operation and breakdown of intergovernmental co-operation in law enforcement. The laws not only took such co-operation between federal and state law enforcement officials for granted, but were based on such co-operation to attain any real effectiveness. When

antislavery sentiment in the North forced the state and local lawmen to desist from aiding in the apprehension and return of fugitive slaves, the entire program broke down. For a view of the constitutional impact of this problem, see Carl Brent Swisher, *American Constitutional Development* (Boston: Houghton Mifflin, 1943), pp. 236-38.

4. See W. Turrentine Jackson, *Wagon Roads West* (Berkeley: University of California Press, 1956), for a discussion of the integration of wagon roads constructed by the federal government into the co-operative system.

5. Federal grants to arm and equip the state militias were initiated in 1808 as the first federal cash grants-in-aid to the states on record. An obvious example of co-operative federalism, the case of the militia has not been dealt with at any length in this volume dedicated to the "hard case." Information on intergovernmental co-operation in maintaining the militia in the nineteenth century is available in William H. Riker, *Soldiers of the States* (Washington, D.C.: Public Affairs Press, 1957).

4. THE FEDERAL SYSTEM

Morton Grodzins

Federalism is a device for dividing decisions and functions of government. As the constitutional fathers well understood, the federal structure is a means, not an end. The pages that follow are therefore not concerned with an exposition of American federalism as a formal, legal set of relationships. The focus, rather, is on the purpose of federalism, that is to say, on the distribution of power between central and peripheral units of government.

I. The Sharing of Functions

The American form of government is often, but erroneously, symbolized by a three-layer cake. A far more accurate image is the rainbow or marble cake, characterized by an inseparable mingling of differently colored ingredients, the colors appearing in vertical and diagonal strands and unexpected whirls. As colors are mixed in the marble cake, so functions are mixed in the American federal system. Consider the health officer, styled "sanitarian," of a rural county in a border state. He embodies the whole idea of the marble cake of government.

The sanitarian is appointed by the state under merit standards established by the federal government. His base salary comes jointly from state and federal funds, the county provides him with an office and office amenities and pays a portion of his expenses, and the largest city in the county also contributes to his salary and office by virtue of his appointment as a city plumbing inspector. It is impossible from moment to moment to tell under which governmental hat the sanitarian operates. His work of inspecting the purity of food is carried out under federal standards; but he is enforcing state laws when inspecting commodities that have not been in interstate commerce; and somewhat perversely he also acts under state authority when inspecting milk coming into the county from producing areas across the state border. He is a federal officer when impounding impure drugs shipped from a neighboring state; a federal-state officer when distributing typhoid immunization serum; a state officer when enforcing standards of industrial

Author's Note: This paper is the product of research carried out in the Federalism Workshop of the University of Chicago. I am indebted to the workshop participants, particularly Daniel J. Elazar, Dennis Palumbo, and Kenneth E. Gray, for data they collected. I profited greatly in writing Part III of the paper from Mr. Elazar's prize-winning dissertation, "Intergovernmental Relations in Nineteenth Century American Federalism" (Chicago, 1959).

From The Report of the President's Commission on National Goals, The American Assembly, *Goals for Americans* (Englewood Cliffs, N.J.: Prentice-Hall, 1960), pp. 265-282.

hygiene; a state-local officer when inspecting the city's water supply; and (to complete the circle) a local officer when insisting that the city butchers adopt more hygienic methods of handling their garbage. But he cannot and does not think of himself as acting in these separate capacities. All business in the county that concerns public health and sanitation he considers his business. Paid largely from federal funds, he does not find it strange to attend meetings of the city council to give expert advice on matters ranging from rotten apples to rabies control. He is even deputized as a member of both the city and county police forces.

The sanitarian is an extreme case, but he accurately represents an important aspect of the whole range of governmental activities in the United States. Functions are not neatly parceled out among the many governments. They are shared functions. It is difficult to find any governmental activity which does not involve all three of the so-called "levels" of the federal system. In the most local of local functions—law enforcement or education, for example—the federal and state governments play important roles. In what, *a priori*, may be considered the purest central government activities—the conduct of foreign affairs, for example—the state and local governments have considerable responsibilities, directly and indirectly.

The federal grant programs are only the most obvious example of shared functions. They also most clearly exhibit how sharing serves to disperse governmental powers. The grants utilize the greater wealth-gathering abilities of the central government and establish nation-wide standards, yet they are "in aid" of functions carried out under state law, with considerable state and local discretion. The national supervision of such programs is largely a process of mutual accommodation. Leading state and local officials, acting through their professional organizations, are in considerable part responsible for the very standards that national officers try to persuade all state and local officers to accept.

Even in the absence of joint financing, federal-state-local collaboration is the characteristic mode of action. Federal expertise is available to aid in the building of a local jail (which may later be used to house federal prisoners), to improve a local water purification system, to step up building inspections, to provide standards for state and local personnel in protecting housewives against dishonest butchers' scales, to prevent gas explosions, or to produce a local land use plan. States and localities, on the other hand, take important formal responsibilities in the development of national programs for atomic energy, civil defense, the regulation of commerce, and the protection of purity in foods and drugs; local political weight is always a factor in the operation of even a post office or a military establishment. From abattoirs and accounting through zoning and zoo administration, any governmental activity is almost certain to involve the influence, if not the formal administration, of all three planes of the federal system.

II. Attempts to Unwind the Federal System

Within the past dozen years there have been four major attempts to reform or reorganize the federal system: the first (1947-49) and second (1953-55) Hoover Commissions on Executive Organization; the Kestnbaum Commission on Intergovernmental Relations (1953-55); and the Joint Federal-State Action Committee (1957-59). All four of these groups have aimed to minimize federal activities. None of them has recognized the sharing of functions as the characteristic way American governments do things. Even when making recommendations for joint action, these official commissions take the view (as expressed in the Kestnbaum report) that "the main tradition of American federalism is the tradition of separateness." All four have, in varying degrees, worked to separate functions and tax sources.

The history of the Joint Federal-State Action Committee is especially instructive. The committee was established at the suggestion of President Eisenhower, who charged it, first of all, "to designate functions which the States are ready and willing to assume and finance that are now performed or financed wholly or in part by the Federal Government." He also gave the committee the task of recommending "Federal and State revenue adjustments required to enable the States to assume such functions." [1]

The committee subsequently established seemed most favorably situated to accomplish the task of functional separation. It was composed of distinguished and able men, including among its personnel three leading members of the President's cabinet, the director of the Bureau of the Budget, and ten state governors. It had the full support of the President at every point, and it worked hard and conscientiously. Excellent staff studies were supplied by the Bureau of the Budget, the White House, the Treasury Department, and from the state side, the Council of State Governments. It had available to it a large mass of research data, including the sixteen recently completed volumes of the Kestnbaum Commission. There existed no disagreements on party lines within the committee and, of course, no constitutional impediments to its mission. The President, his cabinet members, and all the governors (with one possible exception) on the committee completely agreed on the desirability of decentralization-via-separation-of-functions-and-taxes. They were unanimous in wanting to justify the committee's name and to produce action, not just another report.

The committee worked for more than two years. It found exactly two programs to recommend for transfer from federal to state hands. One was the federal grant program for vocational education (including practical-nurse training and aid to fishery trades); the other was federal grants for municipal waste treatment plants. The programs together cost the federal government less than $80 million in 1957, slightly more than two per cent of the total federal grants for that year. To allow the states to pay for these programs, the committee recommended that they be allowed a credit against the federal tax on local telephone calls. Calculations showed that this offset device, plus an equalizing factor, would give every state at least 40 per cent more from the tax than it received from the federal government in vocational education and sewage disposal grants. Some states were "equalized" to receive twice as much.

The recommendations were modest enough, and the generous financing feature seemed calculated to gain state support. The President recommended to Congress that all points of the program be legislated. None of them was, none has been since, and none is likely to be.

[In a section omitted here, Grodzins surveys some of the history of intergovernmental cooperation in the United States. The points made are similar to those of Elazar in the previous essay.—Ed.]

IV. Dynamics of Sharing: The Politics of the Federal System

Many causes contribute to dispersed power in the federal system. One is the simple historical fact that the states existed before the nation. A second is in the form of creed, the traditional opinion of Americans that expresses distrust of centralized power and places great value in the strength and vitality of local units of government. Another is pride in locality and state, nurtured by the nation's size and by variations of regional and state history. Still a fourth cause of decentralization is the sheer wealth of the nation. It allows all groups, including state and local governments, to partake of the central government's largesse, supplies room for experimentation and even waste, and makes unnecessary the tight organization of political power that must follow when the support of one program necessarily means the deprivation of another.

In one important respect, the Constitution no longer operates to impede centralized government. The Supreme Court since 1937 has given Congress a relatively free hand. The federal government can build substantive programs in many areas on the taxation and commerce powers. Limitations of such central programs based on the argument, "it's unconstitutional," are no longer possible as long as Congress (in the Court's view) acts reasonably in the interest of the whole nation. The Court is unlikely to reverse this permissive view in the foreseeable future.

Nevertheless, some constitutional restraints on centralization continue to operate. The strong constitutional position of the states—for example, the assignment of two senators to each state, the role given the states in administering even national elections, and the relatively few limitations on their law-making powers—establish the geographical units as natural centers of administrative and political strength. Many clauses of the Constitution are not subject to the same latitude of interpretation as the commerce and tax clauses. The simple, clearly stated, unambiguous phrases—for example, the President "shall hold his office during the term of four years"—are subject to change only through the formal amendment process. Similar provisions exist with respect to the terms of senators and congressmen and the amendment process. All of them have the effect of retarding or restraining centralizing action of the federal government. The fixed terms of the President and the members of Congress, for example, greatly impede the development of nation-wide, disciplined political parties that almost certainly would have to precede continuous large-scale expansion of federal functions.

The constitutional restraints on the expansion of national authority are less important and less direct today than they were in 1879 or in 1936. But to say that they are less important is not to say that they are unimportant.

The nation's politics reflect these decentralizing causes and add some of their own. The political parties of the United States are unique. They seldom perform the function that parties traditionally perform in other countries, the function of gathering together diverse strands of power and welding them into one. Except during the period of nominating and electing a president and for the essential but non-substantive business of organizing the houses of Congress, the American parties rarely coalesce power at all. Characteristically they do the reverse, serving as a canopy under which special and local interests are represented with little regard for anything that can be called a party program. National leaders are elected on a party ticket, but in Congress they must seek cross-party support if their leadership is to be effective. It is a rare president during rare periods who can produce legislation without facing the defection of substantial numbers of his own party. (Wilson could do this in the first session of the sixty-third Congress; but Franklin D. Roosevelt could not, even during the famous hundred days of 1933.) Presidents whose parties form the majority of the congressional houses must still count heavily on support from the other party.

The parties provide the pivot on which the entire governmental system swings. Party operations, first of all, produce in legislation the basic division of functions between the federal government, on the one hand, and state and local governments, on the other. The Supreme Court's permissiveness with respect to the expansion of national powers has not in fact produced any considerable extension of exclusive federal functions. The body of federal law in all fields has remained, in the words of Henry M. Hart, Jr. and Herbert Wechsler, "interstitial in its nature," limited in objective and resting upon the principal body of legal relationships defined by state law. It is difficult to find any area of federal legislation that is not significantly affected by state law.

In areas of new or enlarged federal activity, legislation characteristically provides important roles for state and local governments. This is as true of Democratic as of Republican administrations and true even of functions for which arguments of efficiency would produce exclusive federal responsibility. . . . A large fraction of the Senate is usually made up of ex-governors, and the membership of both houses is composed of men who know that their re-election depends less upon national leaders or national party organization than upon support from their home constituencies. State and local officials are key members of these constituencies, often central figures in selecting candidates and in turning out the vote. Under such circumstances, national legislation taking state and local views heavily into account is inevitable.

Second, the undisciplined parties affect the character of the federal system as a result of senatorial and congressional interference in federal administrative programs on behalf of local interests. Many aspects of the legislative involvement in administrative affairs are formalized. The Legislative Reorganization Act of 1946, to take only one example, provided that each of the standing committees "shall exercise continuous watchfulness" over administration of laws within its jurisdiction. But the formal system of controls, extensive as it is, does not compare in importance with the informal and extralegal network of relationships in producing continuous legislative involvement in administrative affairs.

Senators and congressmen spend a major fraction of their time representing problems of their constituents before administrative agencies. An even larger fraction of congressional staff time is devoted to the same task. The total magnitude of such "case work" operations is great. . . . Special congressional liaison staffs have been created to service this mass of business, though all higher officials meet it in one form or another. . . .

The widespread, consistent, and in many ways unpredictable character of legislative interference in administrative affairs has many consequences for the tone and character of American administrative behavior. From the perspective of this paper, the important consequence is the comprehensive, day-to-day, even hour-by-hour, impact of local views on national programs. No point of substance or procedure is immune from congressional scrutiny. A substantial portion of the entire weight of this impact is on behalf of the state and local governments. It is a weight that can alter procedures for screening immigration applications, divert the course of a national highway, change the tone of an international negotiation, and amend a social security law to accommodate local practices or fulfill local desires.

The party system compels administrators to take a political role. This is a third way in which the parties function to decentralize the American system. The administrator must play politics for the same reason that the politician is able to play in administration: the parties are without program and without discipline.

In response to the unprotected position in which the party situation places him, the administrator is forced to nurse the Congress of the United States, that crucial constituency which ultimately controls his agency's budget and program. From the administrator's view, a sympathetic consideration of congressional requests (if not downright submission to them) is the surest way to build the political support without which the administrative job could not continue. Even the completely task-oriented administrator must be sensitive to the need for congressional support and to the relationship between case work requests, on one side, and budgetary and legislative support, on the other. "You do a good job handling the personal problems and requests of a Congressman," a White House officer said, "and you have an easier time convincing him to back your program." Thus there is an important link between the nursing of congressional requests, requests that largely concern local matters, and the most comprehensive national programs. The administrator must accommodate to the former as a price of gaining support for the latter.

One result of administrative politics is that the administrative agency may become the captive of the nation-wide interest group it serves or presumably regulates. In such cases no government may come out with effective authority: the winners are the interest groups themselves. But in a very large number of cases, states and localities also win influence. The politics of administration is a process of making peace with legislators who for the most part consider themselves the guardians of local interests. The political role of administrators therefore contributes to the power of states and localities in national programs.

Finally, the way the party system operates gives American politics their over-all distinctive tone. The lack of party discipline produces an openness in the system that allows individuals, groups, and institutions (including state and local governments) to attempt to influence national policy at every step of the legislative-administrative process. This is the "multiple-crack" attribute of the American government. "Crack" has two meanings. It means not only many fissures or access points; it also means, less statically, opportunities for wallops or smacks at government.

If the parties were more disciplined, the result would not be a cessation of the process by which individuals and groups impinge themselves upon the central government. But the present state of the parties clearly allows for a far greater operation of the multiple crack than would be possible under the conditions of centralized party control. American interest groups exploit literally uncountable access points in the legislative-administrative process. If legislative lobbying, from committee stages to the conference committee, does not produce results, a cabinet secretary is called. His immediate associates are petitioned. Bureau chiefs and their aides are hit. Field officers are put under pressure. Campaigns are instituted by which friends of the agency apply a secondary influence on behalf of the interested party. A conference with the President may be urged.

To these multiple points for bringing influence must be added the multiple voices of the influencers. Consider, for example, those in a small town who wish to have a federal action taken. The easy merging of public and private interest at the local level means that the influence attempt is made in the name of the whole community, thus removing it from political partisanship. The Rotary Club as well as the City Council, the Chamber of Commerce and the mayor, eminent citizens and political bosses—all are readily enlisted. If a conference in a senator's office will expedite matters, someone on the local scene can be found to make such a conference possible and effective. If technical information is needed, technicians will supply it. State or national professional organizations of local officials, individual congressmen and senators, and not infrequently whole state delegations will make the local cause their own. Federal field officers, who service localities, often assume local views. So may elected and appointed state officers. Friendships are exploited, and political mortgages called due. Under these circumstances, national policies are molded by local action.

In summary, then, the party system functions to devolve power. The American parties, unlike any other, are highly responsive when directives move from the bottom to the top, highly unresponsive from top to bottom. Congressmen and senators can rarely ignore concerted demands from their home constituencies; but no party leader can expect the same kind of response from those below, whether he be a President asking for congressional support or a congressman seeking aid from local or state leaders.

Any tightening of the party apparatus would have the effect of strengthening the central government. The four characteristics of the system, discussed above, would become less important. If control from the top were strictly applied, these hallmarks of American decentralization might entirely disappear. To be specific, if disciplined and program-oriented parties were achieved: (1) It would make far less likely legislation that takes heavily into account the desires and prejudices of the highly decentralized power groups and institutions of the country, including the state and local governments. (2) It would to a large extent prevent legislators, individually and collectively, from intruding themselves on behalf of non-national interests in national administrative programs. (3) It would put an end to the administrator's search for his own political support, a search that often results in fostering state, local, and other non-national powers. (4) It would dampen the process by which individuals and groups, including state and local political leaders, take advantage of multiple cracks to steer national legislation and administration in ways congenial to them and the institutions they represent.

Alterations of this sort could only accompany basic changes in the organization and style of politics which, in turn, presuppose fundamental changes at the parties' social base. The sharing of functions is, in fact, the sharing of power. To end this sharing process would mean the destruction of whatever measure of decentralization exists in the United States today. . . .

Note

1. The President's third suggestion was that the committee "identify functions and responsibilities likely to require state or federal attention in the future and . . . recommend the level of state effort, or federal effort, or both, that will be needed to assure effective action." The committee initially devoted little attention to this problem. Upon discovering the difficulty of making separatist recommendations, i.e., for turning over federal functions and taxes to the states, it developed a series of proposals looking to greater effectiveness in intergovernmental collaboration. The committee was succeeded by a legislatively-based, 26-member Advisory Commission on Intergovernmental Relations, established September 29, 1959.

5. THE CONDITION OF AMERICAN FEDERALISM: AN HISTORIAN'S VIEW

Harry N. Scheiber

. . . Debate has been colored lately by differences of opinion concerning the actual historic tradition of American federalism. The long-standing view was that throughout the 19th century, and in most respects until the New Deal, "dual federalism"—in which the functions of the three levels of government were well delineated and in which their administrative activities were kept separate and autonomous—was the prevailing system. Only in the 20th century did there emerge a new order, termed "cooperative federalism," in which all the levels of government became "mutually complementary parts of a *single* governmental mechanism all of whose powers are intended to realize the current purposes of government according to the applicability of the problem at hand." [1]

Now there has become popular a new historical view, associated mainly with the late Morton Grodzins, that dual federalism never characterized the American political system. From the beginning, it is asserted, there was a high degree of intergovernmental activity, involving shared functions and responsibilities; indeed, there was "as much sharing" in the period 1790-1860 as there is today. [2] Surprising as it may seem, this historical construct has gained wide currency among political scientists and bids fair to become the new conventional wisdom about American federalism. [3] . . .

I. The Fallacy of Continuity

The model of "cooperative federalism" portrays the present-day federal system as one in which most of the important functions of government are shared. Professor Grodzins argued that the system does not resemble a layer cake "of three distinct and separate planes" so much as a marble cake: "there is no neat horizontal stratification," for both policy-making and administrative functions are shared by Federal, State, and local governments. Grodzins went further, declaring that the marble-cake analogy was applicable no less to American federalism in the 19th century than it is today. "There has in fact never been a time," he wrote, "when Federal, State, and local functions were separate and distinct. Government

From a study submitted by the Subcommittee on Intergovernmental Relations Pursuant to S. Res. 205, 89th Congress, to the Committee on Government Operations, U.S. Senate, October 15, 1966 (Washington, D.C.: U.S. Government Printing Office). Reprinted by permission of the author, Harry N. Scheiber, University of California, Berkeley. All rights reserved.

does more things in 1963 than it did in 1790 or 1861; but in terms of what government did, there was as much sharing then as today." [4]

This historical construct has enormous potential in terms of its political impact. For it lends the weight of historical authority and precedent to the *status quo*, or indeed to any centralization of power that is accompanied by arrangements for the sharing of administrative functions. It has the further advantage of discrediting those who might fear centralization because they attribute the historic strength of representative government in America to the tradition of dual federalism. "One cannot hark back to the good old days of State and local independence," Grodzins declared, "because those days never existed." This refrain was echoed, with good political effect, by Lyndon Johnson during his 1964 Presidential campaign. . . .

Grodzins himself provided little evidence on which to judge his version of historic federalism. He asserted, *ex cathedra*, that "whatever was at the focus of State attention in the 19th century became the recipient of national grants" in the form of cash aid, land grants, or loans of technical personnel. To support such contentions, Grodzins relied heavily on the historical research of his student Daniel Elazar. Elazar in turn has asserted (1) that when government assumed responsibility in specific functional fields, government at all levels "acted in concert"; and (2) that "Federal funds provided the stimulus for new programs throughout the nineteenth century." In his research, he has found that "virtually every domestic governmental program involved intergovernmental cooperation in some form." [5]

There are three main flaws in the Grodzins-Elazar construct. First, it does not cover systematically the whole spectrum of State policy concerns and administrative activities to prove the contention that "whatever was at the focus of State attention" received Federal aid. The Grodzins-Elazar argument can be upheld, in short, only if one accepts a tautological definition of "the focus of State attention"; those programs which *did* receive Federal aid must be viewed as at "the focus." [6]

Second, Grodzins and Elazar do not establish plausible criteria as to what was trivial and what important in the field of "intergovernmental cooperation." Thus they treat the most superficial administrative contacts (for example, State libraries' exchange of legal volumes with Federal agencies, or loan of surveying instruments to the States by the U.S. Coast Survey) as evidence of viable cooperation. [7]

Finally, and most centrally, they do not consider the basic issue of power as it was distributed relatively among levels of government. Indeed, they do not even consider power as it was exercised at different levels in the few State programs that *were* aided with Federal grants of cash, personnel, or land.

The question of Federal cash grants in the 19th century can be disposed of readily: they were of negligible importance by any quantitative measure. [8] The first cash-grant program on a continuing basis, aside from cash aid for maintaining pensioned Civil War veterans in State homes, came in 1887, when the Hatch Act provided $15,000 per year to the States in aid of agricultural research. As late as 1902, less than one per cent of all State and local revenues came from the central government, by contrast with perhaps 20 per cent in 1934 and 14 per cent in 1963. Obviously there was *not* "as much sharing then as today," measured either by the relative magnitude of Federal grants in total State-local financing or by the proportion of State-local policy concerns affected by Federal cash aid. Loans of Federal technical personnel were even less important, comprising mainly the services of the Army Engineers for the brief period 1824 to 1838.[9]

The Federal land grants to the States comprise the only substantial evidence for the Grodzins-Elazar historical construct. These grants were mainly for two purposes: education and transportation.[10] In the field of education, there were two land-grant programs of importance, the cession of portions of the Federal land in public-land States of the West for support of common schools; and the Morrill-Act cessions of 1862, granting scrip receivable for public lands to the States in proportion to their population, for support of agricultural and mechanical colleges.

Neither program, however, comprised genuine sharing comparable to that which characterizes the modern grant-in-aid programs—for neither significantly narrowed the range of policy-making discretion enjoyed by the States. In common education, the States continued to have exclusive control over professional and certification standards, over determination of levels of total support, over curriculum structure and content, and the like. There was no matching formula operative; there were no administrative contacts with agencies of the Federal government charged with policy or administrative functions (the U.S. Office of Education was not even established until 1867); and there was no auditing nor inspection by Federal officials.[11]

Federal grants for transportation offer somewhat more persuasive evidence of genuine "sharing" of 19th century policy-making functions. The grants to the States and to private railroad companies did affect vitally the pace and location of new transport construction. However, supportive and subsidy activity was only one aspect of policy-making in this field. Equally important was regulation of rates and operating practices on the lines of transport. One cannot find government at all levels "acting in concert" (Elazar's phrase) in this policy area. It was the States alone that established basic corporation, property, taxation, and eminent-domain law under which transportation facilities were built, financed, and operated. From the 1830's on, the States had control over railroad charges; and the Granger laws of the 1870's had ample precedent in State regulatory legislation of the preceding decades.[12] Not until 1887, when it established the Interstate Commerce Commission, did Congress first assert its power in the regulatory field. The relative distribution of power over transport costs in the national economy cannot, moreover, be judged alone by reference to statutes and court decisions. For in their administrative operations, the States exercised real control over the ostensibly free internal-transport market. As owners and operators of basic lines of internal transport in the canal era, 1825-1850, the States blatantly evaded Constitutional limitations on their power to regulate interstate commerce. In every major canal State, the public authorities levied discriminatory tolls that favored their own producers at the expense of those located out of State. As a result, the State canal tolls until 1850 constituted a web of effective barriers to free internal trade.[13]

In sum, even if one takes into account the cash value of Federal land ceded to the States, the 19th-century Federal grants did not involve pervasive sharing of policy-making powers. Intergovernmental administrative contracts were casual at best: even in the major land-grant programs, the Federal administrative role was limited mainly to the bookkeeping operations of the General Land Office. It requires tortured semantics and neglect of the critical issue—relative power—to argue basic continuity in the history of the 19th and 20th century federalism on evidence such as Grodzins and Elazar have adduced. If this historical construct of cooperative federalism is fallacious, what, then, is the record?

The federal system may be rather understood as having gone through four major stages of power distribution. The basic pattern of intergovernmental relations has been redefined and reformulated in each of these stages—and the "creative federalism" advocated by President Johnson must be comprehended in a context of successive transformations rather than as a mere variant of a timeless theme.

[The author continues, offering a detailed summary of these historical developments. The clearest statement of Scheiber's views on the stages of American federalism is contained in another article, from which the next seven paragraphs are excerpted.—Ed.]*

The first stage, the era of dual federalism and rivalistic state mercantilism, runs from 1789 to 1861. This is a period when the behavior of the federal system conformed closely to the juridical model of dual federalism. The Supreme Court generally supported dualism in the responsibilities of the central and state governments, and Congress refrained from making innovative policy in many areas formally opened to it by the Court. Moreover, the relatively decentralized character of the economy meant that the states' geographic jurisdiction was congruent with decentralized promotional and regulatory powers.

The second stage, 1861-1890, was one of transitional centralization. Amendment of the Constitution, together with vast expansion of the policy responsibilities of the national government and an increase in the jurisdiction of the federal courts, meant significant centralization of real power. In 1887 Congress undertook national regulation of the railroads, and three years later the Sherman Act marked the beginning of general business regulation. Meanwhile, the Supreme Court's activism was itself a centralizing force, albeit along lines that served to attenuate state initiatives or federal civil rights laws.[14]

The years 1890-1933 constitute the third stage, accelerating centralization. Successive federal laws advanced national regulation; World War I brought intensive, if temporary, centralization; and the Supreme Court continued to "censor" state legislation with a heavy hand. Modern grants-in-aid originated in this period, although on only a small scale.

A residue of dual federalism from the antebellum era was evident in the area of civil rights, as Southern blacks were left virtually helpless against private coercion, state action, and often terrifying violence; the states continued to have almost exclusive control over labor policy, and they have also retained control over such traditional areas as education, family law, and criminal law.

* From "Federalism and Legal Process: Historical and Contemporary Analysis of the American System," *Law & Society Review* 14 (Spring 1980): 679-681. Reprinted by permission of *Law & Society Review*, the official publication of the Law and Society Association.

The New Deal inaugurated the fourth stage, which brought the well-known "Constitutional Revolution" and the transformation of the American political economy. Increases in both the extent and intensity of federal regulation, the establishment of regional planning in the Tennessee Valley, federalization of labor policy, the reorganization of agriculture as a managed sector, and expansion of welfare programs all combined with the adoption of Keynesian fiscal policy and contemporary income and estate taxation policy. It was in this broad context of quick and intensive centralization that Cooperative Federalism emerged as a style or technique of intergovernmental relations.

The fifth phase is the post-World War II era, in which modern centralized government spawned the Creative Federalism of Johnson and the New Federalism of Nixon and Ford while the Warren Court validated enormous extensions of national power in the fields of race relations, criminal justice, and structural reform. Many areas of policy for which state and local government were responsible before 1933 have now become strongly centralized.

Again recognition must be given to vestiges of dual federalism, both in the law and in the dynamics of politics. Thus there is continuing rivalry among the states in the competition for industrial development; there is regional division on some major issues; and the Supreme Court has made some cracks even in the monolithic powers derived from the Commerce Clause (*National League of Cities v. Usery*, 426 U.S. 833, 1976). As Lowi has written, however, the system is now a "modern, positive national state," if also "the youngest consolidated national government," among the large modern nation-states.[15]

[Here Scheiber's Senate subcommittee study resumes.—Ed.]

The American political system has undergone a revolution since 1933, and another major departure appears in process now. This retrospective view suggests, first, a warning that behind us is no homogeneous history of cooperative federalism, and that the Great Society may bring changes no less pervasive than those produced by the New Deal. It may be comforting to assume that cooperative federalism dates from 1790, just as it is comforting to assume that the real power of State-local government has recently grown more rapidly than the Federal Government's, or that issues of relative power are now irrelevant. But such assumptions will foreclose meaningful discussion of how shifts in power distribution (which are not automatically negated by mere administrative sharing) will in the future affect the federal system and the welfare of the Nation. If cooperative federalism from 1933 to the 1960's differs from the projected creative federalism of Lyndon B. Johnson, either in style or specific functional arrangements, the historical record suggests the perils of performance falling short of promise. It also indicates the importance of understanding what changes in power distribution we are prepared to accept—as matters of necessity or matters of choice.

James Madison wrote in 1787:

> Conceiving that an individual independence of the States is utterly irreconcilable with their aggregate sovereignty, and that a consolidation of the whole into one simple republic would be as inexpedient as it is unattainable, I have sought for a middle ground which may at once support a due supremacy of the national authority, and not exclude the local authorities wherever they can be subordinately useful.[16]

We might do well to recall that purpose; for now that creative federalism is focusing on the problems basic to the quality of American life, the stakes are high and the possibility of either failure or stifling uniformity is appalling.

Notes

The author acknowledges with thanks the support of the Public Affairs Center of Dartmouth College during course of research for this study. Prof. Frank Smallwood contributed invaluable criticism and generously shared his own ideas with the author during each stage of the work. Prof. Gene M. Lyons, director of the Public Affairs Center, offered suggestions and criticism, and also a forum: for the paper was first read at the Orvil E. Dryfoos Conference on Public Affairs, Dartmouth College, Hanover, New Hampshire, May 21, 1966. Professors James A. Maxwell of Clark University, Roger H. Brown of American University, and Henry W. Ehrmann of Dartmouth also provided helpful suggestions and criticism.

1. Edward S. Corwin, "The Passing of Dual Federalism," in R. G. McCloskey, ed., *Essays in Constitutional Law* (New York, 1957), p. 205.
2. Morton Grodzins, "Centralization and Decentralization," in R. A. Goldwin, ed., *A Nation of States* (Chicago, 1963), p. 7.
3. For example, in a recent symposium on "Intergovernmental Relations in the U.S.," *Annals*, Vol. 359 (May 1965), many of the contributors quote Grodzins approvingly on the alleged historical continuity of American federalism.
4. Grodzins in *Nation of States*, pp. 3-4, 7.
5. Grodzins, "The Federal System," *Goals for Americans* (President's Commission on National Goals, New York, 1960), p. 270; Elazar in *Annals*, Vol. 359, p. 11; Elazar, *The American Partnership* (Chicago, 1962), p. 338.
6. For a decisive argument supporting the alternative view that power distribution in the American federal system changed markedly over the 19th century, cf. William H. Riker, *Federalism* (Boston, 1964), esp. p. 83.
7. Elazar, *Amer. Part., passim.*
8. Up to 1860, only $42 million in cash was granted by the Federal Government to the States and localities, of which two-thirds comprised the 1837 distribution of the Treasury surplus, a one-time, unique effort. (This was in addition to Federal assumption of State debts in 1790.) Paul B. Trescott, "The U.S. Government and National Income, 1790-1860," in National Bureau of Economic Research, *Trends in the American Economy in the 19th Century* (Princeton, 1960), pp. 337-61. Elazar's own analysis of Minnesota State finance, 1860-1900, supports my contentions. Federal cash payments constituted one-third total State receipts in 1863, a unique instance; all other years computed show Federal payments as 1 to 2 percent of receipts at most *(Amer. Part.*, p. 280).
9. Forest Hill, *Roads, Rails, and Waterways: The Army Engineers and Early Transportation* (Norman, Okla., 1957).
10. Minor programs of aid—measured in terms of personnel and/or funds involved— many of them dating only from the 1890's, are given in Elazar, *Amer. Part.*, pp. 302-303n. Both Grodzins and Elazar treat "19th century origins" of intergovernmental programs in a loose temporal framework, often emphasizing the significance of Federal grants that originated only in the nineties. This, together with their emphases on trivial data (measured in terms of policy-making powers actually shared or in terms

of cash magnitudes involved), is distortive, I think, of the actual evolution of techniques and principles at issue.

11. Harry Kursh, *The Office of Education* (Phila., 1965). Elazar views post-1900 changes as mere "routinization of sharing procedures" (*Amer. Part.*, p. 337). As will become evident, I consider the changes so designated as far more substantive and important in terms of power relationships than Elazar suggests.

12. On early regulation, see Robert S. Hunt, *Law and Locomotives* (Madison, 1958), a study of Wisconsin, and similar studies for other states; also, Frederick Merk, "Eastern Antecedents of the Grangers," *Agric. Hist.*, 23:1-8 (1949).

13. H. Scheiber, "Rate-Making Power of the State in the Canal Era," *Political Sci. Quar.*, 77:397-413 (1962).

14. Laurence Tribe, *American Constitutional Law* (Mineola, N.Y., 1978), p. 5; Harry N. Scheiber, "Federalism and the American Economic Order, 1789-1910," *Law and Society Review*, 10: 100-118 (1975).

15. Theodore Lowi and Alan Stone (eds.), *Nationalizing Government: Public Policies in America* (Beverly Hills, Calif., 1978), p. 25.

16. James Madison, *The Forging of American Federalism,* ed. S. K. Padover (Torchbook edn., N.Y., 1965), p. 184 (letter to Geo. Washington, April 16, 1787).

6. MODELS OF NATIONAL/ STATE/LOCAL RELATIONS

Deil S. Wright

... We can now formulate some simplified models of IGR [intergovernmental relations]. Figure 1 represents graphically three models of authority relationships among national, state, and local jurisdictions in the United States. These models, like most simple models, fall far short of displaying the complexities and realities of governance in several respects—for example, numbers and types of entities, numbers and variations in personnel, fiscal resources, and so on. The three models express visually the three generic types of authority relationships that can exist between political entities—the absence of authority (autonomy), dominant authority (hierarchy), equal authority (bargaining). Despite its simplicity, each model, by concentrating on the essential features of a possible IGR arrangement, guides us in formulating hypotheses. (No two models, of course, will generate identical sets of hypotheses.) By testing these hypotheses we can discover which model best fits the U.S. political system as it operates today.

The Coordinate-Authority Model

In the coordinate-authority model of IGR, sharp, distinct boundaries separate the national government and state governments. Local units, however, are included within and are dependent on, state governments. The most classic expression of state/local relations is Dillon's Rule, named after the Iowa judge who asserted it in the 1860s, which summarizes the power relationships between the states and their localities:

1. There is no common-law right of local self-government.
2. Local entities are creatures of the state subject to creation and abolition at the unfettered discretion of the state (barring constitutional limitations).
3. Localities may exercise only those powers expressly granted.
4. Localities are "mere tenants at the will of the legislature." [1]

For more than a century Dillon's Rule has been a nationwide guidepost in legal/constitutional relations between the states and their local governments. Hidden behind its seeming simplicity is a central issue in IGR and in the models

From *Understanding Intergovernmental Relations*, 2d Ed. by D. S. Wright. Copyright © 1982, 1978 by Wadsworth, Inc. Reprinted by permission of Brooks/Cole Publishing Company, Monterey, California 93940. Pp. 29-42.

of Figure 1: "Who should govern?" This fundamental philosophical question clearly cannot be answered by the model, nor has Dillon's Rule succeeded in resolving it. But the model has helped frame a significant question—and that is one positive result from constructing models.

What does the coordinate-authority model imply concerning national/state power relationships? It implies, again, that the two types of entities are independent and autonomous; they are linked only tangentially. This model received implicit endorsement in the 1880s from Lord Bryce, an eminent Briton who visited the United States and observed its political system.... Bryce's analogy was drawn from observation and experience, but he could have cited an 1871 U.S. Supreme Court decision for a stamp of approval. In *Tarbel's Case* the Court stated:

> There are within the territorial limits of each state two governments, restricted in their sphere of action, but independent of each other, and supreme within their respective spheres. Each has its separate departments, each has its distinct laws, and each has its own tribunals for their enforcement. Neither government can intrude within the jurisdiction of the other or authorize any interference therein by its judicial officers with the action of the other.[2]

Both an impartial foreign observer and the institution charged with interpreting the constitution agreed, then, that *each* of the two units—the national and the state—governs within its respective sphere of authority.

What happened when the respective spheres of action put the national government and a state in conflict—when they ceased to be tangential and clashed directly? The result is well known to students of U.S. federalism. The Supreme Court became the arbiter of national/state relations.[3]... For several decades the Supreme Court, operating on the premise of the coordinate-authority model,

Figure 1 Three Models of Intergovernmental Relations in the United States

Designation:	Coordinate	Overlapping	Inclusive
Relationship:	Independent	Interdependent	Dependent
Authority Pattern:	Autonomy	Bargaining	Hierarchy

attempted to set distinct, insulated spheres of national and state powers. But Court decisions in the 1930s necessitated substantial rethinking of how this model did (or did not) describe the operation of the U.S. political system.

Two scholars, Morton Grodzins and Daniel Elazar, have empirically tested the coordinate-authority model and found it woefully wanting, not simply for the present and recent past but for the nineteenth century as well.[4]... Indeed, many students of constitutional law and history look back at Supreme Court decisions from the 1860s to the 1930s and loudly applaud the discrediting of the so-called "dual federalism" (or what we are calling the coordinate-authority) model. Many U.S. and state courts seemed determined to impose that model on a growing industrial society of increasingly complex and interdependent units.

IGR model builders are probably of near-unanimous agreement that the coordinate-authority model is obsolete and irrelevant, addressed as it is to nonexistent social and political conditions. Before dispatching the model to oblivion, however, consider the Supreme Court decision of June 24, 1976. In *National League of Cities* v. *Usery* the Court, in sweeping language, ruled that the Congress did not have the authority to require that either the states or their local governments observe minimum-wage and maximum-hour laws. In a 5-4 decision declaring unconstitutional a 1974 federal law extending wage and hour requirements to state and city employees, the Court said the legislation violated the "attributes of sovereignty attaching to every state government which may not be impaired by Congress."[5] The Court concluded:

> Congress has sought to wield its power in a fashion that would impair the States' ability to function effectively within the federal system. . . . We hold that insofar as the challenged amendments operate to directly displace the States' freedom to structure integral operations in areas of traditional governmental functions, they are not within the authority granted Congress by [the commerce clause].[6]

The commerce clause (Article I, Section 8), which gives Congress power to regulate interstate and foreign commerce, is the legal basis for enacting the wage and hour laws. The Court's judgment that "state sovereignty" prevents the national government from enacting such laws revives elements of the coordinate-authority model. In this one policy area at least the model has continued, if limited, validity. . . .

The Inclusive-Authority Model

The inclusive-authority model is represented in Figure 1 by concentric circles diminishing in size from national to state to local. Let us suppose that the area covered by each circle represents the proportion of power exercised by that jurisdiction with respect to the others. Suppose also that the national government wants to expand its proportion of power in relation to states and localities. Two strategies are possible: One, reduce the various powers of either the states or localities or both; or, two, enlarge the national government's circle with or without enlarging the state and/or local circles. For obvious reasons this second strategy is often called "enlarging the pie."

Both strategies can be understood by means of game theory: a systematic way of studying behavior in decision-making situations. The theory assumes that all participants strive to optimize their behavior—each trying to maximize gains and minimize losses within the limits of allowed behavior (hence the analogy with games). The outcome is seen to depend not only on the behavior of any one participant but on the responses of other participants as well.

The first strategy above, Type I, is the classic case of a three-person, zero-sum game—like poker: The sum of the players' winnings equals the sum of their losings. An illustration of this in the IGR context is the *Usery* case and the legislation requiring state and local units to meet minimum wage and maximum hour requirements. The national government attempted to exercise (expand) its power at the expense of state/local powers. The gain in national power equaled the power or discretion lost by state and local units. If the Supreme Court had not invalidated the law, states and local governments would have been required to pay increased labor costs. Thus, national gains equaled state/local losses.

In game theory the second strategy above, Type II, or "enlarging the pie," is called a nonconstant-sum game. All participants in this type of game can "win" or make gains. Perhaps the best IGR illustration of the Type II, nonconstant-sum strategy, is fiscal: the conditional grant-in-aid. The national sector can expand by raising more money to offer as grants to states and localities. The funds can be offered with conditions ("losses") imposed on the recipients. But the benefits ("winnings") are so attractive that they appear to outweigh the attached constraints. From these examples of the two strategies we would expect national IGR policies to lean far more toward Type II strategies (such as grants-in-aid) than toward Type I.

Type II strategies assume, however, that the total resources ("winnings") *can* be expanded. That assumption is less likely in a period of fiscal, energy, and other resource constraints similar to that predicted for the 1980s. Indeed, the phrases "cutback management" and "doing more with less" have become common partially as a result of Proposition 13 "fever" and presidential calls for austerity. It would not be surprising, then, to see some movement from Type II to Type I strategies in national/state/local relationships. One policy arena in which such strategies might conceivably emerge is in the energy field.

The inclusive-authority model serves other uses besides allowing predictions of IGR policies. The model also conveys the essential hierarchical nature of authority. The dependency relationships imply power patterns that are similar to Dillon's rule for state/local relations. That is, states and localities would be mere minions of the national government with insignificant or incidental impact on American politics and public policy. To the question of who governs, this model provides an unequivocal answer—the national government.

How well (and in what areas) does the inclusive-authority model describe the realities of present-day American politics, policy, and administration? Curiously enough, conservative and liberal observers alike see this model dominant in many aspects of our public life. Barry Goldwater, Ronald Reagan, and other conservatives see a powerful federal engine rolling over weakened and supine states and localities.

On the liberal side Senator Joseph Clark, as early as 1960, saw, with approval, the inception of a "national federalism": Not only was the federal government in charge (according to Clark) but it *should* be in charge.[7] A more extensive and thoughtful elaboration of the same idea appeared in practitioner/scholar James Sundquist's book, *Making Federalism Work*. Writing in

1969, in the wake of the Great Society programs, Sundquist highlighted the following:

1. "The nation for decades has been steadily coalescing into a national society" (p. 10);
2. "The Great Society was, by definition, one society; the phrase was singular, not plural" (p. 12);
3. There was "close federal supervision and control to assure that national purposes are served" (p. 3);
4. There was "centralization of objective-setting" (p. 13);
5. "Somewhere in the Executive Office must be centered a concern for the structure of federalism—a responsibility for guiding the evolution of the whole system of federal-state-local relations, viewed for the first time as a *single* system" (p. 246).[8]

Sundquist left little doubt that the national government should be in charge, but he was not convinced that it controlled a single, hierarchical system.

Other observers, especially those who have focused on the capacities or incapacities of the states, have also concluded that the states and their localities are governing entities in name only—hence the choice of the term *nominal,* or *centralized federalism.* This conclusion has been reached by four different approaches.

One approach, the power-elite perspective, sees the ship of state guided by a select and cohesive corps of national leaders at the helm. State and local governments and their political leaders are carried along like barnacles on a hull. They are insignificant and powerless to affect important political or societal choices.[9]

A second approach, the technocratic-pluralist position, identifies the dispersal of decision-making power into quasi-public or even private economic fiefdoms that are national in scope. The states or other entities, singularly or collectively, cannot counteract these powerful private-interest groups. This approach argues, for example, that organized medicine and the health industry control the health, welfare, morals, and safety of their citizens.[10]

A third approach, which might be called economic federalism, shares some views in common with the power-elite and technocratic/pluralist points of view. This perspective on the inclusive model can be summarized by excerpts from an extensive 1958 essay on the subject by Arthur S. Miller.

> I do not mean to focus upon the administrative agency, but upon the recipient of economic power—the large corporate enterprise or factory community—probably the most important of the groups in American society. These are the functional units of economic federalism and the basic units of a system of private government.
>
> It takes no fanciful mental gymnastics to say that the factory community operates as the recipient of delegated power to carry out important societal functions. It is the economic counterpart—and superior, be it said—of the unit of political federalism, the forty-eight state governments. It is the basic unit of functional federalism. It is a private governmental system, performing some of the jobs of government.[11]

A fourth approach to the conclusion that states and localities enjoy only a nominal existence is the administrative orientation. The states, it is argued, are little more than administrative districts of the national government, making state governors, in effect, "chief federal systems officers." In the early 1950s L. D. White, discussing "The March of Power to Washington," felt that the states were then well on the way to becoming hollow shells.[12] By the late 1950s Miller reported the district concept as an established fact.

> So far as the traditional federal system is concerned, the implications of this change are clear. Chief among them is that, to a large extent, states today operate not as practically autonomous units, but as administrative districts for centrally established policies. It is doubtless inaccurate to think of them as hollow political shells, but it does seem to be true that the once-powerful state governments have been bypassed by the movement of history. Save for "housekeeping" duties, they have little concern with the main flow of important decisions. When new problems arise, eyes swivel to Washington, not to the state capitol—where eyes also turn to the banks of the Potomac.[13]

The administrative district charge was vigorously challenged by William Anderson on the basis of his and his associates' empirical investigations in the 1940s and 1950s. Specifically addressing the grant-in-aid issue, Anderson contended that the states gained as much as the national government from the fund transfers.

> In short, as administrators of federal programs under grants-in-aid the state governments have acquired something in the nature of an added check upon the national administration. Political power, like electricity, does not run all in one direction.[14]

Whatever the past state of affairs of IGR, another writer, Ferdinand Lundberg, predicts a fully fused centralized system. Lundberg contends that all state and local governments will be operated from an American version of the English Home Office, such as a Department of Internal Affairs. More specifically, he foresees:

> City managers and state executives will probably be appointed or declared eligible from civil service lists by the national government, although there may still be vestigial elections of purely symbolic governors, mayors, and town councilmen.
> Each of the present American states, it seems evident, is destined to become pretty much of an administrative department of the central government, just as counties and cities will be subdepartments.[15]

The hallmarks of the inclusive-authority model should now be clear. One is the premise that state and local governments depend totally on decisions that are nationwide in scope and arrived at by the national government, or by powerful economic interests, or by some combination of the two. A second premise is that nonnational political institutions such as governors, state legislators, and mayors have approached a condition of nearly total atrophy. A third premise is that the functions formerly performed by these now-vestigial organs have been fused into a centralized, hierarchical system.

To what degree or extent is the hierarchical, inclusive-authority model present in the United States today? We cannot say with certainty because our measures of power relationships are poorly calibrated, and the immense body of data required to arrive at such a global conclusion is simply not available. There has been movement toward this model through both court decisions and administrative regulations. . . .

[Wright then presents two cases. The first documents how the national government can acquire leverage via the "strings" on grants-in-aid. The second shows how the U.S. Department of Justice and federal courts intervened to regulate whether San Antonio, Texas, could annex some adjoining territory. The national concern in this latter case was with the effect of the annexation decision on political representation of Mexican Americans.—Ed.]

Do these two examples confirm that the inclusive-authority model best summarizes the contemporary state of IGR in the United States? Despite their close approximation of the hierarchical model (and perhaps the demonstrated need for changes in such relationships), we think that these two examples are not fully representative of the broad spectrum and dominant pattern of IGR in the United States. Instead, we look to a third model.

The Overlapping-Authority Model

The inclusive-authority and coordinate-authority models of IGR are at opposite ends of a spectrum. In the first, hierarchy prevails, while in the second the national and state governments are equal and autonomous. The past, present, or future applicability of either model for IGR in the United States has been sharply challenged. Although there are occasional instances of such hierarchical and autonomous IGR patterns, the weight of academic research suggests that these two models inadequately and inaccurately describe how the bulk of governmental operations are conducted in the United States.

The third and most representative model of IGR practiced is the overlapping-authority model (see Figure 1). The overlay among the circles conveys three characteristic features of the model:

1. Substantial areas of governmental operations involve national, state, and local units (or officials) simultaneously.
2. The areas of autonomy or single-jurisdiction independence and full discretion are comparatively small.
3. The power and influence available to any one jurisdiction (or official) is substantially limited. The limits produce an authority pattern best described as bargaining.

Bargaining is used in the common, dictionary sense of "negotiating the terms of a sale, exchange, or agreement." In the IGR context, sale is far less relevant than exchange or agreement. Wide areas of IGR involve exchanges or agreements. For example, the national government offers more than 1000 assistance programs to states and localities in exchange for their agreement to implement a program, carry out a project, or pursue any one of a wide variety of activities. Of course, as part of the bargain the recipient of assistance must usually agree to conditions such as the providing of matching funds and the satisfaction of accounting, reporting, auditing, and performance requirements.

An illustration of the overlapping-authority model comes from the early 1970s and from efforts by the Nixon administration to innovate and decentralize decision making in categorical grant-in-aid programs. The experiment was called "Annual Arrangements."[16] . . .

About 100 cities participated in the Annual Arrangements (AA) process with the Department of Housing and Urban Development (HUD) between 1971 and 1974. AA was designed to circumvent, by strengthening the hand of the mayor, excessive noncoordination and fragmentation of categorical grant program impacts on the city. A mayor once observed, in dealing with federal agencies, "I feel like I'm the United Fund chairman calling on potential givers." To place the mayor in charge under AA, HUD promised one annual lump sum to a city based on a contract signed by the mayor and HUD after two important prior steps. First was the drafting of a citywide development strategy by the mayor. The second was a series of negotiating sessions between a panel of city officials, headed by the mayor, and a group of HUD administrators, usually region-level officials. In these sessions the city department heads showed how their planned projects related to the mayor's citywide strategy, and the HUD officials determined the level of specific grant program funds they were prepared to commit (in advance) to the city—for example, urban renewal, public housing, open space, and water and sewer funds.

Annual Arrangements was a modest success in its own right, but more significantly, it paved the way for grant reforms and for the consolidation of nine HUD categorical grants into a single block grant program. . . .

This AA example has numerous implications, four of which merit mention. First, exchanges transfer resources and influence across governmental boundaries, making it possible to alter authority relationships among participants (officials). Second, power in the overlapping-authority model tends to be widely dispersed and nearly uniformly distributed.

Third, this model does not presuppose exclusively cooperative or competitive relationships among participants. In this respect it avoids built-in conclusions that collaboration or consensus prevails over conflict and cleavage. It leaves the matter open for case analyses and empirical investigations of IGR operations.

Fourth, as the positioning of the circles in Figure 1 implies, national/ state/local relations are the largest domain, while modest areas of autonomous action (the nonoverlapping areas of the circles) remain to each respective jurisdiction. This distribution reflects the interdependence that appears to permeate IGR. As Professor Catherine Lovell has remarked: "Policy is no longer made mostly in a single governmental unit but is hammered out through a negotiating, bargaining relationship among multiple governmental units."[17]

In sum the chief characteristics of the overlapping-authority model are:

- limited, dispersed power
- interdependence
- limited areas of autonomy
- bargaining-exchange relationships
- cooperation and competition. . . .

Contacts and exchanges between national, state, and local officials may be cooperative or competitive; the determining factors include: the policy issue or problem, the status of the officials, the partisan leanings of participants, and the constituency being represented.

Notes

1. *City of Clinton* v. *the Cedar Rapids and Missouri River Railroad*, 24 *Iowa* 455 (1868). For a recent analysis of Dillon's Rule from a policy orientation, see John G. Grumm and Russell D. Murphy, "Dillon's Rule Reconsidered," *The Annals*, 416 (November 1974): 120-132.
2. *Tarbel's Case*, 13 Wall 397 (1872).
3. John R. Schmidhauser, *The Supreme Court as the Final Arbiter in Federal-State Relations, 1789-1957* (Chapel Hill, N.C.:University of North Carolina Press, 1958).
4. Morton Grodzins, *The American System: A New View of Government in the United States*, Daniel J. Elazar, ed. (Chicago: Rand McNally, 1966); Daniel J. Elazar, *The American Partnership: Intergovernmental Cooperation in the Nineteenth-Century United States* (Chicago: University of Chicago Press, 1962).
5. *National League of Cities* v. *Usery*, 426 U.S. 833, 845 (1976). See also *Wall Street Journal* (June 25, 1976), p. 1.
6. 426 U.S. 852.
7. Joseph Clark, "Toward National Federalism," *The Federal Government and the Cities: A Symposium* (Washington, D.C.: George Washington University, 1961), pp. 39-49.
8. James L. Sundquist with the collaboration of David W. Davis, *Making Federalism Work: A Study of Program Coordination at the Community Level* (Washington, D.C.: Brookings, 1969), pp. 1-13.
9. C. Wright Mills, *The Power Elite* (New York: Oxford University Press, 1956); G. William Domhoff, *Who Rules America?* (Englewood Cliffs, N.J.: Prentice-Hall, 1967); and G. William Domhoff, *The Higher Circles: The Governing Class in America* (New York: Random House, Vintage, 1970).
10. Grant McConnell, *Private Power and American Democracy* (New York: Alfred Knopf, 1966), especially pp. 166-95; Theodore J. Lowi, *The End of Liberalism: Ideology, Policy, and the Crisis of Public Authority* (New York: Norton, 1969).
11. Arthur S. Miller, "The Constitutional Law of the 'Security State,'" *Stanford Law Review* 10 (July 1958): 634, 637.
12. Leonard D. White, *The States and the Nation* (Baton Rouge: Louisiana State University Press, 1953), p. 3.
13. Miller, "Constitutional Law," p. 629.
14. William Anderson, *The Nation and the States, Rivals or Partners?* (Minneapolis: University of Minnesota Press, 1955), p. 204.
15. Ferdinand Lundberg, *The Coming World Transformation* (Garden City, N.Y.: Doubleday, 1963), p. 18.
16. A concise description of cities' experience with annual arrangements can be found in "The New Federalism: Theory, Practice, Problems," *National Journal*, A Special Report (Washington, D.C.: Government Research Corporation, 1973), pp. 32-33.
17. Catherine Lovell, "Where We Are in Intergovernmental Relations and Some of the Implications," *Southern Review of Public Administration* 3 (June 1979): 14. Reprinted by permission.

7.   FEDERALISM

William H. Riker

... Much of the discussion of federalism, like the discussion of all institutions, is moral evaluation. More accurately, it is straightforward ideology in the sense that it is the justification of the advantage of some advantaged interest. Sometimes the moral evaluation or ideology masquerades as science, though of course its nonscientific character is fairly evident, even to the common reader. ... [As] a guide to the reader through that intellectual morass, I offer a brief survey of the ideological issues.

The Beneficiaries of Federalism

Who benefits from federalism? This is the first question one must answer before one can understand the ideology. By its nature, ideology is the justification of an interest served by an institution. To understand an ideology, therefore, it is first necessary to understand who the beneficiary of the institution is. But the identification of who benefits is not easy, largely because the beneficiaries vary over time.

When federations are relatively new, the practical issue in their politics is: Shall the federal system continue to exist or shall it be broken up into the constituent units? When that is the issue, then it is readily apparent that the beneficiaries of the continued existence of the system are those who wanted federalism in the first place. I have earlier argued that those who want it are those who are especially conscious of the need for defense against either external or internal enemies or those who would use the big government of federalism for aggression. For convenience let us call these military beneficiaries "nationalists."

Nationalists are by definition those who put military and police security at the top of their priority list of political goals. Their opponents—for convenience, call them "antinationalists," for they are not necessarily localists—are those who are less concerned about military security and more concerned about other goals such as questions of the distribution of wealth or religious, linguistic, or racial equality.

For example, in the early history of the United States the Federalists were those who first of all wanted to put their house in order against the possible re-

From "Federalism," in Fred I. Greenstein and Nelson W. Polsby, eds., *Handbook of Political Science, Volume 5: Governmental Institutions and Processes* (Reading, Mass.: Addison-Wesley, © 1975), pp. 151-159 (portions only). Reprinted with permission.

opening of the war—it was on that basis that Washington could bring together two nationalist politicians like Hamilton and Jefferson whose secondary goals were so diverse. The Antifederalists, on the other hand, were those who were so especially concerned about political democracy and questions of distribution that they were willing to chance weakness in war to achieve these other goals. . . .

Given this division of politics, at the beginning of a federation, into nationalist and antinationalist impulses, one can say that the initial beneficiaries of federalism are the nationalists, whatever and however contradictory their secondary goals may be.

But the initial circumstances of a federalism do not last forever. In the shifting scene of alliance, both domestic and international, politics make strange bedfellows. Former enemies become friends and former friends become enemies. And these circumstances change the nature of political problems and lead people to reorder their priorities, just as within a couple of years after 1789 Jeffersonians began to become very like the original Antifederalists. On a longer time scale, the circumstances that call forth the original nationalist impulse can even reverse themselves. Thus the United States was formed to fight Great Britain, but in the second century of the American Union it fought two gigantic wars to save England from its political and military mistakes.

With the change in issues, the continued existence of the federation becomes an accepted political premise. It is, of course, possible that the question of existence be reopened, as it was in the United States in 1860 or as it has been recently in Canada or Nigeria. But, aside from such reopening, in mature federations the political issue is no longer whether or not the nation will continue to exist. Rather, political issues are the ordinary nonfederal issues that characterize the politics of any nation: questions of distribution, group influence, racial and religious and linguistic differences, economic policy, etc.

And when these ordinary questions dominate politics, who benefits from federalism then? The answer is, of course, that various minorities benefit. The fact that two levels of government are able to make policy on the same subjects . . . means that the government at one level need not behave the same as the government at another level. If they do behave the same way, then the minority that makes a different policy in a province or state would not be able to make that policy. Federalism permits, indeed guarantees, that there will be some subjects on which policy is made locally. Hence it guarantees also the possibility that such policy may differ from national policy. And if it does, then a minority benefits. . . .

So the question of who benefits from federalism varies with the degree of nationalism and the internal political structure of the federal system. When there is barely enough nationalism to keep the federation going, then the beneficiaries are nationalists, who of course may be of almost any ideological hue. Thus, the victors in the American Civil War contained radical abolitionists and economic conservatives. Or, in Canada, now that the issue of continued existence has been raised to the central position in politics, the beneficiaries of federalism are the English-speaking Canadians and those French-speaking ones who are opposed to a free Quebec. When, however, national feeling is sufficiently strong to guarantee the continued life of the federalism, then the beneficiaries are those who can use constituent governments to enforce minority policies.

Just who these minorities are varies with the political structure of the federalism. . . .

United States. The United States became sufficiently centralized after the Civil War that the issue of continued existence was no longer raised. In the subsequent century the main beneficiaries of federalism have undoubtedly been southern whites, who could use their power to control state governments to make policy on blacks that negated the national policy. It is possible also that business interests used federalism to evade regulation in the era from 1890 to 1935. . . , although it is not clear that a national intention to regulate business in that period ever existed. Clearly, however, in the United States, the main effect of federalism since the Civil War has been to perpetuate racism. Now that race has become a national issue, however, state governments can no longer make policy on race and federalism is irrelevant to racial issues. For the moment the chief significance of federalism in the United States seems to be the protection of some business interests against the juggernaut of the "liberal" bureaucracy in Washington.

. . . One could go on through a list of all well-established federations, but the amount learned would hardly justify the space taken. It is sufficient to conclude with the observation that in every federation there are identifiable beneficiaries and that one can begin to understand the ideology of federalism by identifying these beneficiaries.

It is important to note, however, just what the beneficiaries of a mature federalism get. Since, as I have already shown, the constitutional and administrative features of federalism are accidental rather than essential, it should follow that these do not make a profound difference in political life. And this is indeed the case. Nothing happens in a federation because of the federal constitutional arrangements that could not happen otherwise in fundamentally the same way. One can never blame federalism for a political outcome, for outcomes are the consequences of the preferences of the population. One can only blame federalism for facilitating an emphasis in popular preference. Thus one does not blame an unlocked window for a burglary; the culprit is the burglar. The role of the unlocked window is simply to facilitate entry. So it is with federalism. Federalism itself was never the culprit in American racism, for the real cause of racist behavior is the preferences of whites. All that federalism ever did was to facilitate the expression of racist beliefs and the perpetuation of racist acts. As long as whites strongly prefer racist institutions, one can expect institutions to be racist regardless of whether the country is federal or unitary. But when the preference for racist institutions weakens, then federalism helps racism by rendering difficult the enforcement of an antiracist policy on the minority of white racists. So we can say that the beneficiaries of federalism get only marginal benefits on policy, but marginal or not, they are undoubtedly real.

The Ideology of Federalism

The ideologists of federalism do not, of course, utter arguments justifying the benefits that accrue to these beneficiaries. To do so would be to admit that not everyone gets something out of the institution of federalism. Yet it is the nature of ideology to be a claim of universal benefit . . . the ideology of federalism consists of a claim that everyone gets such and such a benefit from it. Since we know, however, from the examination of beneficiaries just completed, that in fact some people, often a majority, do not benefit at all, it is easy enough to spot an ideology, because it is presented as a claim that everybody gets something good from the institutions of federalism. Let us look at some of these claims.

1. *That federalism promotes democratic polity.* It should be abundantly clear, just from looking at the list of federal governments, that not all of them are democracies or even pretend to be democracies, although their claim to be federations is indisputable. Mexico is one example, Yugoslavia is another. Nigeria was a third, before its civil war. To find an association between federalism and democracy is, on the face of it, absurd. . . . A particularly extreme form of this ideological claim is the argument that the process of federalism, by providing opposition, leads to pluralism. . . . But there does not seem to be much pluralism in the Soviet Union.

2. *That federalism promotes democracy by promoting an interest in state government.* ". . . local government is more responsive to public opinion and more responsible to the people" *(Federalism as a Democratic Process,* 1942, p. 82) is a typical form of this argument, which has been repeated ad nauseam in the ideological literature. Fortunately, this particular claim is subject to direct investigation. One question is whether or not state governments actually are responsive to democratic control. The recent series of studies initiated by Dawson and Robinson (1963) and brought to a considerable conclusion by Dye (1966) and reviewed by Jacob and Lipsky (1968) generally support the proposition that state governments are more influenced in their actions by the state of their economies than by the demands of their citizens (for a different view see Samberg, 1971). Regardless of the apparent lack of responsiveness of the states, which may be an artifact of measurement, it is clearly the case that governments cannot be democratically controlled if citizens know less and care less about state governments than about any other kind: national, local, or international. Jennings and Ziegler (1970) have shown on the basis of survey research that citizens simply do not follow state politics very well. And when people do not know what a government is doing, they cannot hold it responsible. And if they cannot hold it responsible, it can hardly be particularly democratic, especially by comparison with national and local governments, which are more visible.

In general, one would expect that the greatest interest of the citizens would be centered on that level of government that does the most important things. Thus, in a centralized federation one would expect interest to center on the national government, while in a peripheralized federation one would expect the interest to focus on the constituent governments. The evidence from the United States is thus what one would expect from a centralized federalism. Owing to the paucity in the contemporary world of peripheralized federalisms it is difficult to determine if states are more salient in them than is the central government. Perhaps Nigeria before the Biafran revolt is a case of truly peripheralized federation, however. If so, the fact that the main political leaders there preferred state to national office suggests that the states were more salient. . . .

3. *That federalism maintains individual freedom.* This is by far the most popular of the ideological arguments in favor of federalism. . . . Freedom is the right to make rules as one chooses. Rules in turn impose constraints on all those who would not by preference have made exactly those rules. We speak of the per-

son who is constrained by rules as one who has an external cost imposed on him or her. The ideal of freedom is then to minimize the external costs suffered by some person in the society. In an aristocratic society one minimizes the external costs of the well-born; but in the equalitarian society of today, presumably one minimizes the external costs of some representative citizen chosen at random from the whole. The best way to minimize costs for such a citizen is to have policy made by the largest relevant unit of government. For all issues of national concern, then, maximum freedom is attained when policy is made nationally. Conversely, for all issues of local concern, maximum freedom is attained when policy is made locally. . . . Federalism interferes with making policy on national issues nationally. But the converse is not true: nonfederal governments do not necessarily interfere with local policymaking on local issues. Federalism is thus a real barrier to good distribution of the authority to make policy. States' rights guarantee minority governing on national issues, if the minority differs from the majority in significant ways. That is, federalism permits minorities to impose very high external costs on the majority. Thus, for example, in the United States, states' rights from 1890 to 1960 meant that the southern states could develop a tyrannical government that created several generations of poor and uneducated blacks whose maintenance was a charge on the rest of the nation. All this to satisfy the preferences of southern white racists.

In Tarlton (1965), it is argued that federalism works better when the constituent units are alike, "symmetric" is Tarlton's word. The reason for this is that states' rights in an asymmetrical system impose high external costs on national majorities. In general, therefore, in any federal system, but especially in asymmetrical ones like the United States, federalism weakens freedom. So the claim of the ideologists of federalism that the system strengthens freedom is thus false. Indeed federalism . . . weakens freedom. . . .

Moral Evaluation of Federalism

It has so far been shown that the beneficiaries of centralized federalism are those minorities that are permitted to make policy locally on national issues. The contrary assertions of ideologists, that everybody benefits, have been shown to be false. But to show that minorities benefit does not settle the question of moral evaluation. Even if federalism typically hurts a majority, it may well be that a majority might decide to maintain it, especially if the hurt is only marginal.

There are at least two reasons why a majority harmed by federalism might decide to keep it. One reason is that the costs it imposes are relatively low. If, whenever a majority is strongly in favor of a policy, states' rights are overridden, then federalism is only a minor cost on the majority. This well may be the situation in the United States, where in the last generation or so racist states' rights have been fairly consistently denied by a not-very-determined majority in favor of a single national policy on civil liberties. If states' rights can be maintained only when the majority doesn't much care, then the costs of federalism, while greater than the costs of other kinds of government, are not relatively great. In short, then, nations may choose to remain federal simply because federalism doesn't mean very much one way or another. If this is so, then one might well make the moral judgment that federalism is not worth bothering about.

Another reason for keeping a harmful federation is that it might cost too much to get rid of it. To have federalism may be more costly than not having it; yet getting rid of federalism may still be more costly than keeping it. That is, in descending order of cost, the following alternatives may exist for a nation with federal government:

1. dissolving the federation
2. changing (by, e.g., civil war) to a unitary government
3. maintaining the federation
4. maintaining a unitary government.

In such case the *status quo* is preferred, not out of any absolute moral judgment, but out of an instrumental judgment that it is the least expensive of immediate alternatives.

Both these reasons seem to be important in the evaluation of centralized federal governments today. In a federation like Australia the institutions are a minor nuisance and hence not very costly. In a federation like Canada, which may be becoming peripheralized, the costs of transforming to a unitary government may be so great that no one has seriously considered doing so for a generation. In the case of the United States, probably both judgments are relevant.

Both these judgments on federalism are a way of saying that it is not very significant as an institution. Whether or not this statement is factually correct seems to me the most important subject for research on federalism. It would indeed be interesting to know if so much concern for moral evaluation has been wasted on an institution that does not have much effect on political life. . . .

References

Dawson, Richard, and James Robinson (1963). "Inter-party competition, economic variables, and welfare policies in the American states." *Journal of Politics* 25:265-89.

Dye, Thomas (1968). *Politics, Economics, and the Public: Policy Outcomes in the American States.* Chicago: Rand McNally.

Federalism as a Democratic Process: Essays by Roscoe Pound, Charles H. McIlwain, Roy F. Nichols (1942). New Brunswick, N.J.: Rutgers University Press.

Jacob, Herbert, and Michael Lipsky (1968). "Outputs, structures, and power: an assessment of changes in the study of state and local politics." *Journal of Politics* 30:510-38.

Jennings, M. Kent, and Harmon Ziegler (1970). "The salience of American state politics." *American Political Science Review* 64:523-35.

Samberg, Robert (1971). "Conceptualization and measurement of political system output." Ph.D. dissertation, University of Rochester.

Tarlton, Charles D. (1965). "Symmetry and asymmetry as elements of federalism: a theoretical speculation." *Journal of Politics* 27:861-74.

Part One

Review Questions

1. What did the founders of the American system mean by such key concepts as *republican government, federalism,* and *nation?* How did they link these ideas together? How has the meaning of federalism altered over time in the United States?

2. Discussions of American intergovernmental relations frequently include a discussion of federalism. Compare and contrast the two concepts.

3. For the founders, even the office of the U.S. presidency represented an arrangement meant to ensure vitality for both national and state governments. Explain how this could be the case. Identify other institutions in the structure of the national government that were designed by the founders to perform similar functions. Do you believe they do so today? Why or why not? (Take note of the discussions by both Diamond and Riker in this regard.)

4. Basic decisions made in the early years of the nation created substantial ambiguity and opportunities for increased intergovernmental interdependence in later years. Bearing this in mind, explain how Madison's position in his argument with Sherman (summarized in Diamond's essay) could be used to justify substantial expansion of national authority on such policy matters as civil rights.

5. Imagine a debate between Elazar (or Grodzins) and Scheiber on American intergovernmental cooperation and conflict. What would be the major points of agreement and disagreement? Which arguments would be more convincing to you?

6. A friend of yours asserts that history is irrelevant to contemporary events, that it doesn't matter what the founders thought or planned, and that it is a waste of time to try to determine what forms of intergovernmental arrangements were most prominent in earlier times. Can you rebut these claims? (Take special note of Scheiber's discussion here.)

7. Grodzins's essay is properly treated as a classic, but even in 1960 some of his assertions were controversial. It is clear, for instance, that he is far from neutral toward the system he examines. Is his positive evaluation warranted? What problems can you see with the "easy merging of public and private interests at the local level"?

8. When Grodzins wrote more than 20 years ago, a dissenting footnote was appended to his essay by two other intergovernmental analysts, John A. Perkins and Emmette S. Redford. They argued, in part, that

the present system of shared responsibility confuses rather than fixes responsibility. Ascertainable responsibility for policy, administrative performance, and financing is an essential feature of effective self-government. The possibility of achieving it needs to be explored. . . . The chaos of party processes itself impairs leadership for national functions and national aims. Mr. Grodzins's conclusion that the costs of this chaos are tolerable may be drawn too easily.[1]

Looking back on developments in the intergovernmental system during the last two decades (the introductory chapter in this volume may give you some ideas), do you find that these criticisms have been substantiated? Why or why not? (It may be a good idea to review this question again after you have completed readings in later sections of this book.)

9. Which model does Wright identify as the most useful for explaining today's intergovernmental relations? Is his case persuasive? In what ways is this model consistent with the historical descriptions of Elazar and Grodzins? Of Scheiber? Of the introductory chapter of this book?

10. How and why does Riker link American federalism with racism? With business interests?

11. Could or should the United States consider abolishing the system of federalism? What, if any, would be the costs of abolishing it? Would such a change be likely to affect the practice of intergovernmental relations in this country? Why or why not?

Note

1. *Goals for Americans* (Englewood Cliffs, N.J.: Prentice-Hall, Inc., 1960), p. 282.

Part Two

POLITICAL ASPECTS OF
INTERGOVERNMENTAL RELATIONS

The American intergovernmental network is fundamentally a *political* system, or a complex of political systems. As the readings in Part One have suggested, the structure was designed to establish opportunities for different governmental units representing differing interests to stake out positions and exercise influence while also seeking accommodation with one another. Part Two focuses on the question of how that influence is distributed and used. The readings in the following pages examine political aspects of intergovernmental relations; however, as many of the essays make clear, any attempt to analyze separately the political, fiscal, and administrative aspects of the current functioning of the system must be somewhat artificial. Politics and administration are inextricably linked and financial resources are cause and effect of events in both spheres. Nevertheless, these three categories do help to organize some of the basic perspectives and issues of importance for the system.

A comprehensive study of the political aspects of American intergovernmental relations must analyze the roles, behavior, and interconnections of a long list of actors who can substantially influence intergovernmental decisions. This complexity, after all, is one of the hallmarks of the intergovernmental pattern.

Among those likely to be politically important in the system are, of course, the major national governmental institutions: the president, the Congress, and the federal court system. In addition, as the opening chapter of this volume indicated, the national bureaucracy is often an especially significant participant. Also important are public interest groups (PIGs), whether centered on function or representing state and local governments or general-purpose public officials. Political parties can exert their effects on intergovernmental decisions, as can more specialized advisory bodies such as the Advisory Commission on Intergovernmental Relations. The national executive, legislature, courts, bureaucracy, interest groups, and parties all have their counterparts at the state level. And there are numberless institutions and political organizations operating among the various types of local governments. City and county executives and other locally powerful interests are increasingly active in intergovernmental politics. Furthermore, an array of coordinating bodies—councils of government, regional planning bodies, and functionally specific interlocal units (for example, those assisting in transportation planning)—exchange information and sometimes affect policy directly.

Because the participants in intergovernmental politics are too numerous and their relationships too complex to be covered in depth here, Part Two offers an overview, organized into three related but distinct kinds of readings.

The first two excerpts concentrate not on intergovernmental relations and politics per se but rather on a sometimes-neglected but critically important issue: public opinion.

The next five articles examine some of the actors in intergovernmental politics. The first piece in this group concentrates on the sheer diversity of governmental structures in the system and suggests implications stemming from the involvement of many different kinds of governments. Each of the other four readings covers one institution or actor in the intergovernmental political network: PIGs, governors, citizens, and the federal courts.

The focus of the final three pieces is not on individual actors in intergovernmental politics, but on their interrelationships, through which they exercise influence. While intergovernmental theory was one emphasis of Part One, this group of readings also contains profound theoretical insights.

In general, then, the readings in Part Two discuss intergovernmental politics as the interaction of citizens, principal actors, and institutions.

The first two readings in Part Two suggest that people harbor conflicting ideas about the proper distribution of functions among governmental units and about the relative fairness of different governments and taxing methods. Mavis Mann Reeves and Parris N. Glendening examine numerous surveys conducted over several decades. The excerpt here focuses on the substantial and persistent confusion found in the survey results. Their analysis was written before the most recent changes in the system took effect; the second reading, an excerpt from a study conducted by the Advisory Commission on Intergovernmental Relations, adds more recent data to the picture. Of special note in the ACIR study is the large difference between opinions of white and nonwhite Americans on some fundamental aspects of the intergovernmental system.

In the first of the readings on the governmental units Robert Reischauer presents an interesting and somewhat disturbing analysis of the effects of diversity in the network. He documents specific policy consequences and demonstrates that the formal structure *does* make a difference. He asserts that it is impossible to achieve any coherent goal via an intergovernmental grant without encountering considerable problems as well. One other aspect of the diversity discussed by Reischauer, private provision of some "public" services, is covered more thoroughly in Part Five of this book.

The next four readings analyze various actors and their roles in the intergovernmental political system. Donald Haider conducted an extensive empirical study of the PIGs, especially those representing state and local executives, as these organizations sought to influence federal decisions in Washington. Haider generalizes, on the basis of several cases, on the operations and the political strengths and weaknesses of the PIGs. Haider's study is particularly valuable in explaining the different roles exercised by the groups on various kinds of issues, and in exploring alliances and cleavages among them.

Although some of the specific policy issues alluded to by Haider have been resolved, his analysis remains perceptive and timely.

Sarah McCally Morehouse describes the role of the governor in the system. Like other actors who experience the stress of governmental interdependence, the governor feels pressure as someone "in the middle"; role stress results from demands and constraints imposed from above and below. Morehouse's article predates the many system changes effected during the Reagan administration, yet her overall analysis remains important. Indeed, the responsibilities and pressures placed upon the governor have increased rather than decreased during the 1980s.

In intergovernmental relations citizens participate not only by receiving services and by voting at various levels. During the last two decades, many federally established intergovernmental programs have required some form of citizen participation in their operations. These mandates are often designed to include the poor and other underrepresented elements of the society in the decisions made about programs likely to be of special concern to them. The data summarized by ACIR in the report included here raise questions about the efficacy of this channel of access in intergovernmental politics.

There is another infrequently studied but increasingly important channel of citizen access. Flawed though the court system may be, the federal judiciary has generally been an institution more receptive than the overtly political branches of government to well-argued claims of disadvantaged (or any other) citizens. George Brown discusses the growing significance of this institutional actor— especially with regard to the grant system—and incidentally highlights the complexity of the multichannel system.

The final three readings of Part Two are closely linked. In contrast to the current political rhetoric suggesting that the national government has usurped all power in the intergovernmental system, these selections offer more careful, restrained, and realistic analyses. George E. Hale and Marian Lief Palley draw an explicit analogy between government regulation of business and the politics of federal grants. They argue that neither operates on a "command and control," hierarchical model; rather, there is *inter*dependence between participants. This brief excerpt prepares the reader for the two last selections.

Jeffrey Pressman's study of federal-city relations in Oakland, California, claims that intergovernmental disputes do not always or even usually indicate the ,presence of inadequate communication and coordination. Rather, it is the structure of the interaction—that is, the roles people fill and the ways they must deal with one another—that generates persistent conflict. This piece is valuable in a number of respects. Pressman summarizes donor and recipient positions, discusses the problems involved in establishing productive bargaining arenas, and convincingly documents some of the ties between politics and administration in intergovernmental relations.

The final reading in this part is an excerpt from Martha Derthick's seminal book-length case study of one grant program as it was implemented in one state. Derthick's research on public assistance in Massachusetts covered decades of the program's operation in great detail. Her analysis touches upon the strategies and tactics of many participants in the intergovernmental system. In this selection she sketches the patterns of influence primarily between the federal government and the state and, secondarily, between state and local—and federal and local—

governments. Derthick covers the dynamics of intergovernmental influence, including the key roles of the bureaucracies, the limitations on state legislatures, and the possibilities of and limitations on national control, as these are exhibited in the modern system. She also raises some intriguing questions about accountability and democratic government.

8. PREFERENCES FOR AREAL DISTRIBUTION OF FUNCTIONS AND POWERS

Mavis Mann Reeves and Parris N. Glendening

... Nowhere is popular support for pragmatic federalism better illustrated than in the dichotomy between responses to questions about preferences for areal distributions of functions of government, on the one hand, and expressions of philosophy about what powers each government plane should have on the other. Answers to these questions often conflict. They vary over time, perhaps reflecting the economic, moral, or military condition of the country, or the imperfection of the survey instrument.

In general, there appears to be support for an increasing federal involvement in many activities. In education, welfare, establishment of day care centers, unemployment, combating poverty, air pollution control, housing, and urban renewal, citizens have answered in the affirmative when asked if they supported federal participation.[1] Usually the questions asked gave no indication as to whether the public was approving the sharing of functions or a takeover by the federal government.

Sometimes enthusiasm for federal assumption of a new program or an increase in spending on the federal plane wanes if it is associated with an increase in taxes. Illustrative are responses to a 1948 Gallup Poll on whether the Congress should provide money for slum clearance and low-rent housing. A total of 69 percent agreed that the money should be provided but when asked, "Would you, yourself, be willing to pay higher taxes to do this?" only 46 percent were agreeable. This highlights the difficulty of interpreting questions about the desirability of programs when the respondent need not relate them to higher taxes or to the reduction of other services.

Often the public is willing to spend even at the cost of higher taxes. Gallup's surveys ... in 1972 and 1974, for example, emphasized the taxes which would be spent to support the programs. ... [Included in these surveys were questions about a variety of programs, including crime control, education, highways, air pollution control, assistance to the poor, and help for the cities.—Ed.] The

Authors' Note: A revised version of a paper presented at the meeting of the Midwest Political Science Association, Chicago, May 1975. Appreciation for research assistance goes to Sewhan Kim and James Oberle.

From "Areal Federalism and Public Opinion," *Publius* 6 (Spring 1976): 135-167. Excerpted with permission of *Publius: The Journal of Federalism*.

questions were restated halfway through the list of program alternatives in order that all respondents would be aware of costs involved. Nevertheless, there was still strong sentiment for greater government spending. One could speculate that the enthusiasm for increased spending might lessen if it were clear that local property taxes were to pay the costs. It is likely that desires for increased spending for some functions vary over time.

When given a choice of state or local control of an activity, the public often chooses the closest plane of government. Note, for example, responses to a 1961 Gallup question on relief. When asked,

> At the present time most of the regulations dealing with persons on relief come from the state government or Washington. Would you like to have this policy continued, or would you give local communities more say as to which persons should get relief and how much?

55 percent favored giving communities more say, 29 percent opted to continue the present policy, and 16 percent had no opinion.[2]

These apparent fluctuations in public attitudes are shored up by the responses to the 1973 Harris survey for the [Senate] Subcommittee [on Intergovernmental Relations]. Overwhelming agreement with all questions set out in Table 2 appears to indicate some basic confusion in the public mind as to where power should rest. The questions are not necessarily comparable, of course, but it is difficult to agree with both number two and number three and still have a consistent political philosophy about governmental centralization. One could speculate that citizens' philosophies are as pragmatic as the system they have established.

Respondents to the same Harris survey answered the 1973 question set out in Table 3 as to how strong the various planes of government should be. Note that in response to the question as to whether the federal government should be made stronger or have power taken away, more respondents wanted to take away power (42 percent) than to make it stronger (32 percent), while percentages for strengthening the state and local governments are five times those for taking away power. Contrast the responses to this question to the 67 percent in Table 2 who agree with the statement that "It's about time we had a strong federal government to get this country moving again." Harris reconciles these by interpreting "strong" as a reflection of trustworthiness and sense of purpose rather than as a matter of added legal authority over policies and programs.[3] This coincides with attitudes expressed when respondents were asked what ought to be done to restore the public's confidence in government. To this open-ended question a total of 11 percent replied that the government should be decentralized and responsibility for state and local needs given to state and local governments.[4] The wide-ranging choices which could be volunteered may have reduced the percentage recorded in favor of this viewpoint.

The real crux of the dichotomy between functional distribution and power preferences may be reflected in questions directly related to federal-state and state-local relations. Even here, however, the preference for the smaller unit is not always consistent. The citizens appear to be calling on the federal system to shift power in different directions at different times—to centralize today and decentralize tomorrow.

Table 2 Public Attitudes Toward the Way Different [Planes] of Government Should Operate

Question: "Do you tend to agree or disagree with the following statements made about the way different planes of government should operate in this country?"

	Agree	Disagree	Not Sure
1. Local government is closer to the people, so as many government services as possible should be given to local governments to handle.	72%	19%	9%
2. Each state has different people with different needs, so it is mainly the states that should decide what government programs ought to be started and continued.	74	17	9
3. It's about time we had a strong federal government to get this country moving again.	67	24	9
4. The federal government has become so big and bureaucratic, it should give more of its tax money to states and local communities to do what they think is best to do.	73	16	11
5. The federal government should not run the life of the country, but should regulate major companies, industries and institutions to be sure they don't take advantage of the public.	76	16	8

SOURCES: Adapted from U.S. Senate, Committee on Government Operations, Subcommittee on Intergovernmental Relations, *Confidence and Concern: Citizens View American Government* (Washington: U.S. Government Printing Office, 1973), pp. 112-114; Harris Survey, 1973.

Sometimes the responses to different questions defy reconciliation even when they are gathered by the same researchers during a short time period. This is reflected clearly in Table 3. Note especially the contrast between the two questions asked in 1937. Fifty-seven percent of those responding to the first question favored a concentration of power in the federal government, but only 33 percent answering the second question believed that state governments should transfer more of their powers to the federal government. The replies to the 1938 question as to whether the federal government should have more power, indicate that only 31.8 percent believed it should. Responses to the two 1964 questions and the 1973 question suggest a renewed faith in the ability of state and local governments to manage their own affairs, but since the questions are not comparable to earlier ones, the data are not conclusive. Careful examination of them will not reveal a clear picture of what areal distribution of functions and powers Americans deem desirable. There is no attempt in the present study to explain the inconsistencies in answers to these questions. Other scholars have pointed up the problem of divergent responses and have suggested that measurement devices need improvement.[5]

Table 3   How Strong Should Federal/State/Local Government Be?

Date of Survey	Question
1936 1937	"Which theory of government do you favor, concentration of power in the federal government or concentration of power in the state governments?"

	Federal	State
1936	56%	44%
1937	57	43

1937	"Should state governments transfer more of their powers to the federal government?"

	Yes	No
	33%	67%

1938	"In the division of government power between the federal and state governments, do you think the federal government should have more power and the state less, or the state more and the federal less?"

State More Power	Federal More Power	Same as Now	Don't Know
31.8%	27.2%	20.4%	20.6%

1957	"In general, which group do you, yourself, tend to agree with more today—people who believe in states' rights or those who believe that more problems should be turned over to the Government in Washington to try to solve?"

States' rights appears to lead the federal government by at least 2-1.[a]

1964	"Which of the statements listed on this card comes closest to your own views about governmental power today?
	a. The federal government today has too much power.
	b. The federal government is now using just about the right amount of power for meeting today's needs.
	c. The federal government should use its power even more vigorously to promote the well-being of all segments of the people."

Too Much	About Right	Should Use More	Don't Know
26%	36%	31%	7%

1964	"The federal government is interfering too much in state and local matters."

Agree	Disagree	Don't Know
40%	47%	13%

1964	"Social problems in this country could be solved more effectively if the government would only keep its hands off and let the people in the local communities handle their own problems in their own ways."

Agree	Disagree	Don't Know
49%	38%	13%

Table 3 *Continued*

Date of Survey	Question
1966 1970 1972	"Do you think the government (in Washington) is getting too powerful or do you think the government is not getting too strong?"

	Too Powerful	Not Getting Too Strong	Other: Depends	Don't Know	Not Applicable
1966	38.5%	27.0%	3.5%	2.3%	.3%
1970	31.0	33.0	6.0	2.0	0
1972	56.0	36.5	5.0	2.0	.5

1973	"How strong should local/state/federal government be?"

	Made Stronger	Power Taken Away	Kept As Is	Not Sure
Federal government	32%	42%	17%	9%
State government	59	11	22	8
Local government	61	8	23	8

[a] Note: The compilation of total responses was omitted from the Gallup Index on this question. States' rights was favored by all regions and by those of all political persuasions: Democrats, Republicans, Independents.

SOURCES: 1936 data, *The Gallup Poll*, 1:14; 1937 and 1938 data, *Public Opinion, 1935-46*, prepared by Mildred Strunk under the editorial direction of Hadley Cantril (Princeton, N.J.: Princeton University Press, 1951), p. 815; 1957 data, *The Gallup Poll*, 2:1504-5; 1964 data, Lloyd A. Free and Hadley Cantril, *The Political Beliefs of Americans* (New York: Simon and Schuster, 1968), p. 24; Gallup survey; 1966, 1970, and 1972 data from University of Michigan Center for Political Research Election Studies; 1973 data, U.S. Senate Committee on Government Operations, Subcommittee on Intergovernmental Relations, *Confidence and Concern: Citizens View American Government* (Washington: U.S. Government Printing Office, 1973), 1:299; Harris Survey, 1973.

Notes

1. *The Gallup Poll, Public Opinion, 1935-1971*, 2:780-781.
2. Ibid., 3:1730.
3. U.S., Senate Committee on Government Operations, Subcommittee on Intergovernmental Relations, *Confidence and Concern: Citizens View American Government* (Washington, D.C.: U.S. Government Printing Office, 1973), 1:128.
4. Ibid., p. 224.
5. Philip E. Converse, "The Nature of Belief Systems in Mass Publics," in *Ideology and Discontent*, ed. David E. Apter (New York: The Free Press, 1964), pp. 206-261; and Robert G. Lehnen, "On the Existence of Constraints in Mass Belief Systems" (Paper presented at the Midwest Political Science Association, Chicago, 1975). For an

examination of the idea that inconsistent responses do not necessarily reflect random attitude expression, see John C. Pierce and Douglas D. Rose, "Nonattitudes and American Public Opinion: The Examination of a Thesis," *American Political Science Review* 68, no. 2 (June, 1974), p. 627.

9. PUBLIC ATTITUDES ON GOVERNMENT AND TAXES

U.S. Advisory Commission on Intergovernmental Relations

[The material printed here consists of portions of a summary of an ACIR public opinion survey.—Ed.]

White and Nonwhite Divergence

Examining the demographic characteristics of the respondents in this and recent polls indicates that there is an increasing divergence in opinion between white and nonwhite respondents. The 1982 poll shows a higher percentage of nonwhites than whites registering approval of federal programs and spending: 57% of the nonwhites believed that they got the most for their money from the federal government, compared to 32% of the whites; 28% of the nonwhites believed that government services and taxes should be cut, compared to 37% of the whites. In response to a question on attitudes toward federal government power, 45% of the nonwhites believed that the federal government should use its powers more vigorously, compared to 28% of the whites; 21% of the nonwhites believed that the federal government has too much power, compared to 41% of the white respondents. In rating the necessity for various federal grant programs by categories, nonwhites gave a "totally necessary" rating that was 20 or more percentage points higher than that given by whites in each of four categories: providing aid to poor people, to services, to poor states, and to poor cities.

Rating Governments

For each of the past 11 years, the ACIR has asked respondents to choose which level of government—federal, state, or local—provides the most for their money. This year 35% chose the federal government; 28% chose local government; and 20% chose state government.

In nine of the 11 years, the largest number of respondents has selected the federal government. . . .

. . . categories . . . among those giving the highest percentage of support to the federal government in 1982 . . . in order of magnitude . . . were:

- nonwhites (57%),
- persons 65 years and older (46%),

From *1982 Changing Public Attitudes on Governments and Taxes* (Washington, D.C.: ACIR, 1982), pp. 2-9. Reprinted by permission.

- persons with less than a high school degree (44%),
- retired persons (43%), and
- persons with household incomes less than $15,000 (42%). . . .

Rating Federal Government Power

Prompted by the continuing discussion of New Federalism, the 1982 ACIR poll included a question which had been asked in 1978 examining attitudes toward the amount of power possessed by the federal government. The question asked respondents to choose whether the federal government has too much power; or whether it is using about the right amount of power for meeting today's needs; or whether the federal government should use its power more vigorously to promote the well being of all segments of the people. . . .

Responses changed very little between 1978 and 1982, with the only change in the total figures being a drop from 36% wanting a more vigorous use of federal power in 1978 to 30% in 1982. (The percentage having no opinion exactly offset this change, rising from 8% in 1978 to 14% in 1982.) Examination of the demographic groups indicates that most of the changes were relatively minor between 1978 and 1982. One exception was a sharp drop in support for the view that the federal government has too much power by persons in income groups under $25,000.

However, between 1978 and 1982, there was a widening gap in responses of the white and nonwhite population groups to the federal power issue. . . . Nonwhites considerably increased their support (by nine percentage points) for the view that the federal government should use its powers more vigorously, while white support for more vigorous use of federal powers dropped by eight percentage points. The proportions of citizens believing that the federal government has too much power also went in opposite directions, although by only a few percentage points. In 1982, nearly twice as many whites as nonwhites said that the federal government has too much power (41% to 21%), and 28% of the white respondents believed that the federal government should use its powers more vigorously compared to 45% of the nonwhites. In sharp contrast, in 1978, the same percentage (36%) of the white and nonwhite groups had said the federal government should use its powers more vigorously. . . .

Rating Types of Federal Grants

This year for the first time, the ACIR asked a question designed to explore the variation in public support for different types of grant programs:

- aid to *poor* states;
- aid to *poor* cities;
- assisting *all* states and local governments in providing aid to poor people;
- assisting *all* states and local governments to finance public services, such as education, training and health care; and
- assisting *all* states and local governments to finance the construction of major public facilities, including highways, airports, and water and sewer projects.

The ACIR question was prefaced with a statement "when the federal budget is tight, it is necessary to make choices among [federal grant programs serving a number of different national goals]."

. . . It is quite possible that we would have found a considerably lower degree of public support for all or some of the grant programs if the public had been asked to assign priorities to them compared to other federal programs, or to consider their costs.

Our survey found a strong degree of popular support for each category of grant program. . . .

There was a higher degree of public support for all five categories of grants than there was disapproval. For each grant more than twice as many respondents considered them totally necessary than totally unnecessary; for the most popular grants (grants for services), the percent considering them necessary (45%) was five times as large as the unnecessary votes. The percentage considering any of the five grants totally unnecessary . . . peaked at 12% for grants aiding poor cities; the same grant had the second to lowest "totally necessary" approval rate, 25%.

The relative ranking of the totally necessary votes for all five categories indicated a much stronger approval rate for grants directed to individuals (grants for services at 45% and grants for poor people at 39%) than for grants for aiding jurisdictions (grants to poor states had a 24% approval rate, and grants to poor cities had a 25% rate). Grants for the construction of public facilities fell in between the two groups, at 32%.

Of particular interest to students of federalism and intergovernmental relations is the poll's finding that the public apparently does not pay much attention to the traditional separation of functions among levels of government. Grants providing services to people, which were specified as education, training, and health care, scored highest on the necessary scale (at 45%) and lowest on the unnecessary scale (at 8%), despite the traditional theory that such functions as education should not be a concern of the federal government.

Examining the groups considering the grants totally necessary indicates that greater support comes from lower-income groups, younger persons (under 35), the less educated, and nonwhites. Because the percentages of respondents opposed to federal aid were small, there was too little variation in the degree of support by different groups to be statistically significant.

10. GOVERNMENTAL DIVERSITY: BANE OF THE GRANTS STRATEGY IN THE UNITED STATES

Robert D. Reischauer

... The tremendous diversity of governmental arrangements in the United States ... is inherent in the structure of American federalism and makes virtually impossible designing, generating support for, and implementing effective domestic grant programs.

Significant Aspects of Government Diversity

In a nation as physically large and populous as the United States, it is not surprising that subnational units of government are faced with very different sorts of problems, public service demands, and costs. It is surprising—but certainly not unique in federal systems—that the institutional arrangements that have evolved for providing public services are so diverse. Six basic types of government are found in the United States: states, counties, municipalities, townships, school districts, and special districts. From the perspective of the federal government, which is forced by Constitutional constraints to operate through existing governmental institutions rather than revise these structures, a number of characteristics of this diversity are important.

First, none of these governmental types is found everywhere in the nation. Residents of the District of Columbia are not served by a state government. County governments do not exist in two states (Rhode Island and Connecticut) and in 102 separate geographic areas in 21 other states. Municipal governments, which typically provide most local public services in closely settled areas, are nonexistent in rural areas as well as in some urban territories where strong county governments prevail. Townships—a type of local government that, like counties but unlike municipalities, exists to serve residents of geographic areas without regard to population concentration—are found throughout only one state (Indiana) and in parts of only 20 others. Separate independent school districts are the exclusive providers of elementary and secondary education in 30 states, do not exist in 5 others, and provide education in only parts of the remaining 15. Finally, special district governments, which generally have been created to perform a single governmental function, such as the conservation of natural resources or the

From Wallace E. Oates, ed., *The Political Economy of Fiscal Federalism* (Lexington, Mass.: D.C. Heath and Company, 1977), pp. 115-127.

provision of fire-protection services, are not found at all in one state (Alaska) and are lacking in parts of all others.

The second aspect of the structure of subnational government that has implications for a federal grants policy is the vast numbers of governments, their difference in scale, and their overlapping nature. . . .

A third, and by far the most important, aspect of this diversity is that the service and fiscal responsibilities imposed on various types of governments differ tremendously both among and within states. The most important state and local public service, elementary and secondary education, illustrates the variation in governments charged with providing a single service. In Hawaii, the state government alone provides elementary and secondary education, while in Maine schooling is provided in some areas by the state and in others by municipalities, townships, or separate school districts. A wide variety of other patterns exists elsewhere. . . . Education is by no means an isolated case. Welfare-related programs are provided in some areas by state governments and in others by counties or by counties and municipalities; within different areas of some states police services are provided by the state, county, municipal, or township government.

The diversity in the provision of services is matched by the diversity of responsibilities for supplying financial support. The existence of large amounts of intergovernmental grants means that often the jurisdiction responsible for providing a particular service is not the one responsible for its fiscal support. For example, elementary and secondary education in both New Hampshire and Alabama is provided exclusively by local governments, but in Alabama less than one-fifth of the costs are borne by local governments, while in New Hampshire nine-tenths of the support is provided by localities. Similarly, welfare (AFDC) [Aid to Families with Dependent Children] checks are written by local governments in both New York and Iowa, yet local governments in New York must provide over one-fourth of the funds needed to cover these checks, while local governments in Iowa must supply less than one-tenth of the funds.

Differences in service and fiscal responsibility translate into differences in the relative importance of the various types of governments. For example, state government is very important in Hawaii, where it is responsible for 89 percent of the state's direct service expenditures and 77 percent of its revenues; in Nebraska, where the similar percentages are 29 and 36, the state is not anywhere near as important a factor. Among local governments, counties are extremely important in North Carolina, where they are responsible for 70 percent of local government spending, but not so in Massachusetts, where 3 percent of such spending is in their hands. Municipalities and townships are responsible for 94 percent of local-government spending in Connecticut, but only 22 percent in Nebraska, for example.

A final critical aspect of the diversity of subnational government structure in the United States is the variation with respect to both the scope of government activity and the instruments used to raise revenues to support public services. No simple accepted view exists of the proper domain of state and local governments. Most, if not all, services provided by these governments are also available privately. In some areas, private vendors are the primary providers of such services as hospitals, fire protection, sanitation, housing, libraries, public transportation, higher education, and utilities (water, gas, and electricity) that elsewhere are supplied exclusively by the government sector. In general, a mixed situation prevails, but the level of services provided publicly varies tremendously. To take some simple examples: welfare payments per recipient vary by over 6 to 1 among the states; California's system of public higher education provides twice as many slots per high school graduate as that of New Jersey; levels of elementary and secondary public-school services—as measured by per pupil spending—vary by a factor of 10 to 1 within nine states and by over 2 to 1 within all but seven.

The revenue sources relied upon by similar types of governments also vary widely. . . .

The Implications of Governmental Diversity

For a nation that has emphasized grants-in-aid as a mechanism for solving domestic problems, the diversity of governmental structure and policy makers' lack of understanding of this diversity have a number of important implications.

First, the federal government is faced with a dilemma in choosing the appropriate governments with which it should interact when it wishes to act on a particular domestic problem area. One option is to deal exclusively with one type of government: states, counties, municipalities, etc. However, this results in certain areas of the nation not being served by the grant program, because the type of government chosen does not exist there.

More serious is the possibility that in some parts of the country the chosen type of government may lack the experience, ability, or even the legal authority to carry out the intent of the grant program. This situation has occurred to some extent in the new manpower (CETA) and community-development block-grant programs that explicitly designate urban county governments as the recipient governments—all urban areas except within the largest cities. In some regions, these counties have had little or no previous experience with manpower or community-development programs. When faced with the new grant, they tend to create a new, and sometimes duplicative, service structure rather than turn the resources over to another type of government that previously was responsible for providing such programs within that particular geographic area.

Another option for the federal government is to deal with whatever government is responsible for the particular service. This approach also has a number of problems. First, a decision must be made as to whether responsibility is to be judged in terms of providing or of financially supporting the service. In many areas, a focus on service delivery would require interaction between the federal government and local governments; an emphasis on financial support would call for the federal government to interact with state authorities. The former might appear to be more logical if the federal government is concerned with augmenting services directed at a certain problem, but it is of course possible for the states to change their own local grant strategy to blunt, if not negate, the impact intended by the federal government. This approach may also have the drawback of requiring the federal government to deal with an extremely diverse group of governments with different legal powers, constraints, and capacities. In many service areas, it may be impossible to design a grant program that would fit the needs and limits of all, or even a majority, of the governments responsible for providing the particular service in each part of the nation. In fact, in some geographic areas duplicate services are provided by overlapping jurisdictions.

Such considerations partially explain the prevalence of "project grants," which require that the governments interested in a program and capable of providing the specified service apply for part of the resources of federal grant programs. This method allows the federal government to deal with the limited number of governments that have the appropriate responsibility, and it avoids the need to know which governments have this authority. Furthermore, the project method allows the grant to be tailored individually to the resources, legal authority, and experience of the applicant government, whether it is a county, municipality, special district, or whatever. While the "project grants" approach may circumvent some problems posed by the diversity of governmental structure, it has been severely criticized in recent years for several reasons: subjective elements can enter into the distribution of resources; a great deal of red tape is necessarily generated; small and unsophisticated jurisdictions have difficulty competing for projects; and the process leaves considerable control in the hands of federal administrators.

A final option for the federal government is to deal only with the states, relying on them to handle any necessary distribution to lower levels of governments. Until recently, this was the strategy followed by most federal grant programs. . . .

This option may circumvent the problems of diversity and be more constitutionally correct, since local governments are creations of the states and not of the national government. But some suspect it is an option that guarantees that the objectives of a grant program will not be achieved. Many domestic problems brought to the Congress for action in recent years revolve around the distribution of income and the provision of public services to persons who have low incomes and/or who live in declining core cities. Generally, the affected local governments are too poor to tackle the problems alone or cannot deal with them because of the open nature of local economies. In many cases, state governments could deal with the problems but are unwilling to do so. In such instances, providing federal aid to the state for distribution to the appropriate local governments may be like asking the fox to guard the chicken coop. . . .

Dissatisfaction with the "project grant" approach and with the option of leaving federal grants in the hands of state governments has led recently to an increased effort to design mechanisms for dealing directly with the local governments that deliver services in the problem area. These efforts have met several obstacles caused by the diversity of governmental structure. First, the sheer numbers of governments involved make even the most simple programs difficult to administer. A tremendous amount of effort has been required to answer the questions and solve the problems of the 39,000 recipients of revenue sharing, a program that places very few restrictions on recipient governments and therefore was expected to pose little in the way of difficulties. Grants for a specific purpose—such as education or police protection—to a vast number of governments would probably swamp the bureaucracy with problems, questions, and demands from the recipient governments. A related issue involves program design. If thousands of small, unsophisticated jurisdictions are included as recipients, complex demands cannot be placed on them. Nor, given the diversity of governmental arrangements, can the program be too specific in what it requires recipients to do, because they may not have the power to conform. Even the general revenue-sharing program ran into this difficulty: in Illinois, many recipient townships were not empowered to engage in many of the activities required by the law; they spent as much as they deemed appropriate on services that were legal under the revenue-sharing law and their own charters but found it difficult to spend all the money granted to them.

A second obstacle to dealing directly with local governments is the difficulty in developing reasonable methods for allocating grant funds among their large numbers. The kinds of data needed to develop a sensible distribution formula are often unavailable. Considerable costs would have to be incurred to generate data that would allow the federal government to allocate grant funds to local governments in a way that followed the objectives of most programs. Faced with this situation, the federal government has taken a number of approaches. In some cases, clearly inadequate, but available, data have been used to distribute federal grants. This partially explains the use of population to allocate grants for such purposes as law-enforcement assistance, drug-abuse treatment, and other areas where the "need" or magnitude of the problem is correlated only weakly with population size. In other instances, hopelessly out-of-date information is used. For example, in the early 1970s the major federal grant for elementary and secondary education was being distributed according to data gathered in the 1960 census. A more recent approach has been to reduce the number of eligible jurisdictions to a manageable number for which data are available or can be generated at a reasonable cost. . . . While this solution is reasonable, it threatens to undermine the political coalition supporting some grant programs. Governments cut out of direct participation are less willing to fight for larger appropriations or even continuation of the program because the benefits are uncertain from their perspective.

In recent years, increasing concern has been expressed about interjurisdictional fiscal disparities. Many think that these disparities, as they are manifested in the "urban fiscal crisis," will be one of the major domestic problems of the next decade. Preliminary attempts to resolve this problem have been stymied not only by political forces but also by the difficulties posed by the diversity of government structures. While a general consensus can be reached that the amount of aid received by each government under an equalization program should relate positively to the jurisdiction's needs and inversely to its fiscal capacity, there is little agreement on the operational meaning of these terms in a nation where service responsibilities and revenue instruments vary tremendously from jurisdiction to jurisdiction. If all governments relied on similar sources of revenue, a relatively noncontroversial "fiscal capacity index" could be constructed based on a weighted average of the various revenue bases. However, methods of raising revenue are diverse, so such an index necessarily would include revenue sources not used by some jurisdictions either by choice or by lack of legal authority. As a result, federal grant programs have fallen back on the use of per capita income as a crude measure of the relative fiscal capacity of different jurisdictions. In a nation where a relatively small fraction of state and local government revenue is derived directly from income taxes and where states and localities understandably try to export as much of their tax burden as possible, this solution is clearly unsatisfactory. In some local areas, there is no correlation between income and fiscal capacity as measured by revenue sources utilized by the jurisdictions. . . .

The same situation exists with respect to service requirements. Lacking a uniform set of services that are provided by all governments, "needs" have generally been measured by some gross proxy such as population. However, it is clear that the services provided by state and local governments and those which are supported by most grant programs are directed at very specific subgroups of the population—and these are not distributed among jurisdictions in proportion to the general population. . . .

Conclusion

In concluding this discussion, two corollaries of the thesis that the diversity of American governmental structure dooms the grants strategy to failure should be pointed out. The first corollary is that intergovernmental frustration levels tend to rise rather than fall as grant levels increase. From the federal perspective, more is being done to solve a problem when grant levels increase; but, from the standpoint of the recipient jurisdiction and the public at large, the constraints imposed by the government structure may render the programs ineffective. The response of the federal government to the criticism that "things aren't working" is to tighten up the administrative control of the program, then blame the states for mismanagement. This, in turn, increases hostility at the state and local level. The second corollary is that the federal government will increasingly tend to rely on what is called the *incomes strategy*. Faced with its inability to use grants to solve domestic problems and a reluctance to demand structural changes, national policy makers will tend to design programs in which the federal government deals directly with citizens rather than dealing through intermediary state and local governments. This will reinforce the tendencies toward centralization already apparent in American federalism.

11. THE GOVERNMENT GROUPS IN
THE POLICY-MAKING PROCESS

Donald H. Haider

. . . This chapter goes beyond . . . immediate cases to probe the rich variety of tactics and strategies employed by the government groups in influencing government decisions.

General Roles

The government groups confront the usual panoply of external constraints found in the constitutional and political setting of the American federal system. They contend with separation of powers, broad national legislative and appropriative powers, noncentralized governments, interest groups and political parties with their often local bias, and news media focused upon Washington as the center of all things political. They deal with an active court system whose policies have vastly influenced existing relations among government levels. Also, state and local executives, like their federal counterparts, are buffeted by many of the same pressures and forces in their external environment—forces which have significant consequences for government programs and expenditure patterns. Elections, changes in government, and conditions of the national economy affect those inside government as well as those outside, making each susceptible to forces that neither may readily control.

For the government interest groups, their general activities are directed at securing substantial increases in amounts of federal aid made available for distribution by general-purpose governments. Translated into group policy, this means the reduction of federal categorical grants within broad flexible areas (bloc grants, special and general revenue sharing) to be returned to states and localities on a regular, incremental basis with minimum restrictions as to use and maximum discretionary control by elected officials, especially chief executives. These objectives are the cause, quite obviously, of considerable friction between chief executives and the alliances between Congress, the bureaucracy, and interest groups. Federal executive agencies and bureaus as well as their state-local counterparts view the government interest groups' objective essentially as threats to their jurisdiction over "their" programs. Congressional committees and

Reprinted with permission of The Free Press, a Division of Macmillan, Inc. from *When Governments Come to Washington* by Donald H. Haider. Copyright © 1974 by The Free Press. Pp. 213-227.

subcommittees tend to respond with much the same hostility toward loss of influence and control. Most of the program-oriented interest groups surrounding an intergovernmental program also react negatively to these proposed changes. Hence, competition and conflict among these actors is built into their relations.

Each government interest group pursues independently the cultivation of direct federal relations in funding and programmatic support. However, no single government group is self-sufficient in its influence to make decisions or require decisions of others. Every major federal policy involving the groups is consequently the product of mutual accommodation among them. What one group wants is typically desired or held by another, and what all the groups advocate in common is usually what segments of Congress and the bureaucracy have claim upon as well.

In this environment the groups' influence-oriented activities lead them to assume various roles in bargaining for improved position in the intergovernmental decision process. These roles—initiator, facilitator, and obstructor—are not mutually exclusive and often overlap with one another as the groups' strategies and tactics undergo adjustment. Roles are based essentially on expectations of behavior, internally generated and externally imposed. These roles are outgrowths of the groups' institutional and constitutional positions: state and local officials rather than federal; elected, not appointed; generalists as opposed to specialists; and governed by federal-state-local statutes rather than federal exclusively. They also emerge from interorganizational needs, past group experiences, and their relations with other actors in a wide variety of policy areas. Previous outcomes—gains and losses—shape these expectations and strategical choices.

The government interest groups may be the source of new policies and programs. However, diverse constituencies and membership cleavages typically impede them from performing this initiator role, though exceptions are frequent. Membership participation is sustained largely as a consequence of the groups' size and the immediate advantages that accrue from dealing with their federal constituency on this basis. Members pursue immediate payoffs from their activities, leaving to other groups the concern for long-term strategy and future planning. Members have tangible stakes in most policy outcomes, which moderates their activities to an extent and often makes them cautious in their behavior. They are highly protective of previous gains, seeking to expand upon these achievements rather than leap to new programs or policies where outcomes and consequences may be unclear.[1] The groups seek stability in the policy arenas in which they interact, balancing their autonomy as political actors on the one hand with the necessity to form alliances with other claimants on the other. To maintain group consensus, they move deliberately and incrementally, which often prevents them from responding decisively to disruptions in the policy arenas in which they operate.

The groups represent state and local governments as an interest which, in aggregate, means the incorporation of nationwide cleavages and factions within their organizations. Narrow, precise claims, therefore, are often more difficult to generate than broader, more encompassing ones. From a systems perspective the groups provide general demands upon federal actors and institutions. Their initiator and advocacy roles may be diffuse rather than specific. They are protective of the autonomy, fiscal viability, and integrity of the particular level of government they speak for. They are defenders of the interests and prerogatives of political executives. Federal policy makers, on the other hand, perform certain conversion functions by translating group demands into tangible policies and programs. They, too, assume various roles as mediators of group conflict, arbitrators of their differences, brokers for their demands, proponents and opponents of their claims. . . .

. . . another aspect of the groups' advocacy roles [is that] they were united by the common goal, that of greater chief executive control over federal grant programs. . . .

The government interest groups are stimulated into action by public officials as much as they, in turn, stimulate them. The impact of their lobbying effort is generally to reinforce public officials' attitudes and behavior more than to change it.[2] Typically the groups function as facilitators, constantly adapting their agenda and actions in response to stimuli from a well-established network of actors. They seek common grounds for resolution of outstanding differences between them and actors whose assistance they require. The National Association of Counties (NACO) and the National League of Cities (NLC) redirected their activities to the highway program in late 1967, for example, when they expected that the American Association of State Highway Officials' (AASHO's) preliminary report on the future highway program might become a working blueprint for the Federal Highway Administration and the House Public Works Committees. The mayors' most notable legislative achievements in housing are largely attributable to their ability to join with large coalitions which have organized in support of omnibus programs. The United States Conference of Mayors-National League of Cities (USCM-NLC) assisted Congress in drafting strong air and water pollution programs, and later in ensuring that federal funds were available to aid state and local governments in meeting federal standards. . . .

In a highly complex lobbying network, the relation between lobbyists and policy makers frequently is a transactional one. Who is doing what to whom is often blurred. . . .

Groups' roles, as previously argued, are often structured on a routine basis, largely by outside forces. The legislative pace of Congress also affects group roles and the planning of strategies and tactics. While the groups seek to structure the political environment in which they operate to their immediate advantage, more typically they must respond to the workings of Congress and the executive. The groups' carefully articulated national policies, adopted at their annual meetings, may turn out to be a "shopping list" rather than a concrete agenda for daily action. Each group monitors perhaps twenty or so specific legislative items in an average session, but it gives its top priority to substantially less. On programs coming up for renewal or congressional review, the groups may have ample time to plan lobbying activities. On the other hand, where the pace of legislation quickens or the congressional agenda is abruptly changed, the groups may have inadequate lead time to respond or to build a unified group position.

During the prolific 89th Congress, with its major programs in poverty, rent supplements, Model Cities, education, and the like, congressional committees looked to the government groups for detailed responses. The groups had considerable difficulty reacting to a host of new and controversial items of domestic legislation, which fostered organizational disruptions and often indecisiveness. Organizational leaders and staff may find themselves supportive of new legislation, but commitment of the entire association to policies which have not been fully discussed is another matter. In contrast, the 92nd Congress was distinguished by Presidential vetoes over major domestic spending programs passed by Congress. In light of the Nixon administration's budgetary stringency and retrenchment in many domestic areas, Congress called upon the government groups to respond in defending these programs and selecting priorities among them.

The mayors' restraint from an all-out attack on the initial OEO legislation stemmed in a large measure from their own divided membership. Several prominent large-city mayors—Lee, Cavanagh, and Houlihan [their cities were, respectively, New Haven, Connecticut; Detroit, Michigan; and Oakland, California—Ed.]—had served as consultants to the Office of Economic Opportunity (OEO) task force and had actively participated in the Ford Foundation's "Grey Areas" program, the precursor to the federal antipoverty effort. A dozen governors and mayors also had testified favorably before congressional committees in gaining its passage, which neutralized opposition to the program from within their own ranks. The 1966 Model Cities program, with its new towns provisions, supported strongly by the League and opposed by the USCM, sparked divisions within the mayors' ranks, as did the rent supplements program in 1965. The Republican-sponsored bloc grant amendment to the Elementary and Secondary Education Act of 1967, which would have replaced categorical grants directly to localities with bloc grants to be administered by the states, placed governors on both sides of the amendment. State and local executives were divided on the issue of removing tax exemptions from industrial aid bonds, eventually opposing removal more out of fear of the precedent it would set than the issue itself. In the 92nd and 93rd Congresses, in contrast, the groups often reverted to protectionist strategies, anticipating the Nixon administration's budget cuts and planning their defensive moves accordingly. The agenda of one Congress was heavily oriented toward new programs and increased federal expenditures, that of another geared toward program elimination and budget cutting.

What this suggests is how the groups take their cues from Congress and the administration regarding immediate priorities and agenda. Whether acting as facilitators or initiators, they must first build internal consensus for action, which often raises insuperable problems for group leaders. Strong opposition may develop, lead time for response may be lacking, and alternative positions may be wanting. Administration officials are keenly aware of the groups' consensus-building difficulties and thus may seek to coopt or neutralize the groups for short-term partisan advantages. The Nixon White House staff, for example, frequently played upon group cleavages, disrupting consensus-building operations within the groups, among them, and between them and agency-congressional actors. Indeed, several of the Nixon programs set mayors against governors and pitted county officials against mayors. One major indication of the rising importance of the government groups from the White House's perspective is the number of prominent administration officials that frequent the groups' annual gatherings. These officials seek to lobby the groups, neutralize opposition, and play upon partisan cleavages when it is necessary to do so.

Obstructionist or veto roles can be more characteristic of group responses, particularly where the costs, benefits, and possible consequences of policies are not easily discernible. Group leaders generally avoid rendering opinions on new programs or policies in advance of concrete cases or actual legislative proposals. They may specify general guidelines and conditions which would be acceptable to members, but they cautiously await final details, lest the group be recorded supportive of programs that prove unacceptable in the flesh. New legislative proposals are carefully screened with an eye toward details governing implementation, administration, authorizations, and expectations concerning a program's likely funding. Governors and mayors ask the all-important questions of whether this new program will mean less, the same, or more funds for their governments than existing programs. Will it be complementary to, supportive of, or a substitute for existing programs? How long will it take to get it going, what are the start-up costs and how will they be paid for? What will the transition from one program or policy to another involve? Who are the intended and unintended beneficiaries of the program and how does this relate to other programs in the area? Will its passage preclude consideration of other pending programs the groups might feel more strongly about? Can existing legislation be amended to incorporate the principal concepts or benefits of the proposed program?

The questions the government interest groups and their members ask are not categorically different from those that the congressmen consider. However, they do differ in priorities, emphases, and concerns. Legislators generally give greater attention to the politics of "program passage," while state-local executives are far more preoccupied with the politics of taxes and administration. Legislators may value highly the public credit accrued from sponsoring new programs or the benefits attained from new constituencies. They can blame poor administration or inadequate funding when the programs they sponsor fall or go astray. Chief executives, on the other hand, typically concern themselves with revenue acquisition, service delivery, and program administration. Thus the basic differences in views, responsibilities, and electoral needs may lead not only to conflict among them but also to the assumption of contrasting roles.

Considering the innumerable veto points in the policy-making process, distinctive advantages are often gained by those who seek to prevent rather than initiate action. Every major policy change, whether legislative or administrative, entails the fear of costs for some participants as well as the hope of gain for proponents. The legislative process is so structured that defenders of the status quo can block, frustrate, and delay changes more easily than advocates of new proposals can marshal sufficient resources to overcome these pitfalls. The government groups are rarely recorded in opposition to new proposals initially, instead withholding support in the expectation that congressional leaders, committee members, or executive officials will bargain with them to gain their support. Such negotiations may occur within an executive agency in the prelegislative stage. They may begin just after the introduction of legislation and prior to congressional hearings, as occurred in the case of the 1968 Highway Act. Usually, however, the center of bargaining exchanges and accommodation emerges in congressional committees and subcommittees, as in the cases of Model Cities, Juvenile Delinquency, Mass Transit programs, and the Safe Streets amendments of 1970. When demands are not accommodated at this juncture, the groups may resort to the floor stage, where debates and amendments can assist them in attaining their objectives. The governors, for example, were successful at this stage in the crime bill and—to an extent—the poverty program as well. . . .

In the case of general revenue sharing, a supportive coalition of the government groups took several years to form as a consequence of the veto posture one or more exerted in early negotiations. The formulas for distributing federal revenue sharing among states and local governments were constantly being redrawn by the White House and Congress as each sought to reward particular constituencies. In the meantime the groups were hopelessly divided as to which bill offered the greatest potential for building consensus among them. President Nixon first proposed that $500 million be divided roughly 70-30 between states and local government, while Congressman [Wilbur] Mills responded with a version that allocated funds only to local governments. The President countered with a version that divided payments equally between the states and local governments and eventually settled for Congress's alternative, which essentially allocated one-third to the states, with the remainder going to counties and municipalities. It was the latter version that brought the mayors and county officials together. . . .

. . . the government interest groups withhold support or maintain an opposition posture to enhance their bargaining leverage in final outcomes. The line between a facilitator and obstructionist role is often obscured by the fact that the groups may move from one role to another as the situation dictates. A negative stance may be a delaying tactic to allow the situation to clarify, for alternatives and compromises to emerge, or for consensus to form. Such a stance also may be the last extreme where viable options fail to materialize and compromise disintegrates. Once again, no single group is self-sufficient or powerful enough to require decisions of others unilaterally. All cases where the groups were successful in opposition, in fact, involved a coalition of groups and supportive congressional allies.

Fiscal incentives may be the strongest and most compelling justification for policy changes. The governors' reversal on the national highway program in the 1950s from a state-run and financed program to a federal one is no more remarkable than the mayors' turnabout on the poverty program. The governors were relieved of the greater costs in highway financing and thus readily shifted positions with the enticement of federal financing. The mayors were able to cope both with the poverty program and Model Cities, becoming the principal support group of the former and major clientele of the latter. The mayors also reversed themselves on the earmarking of OEO appropriations in the changeover from the Johnson to Nixon administrations. The case against earmarking was predicated on the advantages to cities and their mayors where OEO administrators had flexibility in apportioning funds among various programs. However, under the Nixon administration, Congress's failure to earmark OEO funds into separate categories would likely have led to even further executive impoundment, and hence the mayors reversed their earlier position against earmarking.

The President, Congress, and federal agencies frequently use such fiscal inducements to gain group support. The USCM, for example, was far more enthusiastic about President Johnson's proposed Model Cities legislation in 1966, once the administration agreed to substantial increases in urban renewal authorizations lest this new program threaten to cut into the renewal program's allocations. Once President Nixon proposed to raise the base figure for revenue sharing from $1 billion during the first year to $5 billion, the government groups were prepared to subordinate their outstanding differences in building a strong supportive alliance on the program's behalf.

Thus, in reviewing the groups' record, one finds that their roles are somewhat flexible, susceptible to change, and undergo constant adjustment to new situations. Organization policy provides a bargaining stance, while accommodation to the shifting political arena occurs from program initiation to implementation. It is next important to inquire how the organization and structure of Congress and the executive affect group activities, strategies, and tactics.

Spatial Concerns and Vested Interests

The age-old administrative problem—area and function as competing bases of organization and governance—confronts the groups in their Washington lobbying. The scope of immediate concerns to the government interest groups is influenced by geopolitical boundaries. Policies and problems tend to be defined largely within the context of a spatial setting determined by city, county, and state lines. But since Congress and its committee structure are organized along functional and not geographic lines, the government interest groups confront a chronic and overriding problem. That is, they seek the imposition of spatial concerns on functionally oriented and structured institutions. Not only are committee work groups organized along such functional patterns as agriculture, armed services, public works, education, and the like, but most congressional members' perceptions of public policy tend to coincide with established boundaries between functional programs and committee jurisdictions. Many of the bills to which Congress devotes a large proportion of its time fall easily into what Fred Cleaveland terms "issue contexts." These he defines as the way members of Congress perceive a policy proposal that comes before them, how they consciously or unconsciously classify it for study, and what group of policies they believe it is related to.[3] Such issue contexts strongly influence legislative outcomes because their structure helps determine the approach for analysis, statutory review, and revision, as well as the advice and expertise that enjoys privileged access.

The similarities between the functional organization of Congress and that of the executive reinforce the interdependence and mutual interests which bring together agency officials, congressional committee members, and interest group leaders. They are all concerned with the same area of government activities and programs. The legislative committee-executive agency structure, and attendant policies which link them, often defines, once a bill is introduced and assigned to a committee, the frame of reference guiding policy makers' view of that policy and the arena of action for interest group activity.[4] Therefore the great majority of bills introduced in Congress fall traditionally into readily identifiable and predictable issue contexts. The entire process can be quite predictable in terms of previous experience, interested parties, sources of support and opposition, agency relations with overseeing committees, steps in passage or defeat, and eventual results. New committee-subcommittee chairmen, party alignments, executive reorganization, and other changes may alter this process. So too, media focus, public investigations, and cataclysmic events may move policy concerns into broader, more inclusive arenas of decision making. But such events and actor realignment are the exception rather than the rule. Their impact may be immediate, but their long-term effect is likely to lead to incremental policy adjustments. Thus the functional organization of Congress and its ties with executive agencies and interest groups are crucial not only to understanding group behavior but also to an explanation of the groups' activities.

As previously noted, most government interest groups' policies tend to be worded in a spatial context. They call for a greater role or participation of one level of government as opposed to another—for the expansion of certain programs and benefits. However, as a matter of practice, general group policies are amended to conform to what is realistically attainable in the legislative process. Spatial issues may, deliberately, not even be raised so as not to arouse vested functional interests. Groups have the alternative either to adapt their objectives to the limits fixed by institutional structures and competing claimants or to seek to mold the environment toward acceptance of their objectives.[5] The groups do both, yet they invest greater efforts in the former within the permissible limits of previous policy commitments. Initially the mayors cooperated with the highway lobby interests rather than fighting them. By doing so, the mayors were able to gain highway lobby support for using Highway Trust Funds for "highway related" purposes like fringe parking areas, special bus lanes, and traffic control. They also gained their help in lobbying for separate mass transit appropriations and operating subsidies for mass transit systems. From the mayors' perspective they gained their short-run objectives, while the highway lobby felt that the more funds Congress directly appropriated for mass transit the less pressure there would be for breaking open the HTF for mass transit uses.

The governors, of course, have historical and structural advantages over the other groups. The Senate already is organized on the basis of equal state representation and, in spite of the natural rivalry which flares between governors and senators, a substantial basis exists for accommodating federal programs to state interests. As Matthews observed of the Senate, most lobbyists believe that the best argument for most senators most of the time is in terms of advantage to the senator's state. Quoting a powerful Washington lobbyist, "A Senator won't go along with us because of friendship, or persuasiveness. . . . The real argument is that the bill will do something worthwhile for his state."[6]

Thus the primary advantage the governors have over local government interest groups stems from the historical tendency for allocative programs to be channeled through the states. For the major part of the nation's history, this has been the case. The federal government dealt with the states from the perspective of structure, potential federal influence and leverage, accountability, and tradition. The states were thereby used wherever necessary to deal with their corporate creations—local governments. This had been the case at least with nearly all categorical grant programs including agriculture, welfare, unemployment, higher education, mental health, highways, and conservation.

Because Congress and executive agencies are organized primarily along functional lines, they have a certain bias in doing business with the states. Mayors and their urban allies often must compensate for this by accommodating their strategies to the positions of other actors, previous programs, and the arenas in which they seek benefits. Moreover, the search for political constituencies is frustrated by the complexity of overlapping jurisdictions at local levels. These entail congressional districts, counties, and special district lines which crisscross city maps and state boundaries and rarely correspond to metropolitan problems. Policy for urban areas often emerges indirectly as a result of pursuing other objectives. Public housing programs began, for example, primarily as an employment palliative and stimulant for the building trades, while federal aid to airport construction was adopted to promote civil aviation. Both are considered urban programs with benefits distributed primarily to urban residents.

The government groups also seek geographic inclusion in programs regardless of their original scope and intended beneficiaries. Group admission often requires skillful bargaining and negotiation. Federal investment programs designed to meet specific problems of the inner city are invariably broadened by congressional amendment to include rural areas, while programs targeted to specific rural needs are enlarged to include metropolitan areas. Schultze terms this process "functional logrolling" to point out how trade-offs emerge on a strictly functional basis among urban and rural interests to broaden a program's benefits and expand its constituency.[7] Trade-offs rarely occur across functional lines, though increased rural, suburban, and urban cleavages within Congress may change this. Such characteristic trade-offs also suggest the difficulty in enacting programs, especially those of a public investment nature, that are targeted to a specific geographically limited problem.

... Thus the government interest groups share with the President the problem of dealing with a policy-making process which involves agencies and congressional committees, their constituency orientation as well as functional structures.

Moreover, the government groups generally compete at a disadvantage with more well-established claimants which tend to be more cohesive and possess greater expertise in special areas of public policy. Guilds and functional support groups, organized at all levels, operate with maximum visibility, and usually with maximum effectiveness. They help shape public policy by assisting government agencies and bureaus in developing support groups. Depending on an agency's need for these groups, it may allow these groups considerable freedom in negotiating arrangements with other guilds and allies that benefit directly or indirectly from the agency's programs. Indeed, governors and mayors discover not only the enormous problems they have in gaining admission to policy systems dominated by guild groups but also the fact that they must often rely upon them as interpreters and implementers of public policy. Guild leaders can be found leading and misleading political executives in their relations with higher government levels.

State-local executives have been known to rely on guild leaders for dealing with Washington and may even follow their lead in lobbying. Such dependency has led many an outside observer to wonder exactly who is leading whom. The governors, for example, almost blindly followed state highway officials in advocating more funds for highways—winning the applause of rural and suburban constituents—without much concern for the program's overall impact. The mayors tended to depend upon their housing experts, the National Association of Housing and Redevelopment Officials, for shaping much of their housing policy. The USCM initially echoed NAHRO's opposition to President

Johnson's rent supplements program in 1965 which produced a tremendous uproar among many of the mayors' allies inside and outside of Congress. "How could the mayors follow the public housers in opposing this new program," some asked, "when it offered an opportunity to expand housing specifically and provided a strategy for dealing with urban density generally?" Once again, numerous cases could be cited illustrating the dependency of the government groups upon guilds, which was far more characteristic of group behavior prior to 1968 than after.

Notes

1. See Theodore J. Lowi, *The End of Liberalism,* Norton, New York, 1969.
2. See Raymond A. Bauer, Ithiel de Sola Pool, and Lewis A. Dexter, *American Business and Public Policy,* Atherton, New York, 1963; and Lewis A. Dexter, "The Representative and His District," in Robert Peabody and Nelson W. Polsby (eds.), *New Perspectives on the House of Representatives,* Rand McNally, Chicago, 1963, pp. 2-29.
3. Frederic N. Cleaveland (ed.), *Congress and Urban Problems,* Brookings Institution, Washington, D.C., 1969, pp. 359-360.
4. Ibid., p. 359.
5. See V. O. Key, *Politics, Parties, and Pressure Groups,* 5th ed., Crowell Co., New York, 1964, p. 130.
6. Donald R. Matthews, *U.S. Senators and Their World,* Random House, New York, 1960, p. 182.
7. Charles L. Schultze, *The Politics and Economics of Public Spending,* Brookings Institution, Washington, D.C., 1968, p. 134.

12. THE GOVERNOR IN THE INTERGOVERNMENTAL SYSTEM

Sarah McCally Morehouse

Governors are faced with problems such as growth of crime, poverty, and environmental pollution. Most of these problems have an important urban aspect at a time when more persons live in suburbs than in central cities or rural areas. At the same time the residents of the states are expecting the governor to solve the urban problems, they also expect improved health, educational, recreational, and other services. Yet there is ample evidence of an increasing public resistance to increased taxes necessary to take care of these problems.

The Governor as Federal Systems Officer

The governor plays an important role in the federal system. Although he has been given the title "federal systems officer," he has little choice but to be a political activist. He is chosen by the people of the state to lead and is the undisputed policy innovator. He lobbies for funds in Washington and then strives to ensure that federal dollars entering his state are spent in accord with his goals and conceptions of how the state should develop. He must complement lobbying for funds from Washington with pressures on his own legislature for the authority and money needed to support his programs. He must mediate between the cities and towns and coordinate their actions.

Since 1966, the 50 governors have seen the advantage in maintaining a Washington office to represent their interests before the Congress and the administration. This office was organized by the National Governors' Conference [now Association—Ed.], an organization that has been in existence for some time but has not been energetic enough in representing the interests of the governors vis-à-vis the federal government. Its annual meetings had been ineffective in influencing federal policy. By establishing the Washington office, the Conference embraced new organizational purposes aimed at directly influencing federal-state relations. It created a full-time governors' lobby in Washington. In response to weekly analyses and special research reports, the office receives constant feedback from governors and their staffs on the anticipated effect on state government of pending legislation. To bring the Conference and its members in closer contact

From *State Politics, Parties and Policy* by Sarah McCally Morehouse. Copyright © 1981 by CBS College Publishing, New York. Reprinted by permission of Holt, Rinehart and Winston, CBS College Publishing. Pp. 224-227.

with federal policy makers, an annual midwinter meeting of governors is now held under the aegis of the Washington office. The meetings are attended by nearly all the governors, who put partisan considerations aside for the purpose of acting collectively for state interests. These meetings inform the governors of the major legislative proposals expected to be taken up by Congress during that particular session and alert them to the probable consequences of the action for their state programs and policies. By their fourth annual midwinter conference in 1970, the governors expected their conference to be attended by the president, cabinet officers, and Capitol Hill leaders. They make their collective presence felt by demonstrating their concern with the course of domestic policy.

The demands of the new federalism have also moved at least 27 states to establish their own Washington offices to obtain more federal funds and keep track of them.[1] Since national aid contributes an average 24 percent for a state's budget, the amount and character of such aid is crucial to the states with large urban centers. In these offices, staffs lobby on behalf of the individual states. These lobbyists are attuned to the recent developments with respect to much legislation affecting their states. They keep close check on their congressional delegation, testify before congressional committees, contact government officials, and provide an office where the state officials can convene when in Washington.

When the governors turn their attention to the impact of the federal programs on the cities, towns, and counties in their own states, they are caught in a web of intergovernmental program and policy relationships. These include the assistance state agencies under the governor's policy direction give to local governments and the coordination of federally funded programs at the state and local levels. There has been a trend in federal legislation—for example, the Omnibus Crime Control and Safe Streets Act, the Comprehensive Health Planning Act, the Land and Water Conservation Act, and various regional development programs—to designate the governor as the chief federal planning and administrative officer in the state. For example, the Omnibus Crime Control and Safe Streets Act of 1968 mandates the states to establish a state planning agency created by the governor. The governor and his staff are interested in the development of these programs at the state level. They want to ensure that the direction sought in federally funded programs is compatible with the state's overall goals. The governor desires to use his office to influence the procedural and policy guidelines that accompany the federal programs and to see that they conform to state objectives.

While governors want to oversee the programs that are funded with federal money within their borders, they must often see some localities spending funds for golf courses and marinas while others cannot meet decent standards of housing and welfare. . . . The governors must watch as the cities use their funds to continue operating programs for the poor and elderly while the suburbs use the funds for parks and firehouses. Because the funds are allotted automatically without the governor's option of saying which local governments should receive a portion of such funds and on what basis, the governor loses control over coordinating policy within his own state. For instance, if FHA insurance were to be jeopardized in any state where exclusionary zoning is a problem, the governors would likely do something about it. If local governments can receive federal insurance without such restrictions, the governors have a difficult time initiating such action. Lacking incentives, such action is usually politically impossible.

Until recently, fear, distrust, and disdain characterized the relationship between the states and their localities. This was well deserved in the past. The states tended to let the localities manage with a dwindling tax base. This has been changing as cities see that the states are contributing more money to solve their problems. The state governor may be a better friend than the federal government administrators. In the past two decades, the federal government has developed a host of programs to deal with local problems. Some of these fostered good state-local relationships, and some were detrimental to these relationships. Several programs in the package of federal largesse served to provide the governor and his administration with the few real incentives they had to strengthen state-local relationships. Among these were funding for state assistance to Model Cities and HUD's (Housing and Urban Development) 701 Planning Assistance Program. When this program was initiated, few states except for New York had a community affairs agency through which to establish this relationship. At present there are between 35 and 42 state community affairs agencies.[2] In general, the federal programs that best served the states in the sense that they could control the policies and programs within their borders were those that were channeled through the state.

The "new federalism" concept is supposed to restructure federal aid around block grants or revenue sharing. Supposedly the concept was developed to afford the state and local governments the opportunity to sort out their own priorities and make their own spending decisions. Over the past several years, the states and localities have seen the emergence of block-grant programs in such functional areas as law enforcement (Safe Streets Act), manpower (Comprehensive Employment and Training Act), and community development (Housing and Community Development Act of 1974). The first two programs do provide the governors with a way of planning and assisting the cities in the use of funds. Under the Safe Streets Act, all planning and action grants are made to the state governments, which, in turn, must make 40 percent of the planning monies and 75 percent of the action grant funds available to local governments. While the Safe Streets Act may not have accomplished its end of reforming the criminal justice system, it did lay the groundwork for the cooperation needed between state and local governments. Under the Comprehensive Employment and Training Act, funds are awarded to states, cities, and localities to plan and operate manpower-related programs. Much of the money, however, is channeled directly to large cities and metropolitan areas. It is not as desirable a program from the governor's viewpoint as the Safe Streets Act and does not promote the "new federalism" concept.

The villain with respect to the ability of the states to plan for the health, education, and welfare of their citizens is the Housing and Community Development Act of 1974. The act incorporates federal funding support for a range of community development activities, housing programs, and planning and management efforts. Eighty percent of the funds is allocated to metropolitan areas and 20 percent is earmarked for nonmetropolitan areas. The act itself was developed with little input from the states, and, as a result, the states are largely bypassed.[3] States are not entitled automatically to any funding under Title I of the act, and they have not been assigned specific responsibilities relative to the administration of the Community Development Block Grant Program. The state role in the federal system is weakened as a result of the manner in which the act was written. The previous three cases have served to illustrate the proposition that the federal grants, which provide approximately 20 percent of all state and local funding, have not in all cases provided the proper milieu for allowing the states and localities to cooperate in solving joint problems. . . . The major struggle governors have is trying to convince the Congress that they need to be consulted in the planning and execution of federal programs and in convincing the mayors and local officials that they are willing to assume responsibility with respect to urban problems.

Notes

1. Donald H. Haider, *When Governments Come to Washington* (New York: Free Press, 1974), p. 299.
2. Jay Gilmer, James W. Guest, and Charles Kirchner, "The Impact of Federal Programs and Policies on State-Local Relations," *Public Administration Review* 35 (December 1975): 776.
3. Ibid., p. 777.

13. FEDERAL REQUIREMENTS FOR CITIZEN PARTICIPATION IN THE INTERGOVERNMENTAL SYSTEM

U.S. Advisory Commission on Intergovernmental Relations

In order to determine the impact of federal grant requirements on recipients, ACIR surveyed federal, state, and local officials, examined how citizen participation works in five selected grant programs, and made an extensive literature review.

The Commission found that, as of December 1978, citizen participation requirements were contained in 155 separate federal grant programs—almost one-third of the total—accounting for over 80% of grant funds. Most of these requirements (79%) were adopted since 1970. Over half were in HEW programs [HEW, or Health, Education, and Welfare, has since been split into two cabinet-level federal departments, the Department of Health and Human Services and the Department of Education.—Ed.] and about three-fifths of these were in the Office of Education [now the Department of Education]. Further:

- The establishment of boards or committees and prescription of their membership was the most usual type of mandate—found in 89 programs. The boards or committees were confined to advisory powers, except for 24 programs involving 17 separate committees.
- Public hearings were the next most commonly mandated participation mode and are most prevalent outside HEW.
- Other types of mandated public involvement (found in 114 of the 155 programs) included giving notice of the preparation of a grant application or a plan, conducting workshops, and offering opportunities for giving testimony or review and comment. They varied with respect to the interests involved, the stage of decisionmaking affected, and the types of participation mechanism mandated.

The findings indicate that the variations in forms of citizen participation are substantial. Similar programs within the same department or agency, or programs dealing with like phases of the decisionmaking process differ in respect to whether they do, or do not require citizen participation and how that participation should be encouraged.

From *Citizen Participation in the Federal System* (Washington, D.C.: ACIR, 1979), pp. 4-5. Reprinted by permission.

108

The impact of different kinds of federal citizen participation requirements varies, but overall it is modest. The major participants in the process are the middle class, and even special efforts targeted to certain low income groups often do not produce significant participation by them. For example:

- In the Title XX (social services) program, considerable difficulty was encountered in obtaining widespread involvement by low income consumers of social programs.
- In the Community Development Block Grant, at least in the early years, much dissatisfaction was voiced with the alleged underinvolvement of lower income groups in a program where Congress clearly intended these groups and their urban neighborhoods should have priority attention.
- A study of citizen participation in eight federally aided municipal services found that citizen participants generally were middle class or "aspiring" members of lower income groups. "Ordinary" citizens were influential only in neighborhood health centers. Even the most activist programs of citizen participation—Community Action and Model Cities—involved largely middle class citizens and those with prior leadership experience.

ACIR also found:

- Citizen participation requirements tend to have a stimulative effect on localities' expenditures.
- The amount of influence exercised by the citizen in decisionmaking apparently varies. In some programs, such as General Revenue Sharing and coastal zone management, citizens and policymakers feel that the citizens did affect the setting of priorities. In other cases, particularly programs requiring only public hearings, decisions often were made prior to the citizen participation process and, thus, it was merely a rubber stamp effort.
- Citizen participation processes tend to help citizens feel closer to individual programs, but do not necessarily reduce their overall feeling of alienation toward government generally.

14. THE COURTS AND GRANT REFORM: A TIME FOR ACTION

George D. Brown

Beyond a doubt there is a "law" of federal grants. Its most obvious manifestation is the hundreds—probably thousands—of federal court decisions concerning the award or administration of federal financial assistance. Indeed, the judiciary has assumed such a substantial role in the operation of the intergovernmental aid system that it would seem difficult to understand the functioning of that system—let alone reform it—without an appreciation of what the courts are doing, and why.

Yet, the current intergovernmental reform efforts devote little or no attention to the judicial role. The same is true of many analyses of the grant system and its problems. This article raises the question of whether such "benign neglect" is sound public policy, especially during a period of intense interest in grant issues. Is not the law of federal grants too important to be left to the lawyers (and the courts)? Should not those who design, work with, and analyze grant programs recognize the phenomenon and seek to influence it? . . .

[The author "begins with an analysis of three salient questions in grant law," namely, "Can grantees overturn grant conditions, who can sue to enforce conditions, and what remedies are available?" Then, in the sections reproduced here, he discusses "the volume, causes, and possible impacts of grant litigation" and then renders "some modest proposals for change and for future study."—Ed.]

Grant Litigation: Volume, Causes, and Impacts

Grant law—more precisely, grant litigation—is clearly a "hot" area. The growing volume of cases involves issues which are highly complex and significant to the operation of the grant system.

"A Veritable Explosion"

The rising tide of lawsuits generated by federal grant programs and their administration has been documented. As early as 1972, Professors Frank Michelman and Terrance Sandalow reported a "veritable explosion" in grant challenges by third parties.[1] . . . Others have described and analyzed the growing judicial role in grant programs.

From George D. Brown, "The Courts and Grant Reform: A Time for Action," *Intergovernmental Perspective* 7 (Fall 1981): 6-14. Reprinted by permission of ACIR.

However, it was not until 1979 that an attempt was made to compile and classify all reported grant decisions.[2] . . .

Even this effort was not comprehensive, however. The authors themselves acknowledged that

> the document is not complete and that there are areas of grant law which are not fully covered. Our intent when this project began was to collect all of the caselaw relating to federal grant programs. Our best estimate was that there were no more than 200 cases in the area. When we ended our search, we had discovered over 500 cases, and we estimate that there are still more to be discovered.

It is probably impossible to calculate with any precision the number of decided grant cases, let alone those that are filed but settled or otherwise disposed of along the way. For example, many important district court cases are simply not reported at all. Nonetheless, . . . it seems . . . clear that the number of cases is increasing.[3]

Why are grantors, grantees, and third parties turning, in ever increasing numbers, to the federal courts for resolution of grant disputes? A simple explanation of the phenomenon might be that as the volume of grant dollars increased, a parallel increase in grant related suits was to be expected, especially in a litigious society such as ours. The real reasons are somewhat more complex, however. They can be found, to some extent, in changing doctrines of federal jurisdiction, which have expanded judicial access generally. Other causes lie within the grant system itself.

Judicial Developments and the Grant Litigation Explosion

The judicial doctrinal developments have received considerable attention in the legal literature and will be dealt with only briefly. The important point here is that the three traditional judicial constraints or barriers—standing, right of action and exhaustion of remedies—have in recent years been relaxed considerably. As a result, the floodgates of grant litigation have been opened even wider.

Standing. Standing is a flexible—some might say manipulable—concept. To have standing to sue in federal court a plaintiff must demonstrate harm, causal nexus between that harm and the defendant's conduct, and some likelihood that judicial intervention will alleviate the situation. In the mid-1970s the Court appeared to be turning standing into a formidable barrier, particularly for litigants who complained of harm at the hands of someone other than the defendant. However, recent Supreme Court decisions have taken a much less restrictive approach, requiring, for example, only that a favorable ruling be "likely" to benefit the plaintiff.[4] The lower courts have generally followed the Court's lead in grant suits and other contexts.

Right (or Cause) of Action. In the late 1970s, this obstacle also became a good deal less threatening, as courts were frequently willing to imply a right to sue from the underlying statute. The principal cause of this development is the Supreme Court's 1975 decision in *Cort* v. *Ash*.[5] The Court laid out four factors which determine whether to imply a private right of action: whether the statute creates particular benefits or rights in favor of the plaintiff; the bearing, if any, of legislative history; the effect of private suits on enforcement of the statute; and whether the subject matter is federal or one traditionally left to state law. The lower courts have applied *Cort* very liberally in the grant context, primarily because of the wide range of benefits and rights which grant programs and cross-cutting conditions create. ... [T]he decision in *Thiboutot* [*Maine* v. *Thiboutot*, 100 S. Ct. 2502 (1980)] appeared to remove even the need for this inquiry. ...

Exhaustion of Remedies and Primary Jurisdiction. These interrelated doctrines express a judicially created preference for the administrative process as the first point of recourse when a plaintiff's claims are either against an agency or lie within an agency's special expertise. It might be expected that courts would invoke them frequently in third party challenges to grantee practices. By and large, this has not been the case. A principal reason has been the Court's view that the grievance procedures offered to third parties are inadequate. The Supreme Court in *Cannon* [*Cannon* v. *University of Chicago*, 441 U.S. 667 (1979)] emphasized the fact that the complainant could not participate in the process. The courts seem to feel that requiring recourse to the administrative process would defeat the purpose of allowing a private, third party suit. It is not clear why this should be so, especially if the grantor agency does have something to contribute. No doubt agency ambivalence on this issue has influenced the judges in this direction.

Other elements contributing to the upsurge in grant litigation include judicial and legislative relaxation and ultimate abolition of the $10,000 minimum in federal question cases, and the growing availability of attorney's fees in grant cases. Still, it is also necessary to consider changes within the grant system itself.

The Evolving Grant System As Generator of More Litigation

The major change which is most clearly related to grant litigation is the proliferation of the cross-cutting or national policy conditions. These create substantial new clusters of interests—and interest groups—with which a grantee must reckon. Members of these interest groups—such as the handicapped and environmentalists—are frequently well organized and both willing and able to take judicial action. Frequently, they have the assistance of highly specialized "back-up centers" with great expertise in the relevant area. Third party challenges based on asserted violations of the cross-cutting conditions are probably the biggest single growth area within the overall field of grant litigation. At the same time, the rapid growth of these cross-cutting conditions may well be a principal cause of current dissatisfaction with the system. If so, the availability of the federal courts as enforcers has important systemic consequences.

The volume of third party challenges based on program specific conditions, which prescribe how the money is to be spent, is growing as well. A good example is the body of caselaw under the *Education for All Handicapped Children Act*, based primarily on the act's condition that participating states provide all children a "free, appropriate public education." Thus, it is the case that an increase in grant *programs*—as opposed to grant dollars—will generate more litigation. The point is that here—as in the case of the cross-cutting conditions—Congress has created new interests which can claim judicial protection.

As far as the rise in grantor-grantee disputes is concerned, Prof. Richard B. Cappalli cites the following factors, in addition to judicial developments:

(1) the change in thinking about the grant from the concept of a gift to that of an entitlement; (2) the ever increasing complexity of the grant, as Congress adds more "strings". . . ; (3) tremendous expansion of the world of grantees, primarily through the extension of various grants to thousands of local governments and special districts; (4) movement away from discretionary grants to formula entitlements, thereby lessening grantor leverage over grantee behavior . . . .[6]

The first and fourth factors are perhaps the most significant, in terms of grantee willingness to "fight back." The earlier, highly discretionary grant system was exceedingly one-sided and contained the potential for unbridled exercises of discretion relatively immune from judicial scrutiny. The present system, dominated by formula based programs, creates a sense of entitlement; and since federal funds are an increasingly significant component of state and local budgets, any potential loss is now likely to be contested vigorously.

In sum, the judicial and systemic developments have interacted: Congress has created a plethora of new rights during a period when the federal courts have been increasingly receptive to the assertion of claims based on federal law. The obvious result has been the explosion of grant litigation. What is not obvious is what the effects of this explosion may be on the operation of the system itself.

Impacts of the Explosion

Attempts at an across-the-board assessment of the impact of grant litigation must be somewhat judgmental and subjective. In any given case it may be possible to identify specific results, but the state of the art does not permit empirically based general conclusions. Nonetheless, the subject would appear to warrant *some* consideration, if only because of the pervasive presence of the courts as actors in the operation of grant programs.[7] Since the systemic consequences of grantor-grantee suits may be quite different from those of third party suits, the effects will be considered separately.

Grantor-Grantee Litigation. Some analysts view the recent increase in grantor-grantee litigation as unhealthy. For example, the Office of Management and Budget has stated that "the number of disputes between federal assistance agencies and recipients is growing apace with the growing importance and complexity of federal assistance. Not only is this costly, it is disrupting what should be partnerships to get things done."[8] In a similar vein, Prof. Cappalli has argued that the judicial forum is inadequate, noting that the decision may at best involve a remand, and that suits are costly and time-consuming.[9] He concludes that the "ultimate disadvantage is the hostility which litigation engenders," and expresses a strong preference for the administrative process.

On the other hand, one can make the case that going to court is perhaps only another step, albeit a painful one, in an ongoing relationship and that the ability of grantees to sue obviously introduces an element of equalization into the relationship. The ACIR appears to have accepted this position as early as 1964;[10] and a number of federal statutes authorize appeals by grantees from adverse financial decisions.[11] Availability of the judicial forum is particularly important in cases where the grantee is attacking the grantor's interpretation of the statute itself.

Third Party Challenges.   The arguments in favor of suits by third parties attacking the award or administration of federal grants appear to be substantially stronger. Justice Harlan's opinion in *Rosado* v. *Wyman* [397 U.S. 397 (1970)], suggests two purposes which such suits further: making certain that Congress' will is not ignored by grantees, and protecting the individual beneficiaries of federal aid programs. These justifications overlap but can be examined separately.

Congress attaches conditions to federal aid in order to achieve what it perceives as national objectives. The very presence of any string—program specific or cross-cutting—represents a potential displacement of the grantee's freedom to choose, in that the grantee might well not have chosen to follow the course of conduct "mandated" by the string. That is why Congress imposed the condition in the first place. Yet the grantee may wish to evade or disobey grant conditions due to a desire to cut costs, a legitimate disagreement over how best to operate a program, or an outright desire to convert federal dollars to uses other than those intended by Congress. Thus, allowing third parties to sue to enforce grant conditions is an essential tool to help keep the grantee honest.

It is also important to focus on the types of person likely to bring such suits. In many instances, they will be individuals or groups with little clout in the grantee's political processes. Examples include welfare recipients such as the *Thiboutot* plaintiffs, racial minorities, classes such as the handicapped, low income persons generally, or those promoting a locally unpopular cause such as environmental protection. A fundamental premise which underlies much of the present grant system is that state and local governments cannot be counted on to respond adequately to such interests. Thus, third party grant suits represent one more instance of the federal courts serving as "the primary and powerful reliances for vindicating every right given by the Constitution, the laws, and treaties of the United States." [12]

On the other hand, it may be that third party suits contribute to the "overload" which ACIR has identified as a principal problem of the present grant system. The Commission argues that problems of effectiveness, efficiency, costliness, and accountability are widespread. Third party suits can contribute to the cost of participating in grant programs. There are the costs of defending the suit, increased project costs in case of delays, possible attorneys' fees, and even damages. Third party suits also contribute to the complexity and uncertainty of administering federal aid programs. Grantees are likely to insist on elaborate federal guidance and refrain from innovation out of fear of being hauled into court. Accountability issues also emerge, increasing the opportunity for finger pointing and buck passing. To the extent that participation in grant programs becomes more and more unattractive, the phenomenon of opting out is likely to increase.

Grant suits can also frustrate the achievement of program goals. Take the case of an economic development project involving federal, local, and private funds, which is attacked on the grounds of inadequate citizen participation. If the court agrees with plaintiffs and grants an injunction, the resultant delay will drive up costs. The public funds may no longer be sufficient. The developer may pull out. Which would Congress have preferred: the project without the participation, or the participation without the project? The court is not in any position to make such trade-offs. It must enforce the grant conditions as they are written.

In sum, grant litigation, of whatever variety, raises serious institutional questions. Are the various forms of judicial involvement a good thing? Until now the question has largely been unasked, perhaps because many of those working on grant reform are not lawyers and are understandably perplexed by arcane concepts of federal jurisdiction. Yet the role of the courts seems too important not to be addressed.

The Courts and Grant Reform: A Time for Action

One can argue that a conscious decision should be made *not* to address the issue of courts and grant reform—to leave it to the lawyers and the courts after all. Indeed, cases such as *Pennhurst* [*Pennhurst State School and Hospital* v. *Halderman*, 101 S. Ct. 1531 (1981)] indicate the possibility of judicial self correction. However, if the system is in need of reform—a point generally conceded—that effort ought to at least consider the role of this important, and relatively new, actor: the federal judiciary. (Although the recently enacted block grants may alter the fiscal and political landscape, there is no indication that the judicial role will be significantly altered.)

Short of Congressional action, the grantor agencies might develop accessible and workable grievance procedures. Agency practice in this area varies tremendously but, in general, the administrative avenues available are not viewed as adequate. (Plaintiffs sometimes "exhaust" them anyway, just to be on the safe side.) The availability of such procedures might lead to the resolution of a large number of disputes in a forum more susceptible to negotiation and mediation than a lawsuit. Moreover, the courts would be far more willing to invoke the doctrines of primary jurisdiction and exhaustion of remedies than they are at present.

Still, the primary responsibility rests with Congress. It would be virtually impossible to address the issue of the role of the courts in any across-the-board legislation. The grant programs are simply too varied, and the disputes they generate too dissimilar. Block grants present different issues than categorical programs. It makes a difference whether one is talking about suits to enforce the cross-cutting conditions, or program specific strings. Many different, and difficult, value judgements have to be made. Allegations of racial discrimination in a grant program are more serious candidates for federal judicial review than claims by disappointed vendors that the grantee has violated contractual obligations, while claims of insufficient citizen participation lie somewhere in between. At the moment it is the courts which make these judgments, on an *ad hoc* basis.

Ideally, the role of the courts ought to be addressed specifically each time the Administration and the Congress deal with restructuring or reauthorizing each grant program. It should be possible to identify in advance the types of third-party disputes which a given program will generate. Policymakers could then decide which should be insulated from judicial review, which should receive limited judicial review, and which should receive whole-scale review of the sort awarded in most third party suits as things stand now. For example, citizen participation issues might be resolved using agency forums, while complaints of racial or sexual discrimination would still be able to be heard in the courts, perhaps after exhaustion of administrative remedies. So far, this has happened only occasionally. The most notable example is the General Revenue Sharing

Amendments of 1976, which created an elaborate citizens suit provision including a complaint mechanism and an exhaustion requirement.

As a first step, then, those who deal with grant reform must add the role of the courts to the agenda, recognizing it as a new item. Empirical research is needed to bring to light the judicial impact on categories and subcategories of grant disputes.

The ultimate policy decisions will no doubt rest primarily on a balancing of the relative values accorded to the programmatic and federalism goals to be served by any federal grant statute, and the rights and interests of the individuals affected by such programs. The task is not easy; the trade-offs are difficult. Nonetheless, these issues have been simmering just beneath the surface for some time now. An honest dialogue will be necessary to arrive at an adequate resolution. At the very least, it is time for the dialogue to begin.

Notes

1. Frank I. Michelman and Terrance Sandalow, *Government in Urban Areas*, Supplement, St. Paul, MN, West Publishing, 1972, p. 275.
2. Office of Management and Budget, *Managing Federal Assistance in the 1980s, Working Paper A-7*, "Study of Federal Assistance Management Pursuant to the Federal Grant and Cooperative Agreement Act of 1977 (P.L. 95-224)," Washington, DC, U.S. Government Printing Office, 1979.
3. Thomas Madden, "The Law of Federal Grants" in Advisory Commission on Intergovernmental Relations, *Awakening the Slumbering Giant: Intergovernmental Relations and Federal Grant Law*, M-122, Washington, DC, U.S. Government Printing Office, 1980, pp. 9-10.
4. E.g., *Regents of University of California v. Bakke*, 438 U.S. 265 (1978).
5. 422 U.S. 66 (1975).
6. Richard Cappalli, "Federal Grant Disputes: The Lawyer's Next Domain," *Urban Lawyer*, 11, Summer 1979, pp. 377-88.
7. The role which courts play in establishing the Constitutional parameters of grant programs . . . has received considerable attention.
8. Office of Management and Budget, *Managing Federal Assistance in the 1980s*, Washington, DC, U.S. Government Printing Office, 1979.
9. Richard Cappalli, *Rights and Remedies Under Federal Grants*, Washington, DC, Bureau of National Affairs, 1979, pp. 169-71.
10. Advisory Commission on Intergovernmental Relations, *Statutory and Administrative Controls Associated with Federal Grants for Public Assistance*, A-21, Washington, DC, U.S. Government Printing Office, 1964, pp. 81-83, 93-95.
11. E.g., 31 U.S.C. Section 1245 (revenue sharing).
12. *Steffel v. Thompson*, 415 U.S. 452, 464 (1974) (Brennan, J.).

15. A REGULATORY MODEL OF INTERGOVERNMENTAL RELATIONS

George E. Hale and Marian Lief Palley

Intergovernmental programs and regulatory policies depart from the relatively simple administrative initiatives of more traditional national programs that are administered directly by the federal government. Both involve indirect influence rather than hierarchical or managerial solutions to organizational problems. They represent "command and control" responses, and both aim at affecting the actions of thousands of business firms or units of local government. Each focuses on broad objectives. The formal goals of government regulations are to reduce market domination, alter behavior to curb abuses of public welfare, and establish a national economy. Similarly, grants-in-aid programs are ostensibly designed to reduce fiscal disparities among subnational governments, alter the policies of state and local governments, and establish national programs. Each method of intervention also addresses the "free rider" problem in which voluntary arrangements have allowed some individual firms or governments to avoid paying for their share of collective benefits. In short, both regulatory programs and many intergovernmental grants are far more complex and ambitious than the more traditional government programs. Each represents a fundamental change in the way that government operates.

The regulatory model helps focus our attention on the complex goals and indirect methods associated with many federal grant programs that try to change the behavior of others. In each agency there are limits to federal control; no single agency can monitor all the private transactions by individual businesses just as no grantor agency can fully audit all the expenditures of hundreds of thousands of units of state and local government.

Federal control in each arena is imperfect. Given the clout of private interest groups, and given the complexity of many regulatory actions, most observers agree that, regardless of their original purpose, most regulatory agencies become the protectors or promoters of the regulated interest. According to Pendleton Herring, "the greater the degree of detailed and technical control the government seeks to exert over industrial and commercial interests, the greater must be their degree of consent and active participation." [1] Often the agency is captured outright by those it regulates. In other cases, the process is more subtle. Because

From George E. Hale and Marian Lief Palley, *The Politics of Federal Grants* (Washington, D.C.: CQ Press, 1981), pp. 28-29. Reprinted by permission.

programs are so specialized, there are very few places to seek political support. So, the controller may increasingly need the support of the controlled. Similarly, federal agencies often turn to state and local officials for political support. The price for this support is cooptation and greater delegation of day-to-day administration. Because state and local governments have influence with Congress, administrators will often consult local and state politicians before taking controversial actions. As federal grants increase, so too does the federal government's dependence on the political support and administrative capacity of local and state officials. In the case of both regulatory and grant programs the federal government influences, but also is influenced by those it regulates.

Regulatory administration is also highly political because Congress frequently passes legislation that confers broad discretion upon administrative officials. A good deal of intergovernmental legislation contains broad grants of administrative power. Because these agencies, both regulatory and intergovernmental, have legislative and administrative authority they seem to be especially open to pressures from special interests.

The value of the regulatory analogy is that it places *negotiation, bargaining,* and *compromise* at the core of the policy process. This conception is central to many classic studies of intergovernmental relations. According to Grodzins, "a judgment of the relative strengths of the two planes must take heavily into account the influence of one on the other's actions." [2] In short, national and subnational governments are interdependent.

Notes

1. E. P. Herring, *Public Administration and the Public Interest* (New York: McGraw-Hill, 1936), p. 192.
2. Morton Grodzins, "The Federal System," *Goals for Americans* (Englewood Cliffs, N.J.: Prentice-Hall, Inc., 1960), p. 139.

16.   FEDERAL PROGRAMS AND CITY POLITICS

Jeffrey L. Pressman

. . . If actors and organizations have conflicting policy preferences, then the technical methods of communication, planning, and coordination are unlikely to resolve the differences between them. More discussion and gathering of information might only result in pointing up differences between the organizations. As for coordination, this much-used term is often proposed as a cure for fragmentation, but it does not offer much guidance to one who wishes to make or to understand policy.[1] If organizations disagree about objectives, then coordination may mean that one wins and the other loses. Alternatively, bargaining between them may result in a solution which is somewhere between the opposing preferences. In fortunate circumstances, an integrative solution can make both parties better off than they were. But in no case is coordination among conflicting parties a bloodless and technical process. Certainly, the creation of multiple coordinators and coordinating boards has not eliminated conflict between federal and local agencies.

The differences in perspective between federal and local bodies are due in part to their differing roles as donor and recipient in the grant-in-aid programs. As in foreign aid, a donor's perspective includes a preference for long-term plans, short-term funding, and a number of guidelines regulating how the money may be spent. The recipient's perspective, on the other hand, includes a preference for short-term plans, long-term funding, and relatively few guidelines on spending.

When the problem of conflict has been addressed by designers of intergovernmental structures, it has been treated as a matter of disagreement over goals— to be remedied by collaborative discussion of those goals. Thus, the emphasis has been placed on molding agreement during the formulation of policy, with implementation presumably following in the wake of that initial agreement. This strategy is a perilous one, for, as some recent studies[2] have shown, there are many ways in which initial policy agreement can dissipate during the process of implementation.

If federal-city relations are not characterized by pure cooperation (or by temporary lack of communication between the parties that can be solved by more talking and planning), neither are those relations marked by pure conflict. For the organizations involved have many common interests in operating successful programs and in improving the social and economic health of cities. Thus, federal and city agencies may be seen as engaging in what Schelling calls "mixed motive games," which are combinations of cooperation and conflict.[3] For Schelling, such conflict situations

> are essentially *bargaining* situations. They are situations in which the ability of one participant to gain his ends is dependent to an important degree on the choices or decisions that the other participant will make. The bargaining may be explicit, as when one offers a concession; or it may be by tacit maneuver, as when one occupies or evacuates strategic territory. It may, as in the ordinary haggling of the market-place, take the *status quo* as its zero point and seek arrangements that yield positive gains to both sides; or it may involve threats of damage, including mutual damage, as in a strike, boycott, or price war, or in extortion.[4]

Viewing intergovernmental relations as a bargaining process is useful in keeping us from over-emphasizing either the cooperative or conflictual elements of that behavior. Such a perspective helps us to understand strategic moves made by various players and to suggest policy changes which take into account both shared and divergent values.

Power Asymmetry

A further cause of friction between federal and local agencies is the power asymmetry in the relationship between them. The federal government supplies most of the money for grant-in-aid programs, and it generally insists on a range of guidelines and controls to accompany the financial commitment. A city which desperately needs additional funding is in a poor position to argue about the conditions of a grant. "Cooperative federalism" between relatively wealthy and powerful federal agencies and relatively poor and powerless local agencies is an illusion.

Power asymmetry exacerbates the friction generated by differences in goals and policy preferences. This is not to say that weakness is necessarily a disadvantage in a mixed-motive game. As Schelling notes: "The government that cannot control its balance of payments, or collect taxes, or muster the political unity to defend itself, may enjoy assistance that would be denied it if it could control its own resources."[5] Still, there is no question that city leaders resent their dependence on the federal government and the consequent ability of that government to control so many of their actions.

Mutual Dependence

The federal government's comparative strength does not mean that it can achieve its goals merely by imposing its will on local government agencies. If we follow Dahl's definition of power ("[A] has power over [B] to the extent that he can get [B] to do something that [B] would not otherwise do"[6]), then we can see that federal and city government agencies have power over each other. For just as cities depend on the federal government for money, so the federal government depends on city agencies to build support for and implement a range of urban programs. Because federal and city governments depend on each other, they can each get the other party to do things that that party would not otherwise do.

John C. Harsanyi has written that, in cases in which A has power over B,

it very often happens that not only can A exert pressure on B in order to get him to adopt certain specific policies, but B can do the same to A. In particular, B may be able to press A for increased rewards and/or decreased penalties, and for relaxing the standards of compliance required from him and used in administering rewards and penalties to him. Situations of this type we shall call bilateral or reciprocal power situations.[7]

In such situations, both the extent of B's compliant behavior and the incentives that A can provide for B will become matters of bargaining between the two parties. B can exert pressure on A by withholding his compliance, even though compliance might be more profitable to both parties than noncompliance. B can also exert pressure on A by making the costs of a conflict—including the costs of punishing B for noncompliance—very high.

Even given the supremacy of federal law and the cities' dependence on federal resources, local agencies have a number of bargaining counters. For example, they can threaten to opt out of a federal program; they can threaten a conflict which would be costly for both sides; or they can demonstrate such weakness that emergency federal assistance is made even more likely. Thus, the power imbalance between federal and city governments is not complete; mutual dependence leads to a reciprocal power situation in which bargaining must take place.

The Problem of a Bargaining Arena

For bargaining to take place, the various parties must have some way of transmitting their intentions to each other. As Schelling says, parties to bargaining "must find ways of regulating their behavior, communicating their intentions, letting themselves be led to some meeting of minds, tacit or explicit, to avoid mutual destruction of potential gains."[8] Federal and local officials, with their differing perspectives, career patterns, and associational experiences, sometimes find it difficult to understand each others' policy moves. It has not been easy, therefore, to find effective arenas in which bargaining can proceed. (I will define "arena" as a site at which the exchange of political resources takes place. A list of such resources would include money, authority, information, and physical force, among others.)

Warren Ilchman and Norman Uphoff, whose "political economy" model focuses on exchanges of political resources, speak of such bargaining arenas as "political and administrative infrastructure."[9] They explain that:

infrastructure economizes on the use of political resources by increasing *predictability* or *mobility*. The establishment of certain exchange relationships, whether mutually beneficial, legitimated, or coerced, provides for predictability in the amount and kind of resources available to maintain other relationships. When benefits, sanctions, norms, or simply expectations are established with respect to a given pattern of political competition or exercise of authority, compliance may be achieved with the expenditure of fewer resources because political activities and attitudes can be more reliably predicted. Infrastructure contributes to the increased mobility of resources in much the same way that transport systems contribute to greater efficiency of economic production. . . . Infrastructure is used to gain support, enforce authoritative decisions, gather information, deploy coercion, and confer status at less cost than would be the case if established patterns did not exist.[10]

Examples of infrastructure are political parties, interest groups, bureaucracies, and educational systems. Each of these institutions may be seen as an arena which facilitates the exchange of political resources by increasing predictability and mobility in bargaining relationships.

It would be a mistake to assume that the mere creation of an institution for bargaining means that resource exchanges will be more predictable or mobile, or indeed that any bargaining will take place in that institution. We ought to distinguish between *effective* arenas, in which bargains that take place will have some impact on the distribution of resources (such as money, authority, information) among the relevant participants, and *ineffective* or *pseudo-arenas*, in which no real exchanges of resources take place. Bargaining in effective arenas has consequences for outside actors and organizations with whom arena participants may deal; bargaining in pseudo-arenas involves no meaningful changes for the participants and does not have an impact on the outside world.

Although it is true that numerous intergovernmental relations offices, federal-city liaisons, Federal Executive Boards, and interagency regional teams have been created to facilitate "communication" between federal and city officials, they have not served as effective arenas because decisions made in those bodies have not been binding on governmental policy. Without the authority to approve projects and commit funds, such institutions have served as good examples of pseudo-arenas in which agreements that are made do not necessarily have any consequences for the political world outside. Schelling distinguished between "talk" and "moves," saying that "talk is not a substitute for moves. Moves can in some way alter the game, by incurring manifest costs, risks, or a reduced range of subsequent choice; they have an information content, or *evidence* content, or a different character from that of speech."[11] Federal-local communications channels have often stimulated talk, but they have proved frustrating to local leaders who are more interested in moves (decisions as to which group will receive federal money; approval or disapproval of projects; appropriation and delivery of funds). The difficulty in creating effective arenas in which such moves can be made with more reliability and speed has been a continuing problem of intergovernmental relations. Even if the goals are agreed upon, projects approved, and funds committed, the need for a bargaining arena does not disappear. For the process of implementation—the carrying out of a policy—requires continuing negotiations and exchanges between relevant governmental actors.

Notes

1. Naomi Caiden and Aaron Wildavsky point out that coordination may have various contradictory meanings: efficiency, reliability, coercion, and consent. As a guide for action, they point out, the injunction to "coordinate" is useless. See *Planning and Budgeting in Poor Countries* (New York: John Wiley, 1974), pp. 277-279.

2. See Martha Derthick, *New Towns In-Town: Why a Federal Program Failed* (Washington, D.C.: The Urban Institute, 1972); and Jeffrey L. Pressman and Aaron Wildavsky, *Implementation: How Great Expectations in Washington Are Dashed in Oakland; Or, Why It's Amazing that Federal Programs Work at All, This Being a Saga of the Economic Development Administration as Told by Two Sympathetic Observers Who Seek to Build Morals on a Foundation of Ruined Hopes* (Berkeley and Los Angeles: University of California Press, 1973).
3. Thomas C. Schelling, *The Strategy of Conflict* (New York: Oxford University Press, 1960), p. 89.
4. *Ibid.*, p. 5.
5. *Ibid.*, pp. 22ff.
6. Robert A. Dahl, "The Concept of Power," *Behavioral Science* 2 (June, 1957), pp. 202-203.
7. John C. Harsanyi, "Measurement of Social Power, Opportunity Costs, and the Theory of Two-Person Bargaining Games," *Behavioral Science* 7 (January, 1962), p. 74.
8. Schelling, *Strategy of Conflict*, p. 106.
9. Warren F. Ilchman and Norman Thomas Uphoff, *The Political Economy of Change* (Berkeley and Los Angeles: University of California Press, 1969), pp. 35-37, 208-255.
10. *Ibid.*, p. 211.
11. Schelling, *Strategy of Conflict*, p. 117.

17. WAYS OF ACHIEVING FEDERAL OBJECTIVES

Martha Derthick

The Federal Government in State Politics

In giving grants and attaching conditions to them, the federal government becomes an actor in the state political system. It is a peripheral actor rather than an integral one, for it has no legitimate role within that system—no formal right to make decisions and no recognized informal right to function as a lobby. Nonetheless, it alters the environment within which the integral actors function, alters the distribution of influence among them, and thus itself becomes an actor in state politics.

The selection of subjects for the public agenda—of "issues" for consideration—is the first step in determining the content of public policy, and it is at this point in the process of state politics that federal influence begins to be felt. By offering grants for specified activities, the federal government places an item on the political agenda: should the aided activity be undertaken or not? The setting of conditions works in parallel fashion. By saying to the state that it will not give money unless a certain rule is adopted (or, if the grant program is already under way, by saying that money will cease to be given), the federal government causes the state to consider whether the required action should be taken. An issue is raised that might not have been raised in the absence of federal action. Strictly speaking, of course, the federal government does not itself place the question on the agenda of state politics. What it does is to stimulate proposals by actors integral to the state political system, such as elected executive or legislative officials, party officials, appointed administrators, or executives of pressure groups. For state political actors who independently share some or all of the federal goals, federal action creates opportunities ("excuses") for the making of proposals.

For these elected officials and for appointed administrators—who together are ultimately the objects of federal influence because they are possessors of authority to act within the state government—federal sponsorship reduces the cost of making a proposal and taking the subsequent action. Not only are monetary costs transferred to the federal level; if opposition arises, state officials may be able

Reprinted by permission of the author and publishers from *The Influence of Federal Grants: Public Assistance in Massachusetts* by Martha Derthick, Cambridge, Mass.: Harvard University Press, Copyright © 1970 by the President and Fellows of Harvard College, pp. 201-214.

to transfer political costs as well, by imputing responsibility to the federal government. Moreover, federal action increases the cost of inaction—that is, the cost of *not* proposing or taking the actions the federal government seeks to stimulate. Officials who do not respond to federal stimuli become vulnerable to criticism for failing to act—for "failing to take advantage of federal funds" or "failing to meet federal standards."

Federal influence continues to operate as consideration of the federally stimulated proposal proceeds. The terms of the federal offer or requirement affect the content of proposals and discussion within the state. The proponents or action takers have as one important resource of influence, perhaps their principal resource, the claim that action is desirable or necessary because it will secure federal funds. The "normal" distribution of influence among political actors in the state—that is, the distribution that would prevail in the absence of federal action—thus is altered to the advantage of those with whom the federal government is allied.

In summary, the federal government exercises influence in large part by stimulating demands from groups within the state and by placing "extra" resources of influence at their disposal. It works through allies.

The State Agency as Federal Ally

Temporary allies—that is, more or less accidental allies, intermittently active for limited purposes—may contribute substantially to the attainment of federal objectives. In Massachusetts the federal public assistance administration has at various times and for limited purposes been allied with the old-age lobby (the two have also been at odds) and with professional and good-government groups such as the National Association of Social Workers and the League of Women Voters. But the dependence of the federal government on support within the state is such that it needs a permanent ally, one always organized and prepared to take action, always receptive to federal communications, and having interests thoroughly consistent with those of the federal administration. From the perspective of the federal administrative agency, this is ideally the role of its state counterpart. As the formal recipient of federal funds, the formal channel for federal communication with the state, and a possessor of authority within the state government, the state agency has a combination of obligations to the federal administration and assets of influence at the state level that make it by far the most suitable and efficacious of potential federal allies. Much federal activity—some of it designed for that purpose and some not—contributes to making the state agency into an ally, an organization not simply accountable to the federal agency (responsible for the state's conduct and capable of reporting on it), but also *responsive* to it (disposed to make state conduct conform to federal preferences). Such activity is one of the major techniques of federal influence.

The first step in creating a state-agency ally is often to call an agency into existence. Many state and local administrative agencies, especially those in urban renewal, public housing, and antipoverty programs, have been created for the purpose of receiving and administering federal grants. The next step (likely to be more difficult with an established agency than a new one) is to shape its values and conceptions of purpose so that they are consistent with federal objectives, and to enhance its power and autonomy at the state level. To the extent that the state agency shares federal goals, is willing to commit its power to attaining them, and has power so to commit, the probability that federal goals will be achieved is greatly enhanced.

Federal patron agencies and their state counterparts might be expected to have shared values and goals without the federal agency's taking steps to assure this, if only because they share programmatic functions. The sharing of functions, however, is not necessarily sufficient to assure the congruence of a wide range of values among a high proportion of administrators in numerous governments, the governments themselves being representative of diverse value systems and regional subcultures. If federal preferences are to prevail, then, the core of shared values and goals that federal and state administrators derive from the sharing of a function must be elaborated and perfected, in ways of federal choosing, until a high degree of congruence has been achieved. The professionalization of personnel, through which a common body of values and doctrines is disseminated, has been the principal means of doing this.

To the extent that the federal effort to bring about a sharing of values between governments is successful, difficulties of obtaining conformance are much reduced. The state agency becomes highly responsive to federal preferences, and responsive for what federal administrators can only regard as the right reasons. That is, it responds not just because it seeks to maximize the receipt of federal funds (and thus is willing to act as if it shared federal goals); rather, it responds because it does in fact share them. Indoctrination of the state agency is the federal administrators' only defense against the persistent and pervasive problem that arises from the tendency of state governments to agree to federally stipulated actions because doing so will enlarge the flow of federal money. At most, the spread of professionalism at the state level may altogether eliminate the problem of nonconformance. If state agencies come to share federal values and have power to embody them in state policy, they become something more than responsive partners of the federal agency. They also undertake to pursue shared goals independently. The values expressed through public action at the state level then become identical to those that prevail within the federal administration. The result is the elimination of federal-state conflict and hence the elimination of the necessity for the exercises of federal influence. The federal effort to professionalize and to render autonomous the state agency is thus in a way the ultimate adaptation to limits on that influence.

Federal action contributes to state-agency power and autonomy in various ways, of which the most obvious, in the public assistance program, has been the "single state agency" requirement. On the basis of this statutory provision, federal administrators have insisted that the agency possess enough authority to assure that federal conditions are met. Very early in the federal grant program, this resulted in amendments to Massachusetts law that much increased the rule-making powers of the state welfare department.

In the case of the "single state agency" requirement, enhancing the counterpart's power is the primary end of federal action. Although most federal actions obviously do not have this as their major goal, virtually all federal-state interaction through the grant system incidentally yields that result.

As the recipient of federal grants, the counterpart is endowed with resources that would not otherwise be available to it and that come to it more or less independently of action by the governor or legislature, upon whom it would otherwise be altogether dependent for monetary support. How much power the agency thereby gains depends on how much discretion it has in the use of federal money. This use may be closely circumscribed by federal action or by the action of the state legislature. In the Massachusetts public assistance program, the state welfare department was more a passive channel for the routinized flow of federal funds to local agencies (and ultimately to assistance recipients) than an independent allocator of the funds, the crucial decisions about allocation having been made by the legislature (once the cost-of-living formula was passed, at least). Nevertheless, the result of federal grants was to increase, in a subtle way and to an unspecifiable degree, that state agency's power vis-à-vis local agencies. The agency gained leverage in its role as rule maker and supervisor of administration, since its right to function in this role depended both on grants of authority from the state legislature and on the state's sharing of assistance costs. And the "state" share of costs, from the perspective of local agencies, was the equivalent of the state *and* federal shares combined, for the state welfare department disbursed federal grants to local agencies and had authority to supervise their spending. "Federal" money, having been so channeled, from the local perspective acquired the character of "state" money.

The stipulation of federal conditions or rules to accompany grants had the same effect. Given the nature of a federal system, federal rules can be effective within the state only after being reincarnated as state rules. Therefore the making of federal rules for the grant program stimulates the making of state rules; it stimulates the usage of the counterpart agency's authority. Again, whether the result of this process is to increase state-agency "power" depends on the particular circumstances of the rule making and the particular relationship of power. When the state rule simply repeats verbatim a federal rule and does not entail the use of state discretion, state-agency power in relation to the federal administration is decreased. On the other hand, whether the state agency exercises discretion itself (typically the case) or merely repeats what the federal administration has stipulated (less often the case), its rule-making authority within the state political system has been enhanced by usage. In Massachusetts, for the perspective of the local agencies to which public assistance rules were addressed until 1968, all rules were state rules no matter what the origin of their content. All were experienced and interpreted as manifestations of state authority. All therefore tended to enhance state power as it was exercised in relation to local agencies.[1]

An alliance between federal and state administrative agencies, formed and perfected through the working of the grant system, can become a powerful force in state politics, perhaps the dominant force in the making of policy for the program in question. When federal and state agencies work together, each reinforces the influence of the other, the state agency gaining as a result of the federal partnership, the federal agency being compensated for deficiencies in its ability to exercise influence directly in state affairs. The result is that a relationship of mutual dependence develops such that each accommodates itself, perhaps unconsciously, to the interests of the other. What the federal agency undertakes depends in part on what its state counterpart desires or can be expected to concur in, for the state agency's cooperation is essential to the realization of any federal goal. Similarly, a state agency learns to accommodate its goals to federal ones. Where, as in Massachusetts before 1968, a state agency has little independent strength within the state political system, its dependence on federal patronage becomes very great. It must rely on federal action to create opportunities for action and on the justification of "federal requirements" or the "availability of federal funds" to rationalize and legitimize all that it does. Whatever power and autonomy the Massachusetts welfare department possesses derive very largely from the relationship with its federal patron.

Federal influence, in summary, operates mainly through the agency that receives grants, and with the agency's self-serving cooperation. It operates by enhancing the role that the agency plays in the state political system and by shaping the agency's values, goals, interests, and actions. It operates primarily on the structures and processes of policymaking and administration rather than directly on the substance of policy. This may be a critical limitation, but if the influence on structures and processes is extensive and enduring enough, the result must be to influence policy outcomes as well—*all* policy outcomes, not just those in which the federal government is actively interested. If the federal government can influence the locus of policymaking authority in the state government, how the policymakers perceive opportunities for action, what values prevail among the policymakers, and what resources of influence are at their disposal, it has gone far in influencing the content of policy. It has, in any case, increased the disposition of the state to respond to federal action and to undertake, independently, actions consistent with federal preferences.

The Withholding of Funds

The ultimate resource of federal influence is the withholding of the grant, but this is almost impossible to use, for withholding serves no one's interests. Objections are bound to come from Congress.[2] Although Congress agrees with the administration on certain general statements of federal conditions when the effects on particular constituencies are impossible to foresee, withholding is a specific act, threatening to a particular constituency; this automatically brings a response from that constituency's representatives in Congress and evokes the sympathetic concern of other congressmen, who are made aware of a potential threat to their own constituencies. Even apart from the possible difficulties with Congress, administrators are reluctant to withhold funds because of the damage it might do to program goals and to relations with state governments. Given the limits on its influence, the federal administration is—or at least perceives itself to be—heavily dependent upon maintaining their good will and disposition to cooperate. Partly for this reason, it seeks to avoid direct, hostile confrontations with state governments such as the withholding of funds entails. Above all, it wishes to avoid public sanctions against the state agency (which, at least *pro forma*, must be the object of withholding), for one way of maintaining the state-agency alliance is to avoid embarrassing the agency in public.[3]

These objections to the manipulation of funds as an enforcement technique apply to the withholding of the entire grant, which in principle is the penalty for nonconforming policies or recurrently nonconforming administrative practices, more than to the taking of audit exceptions, which in principle is the penalty for specific nonconforming acts of expenditure. Because they are more feasible to use than withholding, the federal administration is sometimes tempted to use audit exceptions on a large scale as a substitute for withholding; that is, audit exceptions may be applied to a whole class of expenditures in an effort to bring about change in a nonconforming policy or practice, as when the regional representative decided to apply them in Massachusetts in the later 1940s to the salaries of elected board members who were engaged in administration. However, using audit exceptions in this way is subject in some degree to most of the same objections, and to others besides. An audit exception is inconvenient to administer, and as a *post hoc* action that applies only to particular acts of expenditure (selected acts, in the normal case, for not all expenditures are audited) its range of effectiveness is limited. It is particularly difficult to apply to acts of omission. The difficulties of withholding or of taking audit exceptions on a large scale help to explain why the whole aim of federal enforcement activity is to bring about compliance in advance and thus to avoid confrontations in which financial penalties will have to be invoked. Federal administrators consider that they have done their jobs well when the volume of audit exceptions is low.

It would be wrong, however, to infer that the federal ability to withhold funds is of no effect. It is in fact one of the major resources of federal influence—but it is of use mainly as a potential resource. It lies at the foundation, as a weapon in reserve, of all federal enforcement activity, and the nature of that activity is such as to make the best possible use of it.

Federal enforcement is a diplomatic process. It is as if the terms of a treaty, an agreement of mutual interest to the two governmental parties, were more or less continuously being negotiated. In these negotiations, numerous diplomatic forms and manners are observed, especially by the federal negotiators. Typically they are in the position of having made a demarche. Negotiations become active when a new federal condition is promulgated or an old one is reinterpreted, or when a federal administrative review has revealed a defect in the state's administration. Negotiations are carried on privately. The federal negotiators refrain from making statements in public, for they want to avoid the appearance of meddling in the internal affairs of the states. They refrain from making overt threats. They are patient. Negotiations over a single issue may go on steadily for several years and intermittently for decades. They are polite. In addressing state officials, they are usually elaborately courteous. They make small gestures of deference to the host government, as by offering to meet at times and at places of its choosing.

The objective of the negotiating process is to obtain as much conformance as can be had without the actual withholding of funds. Because federal requirements are typically stated in general terms, administrators have a high degree of flexibility in negotiating terms of conformance. Within the broad guidelines they have laid down, they have been able to adapt to the political and administrative circumstances of each state. If the constraints of the situation so require it, federal administrators may consider conformance to have been achieved even if state action falls considerably short of the federal ideal. As long as federal requirements are vague and general, conformance, though difficult to prove, is equally impossible to disprove. The federal administration may therefore avoid outright defeat no matter what concessions it makes to state political and administrative realities. (The situation changes, of course, if federal requirements are highly specific. Federal administrators then may feel compelled to accept merely formal proofs of conformance that falsify reality and that they *know* to falsify reality, as with caseload standards in Massachusetts.)

The function of intergovernmental diplomacy in a federal system, like that of international diplomacy, is to facilitate communication and amicable relations between governments that are pretending to be equals by obscuring the question of whether one is more equal than the other. In the case of federal-state relations in the United States, that question is obscure in any event, and the function of diplomatic processes may merely be to keep it that way or to obscure, and thereby facilitate, changes in power relations. That this be done is important primarily to the federal government, for it is the aggressive, the states the defensive, actor in intergovernmental relations. It has the greater interest in seeing that change is facilitated. But perhaps the principal advantage of a diplomatic style to federal administrators (and the choice of that style is essentially their choice), is that this mode of behavior makes the best possible use of the technique of withholding funds. It enables federal officials to exploit, without actually using, this basic resource. In cases of federal-state conflict, federal negotiators keep open the possibility of withholding during the process of negotiation, referring to it in oblique and subtle terms. They seek to obscure the low probability that they will actually use it. By not making overt threats to withhold, federal administrators protect their credibility; the state is kept guessing. Diplomatic behavior is thus an adaptation to the impracticability of withholding, as well as to other constraints on federal influence, especially the widespread belief that the federal government ought not to interfere in state and local affairs. By relying so heavily on private negotiations, federal officials avoid "meddling" in public. At the same time, they avoid exposing the state agency to public embarrassment or more tangible federal penalties so that the agency's disposition to cooperate is not discouraged.

It might seem that, as time passes, the federal administration's failure to withhold funds would undermine its credibility and render withholding useless even as a negotiation weapon. In fact, the federal willingness to withhold funds itself diminishes with time. It is much easier to withhold (or delay the granting of) funds at the outset of a grant program, when the volume of the grant is low and the program not yet routinized. In the first five years of the public assistance program, the federal administration did make several attempts to withhold funds, and it was not altogether implausible, when a dispute with Massachusetts arose in 1939-40 over the merit-system requirement, that it would try to do so again. The welfare commissioner, apparently believing that it would, gave in to the Social Security Board very quickly. Ten years later, when the issue over board member-administrators arose, it was much less plausible that withholding should be tried, and by 1964-65, when the dispute over the educational requirement developed, withholding was altogether implausible. But not everyone knew this (many state legislators did not), and some people who did know it, especially the welfare commissioner, preferred to pretend that they did not. Withholding would probably not remain effective as a resource of influence were it not for the federal alliance with the state agency; when the two cooperate in pursuit of a shared goal, the state agency exploits the possibility of federal holding and vouches for the credibility of it.

The fact that the state agency is the sole official recipient of federal communications and the official interpreter of them within the state gives it an important advantage. It can make decisions about dissemination and interpretation in such a way as to facilitate attainment of its own ends. This is likely to mean, as in the dispute over the educational requirement, that the state agency will encourage the belief that a serious threat of federal withholding exists. The federal administration, which alone might provide an accurate interpretation of its own intent, refrains from doing so as a tactical necessity. Attempts to elicit clear statements of intent are unavailing, whether they come from the state agency or other sources. But whereas the federal agency refrains from issuing threats of withholding itself, it does nothing to dispel threats that others issue in its name. Its interests will best be served if those statements are believed. In these circumstances, federal intentions may be difficult for anyone to evaluate, even those who, like state administrative officials, have direct access to the federal agency and experience in the administration of grant programs. For others, such as state legislators, who have no such access and no such experience, federal intentions are virtually impossible to evaluate. In any case, it is always impossible for the opponents of federally sponsored action to demonstrate that the federal administration will *not* withhold funds.

The limited capacity of state legislators to appraise federal intentions with respect to withholding is one advantage the state agency has whenever it undertakes an action with federal sponsorship. It might be supposed, however, that opponents of federally sponsored action would get help from Congress, which is thought to be responsive to the appeals of parochial interests and skilled at overturning the acts of federal administrators. Judging from the Massachusetts experience, however, appeals to Congress appear to bring few results to those who make them. When federal and state agencies act cooperatively, they have much protection, individually or together, against unwanted intervention from legislatures at either or both levels of the federal system.

They have, of course, the usual assets of administrators confronting legislators: they are the full-time specialists in their function, while legislators have only a part-time interest in that function. For a congressman to intervene successfully once the federal administration has committed itself to a particular action in a particular state requires an intense and sustained interest in the matter and a great mastery of administrative detail. The Massachusetts case suggests that these conditions will rarely be met. Although congressmen, in response to constituents' requests, at critical times inquired of the federal administration about its intentions in Massachusetts, these inquiries almost without exception were routine and perfunctory. The letter from the constituent was forwarded to the administration with a form letter from the congressman requesting a response. A response—couched in oblique, noncommittal language that tended to minimize the degree of disruption being experienced within the state and the degree of the federal administration's responsibility for it—then went to the congressman, who presumably relayed it to the inquiring constituent as proof that he had acted on the constituent's request. Typically, these congressional inquiries revealed little knowledge or specialized interest in the case on the part of the congressman, and the replies from the administration were designed to avoid increasing either.

The only important exception to this pattern was the activity of Congressman [John] McCormack with respect to the directive on educational requirements. If ever there was a situation in which congressional intervention might be effective, this seemed to be it. Here was a congressman—the Speaker of the House, no less—who was opposed to an important action of the administration, an action profoundly damaging to the career prospects of perhaps eight hundred local government employees in his state. His objection was largely spontaneous and strongly enough felt to produce protests to the secretary and the undersecretary of health, education, and welfare. But in the end it had very little effect on the administration's action. None of this means that federal public assistance administrators are not subject in profoundly important ways to congressional controls. What the administrators undertake to do depends heavily on what Congress has authorized and on the administrators' guess of what Congress will tolerate. Contrary to what is perhaps the usual impression of Congress' performance, the evidence from public assistance suggests that Congress is more effective in making broad policy than in doing "casework" for particular individuals or groups of aggrieved constituents.

In addition to the defenses that administrators normally have against legislators, the grant system offers special ones, a result of the diffusion of responsibility it entails. When called to account for controversial actions, administrative agencies at both federal and state levels can escape responsibility vis-à-vis their own legislatures by attributing responsibility to a counterpart at the other level. In parallel fashion, each legislature can escape responsibility vis-à-vis its own constituents. The ability of all major official actors to deny responsibility very much reduces the chances of successful opposition.

Notes

1. From the perspective of the state agency, federal efforts to enhance the agency's authority and to stimulate exercise of that authority are not unambiguously beneficial. How welcome they are depends on how highly the state agency values the ends prescribed by the federal administration; on the amount of resistance pursuit of them is likely to provoke within the state; and on the federal ability to endow the agency with resources of influence to overcome the resistance. The danger is that federal action will force the state agency into situations of conflict without sufficiently compensating it.
2. See U.S. Senate, *Proposed Cutoff of Welfare Funds to the State of Alabama*, Hearings before the Committee on Finance, 90 Cong., 1 sess. (1967), for a recent example.
3. In doing research for this book, I found that the one restriction on the cooperation of federal regional officials was a concern that their relations with state officials might be damaged. I was given access to federal files with the understanding that I would not use them to attack or gratuitously embarrass the state agency. I was asked to use the material "objectively," a condition that I was of course happy to accept. When the completed manuscript was made available for comment, the federal office did not ask for any deletions.

Review Questions

1. What would be a plausible explanation for the clear racial differences in public opinion about intergovernmental matters? What is the significance of this split? In your answer, draw from not only the readings of this section but also Riker's analysis in Part One.

2. What intergovernmental policy implications follow from the fact that American government structures are bewilderingly diverse? Are rational action and reform possible in such an intergovernmental system? In your answer, consider Reischauer's discussion of the negative consequences of this diversity; can you suggest any positive ones?

3. What political and structural impediments stand in the way of efforts to attempt equalization of governments' resources through the grant system?

4. What are the sources of potential strength and weakness for the PIGs?

5. What political behavior would one expect to see on the part of the PIGs if a president were to propose a shift of funding from categoricals to block grants and a cutback in total assistance? Why would the PIGs react as you predict?

6. Why do opponents of intergovernmental change have a strategic advantage in intergovernmental politics?

7. Explain the link between the increasing use of formula entitlements by the federal government and the growth in grant litigation in recent years.

8. Does Pressman's bargaining framework and analysis of the donor-recipient relationship conflict with Elazar's interpretation of intergovernmental relations in the nineteenth century? If so, explain the divergence.

9. Your friend is very concerned with the apparently overpowering role of the federal government in intergovernmental relations since the 1960s. On the basis of the analyses presented by Hale and Palley, Pressman, and Derthick, how would you explain to your friend the sources of strength and weakness in both the national government's role and the states' role?

10. Derthick claims that the federal government hardly ever cuts off funding for a grant program, despite the fact that frequently states and locals fail to meet federal requirements. Why not? Does this mean that the threat to eliminate funding is empty?

11. Derthick says, "The function of intergovernmental diplomacy in a federal system, like that of international diplomacy, is to facilitate communication and amicable relations between governments that are pretending to be equals by obscuring the question of whether one is more equal than the other." Is the diplomacy analogy a reasonable one? Why or why not?

12. Compare Derthick's analysis of the troubling implications of the pattern of influence in intergovernmental politics to Grodzins's more sanguine assessment. Be sure to analyze the topics of diffusion of responsibility and bureaucratic barriers to outside influence.

Part Three

FISCAL ASPECTS OF INTERGOVERNMENTAL RELATIONS

There may be no better way of seeing the complexity and interdependence characteristic of today's intergovernmental system than by examining its fiscal aspects. Nowadays, by virtue of various financial instruments—especially the grant-in-aid—American governments at all levels are tied together in a bewilderingly intricate and dense set of obligations, opportunities, and dependencies.

As of fiscal 1983, for instance, and despite cutbacks in aid during the Reagan years, federal dollars constituted 20 per cent of state and local budgets. Estimated 1984 intergovernmental aid from Washington totaled $97.8 billion, while in 1982 intergovernmental aid from the states and national government to local units amounted to a massive $116 billion. For each dollar that cities, counties, and other local units raised on their own in 1982, they received 71 cents in intergovernmental revenue.[1] Clearly, then, these indicators suggest considerable financial complexity and interdependence.

The readings in Part Three document some of the fiscal developments in the system during recent years, explain the significance and purposes of intergovernmental fiscal instruments, and analyze some of the donor and recipient behaviors generated by intergovernmental fiscal activity. Once again, however, it will prove impossible to cover these aspects of the American system without paying considerable attention to other features, especially the *political* significance of fiscal mechanisms. Thus a lesson in this section, as in the preceding one, is that the various dimensions of the intergovernmental pattern are inextricably related.

Even with the wide range of issues and topics addressed in the readings that follow, some important fiscal issues receive little or no attention. Most of the newer block grants initiated in Washington are not treated here, nor is the contentious topic of urban-suburban fiscal disparities. The Reagan cutbacks and reforms are included only insofar as they illuminate the issue of urban dependence on Washington. Block grants and the Reagan changes are discussed in the last part of the book, which concentrates on a few issues of special relevance today. But there remain plenty of important matters to explore first.

Part Three begins with an excerpt from a report of the Advisory Commission on Intergovernmental Relations (ACIR). In a multivolume study of the intergovernmental system, the ACIR concluded that recent decades have seen a noticeable centralization of responsibilities, fiscal and otherwise, in the United States. The reading included here presents some general data on fiscal interdependence in the intergovernmental system, with emphases on the financial role of the national government and on the apparent increase in federal influence. This piece also documents the accentuated importance of intergovernmental fiscal affairs for many local units that, until recently, were financially independent of Washington.

The introductory chapter of this volume identified some of the most important fiscal instruments. Categorical and formula grants, block grants, and revenue sharing are all significant today. Several readings in this part address the economic and political purposes of these tools from different perspectives.

George Break classifies grant and revenue sharing mechanisms according to their expected economic effects. Break's discussion is especially helpful because it treats not only fiscal mechanisms employed by the national government but also the economic impact of state aid to local governments.

Break's analysis is grounded in economic theory. But one can also examine empirically the actual operations of fiscal instrumentalities. Three readings included in this part do so by comparing the conventional justifications for aid with the aid's practical impact.

Richard Nathan, Charles Adams, and a large team of field researchers, working through the Brookings Institution, studied one of the most important intergovernmental fiscal innovations in this century—revenue sharing. Their study, funded by the Ford Foundation, examined effects in 65 state and local jurisdictions over a several-year period in the mid-1970s. (At the time of this research, states as well as local governments were recipients. Since 1980 only the latter have been beneficiaries of this program.) Revenue sharing has been strongly supported by PIGs at the state and local levels, and participants and analysts have advanced a number of claims (as well as criticisms) concerning its impact. The Brookings group looked systematically for fiscal consequences of revenue sharing, for the effects on central cities, and for alterations in the structure and decision-making processes in recipient units. In this excerpt, the researchers report on some of their most general and significant findings.

Next, in a frequently quoted essay Phillip Monypenny analyzes the effects of the intergovernmental grant system in toto. Writing during an earlier debate about the nature and future of the intergovernmental network, Monypenny finds that the oft-cited economic and fiscal ends attributed to the grant system are not supported by the data. In other words, most of these justifications for the system are unfounded. He then argues that this system of fiscal instruments actually serves some political functions. His logic supports the view, advanced in the introductory chapter of this book, that American intergovernmental relations constitute an amalgamated pluralism and that there are indisputable links between fiscal and political aspects of the system.

Michael Reagan and John Sanzone offer a clear and useful summary of specific economic and political objectives often intended by the use of the grant-in-aid. Their conclusions about the overall rationality of the grant system in practice, informed by some experience since the time of Monypenny's evaluation, are relatively positive. The careful reader will likely be able to detect that Reagan and Sanzone's evaluation derives in some measure from their implicit view of the national government as the most appropriate and most enlightened policy maker in the intergovernmental system.

Regardless of evaluations such as those just discussed, despite the variety of fiscal instruments available, and despite the recent interest in block grants and revenue sharing, *categorical* aid still dominates the system and is likely to do so for the foreseeable future. Why? Part of the reason is found in the excerpt from an ACIR study of categorical grants, which examines economic and political inducements to adopt this form of financial assistance.

The fiscal operations of the American intergovernmental system also affect the fiscal and nonfiscal operations of participating governments. The final four readings explore some of these effects.

Ann Michel describes her own role and the role of her bureaucratic unit in the pattern of intergovernmental aid. At the time this essay was written, she directed the Office of State and Federal Aid Coordination in a typical medium-sized American city, Syracuse, New York. As she describes the operations of this office, a type of dependence experienced by many of the nation's cities becomes clear. Cities often are heavily reliant on fiscal decisions in the state capitals and in Washington, yet they feel a tremendous incentive to devote significant resources to the task of attracting even more resources and, consequently, more dependence. Especially when it comes to discretionary aid like project grants, research has shown that localities that do not gear up to compete with one another as Syracuse has done often lose in the fiscal game.[2]

As discussed earlier, however, not all intergovernmental aid is distributed in this fashion. Increasingly popular in the last dozen years have been programs based upon formulas. Because of the absence of overt unit-versus-unit competition, formula grants may seem a more civilized, less political method of channeling intergovernmental aid. However, this is an oversimplified view. Rochelle Stanfield demonstrates this point in an essay on the "computer politics" that now accompany any effort to establish a formula grant. She concentrates on issues surrounding the revenue sharing program (as they emerged prior to the 1980 reenactment) and some of the major block grants. As her analysis makes evident, the process of establishing formula-based aid involves a complex interplay of technical and political considerations. This essay may also help to explain the finding, reported by Monypenny, that the system does not accomplish much financial equalization across jurisdictions; Stanfield shows that values like "equalization" may be complicated blends of competing considerations.

James Skok discusses a different sort of impact of the detailed fiscal ties among governments. State legislatures, like the national one, jealously guard their authority over the public treasury; yet, as was clear in Derthick's essay, intricate financial agreements and transfers between governments may make this control especially difficult to retain. Skok discusses state legislatures' recent efforts to gain more control over fiscal aspects of intergovernmental relations, specifically during a reform of state financial procedures in Pennsylvania. His analysis documents an irony: complexity and interdependence have stimulated some actors (like state legislatures) to become more involved in and acquire more control over intergovernmental processes; the results may be even more complexity and expanded patterns of interdependence.

In the final reading of this section, James Fossett presents a controversial interpretation of the fiscal dependence of big city governments. Drawing on 11 case studies from a federally funded Brookings research project, Fossett summarizes the effect on cities of fiscal developments in intergovernmental relations over the last decade. He suggests that some conclusions about the degree of cities' dependence on federal pursestrings may have been overstated by earlier and present-day researchers. Using a refined measure of dependence, he finds the overall pattern to be a complex one: some cities *are* heavily dependent on intergovernmental aid and find themselves in precarious fiscal situations today; others are more able to handle changes induced by other levels. In short, the impact on cities of changes in fiscal intergovernmental relations—for example, the cutbacks of recent years—may vary considerably.

Notes

1. Advisory Commission on Intergovernmental Relations, *Significant Features of Fiscal Federalism, 1982-83 Edition* (Washington, D.C.: ACIR, January 1984), pp. 1, 120, 124.
2. Robert Stein, "Federal Categorical Aid: Equalization and the Application Process," *Western Political Quarterly* 32 (December 1979): 396-408.

18. FISCAL INTERDEPENDENCE AMONG AMERICAN GOVERNMENTS

U.S. Advisory Commission on Intergovernmental Relations

Relative Growth of Federal Aid

Federal payments to state and local governments as a percent of GNP peaked in the 1930s as GNP bottomed out, and again in the late 1970s as a result of the rapid growth of federal aid programs. Figure 2 shows these peaks.

Figure 3 reveals that federal aid grew as a percentage of federal outlays, both in terms of the domestic sector and total. But Figure 4 demonstrates that federal aid increased even more rapidly as a percentage of state and local expenditures. Both of the figures indicate that federal aid has begun to level off or decrease in relative terms, however, as the 1970s ended. This is confirmed by Figure 5, which shows a late 1970s drop in the constant dollar value of federal aid. Figure 6 discloses that the growth of federal aid had its biggest impact on state government in the late 1950s, but the local impact was delayed until the mid-1960s and 1970s. These trends reflect a mixture of: (1) improved state revenue capacity, (2) increased federal aid going directly to local governments or having a required pass-through from the states to localities, and (3) weakened revenue capacities at the local level. Figure 7 shows the growing importance of state aid in the overall mounting reliance of local governments on outside aid. Thus even as the real buying power of federal aid begins to slacken, local dependence on outside aid (from all sources, including a large state component) continues its rapid rise. . . .

Incidence of Federal Influence

. . . Most state and local governments also are under heavy federal influence, often at their own request. Nothing demonstrates this better than the growth of federal aid. . . . Prior to 1972 many of the smaller counties, municipalities, and townships did not receive federal aid, perhaps largely because of constraining eligibility requirements and the specialized staff effort required to apply for, and administer the available funds.[1] With the advent of the General Revenue Sharing program in that year, however, all the states and virtually all of these general purpose local governments now receive and spend regular quarterly payments from the federal government without even applying for them. At latest count

From *The Federal Role in the Federal System: The Dynamics of Growth—A Crisis of Confidence and Competence* (Washington, D.C.: ACIR, July 1980), pp. 60-61, 84, 87. Reprinted by permission.

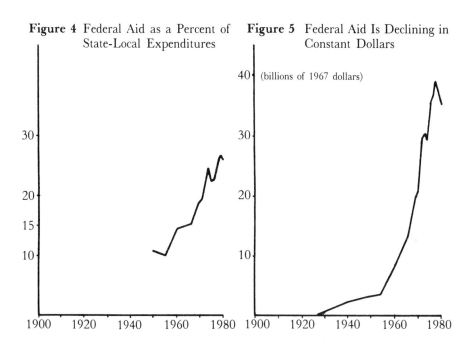

Figure 2   Federal Payments to State and Local Governments as a Percent of GNP

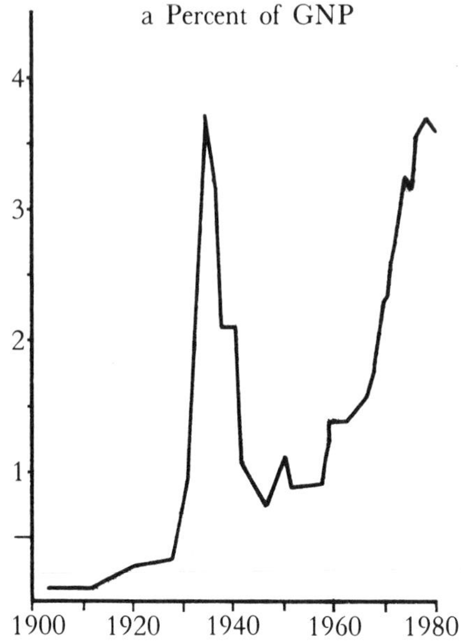

Figure 3   Federal Aid as a Percent of Federal Outlays

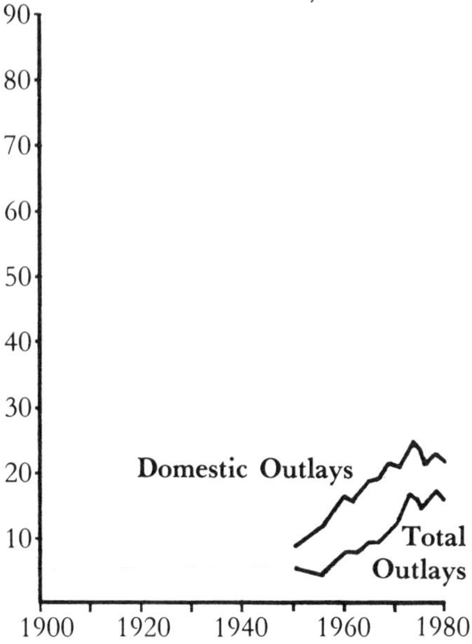

Figure 4   Federal Aid as a Percent of State-Local Expenditures

Figure 5   Federal Aid Is Declining in Constant Dollars

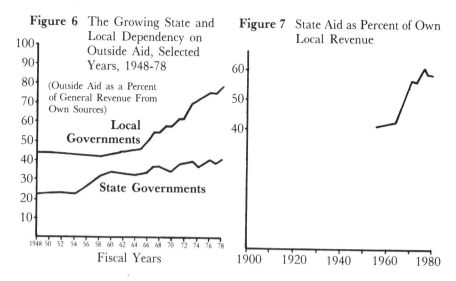

Figure 6 The Growing State and Local Dependency on Outside Aid, Selected Years, 1948-78

(Outside Aid as a Percent of General Revenue From Own Sources)

Local Governments

State Governments

Fiscal Years

Figure 7 State Aid as Percent of Own Local Revenue

37,704 state and local governments receive these payments, out of a total of 38,776 such governments.[2]

Public school districts also are deeply embedded in the federal aid system. Virtually all of the nation's 16,500 public school systems receive federal funds. About 80% of this aid is distributed through the states, while the remaining 20% goes directly from the federal government to the school system.[3] Federal aid distributed by the states is virtually universal among the 15,174 independent school districts, and also is quite prevalent among the 1,386 dependent school systems. Even private schools are deeply enmeshed in federal aid; almost 82% of those at the elementary and secondary levels receive such aid.[4] Yet according to the *1977 Census of Governments,* only 8.1% of all public school system revenue is derived from federal aid. Still, this small amount brings these units under numerous detailed grant requirements.

Finally, special districts, which are the most numerous type of government in the United States, also share in federal aid to a large extent. The figures are imprecise, but it is known that intergovernmental revenues (including state and local as well as federal) account for 30.1% of special district revenues,[5] and about 10,000 of the 26,000 special districts (38%) are eligible for federal aid. These include districts for soil conservation, housing and urban renewal, sewerage, hospitals, libraries, and transit systems.

Adding the 50 states and totaling the above mentioned governments yields an estimate that about 63,000 of the nation's approximately 80,000 units of state and local government (nearly 80%) probably are receiving federal funds. In addition virtually all of the increasingly numerous substate regional organizations are dominated by federal aid, which contributes well over 80% (on the average) of their budgets. This adds almost another 2,000 governmental organizations to the total public recipients of federal aid.[6]

Federal aid obviously has a pervasive effect on state and local government. The substate regional organizations, with such a high percentage of their budget coming from federal aid, probably are the most greatly influenced of the state and local units. Their funds are mostly categorical grants which have quite firm and detailed program requirements, as well as a number of general requirements affecting virtually the whole federal aid system. . . . The broad range of these generally applicable grant requirements . . . cover[s] nondiscrimination, environmental protection, planning and project coordination, relocation and real property acquisition, labor and procurement standards, public employee standards, and access to government information and decision processes. Even the school districts . . . are subject to many of these same requirements. And the General Revenue Sharing program, which affects almost 38,000 state and local units and was designed specifically to have the fewest possible federal requirements on recipients, carries with it the following restrictions: a prohibition on the use of funds for lobbying purposes, requirements for citizen participation, restrictions on debt retirement with revenue sharing funds, compliance with the prevailing wage provisions for construction projects under the *Davis-Bacon Act,* requirements with respect to wage rates for employees of recipient governments, protections against discrimination in recruitment and employment of various sectors of the population, prohibitions against discrimination by subcontractors, and restrictions against discrimination in the provision of municipal services or the selection of facilities to be financed with federal funds. Although this list leaves out some of the generally applicable requirements, there is still a very substantial federal presence in even this "least intrusive" federal program, and it affects more subnational governments than any other.

. . . About 74% of the total state agencies now receive federal aid. . . . The percentage of state agencies receiving 50% or more of their budget from federal aid has increased from about 10% in the mid-1960s to over 25% in the late 1970s. Thus the states also face growing federal influence within their programs.

Notes

1. Richard P. Nathan, Allen D. Manvel, Susannah E. Calkins, and Associates, *Monitoring Revenue Sharing*, Washington, DC, The Brookings Institution, 1975, p. 281. See also: Robert D. Lee, Jr., *The Impact of General Revenue Sharing on Local Jurisdictions in Pennsylvania: Initial Findings*, University Park, PA, Institute of Public Administration, The Pennsylvania State University, October 1974, p. 3; and G. Ross Stephens and Gerald W. Olson, *State Responsibility for Public Services and General Revenue Sharing*, Final Report, Kansas City, MO, University of Missouri, June 15, 1975, p. vii.
2. U.S. Department of the Treasury, Office of Revenue Sharing, "Revenue Sharing Funds Distributed," News Release dated October 11, 1979, Washington, DC.
3. U.S. Department of Commerce, Bureau of the Census, *1977 Census of Governments: Finances of School Districts*, Vol. 4, *Governmental Finances*, No. 1, Washington, DC, U.S. Government Printing Office, March 1979.
4. U.S. Department of Health, Education, and Welfare, Education Division, National Center for Education Statistics, *The Condition of Education*, 1978 Edition, Statistical Report, Washington, DC, U.S. Government Printing Office, p. 49.

5. U.S. Department of Commerce, Bureau of the Census, *1977 Census of Governments*, Vol. 4, *Governmental Finances*, No. 2, *Finances of Special Districts*, Washington, DC, U.S. Government Printing Office, May 1979, p. 2.

6. U.S. Department of Commerce, Bureau of the Census, *1977 Census of Governments*, Vol. 6, *Topical Studies*, No. 6, *Regional Organizations*, Washington, DC, U.S. Government Printing Office, August 1978, p. 74.

19. THE ECONOMICS OF INTERGOVERN- MENTAL GRANTS

George F. Break

. . . Grants-in-aid may be classified in numerous ways.[1] The classification in Table 4 highlights both the flexibility of grants as a fiscal instrument and the diversity that complicates the assessment of the effects of different grant programs. Four basic types of grant are widely used.

Categorical grants of the open-ended matching variety (3e) have the economic effect of stimulating state and local expenditure in designated functional areas (1d) by lowering the price at which grantees can acquire the program benefits; grantees are free to buy as much as they like at that lower price. The grants are allocated by formula with administrative checks on their use (2c). Federal grants for public assistance and medicaid, which accounted for about 18 percent of total federal grant expenditures in fiscal 1978, fall in this category. State matching grants of any kind are rare.

Unconditional general grants allocated by formula fall at the opposite end of the economic spectrum. Their effect is to increase the money income of recipient governments but not to change the prices at which they can purchase goods and services for their citizens. Though there are no examples of a completely unrestricted federal general grant (1a, 2a, 3a) in the United States, general revenue sharing (1b, 2b, 3b) comes close.[2] About 10 percent of state grant funds goes for general support of local government.

Fixed-amount grants for specified purposes are the most popular type of grant in the United States, accounting for 88 percent of federal grant expenditures in fiscal 1978 and over 85 percent of state grant expenditures in fiscal 1972. This category includes the traditional federal categorical matching closed-end grant (1d, 2c, 3cd), federal block grants (1c, 2bc, 3b), and most state grants for education and highways.[3] Though messy in the eyes of many economists because they combine income and price effects in ways that are difficult to disentangle, these fixed-sum special-purpose grants have numerous attractions. Not the least of these may be their ability to conciliate appearance and reality, seeming to support some function close to the heart of the grantor while in reality allowing the grantee to use the funds for any local purpose desired. Closed-end grants have the further advantage of greatly simplifying the budgetary and administrative

From *Financing Government in a Federal System* (Washington, D.C.: Brookings Institution, 1980), pp. 73-76.

Table 4   The Many Dimensions of Intergovernmental Grants

1. **How funds are used by recipient**
   a. Unrestricted
   b. General, with limited restrictions
   c. Block, within broad program areas
   d. Categorical or functional, within narrow program areas

2. **How funds are allocated to recipient**
   a. Formula, unrestricted
   b. Formula, subject to limited restrictions
   c. Formula, with administrative checks
   d. Competitive applications by grantees (project grants)

3. **Degree of participation by grantor**
   a. None (beyond provision of grant funds)
   b. Administrative oversight
   c. Technical services; cooperative management
   d. Grantee matching requirements up to the limit of grantor funds (closed-end matching grants)
   e. Grantee matching requirements with unlimited grantor funds (open-ended matching grants)

problems of the grantor. Open-ended grants, in contrast, create budgetary uncertainties by committing the grantor to the provision of whatever funds grantees choose to match. And if the aided activities are not tightly defined, recipients may exert explosive pressures on spending levels by diverting open-ended grant funds to programs the grantor had neither intended nor wished to support.[4]

Project grants are distinguished by the requirement that donees compete for the available funds by submitting detailed plans concerning their use (2d). Some potential recipients may choose not to compete, either because they lack the technical expertise needed to prepare the required plans or because they regard the risks of failure as too high to justify the costs of applying. For the grantor, on the other hand, project grants provide welcome opportunities to reject low-priority proposals and to adjust the terms of support for others so as to maximize the public benefits to be obtained from the funds expended. In fiscal 1972, project grants accounted for 21 percent of federal grant expenditures but less than 2 percent of state grant spending.

The greater importance of project grants in the federal grant system suggests that the relationship between the two parties to a transaction may have a significant impact on grant design. The degree and type of controls exercised by grantors might well be different on grants between two independent powers than on grants between superior and subordinate powers or grants involving a mixture of independent and subordinate powers.

Notes

1. See, for example, Jesse Burkhead and Jerry Miner, *Public Expenditure* (Aldine, 1971), p. 285; ACIR, *Federal Grants, Their Effects on State-Local Expenditures, Employment Levels, Wage Rates: The Intergovernmental Grant System: An Assessment and Proposed Policies*, Report A-61 (GPO, 1977), pp. 25-29.
2. In Canada, federal-provincial tax equalization grants fall in the completely unrestricted category. Australia also uses unconditional financial assistance grants. See ACIR, *In Search of Balance: Canada's Intergovernmental Experience* (GPO, 1971); David B. Perry, "Federal-Provincial Fiscal Relations: The Last Six Years and the Next Five," *Canadian Tax Journal*, vol. 20 (July-August 1972), pp. 349-60; James A. Maxwell, "Revenue-Sharing in Canada and Australia: Some Implications for the United States," *National Tax Journal*, vol. 24 (June 1971), pp. 251-65.
3. In states with separate school districts, education grants looked at from the point of view of the state government are grants restricted to one function; but from the point of view of the school district, they are general-purpose grants unless their use is restricted to particular education programs.
4. Martha Derthick, *Uncontrollable Spending for Social Services Grants* (Brookings Institution, 1975).

20. THE RECORD OF REVENUE SHARING

Richard P. Nathan, Charles F. Adams, and Associates

... Judgments about a program's effectiveness depend on one's point of view. Program evaluation requires a set of criteria against which performance can be measured; but, like many government programs, revenue sharing encompasses a number of diverse and sometimes contradictory objectives. The goals most frequently cited for the program can be characterized as follows: (1) to reduce fiscal disparities between states and among local governments; (2) to stabilize state and local taxes and thereby help produce a more progressive national tax structure; (3) to assist in the financing of needed state and local services; and (4) to move in the direction of governmental decentralization by increasing the discretion of state and local governments in determining the uses of federal grants. The extent to which each of these objectives has been achieved is briefly discussed below.

Reducing Fiscal Disparities

Because the formula established in 1972 for distributing general revenue sharing funds was not basically changed by the new law [in 1976], we will not repeat here the discussion of the formula already presented in *Monitoring Revenue Sharing* [an earlier study of general revenue sharing—Ed.]. There particular attention was given to the distributional impact of the revenue sharing allocation system on large central cities and poor states. The general policy issue raised was whether these and other "needy" jurisdictions received "appropriate" treatment under the formula contained in the original law. Taking into account the way in which most of the framers of the original program described their aims, we concluded that some provisions of the law appeared to work in ways that were not anticipated and that these features should be changed. Our analysis also indicated the need for better measures of certain variables included in the original allocation system.

... The overall distributive pattern of the federal revenue sharing program is a function of the "something for everyone" philosophy of the program. In other federal countries—notably West Germany, Canada, and Australia—the equalization effects of general grant programs tend to be much more pronounced because the allocation systems used involve a redistribution from wealthier

From *Revenue Sharing: The Second Round* (Washington, D.C.: Brookings Institution, 1977), pp. 160-166.

(donor) jurisdictions to a limited number of recipient jurisdictions, defined as having special and acute problems and fiscal deficiencies.[1]

This is not to say that revenue sharing fails to reduce disparities, only that its equalizing impact is relatively limited. Many proponents of the existing formula, although it is not often expressed in these terms, regard other federal programs as more appropriate equalization devices, particularly income-transfer programs and social service grants. In debates on revenue sharing, spokesmen for local governments that would be considered fiscally healthy, particularly suburban jurisdictions, have argued that their units also have needs and that inflation has reduced their ability to respond to these needs; thus, while other federal programs should focus on poverty needs, revenue sharing should give recognition to the financial problems of *all* governmental units.

The distributional effects of revenue sharing are closely related to the next objective to be discussed.

Impact on the Tax System

One of the ideas important to backers of the original revenue sharing program was that it would have a desirable effect on the national tax structure by causing a heavier reliance on more progressive and efficient federal tax sources and, in turn, less reliance on state and local sales and property taxes. The research to date shows significant indications that this has occurred. Revenue sharing has been an important factor in allowing some governments to stabilize or limit tax increases; . . . this effect has been particularly pronounced among hard-pressed municipal governments. At the same time, however, sample jurisdictions characterized as being under no fiscal pressure are also reported to have used a relatively high proportion of their shared revenue to cut or stabilize taxes.

Some regard this tax stabilization effect as generally desirable; others criticize the revenue sharing program because in some instances it may increase rather than reduce fiscal disparities among recipient governments. For example, the efforts of hard-pressed central cities to improve their fiscal position by using shared revenue to stabilize taxes may be significantly or fully offset as more fiscally healthy suburban jurisdictions take similar measures. The competitive position of the central cities could as a result be relatively unchanged or even worsened. This issue of the extent to which revenue sharing should be oriented to urban or poverty needs has been extensively debated. The point of view that appears to have prevailed, or at least been dominant, is that revenue sharing is a *general purpose program.*

Expanding Public Services

Another purpose of revenue sharing advertised by its supporters in 1972 was that it would expand the capability of state and local governments to meet public needs. This objective, of course, conflicts with the idea that revenue sharing should cause a heavier reliance on federal taxes and provide tax relief at the state and local levels. It implies a pro-spending orientation and emphasizes the impact of revenue sharing at the local level on the public, as opposed to the private, sector.

Persons with this pro-spending orientation may be encouraged by the significant amounts of new spending uses reported for the sample jurisdictions.

For the vast majority of jurisdictions, at least some portion of revenue sharing has been used for new spending. Smaller local governments experiencing relatively little or moderate fiscal pressure were observed . . . to be the most likely to use a significant portion of their shared revenue in this way. For these governments, capital projects accounted for the bulk of their new spending uses. This bricks-and-mortar emphasis has also generated controversy. Critics of capital-intensive patterns in the use of shared revenue have urged instead that the funds be channeled into operating programs to improve and increase basic services. Among local jurisdictions, only county governments' have evidenced any significant tendency to use shared revenue for new or expanded operating programs.

Decentralization

Although it is discussed last in this section, the decentralizing objective of revenue sharing was the most prominent reason for its enactment in 1972. As in the case of other purposes of the program, however, decentralization has different meanings for different observers. Generalist officials (governors, mayors, managers, legislators) regard the basically "no-strings" character of these grants as an important means of allowing them greater discretion. Above and beyond the dollars and cents, these officials and supporters of decentralization generally see revenue sharing as a symbol of a new willingness on the part of the federal government to reduce the level and specificity of the controls placed on federal subventions in order to give greater emphasis to the role and significance of subnational governmental units in contemporary federalism. The fact that the program allows a high degree of discretion to generalist officials in determining the uses of these funds is reason enough for some observers to judge the program a success.

However, the experience to date suggests that the program has not decidedly changed the nature and type of participation in the political processes of recipient governments. In only about one-fifth of the local jurisdictions in the sample has there been either a broadening of the decisionmaking process, with new groups gaining access, or some shifting in relative influence among generalist officials.

Under the decentralization heading, one body of opinion measures the success of revenue sharing in terms of its ability to increase the role and leverage at the state and local level of citizens' groups with a decidedly social-service orientation and purpose. Of the twelve cases where there was a broadening of the decisionmaking process, nine involved social action organizations. There is also evidence that other grant-broadening programs of recent vintage, especially the block grant for community development, have had a greater effect in these terms.[2] . . .

Notes

1. Considerable research on comparative fiscal federalism has been conducted recently by the Directorate-General for Economic and Financial Affairs of the Commission of the European Communities. This work is under the supervision of its Study Group on the

Role of Public Finance in European Economic Integration. See especially "Budget Equalization and Other Unconditional Redistribution between Federal and State Governments" (Brussels, June 13, 1975; processed). The authors are indebted to Klaus Schneider of the EEC for his assistance in obtaining and working with these materials.

2. See Richard P. Nathan and others, "Block Grants for Community Development" (Department of Housing and Urban Development, 1977).

21. FEDERAL GRANTS-IN-AID TO STATE GOVERNMENTS: A POLITICAL ANALYSIS

Phillip Monypenny

The federal system is always in danger and it is always rising anew from the ashes of its earlier existence. The current concern about the federal system, which has an obvious base in the party battle, is indicated by the number of reports and studies, non-partisan, if not non-political in character, which are concerned with it. Though these contribute a great deal of information about the current state of federal-state relations, it cannot be said that they settle any of the questions currently in dispute, in particular the question of whether the position and significance of the states as policy making centers has been significantly changed by the changing scope of the activity of the national government. . . . It is to the scope and character of the grants system, and to its political conditions, that this paper is directed. Incident to this discussion there may be an opinion, if not a conclusion, as to the effect of the grant system on the policy making freedom of state government.

[The author analyzes developments in the grant system, documents the patterns of grants-in-aid, and then compares the results with some of the most frequently cited justifications for the American system of fiscal interdependence.—Ed.]

. . . The picture presented, both in terms of the distribution of aid among the states, and the apparently arbitrary selection of purposes for which aid is extended do not square very well with the textbook justifications for a grant-in-aid system. The classic case for the extension of financial assistance by one government to another is that it provides money for local units which need it in order to support essential activities at a minimum level. This implies a larger measure of support for some units than for others, depending on the relative ability of units to finance the programs supported. No *major* federal grant is based primarily on an equalization factor, and those which include such a factor do not begin to produce a uniform level of service. . . . Perhaps the most comprehensive justification of the federal grant system would be that it provides a measure of service which national interest requires without complete federal assumption of the function. . . . Every grant, from the construction of wildlife refuges to the piddling expenditures for civil defense, serves some purpose which

From *National Tax Journal* 13 (March 1960): 1, 11-16. Reprinted by permission of the National Tax Association.

its defenders regard as properly national. The only difficulty is that the attributes of matters of national concern are by no means obvious. . . .

The stimulation of state and local activity in fields of national interest is often cited as a proper basis of federal aid. Apart from civil defense, in which the national expenditure is minute, there are no grant fields which had not developed prior to the grants as activities of state governments under their inherent powers. This is true of higher education, of the agricultural and home economics extension service, of orthopedic care for crippled children, of state financing of highway construction, of unemployment compensation, or whatever. It is true that federal aid may have been a factor in persuading the less ready states to undertake what had already been undertaken elsewhere. It is hard to make a case for federal aid as a pioneering measure.

Finally, the difficulties which state and local governments face in raising revenue is often urged as a basis for increased federal assistance. The enormously wide variations in the ratio of resources to populations among the states makes this absurd if it requires aid to all states on a uniform basis. Admitting the greater difficulty of tapping wealth in a smaller area than a large one, in dealing with a national system of production and distribution, most of the difficulties of the states in raising revenue are self-imposed. The states increased revenue drastically in the middle of the depression, at a time when it would seem to have been economic folly to raise taxes, and expanded their own scale of operations equally drastically. If a tax on real estate remains the prime resource of local governments to support their ever more expensive functions, this is the doing of the states, not the federal government. Those cities whose fiscal difficulties are most prominently displayed house the greatest concentrations of wealth.

The claim of greater administrative competence on the part of federal authorities may be viewed with some scepticism. Wisconsin supplied key members of the federal staff in the early days of employment security, and the states have contributed a considerable contingent of public health officers to the U.S. Public Health Service. It is true that the federal service escapes some of the impediments which hamper administrators of state programs. They are freer of the fear of political reprisals from minor political figures, and they are able to handle the recruitment and assignment of personnel with far less concern about the patronage obligations of executive and legislative leaders. On the other hand the introduction of federal aid administration imposes another administrative and legislative layer, and to that extent dilutes responsibility, slows action, and increases the necessity of documentation. A great many states could probably build highways just as well without the oversight of the [federal bureaucracy], and administer unemployment compensation and the public employment services without the watchful eye of the [national agency responsible].

Nevertheless, federal aid is here to stay and it is not likely to become any more consistent from one program to another. The balance of federal to state authority, which varies from one program to another, is not likely to shift very much.

The standard explanation of taxpayers' organizations for the federal aid programs is that they represent the triumph of expenditure without responsibility. There is an element of truth in that, but it is not the whole story. It is obvious that many states choose to spend less than others in the very fields in which federal aid pays the highest bonuses for state expenditure. A dollar raised from taxes is still a dollar, whether it brings additional money in federal grants or not. The pressure against the tax is just as heavy by those who have no interest in the expenditure. Obviously, too, Congress has not escaped the need to tax to support these programs, and what its members stand to gain by satisfying demands for larger grants they lose by imposing taxes. The increase in state tax revenues has been dramatic, and it has been incurred to meet increasing state responsibilities in the very fields in which federal aid has been least available—public education, mental hospitals, and, in the wealthier states, general assistance.

Nor is there much evidence that federal aid causes costs to be incurred for certain purposes despite a lack of interest in them by people in the state. In many of the fields where state expenditure is relatively low, . . . federal grants have been unsuccessful in luring increased expenditure. Where there is local support for the activity as in highways and vocational education, expenditures in many states are far larger than the minimum that would be required just to match federal allotments. On the other hand in the fields in which excessive expenditure is alleged to be created by federal aid, public assistance, especially for the aged, there is the strongest local support for large expenditure, and the state programs long preceded federal grants.

It is unlikely therefore that the prospect of free expenditure by the states, without the assumption of concomitant tax obligation is the chief root of the grants system. What is then the root of this apparently contradictory phenomenon of patchwork assistance to states in which each field of activity has its own basis for granting money and its own set of administrative requirements, varying from very stringent, to very undemanding? It must be sought in the political system of the United States itself, which refuses to conform to the nice legal distinctions of a federal system, or to the logical consistencies of the advocates of executive responsibility and responsible party government.

That system has been adequately sketched in other places and by more skillful hands than those which shape these paragraphs. The population of the United States is divided by loyalties to a thousand different causes. People look to the complex fabric of government for means to pursue these causes, acting at points which are responsive, whatever the formal jurisdiction of the officials who respond. Groups within the population use their influence in one part of the fabric to negate the influence of their opponents at other points, to impose controls, or to escape them. The population acts through political parties and outside of them; it divides in elections for office, and recombines in pursuit of more particular goals. It uses the weapons of numbers, or of status, of publicity, or of intensity of organization, of money, or of familial and personal connection, as they are appropriate.

For such a population the federal grant-in-aid is a made-to-order device for securing unity of action without sacrificing the cohesiveness which is necessary for political success. The great obstacle to effective political action in a country such as the United States is the particularity of the ends of a great part of the politically active public. There are political organizations which will gladly lose national elections if they can keep their hold on local office, and followers of a national leader who are indifferent to the local office base of the party leadership whom they wish to enlist in their campaign. There are local labor organizations which will sacrifice any doctrinal commitment which their parent organizations may have if they can maintain their jurisdiction over jobs which members hold in public employment or in the work under government contract. There are wheat farmers who see farm programs in terms of wheat, and growers of perishable commodities who are more interested in the financing of production and distribution and in cooperative marketing than they are in price supports. Specificity of aim limits the possibility of getting sufficient support to outweigh opposition. Commitment to a political party as a means of political action is not binding enough to make parties a means of achieving unity of program.

Action through a single government, whether it be state, nation, or local unit, obviously requires some specificity of aim. Legislation must be drafted so as to embody with some precision the aims of those who promote it. Once drafted, it is apt to estrange some of those who were linked in the coalition when it had only partially defined aims. Once drafted, the legislation also defines the opposition, which before lacked a firm base of coalition. The course of legislation may unite persons of very different views because of what they dislike.

The situation changes at once when it is proposed to act through grants to another governmental unit rather than by direct action. By state grants to local units, as in the field of education, a minimum state program is assured, but wide room may be left for differences of local emphasis. The obstacle to the realization of educational goals which lies in local tax limits is the common problem of persons with very divergent educational goals. They can unite to escape this common problem without reconciling their divergences on program.

If this is so in the states, where there is an extensive legal power of regulating the policy, as well as the structure and finance of local units, it is the more so in the federal government. The fiscal power of the federal government can be invoked without bringing to play its policy making powers, except for that minimum on which those desiring the fiscal assistance can agree. This does not imply that those who support federal financial assistance escape the problem of levying taxes to support the expenditure they sponsor. At the federal level, however, they can both spend and tax; at the state level claims on fiscal resources are less successful. It is possible to get unemployment compensation on a virtually national basis without battling to the wall every combination of employers determined to pay for no more than a minimum program, and yet get a more extensive program in those states where there is support for it. It is possible to get the semblance of a national highway program while still enabling each state to decide whether it will support a more extensive or an intensive program of highway construction; to have many miles of roads to a less high standard, or fewer to a higher. It is notable that in approving the interstate system, which is built with 90 per cent federal money, and very extensive federal controls over routes and design, Congress attempted to box in the [federal agency charged with execution] with requirements of Congressional approval of specific administrative decisions not present in earlier highway legislation.

It can be asserted therefore that politically speaking, federal aid programs are an outcome of a loose coalition which resorts to a mixed federal state program because it is not strong enough in individual states to secure its program, and because it is not united enough to be able to achieve a wholly federal program against the opposition which a specific program would engender. In this connection the uneven responsiveness of governmental units to various population segments undoubtedly plays a part in the resort to federal or to state action, or to a combination of both. Mayors expect Congress to support housing programs which do not get sympathetic attention in state legislatures. Water, wildlife, forest, and soil conservationists generally look to Washington rather than to the states. Characteristically taxpayers federations concentrate their attention on state governments, and resist the transfer of questions from that arena to another in which they have less confidence.

Viewed in this light, the grant-in-aid programs make sense. Each is the product of a specific coalition and the terms of that coalition are evident in the statute and in the administrative practices which result from it. . . .

. . . The grant-in-aid system is by no means an undermining of federalism, but rather a refinement of it. It corresponds to a pragmatic pluralism, which has long been remarked as a characteristic of politics in the United States. It has built into it the characteristically different policy tendencies of states and of the national government. It is scarcely a means of enforcing similarity between them. Although direct administration by either government would have the advantage of political and administrative clarity and consistency, the choice of federal aid schemes as an alternative to either is sufficient evidence that these simpler measures were not a practical means for the attainment of political objectives whose achievement was only possible if they were not too minutely specified.

22. PURPOSES OF GRANTS

Michael D. Reagan and John G. Sanzone

Decisions regarding when to use formula grants and when to use project grants, and evaluation of the merits of each type, depend partly on the purposes for which one has a grant at all. We sometimes assume that the purpose of all federal grants-in-aid is financial in nature: to supplement inadequate state-local resources. This is too simple. At least as important as the purely financial objective are the following:

1. *To establish minimum national standards in some program that exists in all states, but at widely differing levels.* Examples would include air and water pollution control programs that set parts-per-million standards regarding allowable levels of pollutants, and pesticide controls (as with DCPB), which grower pressures might well emasculate in some states in the absence of a federally mandated minimum standard.

2. *Equalization of resources.* This objective is closely related to the first one. The emphasis here is upon the use of the federal tax system to apply the Robin Hood principle: to take more money from the states with higher per capita incomes and transfer it to those with lower per capita incomes, enabling the latter to upgrade their public services. Many federal formula grant programs have had sliding scales that vary federal contributions from one third to two thirds, inversely related to the capacity of receiving states to raise their own funds. The trend, however, is away from equalization.

3. *To improve the substantive adequacy of state programs.* Under project programs particularly, in the process of inviting, aiding in the design of, reviewing, and approving proposals from state-local agencies, officials of the grant-giving agency have an opportunity to provide technical assistance in accordance with the highest professional standards. Inasmuch as only a few states are able to compete with the national government in attracting outstanding professional talent, such technical assistance can be an important vehicle for upgrading the quality of public services at the state level. Graves evaluated the standard-setting impact of the Hill-Burton Program for planning and constructing hospitals with federal aid with these summary comments:

> The introduction of a continuing state-wide planning program is a landmark in
> the field of hospital and medical facility planning and construction, while the

From *The New Federalism, Second Edition* by Michael D. Reagan and John G. Sanzone, pp. 60-66. Copyright © 1981 by Oxford University Press, Inc. Reprinted by permission.

utilization of standards of adequacy and the development of patterns for distributing facilities within a State has resulted in important gains in hospital planning and better distribution of health facilities. Another important accomplishment of the program has been the development for the first time of minimum standards of design, construction and equipment for hospitals and other types of medical health facilities.[1]

4. *Concentration of research resources.* A related way in which the federal government may improve state programs, concentrate a "critical mass" of attention in a given area, and avoid useless state duplication and the frittering away of energies in many efforts is exemplified in air pollution research grants from the Environmental Protection Agency. If California, New York, Idaho, and other states with air pollution problems were to go their independent ways on their research, there would be a great deal of money wasted, and no state alone could afford to spend enough to do an adequate job. Federal grants can be the catalyst for bringing a unified research program into being out of the cooperative efforts of all interested states.

5. *The stimulation of experimentation and the demonstration of new approaches* are major objectives of a high proportion of the project grant programs in the areas of health care, education, human resources development, and community development. Sometimes the stimulus is not for an innovative program but simply to get more communities to do something quite ordinary that they don't get around to on their own. The sewage treatment plant program inaugurated in the late 1950s is a good example. The number of treatment plants under construction jumped several-fold in the first three years of operation of this grant program. Apparently federal money stimulated the cupidity of local governments, if nothing else, making it hard for them not to do something for which the federal government would pay half the cost.

Perhaps the most experimental and stimulative—too much so for many politicians involved—of all federal grant programs were the community action programs under the Office of Economic Opportunity in the late sixties. OEO grants encouraged substantive experimentation in treating the symptoms and causes of poverty in more free-wheeling ways than the traditional social welfare agency pattern had permitted. Class action law suits on behalf of the victims of finance companies and installment merchandisers also sufficiently proved their worth so that President Nixon initiated separate institutionalization for this concept.

Even more stimulative of experiment than the substantive programs undertaken by OEO was the unheard-of process of encouraging the poor to participate in the design and implementation of their own programs. OEO grants also encouraged recipients to organize to work their way into American politics, or, as the late E. E. Schattschneider put it, to work their way into the pressure system from which they had traditionally been excluded.[2] It is safe to say in the case of OEO grants that the experimentation in clientele policy making generated by the innocuous-sounding phrase *maximum feasible participation* ended up being a good deal more experimental than nine tenths of the government officials and legislators associated with the program ever expected—or wanted. The perhaps quixotic ideal of "participatory democracy" has been at least partly realized in actual practice: through the operation of grants to community action programs, participatory democracy is more than a theory.

Let us note here an interesting point about the thesis of federalism as a system that encourages the use of the constituent units as laboratories, with an opportunity for successful results to be applied through the national level of federalism to other constituent units. The induced changes in political structure and in substantive policies that made OEO grants so controversial did not take place according to the mythological formula. Instead of a few states or localities trying out an idea that had welled up spontaneously at the local level, these astonishing experiments came about because an agency of the central government (drawing upon some expertise developed in a foundation-sponsored program for dealing with youth problems) *mandated* a new kind and degree of local citizen participation as a condition for receiving national government funds. Alliances developed between functional professionals working in the local Community Action Programs (CAPs) and in OEO headquarters—alliances that constituted a kind of functional federalism as a conscious alternative to the predominantly status quo orientation of the regular government structures under the control of local elites. In short, the OEO grant program conclusively proved that experimentation *can* be directed from above. Indeed, sometimes that is the only way it can be started at the local level. Two very significant examples of social experimentation that were directly developed by the federal government, and probably could not have come about otherwise, are the Housing Allowance and Negative Income programs. These are important both as examples of national leadership in programmatic innovation and as constituting perhaps the largest-scale social science equivalents to physical science R&D (research and development) that America has ever seen.

6. *Improvement of state-local administrative structure and operation.* Since the adoption of the public assistance grant programs in the mid-thirties and the 1939 amendment to the Social Security Act that established a merit system requirement for participating state agencies, the general administrative requirements attached to a great number of federal grants have induced grant-receiving governments to professionalize their organizational structures and their personnel and financial practices. Merit system and auditing requirements have had double effects. Directly, they have established new standards of competence and accountability in the agencies handling federal funds. Indirectly, these standards have constituted, if only by contrast, benchmarks against which to measure the quality of operation of state agencies not subject to federal supervision. While a few states have always been the equal (even occasionally the superior) of the national government with regard to administrative quality, the great majority have been extremely laggard in adopting modern management knowledge. The national government has therefore played an indispensable role in relaying to the states the management knowledge it has itself developed and assimilated from the most advanced private business practice. From the standpoint of maintaining a healthy federalism, the administrative improvement impact of the federal grant system upon the states may have been at least as important (by improving state-local government effectiveness) as the provision of funds.

7. *Encouragement of general social objectives.* The "boilerplate" provisions of federal programs (those provisions that are automatically included in every

grant agreement between the grantor agency and the grantee government) have also been used as inducements to attain unrelated social objectives. The most notable among these is, of course, the nondiscrimination clause that has made grants-in-aid a potent lever in the struggle to persuade the more recalcitrant state governments to provide public services equitably to their minority populations.

8. *Minimize the apparent federal role.* Perhaps the most important political achievement of the grant system is to have solved the apparent dilemma arising from the American electorate's contradictory desires (a) to attack problems that the state and local governments lacked the resources to handle while (b) not enlarging the federal government. The solution to the dilemma is that the federal role is in fact enlarged, always in financial terms and often in programmatic terms, without that enlargement being apparent either in the size of the federal civil service or in the number of occasions upon which the individual citizen deals with a national functionary. It is a nice way of having one's cake while eating it. Recent Presidents of the United States have prided themselves on reducing the size of the federal bureaucracy, or at least in reducing its rate of growth to very minimal proportions. They have also prided themselves on the increasing help they have given to the solution of domestic problems through new and enlarged grant programs. They have never, however, put the two together so as to acknowledge that the first claim could be made only because a result of the second claim was to increase greatly the size of the bureaucracy at the state-local levels (as mentioned earlier). Of course, we shouldn't push this too far. It is certainly still true that direct federal operation of the funds and programs represented by the $80 billion plus [$97.8 billion in 1984—Ed.] of current federal grants-in-aid would considerably increase the federal "presence."

Notes

1. W. Brooke Graves, *Intergovernmental Relations in the United States* (New York: Scribner's, 1964), p. 546.
2. E. E. Schattschneider, *The Semi-Sovereign People* (New York: Holt, Rinehart & Winston, 1961).

23.   WHY CATEGORICAL GRANTS?

U.S. Advisory Commission on Intergovernmental Relations

The development of American federalism since the Civil War, which settled the most fundamental issues, is in large part the story of an expanding system of categorical aids....

Cumulatively the events over this period of a century established an intergovernmental system in which, by 1976:[1]

- 24.7% of state and local expenditures were supported by federal assistance;
- 21.7% of federal domestic outlays were made through state and local governments by means of grant programs;
- the federal government had some financial involvement in almost every major field of state and local activity; and
- more than 448 separate programs of federal assistance to state and local governments existed, almost all of which were conditional grants for narrowly defined services and activities.

These features of American federalism were not, in any clear sense, preordained. Other advanced democracies having a federal constitution have followed different developmental patterns.[2] Among the most obvious historical alternatives that might have been, but were not, adopted are: a pattern of financial self-sufficiency on the part of state and local governments; direct performance by the national government of all its domestic functions; a clear distinction between national and subnational services and responsibilities; and the use of broad-gauged general support and functional (or block) grants for the equalization of fiscal capacities and service levels among the states. In the light of such alternatives, the question to be considered is: Why was the development of the American federal system characterized by the extensive use of categorical assistance programs rather than by the alternative federal-state-local relationships?

Possible answers to this query ... suggest the importance of at least three factors: (1) economic and fiscal considerations; (2) the constitutional and philosophical traditions of the United States; and (3) features of the decisionmaking process in the American political system....

From *Categorical Grants: Their Role and Design* (Washington, D.C.: ACIR, 1977), pp. 49, 51, 53-57. Reprinted by permission.

Economic and Fiscal Factors

[Most of the economic and fiscal factors covered by the author, including the tax structure at various levels of government in the United States, the depression, and the economic diversity of the country, were summarized in the introductory chapter to this volume. This excerpt resumes with a discussion of one economic/fiscal factor not explicitly covered thus far in this book.—Ed.]

Some economists have suggested another conceptual framework for the growth of categorical aids. This explanation involves recognition of the "spillovers" or "externalities" that occur in the provision of many state and local government services. The benefits flowing from public programs are not necessarily restricted to residents of the jurisdiction that provides and finances them through its taxes. Some spill over to the residents of nearby areas or to the general public. Waste water treatment is one clear case; the beneficiaries of cleaner water often are those who live downstream from a source of pollution, not those whose effluent is treated. Highways that carry a large volume of interstate traffic are another obvious example of a state service that benefits nonresidents. Higher education, because of the frequency with which college graduates migrate to other states, might be a third instance.

The danger in these situations is that the amount of public services provided will be inadequate, because local voters and taxpayers have no incentive to pay for activities that benefit others. One solution is to have a share of the costs proportional to the actual distribution of benefits borne by a higher level of government, which can be accomplished by a properly designed grant-in-aid. In 1967 George F. Break concluded that:

> . . . external benefits, which will probably continue to grow in importance, are already pervasive enough to support a strong prima facie case for federal and state functional grants to lower levels of government.[3]

Grants aimed at correcting these spillovers usually are categorical and would be necessary even if a state or locality possessed a strong fiscal base.

This theory, although accepted by many experts in public finance, is subject to certain criticisms. First, it is based upon the somewhat tenuous assumption that state and local governments know the needs or preferences of their citizenry and act to maximize their residents' economic welfare.[4] Other economists, although accepting the basic argument in certain instances, suggest that many existing grants are not actually based upon the externality principle. Concerning this interpretation, Charles L. Schultze concludes that externality:

> . . . is not very useful for analyzing most of the existing social grants. Rather, many of these grants are a means by which the federal government uses state and local governments . . . as agents or subcontractors to produce centrally determined amounts and kinds of collective goods, since, for a number of reasons, principally historical and political, the federal government itself virtually never delivers collective goods or services at the local level.[5]

. . . One set of estimates of the importance of the externalities involved in various functional fields [indicates that] the federal government makes financial contributions to some fields in which externalities are slight (police protection, libraries), while the states and localities retain substantial fiscal burdens in activities that involve the largest externalities (education, welfare). Moreover, as Schultze adds, most federal grants do not have the specific characteristics that the externality theory suggests are desirable. . . .

[Constitutional and historical factors, which are discussed next, have been summarized in the introductory chapter.—Ed.]

Political Factors

The categorical grant program also appears to many analysts to be an expression of basic American political patterns and institutions. Important influences may be found in the operations of interest groups, the attitudes of federal officials, the structure and procedures of Congress, and the social and political diversity of the population.

Interest Group Influences

A political interpretation of grants-in-aid, based on observations about interest group activities, was offered several years ago in an article by Phillip Monypenny. Monypenny found that the growing grant system largely failed to satisfy the standard textbook justifications for federal aid. It did not provide for substantial fiscal equalization among the states, for example, and the programs did not appear to fall into areas of special national interest or concern by any consistent definition.

Monypenny believed that the actual source of the grant programs lay in features of the political system. A sharing of program responsibility, using federal fiscal resources but offering some discretion through administration by the states, was produced when an interest group lacked sufficient strength to gain all of its objectives in either the state capitals or Congress. . . .

Federal Distrust

The use of categorical aid programs also has been encouraged by a set of attitudes shared by many officials in the national legislative and executive branches. In its most moderate form, this attitude appears in the view that the government that raises money via taxation should also control the expenditure of that money. A preference for categorical aid reflects the judgment that this instrument maximizes accountability in the use of federal funds. Not infrequently, however, a more extreme position is taken, based upon a deeply felt distrust regarding the intentions, performance, and general competence and representativeness of state, municipal, and county governments.

The 1955 report of the Kestnbaum Commission highlighted the need for accountability through categorization, concluding that:

> . . . when federal aid is directed toward specific activities, it is possible to observe the effects of each grant, to evaluate the progress of aided activities, and to relate the amount of financial assistance to needs. There is more assurance that federal funds will be used to promote the nation's primary interests.[6]

More recently, a Congressional committee professional staff member, Dr. Delphis C. Goldberg, has described this position from the legislative perspective, contrasting categorical programs with broader purpose grants:

There are practical disadvantages to assistance mechanisms that carry few or no conditions. The federal government may become locked into supporting ineffective and inefficient activities, and the information needed to evaluate programs becomes difficult or impossible to obtain. In discharging its responsibilities, Congress generally desires more than assurance of fiscal probity; it wants to know how well the money is spent and who benefits.[7]

Distrust or actual hostility toward subnational governments was indicated in the views expressed by Wilbur J. Cohen, a former Secretary of the Department of Health, Education and Welfare, in an interview in 1972. Secretary Cohen described his comments on the revenue sharing proposal to a group of Democratic mayors.

> I told them, I found it hard to argue—in fact I am very unsympathetic with all you fellows asking for this federal revenue sharing when most of you run political machines that don't allow competent people to administer programs and you're shackled to a lot of political hacks.[8]

Only the federal government, in Secretary Cohen's view, could guarantee rapid action on pressing social problems.

> . . . I think in the nature of problems we face in our society, there's no question in my mind that we wouldn't be where we are today if there were no federal people pushing civil rights, desegregation or equal treatment for women. Take big, social-economic-ideological problems, and if left to just disorganized state and local action, or citizen action, I'm not saying that they might never get done, but they might take 100, 200 years. Whereas, the federal government action in the problems, whether it's against mental retardation, old-age assistance or whether it's building libraries—take any of the categories I think have resulted in faster, more effective meeting of the nation's social problems.[9]

Historically these criticisms have had both administrative and political dimensions. In the 1920s and 1930s, the former was paramount, and federal aid was widely credited with improving the administrative practices of the states.[10] Many grant requirements were directed specifically toward this end. The Kestnbaum Commission, along with many other students of government, concluded that, "When used effectively, the (categorical) grant not only has increased the volume of state and local services, but also has promoted higher standards both in service and administration. . . ." [11]

In the 1960s and 1970s certain political issues received greater stress. States were regarded as unrepresentative and unresponsive to urban needs, encouraging the development of direct federal-local project grant programs.[12] Yet many policymakers believed that cities also neglected the interests of their least fortunate citizens. As noted by Edward R. Fried and his associates in the 1972 Brookings Institution report, *Setting National Priorities:*

> . . . states and localities may fail to meet the needs of some groups of citizens, especially those with little power and status in the community. Although a few states and localities have at times been more progressive than the national government, most have been relatively unresponsive to the needs of the poor minorities. Disadvantaged groups (for example, labor unions in the 1930's and the blacks and the poor in the 1960's) have often turned to the federal government for help after failing to arouse state and local governments to

awareness of their plight. The goal of providing more nearly equal opportunities for the disadvantaged—which was a growing national concern in the 1960's—cannot be met by relying on the highly unequal resources of state and local governments or on their willingness to provide the services that the disadvantaged require.[13]

One expression of this critical view under the Great Society was the provision of federally funded services through limited purpose governments and private nonprofit organizations, thus bypassing the traditional state-local system entirely.

The federal government, however, has sometimes stepped into fields in which states actually have served as innovators, as well as those in which they seem to have lagged. Morton Grodzins has pointed to instances in the historical record (such as unemployment compensation, aid to the aged and blind, and road construction) in which the federal government has acted as an emulator of state programs by making national programs of their successes. Thus, he notes, "the states can lose power both ways." [14]

Congressional Influence

Certain features of the structure and milieu of the national legislature also encourage the heavy use of categorical grants. Students of the legislative process indicate that specialization is a dominant feature of the modern Congress, particularly the House of Representatives. Power is concentrated at the committee and subcommittee level, while the central organs of leadership have limited control over activities in either chamber. Individual Congressmen are expected by their peers to become expert in some narrow, particular field of public policy, normally a field related to their committee or subcommittee assignments. In this manner Congress as a whole gains the expertise necessary to deal with complex social and economic issues.

This norm of legislative specialization is accompanied by another—that of deference. Next to their own personal judgment, Congressmen rely most heavily in determining their issue positions on the opinions of their colleagues. Those thought to be most expert in a field, quite naturally, are usually the members who sit on that particular area's committee or subcommittee, and their views are respected.[15] Deference goes beyond this respect for one's colleagues, however. At least in the past, freshman legislators were expected to refrain from even speaking out on matters outside their committee work unless their home district was affected directly.[16]

Specialization also is tied to the practice of decisionmaking by "logrolling." Individual Congressmen generally seek committee assignments that relate to the interests of their constituents and, therefore, their own reelection prospects. For this reason they often have a direct stake in the promotion of new and beneficial programs. Other Congressmen hesitate to undercut the electoral base of their colleagues and expect this favor to be returned.

A consequence of these practices is that in many fields, the basic decisions are made at the committee or subcommittee level and are seldom challenged on the floor. This situation appears to have had a direct impact on the development of the grants system. The fragmentation of responsibility in Congress inclines it toward the creation of a large number of specialized grants, which may provide duplicative or even conflicting services. Harold Seidman stated:

> It's no accident that we have four different water and sewer (grant) programs, because these come out of four separate committees of Congress. These are very important programs for a Congressman's constituency, and a Congressman wants to be sure that it will remain in an agency under the jurisdiction of his committee.[17]

Similarly the weakness of central legislative organs means that each committee is largely free to follow its own inclinations regarding procedural matters, such as planning requirements, recipient administrative organization, matching and allocation formulas, and so forth. As a consequence grant programs vary greatly in these administrative particulars.

Although some specialization is certainly necessary in dealing with complex legislative problems, the fragmentation of Congress fails to provide for an equally urgent requirement—the task of integrating the manifold activities of government. As Samuel P. Huntington has stressed, the complex modern environment requires both a high degree of specialization and a high degree of centralized coordinative authority. Congress has adjusted only half-way by accommodating the former but not the latter function.[18]

Although establishing a direct cause-and-effect relationship would be difficult, the dispersion of authority in Congress has increased over the course of this century along with the expansion of the intergovernmental grant system. The increased development of categorical aid during the World War I era followed a revolt in 1910-11 against Rep. Joseph G. "Boss" Cannon, who as Speaker of the House had acquired extensive control over the House of Representatives. The effect of this revolt was to strengthen the position of committee chairmen.[19] The post-World War II growth of assistance occurred after another set of reforms embodied in the *Legislative Reorganization Act of 1946*. That act, which reduced the number of Congressional committees and was intended to strengthen them, had what was in many respects the contrary result, because it led to a proliferation of subcommittees and actually intensified the dispersion of power. At the same time Congressional committees acquired their first permanent professional staff positions.[20]

The number of subcommittees grew steadily in the 1950s and their autonomy increased. Earlier struggles for control between committees and the central legislative leadership were replayed between the subcommittees and committee chairmen. As in 1910 the forces for dispersion proved the more powerful. By 1962—just before the period of the most rapid increase in categorical programs—it could be said that,

> ... given an active subcommittee chairman working in a specialized field with a staff of his own, the parent committee can do no more than change the grammar of a subcommittee report.[21]

This trend has continued. In the 94th Congress (1975-76), 144 subcommittees were in existence, a significant increase from the 83 functioning 20 years ago. Moreover each subcommittee now possesses some staff. Most authorization hearings in recent years have been held at the subcommittee level, rather than by the full committee as had been the practice in the past.[22] According to a recent observer, the problem of overlapping jurisdictions has increased. Duplication in hearings and frequent legislative delays occur, and a situation has arisen in which legislation is drafted in isolated environments that may not reflect the views of the membership at large.[23]

The growth of the modern executive bureaucracy has paralleled the structure of Congressional subcommittees established since 1946.[24] The administrative agencies, in turn, reinforce the pattern of Congressional organization. Bureaus and subcommittees closely work together and with the interest groups concerned with their specific policy areas. These "subgovernments," as they have been termed, are the spawning ground of many new aid programs. They form "iron triangles," which have often been criticized for operating beyond the control of the Congressional leadership, the Presidency, and the public-at-large.[25]

Social Pluralism

The great social diversity of the United States also has had an impact upon the nature of its public policy. The nation is composed of a very large number of cultural and economic groups, each possessing different political objectives and concerns. As a consequence the existence of a large national majority actively committed to any specific major social policy change would be unusual. This fact is reflected in Congress, where modest, incremental programmatic steps, typified by the smaller categorical grant programs, are most readily accepted. Gary Orfield, an analyst of Congress, indicates:

> For a number of readily understandable reasons, Congress is far more responsive to the need for new (categorical) programs than to basic fiscal or social rearrangements. Redressing general social or economic imbalances always means helping some while denying to others a portion of their goods or of their social objectives. . . . Most new grant programs, on the other hand, give additional benefits to some groups while seldom disturbing the others. When a Senator fights for more housing or better health care for old people, or for better education benefits for veterans, he usually gains strength from a segment of his constituency without deeply offending anybody else.[26]

Education provides an example. This field was the first area of federal assistance, and it is one in which programs have been particularly numerous. The current variety of categorical education programs reflects the inability in past decades of the supporters of federal aid to education to agree upon a system of general education support. Legislation to create a program of general assistance for education was considered repeatedly by Congress after 1870, with bills introduced into the House or Senate during most sessions over this period of nearly a century.[27] However division among the advocates of aid—especially those within the Democratic party—made passage impossible, with religion and race the most divisive issues.[28] The result was that consensus could be reached on the desirability of programs for specific education purposes but not for general aid. Jesse Burkhead has commented:

> Specific grants for special purposes can be devised which avoid the problems that block the approval of (general) federal aid (to education). The past experience has been that pressures for federal aid have most frequently found expression in the passage of just such specialized programs. The agitation of the 1870s and 1880s was capped by the enactment of a vocational education law. The struggles

of 1948 and 1949 brought educational legislation for impacted areas. And the 1956-57 House battles culminated not in a construction bill, but in the (National Defense Education Act).[29]

Similarly in the early 1960s, attention was initially focused on assistance for higher education, which generated less opposition than aid to elementary and secondary schools.[30]

Social pluralism and divergent interests also abet the enactment of comprehensive bills, including a number of distinct programs. Title after title is added in the process of building a supportive coalition. The 1965 *Elementary and Secondary Education Act* (ESEA) provides an example. In five titles ESEA provided aid to the educationally disadvantaged, authorized funds for school textbooks and libraries, established supplementary education centers for adults and children, developed a national network of regional educational laboratories, and assisted the strengthening of state departments of education. U.S. Commissioner of Education Francis Keppel, who served as a "broker" among various interests in developing the legislation, developed a coalition that fit together as intricately as a "Chinese puzzle."[31]

Notes

1. Office of Management and Budget, *Special Analyses, Budget of the United States Government, 1978*, Washington, DC, U.S. Government Printing Office, 1977, p. 273.
2. See R. J. May, *Federalism and Fiscal Adjustment*, London, Eng., Oxford University Press, 1969.
3. George F. Break, *Intergovernmental Fiscal Relations in the United States*, Washington, DC, The Brookings Institution, 1967, p. 63. Break's text provides a full discussion of the externality rationale for categorical grants. See especially pp. 63-68.
4. Wallace E. Oates, *Fiscal Federalism*, New York, NY, Harcourt Brace Jovanovich, Inc., p. 73. Oates comments that although these weaknesses are such that some might believe that the Pigovian prescriptions for intergovernmental grants to correct spillovers should be rejected entirely, his own view is that a case for such grants does remain in many instances.
5. Charles L. Schultze, "Sorting Out the Social Grant Programs: An Economist's Criteria," *American Economic Review*, 64, May 1974, pp. 182-83. He defines "collective goods" as "those goods actually produced and distributed free (or at highly subsidized prices) by governmental organizations."
6. *Commission on Intergovernmental Relations*, U.S. House of Representatives, 84th Cong., 1st Sess., June 28, 1955, p. 122.
7. Delphis C. Goldberg, "Intergovernmental Relations: From the Legislative Perspective," *Annals of the American Academy of Political and Social Science*, 416, November 1974, p. 63.
8. "Wilbur J. Cohen: A Defender of Categorical Grants," *National Journal*, Dec. 16, 1972, p. 1912.
9. *Ibid.*
10. For example, see V. O. Key, Jr., *The Administration of Federal Grants to States*, Chicago, IL, Public Administration Service, 1937, pp. xiv, 368.

11. *Commission on Intergovernmental Relations, op. cit.,* p. 126.
12. For a summary of this view, see Roscoe C. Martin, *The Cities and the Federal System,* New York, NY, Atherton Press, 1965, especially *Chapter 3.*
13. Edward R. Fried, et al., *Setting National Priorities: The 1974 Budget,* Washington, DC, The Brookings Institution, 1973, p. 173.
14. Morton Grodzins, *The American System: A New View of Government in the United States,* Chicago, IL, Rand McNally & Co., 1966, p. 317-18.
15. Charles L. Clapp, *The Congressman: His Work as He Sees It,* Washington, DC, The Brookings Institution, 1963, p. 149.
16. Ibid., pp. 20-24.
17. Seidman's remarks are contained in Douglas M. Fox, "A Mini-Symposium: President Nixon's Proposals for Executive Reorganization," *Public Administration Review,* 34, September/October 1974, p. 489.
18. Samuel P. Huntington, "Congressional Responses to the Twentieth Century," *The Congress and America's Future,* David B. Truman (ed.), 2nd Ed., Englewood Cliffs, NJ, Prentice-Hall, Inc., 1973, p. 22.
19. Gary Orfield, *Congressional Power: Congress and Social Change,* New York, NY, Harcourt Brace Jovanovich, Inc., 1975, p. 16.
20. Michael J. Malbin, "Congressional Staffs—Growing Fast, But in Different Directions," *National Journal,* July 10, 1976, p. 958.
21. George Gordon, Jr., "Subcommittees: The Miniature Legislatures of Congress," *American Political Science Review,* 56, September 1962, p. 596.
22. Bruce I. Oppenheimer, "Subcommittee Government and Congressional Reform," *DEA News Supplement,* Summer 1976, p. S-8.
23. *Ibid.,* p. S-11.
24. Richard E. Neustadt, "Politicians and Bureaucrats," *The Congress and America's Future, op. cit.,* p. 120.
25. The "subgovernment" system is discussed in *Chapter I* of another Commission report in this series: Advisory Commission on Intergovernmental Relations, *Improving Federal Grants Management* (A-53), Washington, DC, U.S. Government Printing Office, February 1977.
26. Orfield, *op. cit.,* p. 262.
27. Jesse Burkhead, *Public School Finance: Economics and Politics,* Syracuse, NY, Syracuse University Press, 1964, pp. 237-38.
28. Orfield, *op. cit.,* pp. 126-27.
29. Burkhead, *op. cit.,* p. 265.
30. *Ibid.*
31. Jerome T. Murphy, "The Education Bureaucracies Implement Novel Policy: The Politics of Title I of ESEA, 1965-72," *Policy and Politics in America: Six Case Studies,* Allan P. Sindler (ed.), Boston, MA, Little, Brown and Co., 1973, pp. 162-65.

24. INTERGOVERNMENTAL AID:
A LOCAL PERSPECTIVE

Ann Michel

The "Dependent" City

I'll start by reviewing briefly the financial condition of the City of Syracuse, and how that condition is affected by state and federal revenues. The first comment here is simply that the city is unable to raise its own revenues beyond a certain level dictated by the State of New York. Any activity above that level must be financed with non-city raised revenues. In the City of Syracuse we have been within $25,000 of our constitutionally imposed tax ceiling for the last four years, and have been unable to persuade the State of New York to permit us to exceed that ceiling in the same way the cities of Buffalo, Rochester and Yonkers have been able to. As a result, our tax rate is considerably lower than the rates in those communities. We have been cutting back local staff for years, and therefore are not confronting their bonding and credit problems. On the other hand, we do not provide the same level of service that those three cities do because we have not been able to raise local revenues to permit such extensive service delivery. Last year we adopted a balanced budget of $103 million. This is considerably lower on a per capita basis than the other three communities. The city budget stayed in balance until the Governor chose to impose, or tried to impose, cutbacks in local assistance in this year's state budget. The Governor's proposals included substantial cutbacks in three categories of aid: (1) State revenue sharing, (2) municipal overburden assistance grant, and (3) the education formula. . . .

This discussion is an attempt to show our extreme dependence on state and federal aid—though school aid is often more available for special purpose programs than for general operating items. The only real federal program that gives us general purpose revenues which can be used against our basic service requirements is general revenue sharing. For Syracuse, that involves only $2.4 million a year, or slightly more than two percent of our annual expenditures for basic city services. There is dramatic difference between that two percent and the 35 percent we get from the state government in revenue sharing funds.

Federal funding tends to be more oriented toward "special purpose activities" to meet national objectives as defined by Washington. While we get

From James D. Carroll and Richard W. Campbell, eds., *Intergovernmental Administration* (Syracuse, N.Y.: Maxwell School of Citizenship and Public Affairs, Syracuse University, 1976), pp. 241-244, 250-253.

close to $20 million a year from the federal government for local activities, we don't get the discretion to the same degree we do with state financing.

For 1976, in Syracuse, we will receive approximately $55 million from either the state or federal governments, or 45 percent of city expenditures. The reason that $55 million translates to 45 percent rather than a slightly higher percentage is that the $103 million figure that I've been using for the city's budget does not include the special federal categorical aid programs. We do not place them in the city budget because of their lack of reliability and because of the inability to generally apply such funding to the provision of basic city services.

This dependency within the City of Syracuse on intergovernmental aid is representative of cities across the country. . . .

Office of Federal and State Aid Coordination

Our first function is to manipulate the system to get as much of the money as we can into the City of Syracuse, in the first instance, at least, to be used to meet city priority budget needs. That includes grant negotiations, most heavily in the categorical grants and block grant systems; it includes the preparation of our applications, some of them more intelligible than others. It also includes the development of a state legislative program and the follow-up lobbying effort, which has become a much more important aspect of our activities than it used to be and takes a great deal of my own time. It is extremely important to the cities— at least in New York State—because so many of the laws for the cities are really state laws. And as I indicated earlier, so much of the money we spend in the course of a year is state raised revenue. Not to pursue the state legislative program aggressively would be short-sighted and in the long run would cost us money and flexibility in terms of the way we operate city government.

An additional activity related to procuring maximum outside aid is fairly active participation in federal legislative lobbying efforts, though that tends to be less intense than the state process. (If for no other reason than it seems to take two years to get any sizeable piece of federal legislation passed.) So, what at the state level requires week after week persistence, at the federal level may take two years and only require quarterly trips to Washington as the bills make their way through the Congressional process. This year's major defeat, and there always seems to be one, was the Public Works Bill into which the city lobby put about 18 months only to have President Ford veto it. The Senate upheld the veto by very few votes. The public works bill is an example of legislation that was really important to cities. In Syracuse's case it would have meant $970,000 in general revenue in a 12-month period. It might also have produced as much as two or three million dollars in specialized public works kinds of construction efforts which would have meant jobs for city residents. So lobbying is an important part of our activities, though it is not one which always produces overwhelming success.

Finally, this effort of procuring outside aid includes city-county negotiations. As cities become less able to support functions with their own revenues you will see increasing efforts on the part of city governments to try to get the county governments with their broader suburban-financed tax base to pay for a larger share of services. One of this year's issues in Syracuse is an attempt to get the county to finance half of the Burnet Park Zoo expenditures. If it works out it will mean a savings in the city budget of a quarter of a million dollars a year. Not a lot of money, but, when you are at your tax ceiling and there is nowhere else to go for revenue, every $25,000 or $50,000 saved is one less fireman, policeman or teacher who has to be laid off. City-county negotiations do not generally involve large sums of money—but every resource is needed—no matter its size—to keep the cities solvent.

The second category of activity within O.F.S.A.C. is fiscal management and oversight. The quickest way to lose credibility with funding sources is to have an audit exception. If we are going to retain our reputation the city must manage its monies well and demonstrate a capacity to effectively use state and federal resources. It is very important that our fiscal systems be tight and accurate. While one often thinks of an office like ours solely in terms of getting the money, the whole fiscal management effort is really much more important than one might initially suspect because it helps us retain the reputation we need to continue to get the money—to stabilize our funding.

The third category of activity in O.F.S.A.C. is a function we've only recently added, a division of program evaluation. It is done for several reasons. Partly it's an attempt to stay one step ahead of the funding sources, because if we discover the problems before they do and get them corrected then we continue to have the reputation we feel we need to strengthen our negotiations. It is also an attempt to meet funding source requirements for evaluation—requirements which are increasing in interest and importance. The third reason is probably of more value to the way we administer city programs: evaluation activity serves as a means to help develop prototype systems for city service delivery. As the City of Syracuse finds itself in the position of less money to spend, it is important that we maximize profitable activity from every dollar. It is important to try to develop prototype systems to evaluate just how cities do deliver services and develop management and productivity approaches accordingly.

Finally, O.F.S.A.C. is also responsible for human services planning and program operation. In most communities your human services program operation effort is in a separate department, and that is generally the way it ought to be done. But in Syracuse that's not possible because of the general attitude that local government should be small, invisible, and not involved in extraneous issues. Thus, we operate our human services efforts under the state and federal aid umbrella. We operate, through O.F.S.A.C., a range of human service programs from manpower to youth services, to neighborhood facilities development, to summer programs, etc. The Syracuse O.F.S.A.C. goes well beyond the basic state and federal aid negotiating responsibilities that you would normally identify with the typical federal/state aid office.

In summary, then, the Office of State and Federal Aid for the City of Syracuse is responsible for procuring as much outside aid as we can through the range of mechanisms I've described. We place a great deal of emphasis on fiscal management and oversight; we try to place reasonable emphasis on program evaluation, and we are also involved in the whole range of human services, planning, and program operation activities directly administered by the City of Syracuse. The objective, or the basic thrust of this structure, is an attempt to integrate a broad range of planning and program operation and negotiating efforts under one single administrative entity. . . .

25. PLAYING COMPUTER POLITICS
WITH LOCAL AID FORMULAS

Rochelle L. Stanfield

Members of Congress have a new weapon in their hands when they gather to vote on federal aid programs: thick computer printouts showing how much money their districts would receive under the various proposals before them.

This is the era of "politics by printout," a phrase coined by Richard P. Nathan, a senior fellow of the Brookings Institution, to describe the need for district-by-district printouts showing the results of the complex formulas that the federal government uses to distribute billions of dollars of aid to states, counties and cities.

Computers entered politics in a big way with the enactment of general revenue sharing under the State and Local Fiscal Assistance Act of 1972 (96 Stat 919). When Congress considers renewing it in 1980, the printouts are bound to play an even more prominent role in the proceedings. Even though the renewal fight is more than a year away, computers on all sides of the revenue sharing debate are already whirring away, looking for modifications to accomplish any number of political and fiscal purposes.

Revenue sharing is by no means the only program that depends on a complex distribution formula. Community development, economic stimulus, education, [and] transportation . . . aid are among a growing number of programs also allocated according to mathematical fiat.

The formula is merely a tool for performing a very old political balancing act: putting the money where the needs are while making sure that every congressional district gets something. Formulas are supposed to provide a fair, objective distribution of federal aid. But formula elements are chosen politically, and seemingly minor changes can mean boom or bust for some recipients of aid.

When printout politics was in its infancy . . . the side with the computer had a tremendous advantage and could reap enormous benefits by manipulating minor factors. That day has passed.

"At first, the one side that had the strategic weapon could measure the potential impact of different formula distributions," explained Robert D. Reischauer, assistant director of the Congressional Budget Office (CBO). "Now every side has the new weapon. The level of information is very high and the result is a more even battle."

From *National Journal*, Dec. 9, 1978, pp. 1977-1981. Reprinted by permission.

A Lasting Formula

The complex general revenue sharing formula survived its first renewal test in 1976 because it distributes money to nearly all the state and local governments in the country, with small bonuses for jurisdictions regarded as needy. In addition, the factors that make up the formula are regarded as fair and relevant and are based on reasonably recent data. The formula will probably remain substantially intact if the program is continued after its current expiration date, Sept. 30, 1980. [The formula has remained the same through the mid-1980s.—Ed.]

"When revenue sharing came up last time, the Office of Revenue Sharing did more than 100 trials of different formula variations," said Bernardine Denning, director of the Treasury Department's Office of Revenue Sharing. "After all that discussion, Congress came back to the same formula—probably because it was the best available."

Former President Nixon proposed revenue sharing so that states and localities could take advantage of the federal government's ability to raise money through the progressive income tax. The formula builders tried to reflect state and local governments' relative difficulty in raising their revenues.

They built the formula around three key factors: tax effort, to scale the grant according to how hard the local governments already were trying to raise their own money; personal income, to reflect need and indicate the potential for raising additional money; and population, to divide the funds according to the number of people served by each jurisdiction.

If it stopped there, the revenue sharing formula would be simple and logical. But the simple formula produced weird results for some of the 39,000 state and local governments—and some Members of Congress wanted more for their constituents.

"You choose a bunch of variables which any reasonable person might suggest and come out with a distribution formula," said Reischauer. "But politicians must decide whether they like the distribution or not. It is a value judgment, a political decision."

So the simple formula was modified to accommodate some statistical and political realities.

One modification puts more money into urban areas by providing an alternate five-factor formula. Other changes tend to spread the funds around. Because localities compete with each other for funds allocated to their states, Congress decided to limit each city's share of revenue sharing, to prevent poor big cities from getting most of their states' funds.

The formula also recognizes power politics. There is a separate pot of money for sheriffs in Louisiana, the home state of Sen. Russell B. Long, chairman of the Senate Finance Committee and gatekeeper of the revenue sharing programs in the Senate.

These compromises illustrate a tension in formula building between the technician's desire to draft a theoretically pure statistical model based on objective data and the politician's need to find a mathematically plausible way to put money where both the needs and the votes are.

"In designing a formula, we try by sophisticated means to apply what our perceptions tell us the needs are," said Peggy L. Cuciti of the CBO. "But after we're finished, we'd better see how many places are on the list to get money and whether those places meet perceptions of need. After all, a Congressman is going to look at the list and say, 'I know this county and it's really wealthy and doesn't need the money.' " . . .

Measuring Need

Putting the money where the needs are is the reason given for using a mathematical formula for dividing up federal aid. But need is an elusive quantity and no standard gauge will measure it for all situations.

"It's not hard to design a formula based on need," said Nathan. "There are an infinite number of possibilities, but you have to start with an essentially political decision: what dimension of need do you care about?"

There are urban needs and rural needs, government needs and people needs. Need varies from region to region and between growing and declining and new and old areas within regions.

"Informed observers disagree over which problems or conditions ought to be included in calculations of urban need. . . . Not all problems are distributed in a similar fashion," Cuciti of CBO warned in a recent report on the responsiveness of revenue sharing and four other federal programs to city needs ("City Need and the Responsiveness of Federal Grant Programs," prepared for the House Banking, Finance and Urban Affairs Subcommittee on the City). "Whereas economic decline may be the major problem in New York, low levels of income and education may be the difficulty in Tampa."

The CBO report identifies three kinds of need: social, economic and fiscal. Revenue sharing ranks high in meeting the fiscal needs of the cities—which was the original intent of the program—but near or below the other programs in responding to social and economic needs.

Many of the program's opponents long have objected to the fact that revenue sharing does not focus more attention on poverty, included in CBO's social need comparison.

"Before you talk about increasing the targeting on revenue sharing, you have to ask whose need are you looking at," said Treasury's Denning. "A city might have a lot of poor people, but the government could be wealthy and not hand it out to the poor."

An attempt was made to retarget some of the revenue sharing money to the poor when the program was renewed in 1976, but it backfired. That fight provided a lesson in relative measurements of need.

"We were trying to shift the money on the basis of need, but we lost our strongest support in the House," said Leon Shull of Americans for Democratic Action, one of the leaders of the coalition that put together the proposal. "Too damn many people were going to be hurt."

The proposal, which was introduced by Rep. Dante B. Fascell, D-Fla., would have substituted numbers of poor individuals for the relative income factor in part of the formula. It sounded good in theory, and the coalition that put it together went around Capitol Hill, trying to sell the idea to House liberals, many of whom came from northeastern and midwestern big cities.

Then the computer printouts were released. They showed a significant shift of the money from the Northeast and Midwest, where incomes tend to be higher on a national scale, to the South, where more people fall below the poverty line. Support evaporated.

"We produced a formula more valid than one using per capita income," said William Taylor, director of the Washington-based Center for National Policy Review, and another leader in the coalition. "But it may be necessary to modify it to one perceived as more equitable among the regions."

Before the 1976 debate, poverty and need had been linked in most minds. But the Fascell proposal taught representatives of older, declining cities a lesson in statistics.

"As a general rule, the people who represent older cities ought to be very careful when income statistics are used in a proposed formula," warned [Donna E.] Shalala [assistant secretary for policy development and research at the Department of Housing and Urban Development].

This may be changing. A new census study shows per capita income rising in the South and projects the closing of the poverty gap by 1988.

The Frostbelt forces had not been organized at the time of the revenue sharing debate. But partly because of it they formed the Northeast-Midwest Economic Advancement Coalition (now the Northeast-Midwest Congressional Coalition) to fight for regionally beneficial formulas.

The coalition has fought for regional cost-of-living differentials and the indexing of poverty by region. For the most part, it hasn't won those battles, but it has succeeded in inserting in several formulas new measures of need that relate to high-density, declining areas.

In the recent renewal of the Elementary and Secondary Education Act, Congress defined poverty in terms of local median income, for example.

A major victory was the adoption in 1977 of a dual formula for the community development block grant program, which features two factors that benefit older, declining cities: population growth lag and housing built before 1940. . . .

The older housing factor, particularly, continues to be quite controversial. "It's a steal for large old cities," said Delphis C. Goldberg, a staff member of the House Intergovernmental Relations Subcommittee. "It has absolutely no relevance to actual need."

The factor's supporters are just as adamant. "Pre-1940 housing gives you a very good indication of how old the rest of the infrastructure is," Nathan said. "As for expensive, restored mansions, you can write the formula to take out all houses worth more than $40,000. Those statistics are available."

Spreading the Wealth

Mathematical formulas, which in theory are designed to target money to needy places, in practice have been used to make sure that everyone gets a share of the federal aid pie.

In fact, until the recession-spawned economic stimulus programs of 1975-76, most formulas spread the money widely, rather than pinpointing it according to need. The general revenue sharing formula, a key Nixon effort, assures that all but the very smallest local governments get a quarterly check.

The economic stimulus programs—anti-recession fiscal assistance, the public jobs programs of the Comprehensive Employment and Training Act (CETA) [now eliminated in favor of the Job Training Partnership Act—Ed.] and local public works—as well as the 1977 dual formula for community development block grants were remarkably well targeted to need. But the intergovernmental experts see this as a temporary aberration caused by the recession.

"In my view, we've seen the high point of redistribution in this country," said a congressional aide. "Political pressures dictate more equalizing of federal grants than a stress on meeting social needs. I think we are going to see this played out in more spreading of federal aid over the next decade."

One indication of this is that the 95th Congress allowed two of the economic stimulus programs, anti-recession aid and local public works, to expire on Sept. 30. Ironically, a major argument against the renewal of these programs was that proposed new formulas—particularly in the case of anti-recession aid—wouldn't target the money to the neediest places.

The anti-recession aid story illustrates the political pitfalls of trying to balance targeting and equalization goals in formula writing.

The anti-recession formula had distributed more than $1 billion a year for 2½ years to about 17,000 state and local governments based on their unemployment rates and their general revenue sharing payments. The CBO study of responsiveness to city needs found anti-recession aid to be highly responsive to all three kinds of urban needs: social, economic and fiscal.

But the House Intergovernmental Relations Subcommittee staff rejected that finding. In a memo to subcommittee members, Goldberg maintained that the program appeared to be responsive because responsiveness was measured by the same unemployment statistics that were used to distribute the funds. He argued that if an independent gauge of need, such as tax effort, were used to evaluate the program, it would not appear to be so responsive.

Goldberg's bosses, subcommittee chairman L. H. Fountain, D-N.C., and committee chairman Jack Brooks, D-Texas, didn't like the anti-recession program for a number of reasons, not the least of them being the fact that it didn't provide much aid to small communities in North Carolina and Texas.

On two previous occasions when anti-recession aid was before Congress, the House leadership used parliamentary tricks to get around the Government Operations Committee. This time, the Carter Administration tried unsuccessfully to win Brooks and Fountain over by changing the formula somewhat. Treasury proposed adding three factors—below-average growth in population, per capita income and employment—to the unemployment rates in the formula.

While these three factors look as if they would target the money to economically lagging communities, in fact they would have spread the program to an additional 10,000 localities (including many small towns in Texas and North Carolina).

The ploy backfired. Not only did the new formula fail to impress Brooks and Fountain, but it was dismissed by the Senate and attacked by members of the urban lobby because the three new factors accidentally allowed in a number of very wealthy suburban communities. The town of North Hills, N.Y., for example, which had a 1974 per capita income of $46,577, was slated to receive anti-recession aid because its per capita income had grown at a slower pace than the national average.

In the end, the Senate approved a bill with a formula similar to the old one and the House leadership tried to get it passed by circumventing the committee. The strategy didn't work.

Shaken by the failure of Congress to reenact anti-recession aid, state and local governments have nightmares about revenue sharing expiring in the same way.

"The reenactment of revenue sharing is not a sure thing," said a staff member of one of the government groups.

A Treasury official, noting the rising panic among the state and local organizations, said, "That kind of talk could become a self-fulfilling prophecy."

But others in the state and local lobby are putting up a brave front.

"We don't see countercyclical as an omen," said Stephen B. Farber, director of the National Governors' Association. "But the experience is a clear indication that we must marshal our forces early and effectively. There are clear lessons to be learned from countercyclical."

One of these lessons might be not to play with the formula. The government groups were able to mount a strong effort in favor of revenue sharing last time because they didn't get bogged down in a formula fight. But the Administration did try to change the formula for anti-recession aid—and that's when all hell broke loose.

"I think this whole urban policy experience, including the countercyclical fight, has demonstrated that the name of the game is formulas, but by putting targeting up front you open a Pandora's box," said Nathan. "The analytical right answer is not always the tactical right answer."

26. FEDERAL FUNDS AND STATE LEGISLATURES: EXECUTIVE-LEGISLATIVE CONFLICT IN STATE GOVERNMENT

James E. Skok

As problem-solving institutions in modern American society, state legislatures hold great potential for developing solutions to the vast array of public policy problems facing our nation. In the public's perception, however, the performance of the 50 legislative bodies has not been impressive. The Citizens Conference on State Legislatures observed in 1971 that "State legislatures would undoubtedly rank low on most Americans' lists of governmental institutions that make a difference in dealing with the issues and problems that bother us." [1] With the momentum given to legislative reform by the reapportionment decisions of the 1960s, various groups such as the National Conference of State Legislatures (NCSL) and the Advisory Commission on Intergovernmental Relations (ACIR) have called for broad reforms of state legislatures designed to improve their policy-making capabilities.

Focusing upon one problem currently facing many state legislatures—their inability to control the use of federal funds coming into the state—the ACIR has recommended that state legislatures specifically appropriate all federal aid, prohibit spending of federal funds over the amount appropriated, and establish sub-program allocations. [2] This proposal has caused state legislatures across the country to reexamine their procedures for appropriating federal funds and has sparked a debate in state government and academic circles over the proper relationship between the executive and legislative branches in the administration of federal grant programs. Controversy has developed over proposed changes in the traditional relationship with legislators advocating more explicit procedures to improve their policy control and executive officials fearing legislative interference with the governor's constitutional powers over administration. . . .

Current State Practices

Methods of administering federal funds vary widely among the states with variations ranging from a "boilerplate" approach (virtually no legislative involve-

From *Public Administration Review* 40 (November/December 1980): 561-564, 566-567. Reprinted with permission from the author and *Public Administration Review* © 1980 by The American Society for Public Administration, 1120 G Street, N.W., Washington, D.C. All rights reserved.

ment) to a legislative control-oriented approach. According to recent surveys by the National Association of State Budget Officers (NASBO) and the National Conference of State Legislatures (NCSL), the legislatures in 43 of the 50 states appropriate federal funds in some degree of detail.[3] When examined more closely, however, the NASBO study indicates that this apparent legislative power seems illusory in many cases. In 19 of these states the appropriations of most federal funds were made only in general, open-ended language leaving much discretion over use of federal monies to the state's executive branch. In 27 of the 43 states lump sum appropriations were used for federal funds, a practice which normally allows executive branch officials to authorize transfers among programs covered by the appropriation. Finally, in 24 of these states, unanticipated federal monies which became available in mid-year (after legislative enactment of the budget) were automatically appropriated or made available for expenditure solely by executive branch officials. In only four states were legislative powers extensive in all three of these aspects; that is, the legislatures reported power to appropriate federal funds, including interim funds, in specified amounts by object-class or line item detail. Getting beyond these formal power arrangements, only seven states in the NCSL survey reported an active legislative review of federal funds, while 22 reported a moderate review and 16 a limited review.

Typical of the limited review or "boiler-plate" approach is the set of procedures used in Pennsylvania prior to 1976. Executive branch agencies in preparing annual budget requests would estimate the amounts of federal funds to be received during the forthcoming fiscal year. State funds were appropriated in lump sum amounts; however, the appropriations act did not list specific amounts of federal funds. Rather, each agency was simply authorized to spend whatever federal monies were received during the year. The nature of the federal grant program generally would determine the nature of the agency's state budget presentation and the information presented to the legislature.

For categorical entitlement or formula grant programs (Aid to Families with Dependent Children, for example), the agency would calculate a total amount needed to fund the estimated case load at a given level of support (a percentage of the state standard family subsistence income). The federal entitlement formula would then determine the state appropriation needed and the expected federal grant level. Both amounts and the calculations used would be shown in the agency's budget request forms. These types of programs caused few problems from the standpoint of legislative control under the "boiler-plate" approach since the agency's discretion was severely limited by federal regulations and the options were clear to all involved. Funds could not be transferred to any other use.

In the case of more open-ended categorical assistance grants (Social Services grants, for example) and block grants, the problems of legislative control become infinitely more complex. To illustrate, Title 20 Social Services Grants may be used for a wide range of projects (day care, homemaker/housekeeping services, counseling, family planning, health diagnosis and help in securing treatment) subject to approval of a Comprehensive Annual Services Plan by the U.S. Department of Health, Education and Welfare [now Health and Human Services]. Traditionally such plans have been developed by the state welfare agency with little or no state legislative involvement. Mid-year amendments to the state plan may be made with HEW approval and frequently additional unallocated federal monies become available during the fiscal year. Under these circumstances, the "boiler-plate" procedures are highly unsatisfactory from the standpoint of legislative control. The agency budget submission would show the total amount of social services funds expected, and break the total amount down into specific amounts for the various projects to be funded. The agency, however, had great discretion over the projects in which federal funds should actually be used. Since all federal funds were appropriated in a general, open-ended grant of authority, the agency was free to make shifts from one use to another during the fiscal year with approval of the Governor's Budget Office. Additional federal monies that became available during the year were budgeted and expended without additional legislative approval as long as the 25 percent state matching requirement could be met from existing state appropriations. The problems associated with federal block grants . . . were similar to those of the Title 20 grants.

While the "boiler-plate" approach had the advantage of allowing agencies much administrative flexibility to seize opportunities to capture federal funds as soon as an occasion arose, it also produced among legislators a feeling of impotence when trying to control state spending. In 1976, the Pennsylvania General Assembly enacted legislation (over Governor Shapp's veto) forbidding expenditure of federal funds or state matching funds unless both were specifically appropriated by the General Assembly.[4] Since 1976, the annual General Appropriation Act has provided state funds only. Federal funds are now appropriated annually in a separate act by specific amount, department, and grant category. To illustrate, in 1976 the state Justice Department received 17 specific appropriations from state funds and 24 additional specific appropriations from federal funds. Funds now may not be transferred among the specified purposes nor may additional federal funds which become available during mid-year be allocated for expenditure without enactment of new appropriations by the legislature.[5]

The Arguments:
Proponents of Executive Power Versus Legislative Partisans

Proponents of increasing state legislative control over the appropriation of federal funds argue that current budgetary practices were established during a time in which federal funds made up only a very small part of total state budgets.[6] Increases in the amounts of federal funds and the development of new federal discretionary grants such as General and Special Revenue Sharing, the proponents argue, have been used by administrators to increase their control over policy at the expense of the state legislatures. The representative character of state government, they continue, is lost if executive agencies, which do not have to face the voting public, can use federal funds to finance activities which their legislatures have refused to fund. Legislatures, this argument continues, lose oversight control if executive agencies feel they alone control the allocation and expenditure of federal funds totaling from 20 percent to 30 percent of the typical state budget. Finally, program administrators at the state and federal levels develop channels of communication and a common professional-agency bias which often ignores the general public interest and excludes the state legislatures from significant areas of policy making.

To illustrate, a state legislator in Pennsylvania has claimed that agencies in his state have: (1) purposely expanded their staffs on "soft" federal money, thus forcing the legislature to provide additional state funds when federal funds expired (Board of Probation Parole); (2) purposely overestimated federal receipts for mental institutions, thus forcing the legislature to appropriate state funds to cover the deficit (Welfare Department); and (3) shifted federal Title 20 funds from day care after the legislature had increased the state day care appropriation above the amount requested by the agency (Welfare Department).[7] In Pennsylvania, as well as other states, many legislators perceive administrators as being deceitful, arrogant, and overbearing in their attempt to exclude legislators from effective participation in the policy-making process.

Countering these arguments, opponents of extending state legislative appropriation powers over federal funds contend that handling these funds at the state level is an administrative function and emphasize that state governors generally have constitutional powers as chief executive.[8] Congress, they argue, has already made the critical policy decisions guiding the use of federal grants; and subsequently, federal executive branch agencies enter virtual contractual relationships with state administrators controlling the use of federal grant funds. Echoing the thoughts of some of the early writers on public administration, these advocates of executive power articulate the following arguments.

Structurally and functionally legislatures are policy-making institutions. They are neither designed nor staffed to perform efficient, non-partisan administration. Many state legislatures meet only a limited number of days each year; are prone to partisan deadlocks; and are characterized by bargaining, logrolling and other types of "nonrational" decision making. State legislatures are subject to the demagogic behavior of vocal minorities advocating racial discrimination or narrow partisan and personnel objectives which would threaten to undermine national objectives established by Congress in federal legislation. State legislatures are unable to act with dispatch when rapid decisions upon federal funds are required. Their participation in the federal funds process presents a threat to the constitutional principle of federal supremacy. Executive branch agencies are structurally and functionally efficient decision-making systems, and to force the governor's guardianship of federal funds to become subject to partisan state legislative control violates the intent of many federal grant programs and reduces the governor's constitutional power as chief executive to, merely, a ministerial function. Finally, allowing state legislatures to control federal funds through the appropriation process creates inefficiency, delays, and excessive red tape; and, ultimately, it raises the possibility that program administration will become politicized.

Evaluating the Arguments: Executive-Legislative Conflict in Pennsylvania

Interviews with 15 executive and legislative staff officials subsequent to the enactment of Act 117 in Pennsylvania have revealed information useful in evaluating these arguments. All officials interviewed conceded that legislators are within their constitutional powers in requesting greater involvement in the federal funds process. The consensus of those persons interviewed is that the new procedures seem workable but cumbersome—capable of producing massive amounts of detail but at the expense of administrative flexibility. The following range of problems has been experienced by the commonwealth agencies receiving federal funds: minor conflict situations, policy confrontations between the executive branch and the legislature, constitutional confrontations between the state legislature and the federal government, and, finally, the politicization of state administration. . . .

[In his complete essay, Skok provides explanations for and examples of each of these difficulties.—Ed.]

Conclusion

The assertion of state legislative powers over federal funds is a reform national in scope undertaken in good faith throughout the country. It has the support of "good government" groups such as the National Conference of State Legislatures and the Advisory Commission on Intergovernmental Relations. Indeed, ACIR's vocal support of the reforms in Pennsylvania was cited by the court majority in *Shapp v. Sloan* as a factor influencing their decision to uphold the constitutionality of Act 117.[9] The political nature of the Pennsylvania case should not be used to discredit the legislative reform movement. Ultimately, each state must consider the facts and circumstances of its particular case. To those states considering adopting procedures similar to the Pennsylvania process, the conclusions drawn from this study might prove informative.

All persons interviewed supported the right of the legislature to improve its policy-making capability in relation to federal funds. Likewise, all interviewees concluded that the Act 117 procedures are being complied with by the bureaucracy and that minor delays and increased paperwork are the most common operational problems. By a large majority, however, the interviewees felt the new procedures are cumbersome, time consuming, and not productive of real improvement in the policy-making process. During periods of legislative recess or deadlock there is an inability to act upon federal funds. While the legislature does receive much more detailed information under the new procedures, there is the danger that legislators, deluged by detail, might actually be diverted from larger policy questions. Adequate legislative staffing to cope with the additional flow of paper is essential. Finally, the potential for politicization of matters that have been considered essentially administrative in character is underscored by the Pennsylvania experience.

Notes

1. *The Sometime Governments* (Kansas City: Citizens Conference on State Legislatures, 1971), p. 2.
2. "State Legislatures and Federal Grants," *Information Bulletin* No. 76-4 (Washington, D.C.: Advisory Commission on Intergovernmental Relations, November 1976). (Hereinafter cited as *ACIR Information Bulletin.*)
3. The National Association of State Budget Officers, *Federal Funds Budgetary and Appropriations Practices in State Government* (Lexington Ky.: Council of State

Governments, 1978), p. 7 . . . ; *State Legislative Oversight of Federal Funds: Preliminary Report and Suggested Activities* (Denver, Colo.: National Conference of State Legislatures, 1979). (Hereinafter cited as the *NCSL Survey*.)

4. Act No. 117, July 1, 1976; 72 P. S. 4611.
5. Unlike some states, the Pennsylvania law does not designate the Appropriations Committee or some other unit as a joint clearing house to act for the entire legislature in approving changes to the federal funds appropriation throughout the fiscal year. A process similar to this is currently used in 12 states although at least three states have constitutional prohibitions to such a procedure. *NCSL Survey*, Appendix A, Table 11.
6. These arguments are abstracted from various sources. See for example, the comments of Michael Hershock of the staff of the Pennsylvania House of Representatives in *ACIR Information Bulletin*, p. 2. See also the testimony of Representative Stanley Steingut of the New York State Assembly in "Role of State Legislatures in Appropriating Federal Funds to States," Hearings before the Subcommittee on Intergovernmental Relations of the Committee on Governmental Affairs. U.S. Senate, 95th Congress, First Session, June 16, 1977, pp. 2-50. (Hereinafter cited as *U.S. Senate Hearings on Role of State Legislatures*.)
7. These situations are summarized from testimony by Representative James P. Ritter of the Pennsylvania General Assembly in the *U.S. Senate Hearings on Role of State Legislatures*, pp. 56-60.
8. These arguments are abstracted from various sources. See, for example, the testimony of John P. Mallan of the American Association of State Colleges and Universities in *U.S. Senate Hearings on Role of State Legislatures*, pp. 114-203. See also the brief for appellants in *Shapp v. Sloan* in *U.S. Senate Hearings on Role of State Legislatures*, pp. 134-197. These arguments are primarily those of lawyers and practicing governmental officials rather than academicians or administrative theorists; however, the influence of the early literature of public administration is apparent. For a review of this early literature see: John A. Worthley, "Public Administration and Legislatures: Past Neglect, Present Probes," *Public Administration Review*, Vol. 35 (September/October 1975), 486-490.
9. Pa. 391 A2d. 595, 605. One wonders whether the ACIR would have been so vocal in its support if all the facts had been available to them at the time.

27. FEDERAL AID TO BIG CITIES

James W. Fossett

Recent cuts in federal grant programs and Reagan administration proposals to delegate control over most urban programs to state governments seem likely to reopen debate about the extent to which state and local governments—particularly big-city governments—have become "dependent" on federal funds. A number of observers, noting the major build-up of federal grants to cities during the 1970s and the increasing size of these funds relative to local revenues, have argued that many city governments were in danger of becoming, in the words of one observer, "creatures of the state and wards of the federal government."

The changes during the 1970s were indeed substantial. The most important was a major increase in the amount of federal funds going to cities. This growth resulted from two initiatives: (1) the New Federalism proposals of the Nixon administration, which resulted in the adoption of federal revenue sharing and the community development block grant (CDBG) and comprehensive employment and training (CETA) programs, and (2) the Carter administration's 1977 economic stimulus package, which substantially expanded funding for public service jobs, local public works, and countercyclical revenue sharing. Federal grants to cities grew by almost 700 percent over the 1970s, or almost twice the growth in nonwelfare grants and better than twice the growth rate in the grant system as a whole. Grants reached their peak as a city revenue source in 1978, when they provided funds equivalent to 26 percent of the revenue provided to cities by state governments. While the rate of growth in direct federal grants has declined sharply in recent years, federal dollars remain a substantial revenue source for city governments. In 1980, the most recent year for which data are available, direct federal grants amounted to $10.9 billion, the equivalent of 23 percent of city-raised revenue.[1]

There were also noteworthy changes during the seventies in the geographic allocation of federal funds to cities. Under earlier categorical programs such as urban renewal and model cities, federal administrators reviewed applications from local agencies and granted funds to those that ranked high on various criteria. This method tended to concentrate federal funds in larger cities, particularly in the Northeast, whose officials were willing to invest substantial

From *Federal Aid to Big Cities: The Politics of Dependence* (Washington, D.C.: Brookings Institution, 1983), pp. 1-3, 20, 52-59.

effort in developing applications and lobbying federal agencies to secure their approval.

The new programs of the seventies, by contrast, allocated funds automatically on the basis of formulas to all cities that met simple eligibility criteria. The general revenue sharing program, for example, distributes funds to all 38,000 units of general-purpose local government in the country. The community development block grant program provides nearly automatic funding to any city recognized as the central city of a Standard Metropolitan Statistical Area (SMSA). Governments do not have to compete for funds with other governments, but rather receive allocations based on characteristics of the city's population, housing stock, or finances. The increased use of formulas has had the effect of spreading funds to smaller cities and to larger cities located in the South and West, many of which had received little or no money from earlier programs.[2]

These new programs also produced a major change in the types of recipients within cities. Earlier categorical programs made large numbers of grants to special authorities and community organizations. The formula-based programs of the seventies, by contrast, provide federal funds to city governments, which have a substantial amount of discretion in deciding how to spend them. Organizations such as urban renewal authorities and community action agencies that once dealt with federal agencies are now compelled to work through city hall to obtain federal support.

There is, in brief, some plausibility to the argument that cities may have become "dependent" on federal dollars. More money is being provided to more cities than earlier, and being provided in a form that makes it relatively easy for city officials either to cut local taxes or to increase services with no increase in taxes. Further, redirecting federal funds through city hall may have provided mayors and council members with the opportunity to use federal funds to maintain or broaden their base of political support. If local officials have availed themselves of these opportunities for fiscal or political relief, then many cities may have in fact become "dependent" on these funds and stand to lose substantially from aid cutbacks of the magnitude contained in recent administration proposals.

The extent to which cities have, in fact, used federal dollars in ways that have made them financially or politically "dependent" on these funds is, however, far from clear. Because the federal programs enacted during the seventies presented local officials with a considerable amount of discretion in how to use federal dollars, a reasonable assessment of "dependence" requires some understanding of the uses of federal dollars and the attitudes of state and local officials toward them.

This essay presents such an assessment, drawing on case studies of the impact of federal funds on eleven large American cities in 1978. . . .

[In the full study the author "indicates the difficulties associated with current definitions of city 'dependence' on federal funds, and then advances an alternative definition of dependence based on city use of federal funds to support 'basic' city services." He "presents a set of propositions about the political and financial conditions under which cities become 'dependent' on federal funds. . . ." In the concluding portion of the study, Fossett summarizes the findings and "suggests the likely consequences of recent budget cutbacks on the finances and politics of big cities."—Ed.]

This analysis has identified three distinct patterns in federal aid's budgetary and political impact among the eleven cities under consideration. . . .

In the six cities classified as financially hard pressed [New York, Detroit, Cleveland, Boston, St. Louis, and Rochester, N.Y.], federal funds have become major sources of support for ongoing city activities, particularly basic services, and have become major sources of political capital for city officials. Federal funds were the fastest-growing source of city revenue over this period and local officials were unable to maintain politically acceptable levels of basic services from local revenues. As a result, mayors and budget officials made considerable use of federal funds to support such basic city services as police, fire, and sanitation, which might otherwise have been reduced. Federal funds were allocated through the same decision-making processes, and by the same actors, as other local revenues, and were spent in ways that resemble the ways in which locally raised dollars were spent.

The second major pattern appears in Chicago and Los Angeles, where federal funds have not been used to support basic city services, but have become integrated into local politics. During the mid-1970s, both these cities were in relatively strong financial condition, making it possible for city officials to follow a relatively cautious policy of segregating the activities supported by federal funds from those supported by local revenues. Federal funds were used to support activities in departments that provide basic services, but these activities have been nonrecurring expenditures or activities that could be discontinued with relatively little difficulty if federal funds were terminated. By the same token, officials in both these cities avoided committing local funds to human service activities supported primarily with federal dollars, in order to avoid creating any local liability for these programs.

In these two cities, however, the process of allocating federal funds has been closely tied to local politics, for much the same reasons as in the hard-pressed cities. Relatively large areas of these cities are eligible to receive federal funds, and program constituents are relatively well organized and politically important. Under these conditions, decisions on allocating federal aid are made by the same actors—the upper levels of department bureaucracies in Chicago and the city council in Los Angeles—and in response to much the same set of political demands and constraints as decisions on allocating local resources.

The third major pattern of federal aid use appears in Phoenix, Tulsa, and Houston, where federal funds have become neither a major source of support for normal city services nor an important political issue. Because these cities have been financially strong, they have generally kept federal funds segregated from local revenue and have avoided using grants to support ongoing city services. Instead, they have used federal funds largely to finance new services, such as manpower or community development, which they were not providing before federal support became available for these purposes. Federal dollars have also enabled these cities to provide capital facilities or expand services to keep pace with population growth without increasing local taxes.

By contrast with the situation in the first two sets of cities, federal funds have not become political issues in these three cities. Federal regulations have the effect of limiting the areas within which funds can be spent in these cities, and program constituents are less well organized and have less political power than in the other cities in this study. The allocation of federal dollars has not become a major concern of local elected officials, but has rather been largely determined by professional program staff and local service agencies.

Three points are particularly worthy of note. First, the amount of federal money a city receives—whether compared with its own revenues or judged against any other standard—has little relation to its dependence on these funds to support ongoing city services. Hard-pressed and more prosperous cities have used federal funds to support very different activities, but these differences are not reflected in the amount of federal money these two kinds of cities receive. According to the figures in Table 5, the cities classified as prosperous are more "dependent" on federal money than the hard-pressed cities, because the federal aid they receive is larger relative to local taxes than the comparable figure for the hard-pressed cities.

Second, there is considerable variety in the politics surrounding the allocation of federal funds, and these different political conditions appear to influence the way federal aid is spent. In some cities, decisions about how to spend federal dollars are made primarily by elected officials, in others by professional staff. In cities where elected officials are the major decision makers, federal funds are more likely to be used to support basic services and to benefit the population at large than in places where professional staff have more to say about what is

Table 5 Three Measures of Dependence on Federal Funds, 1978

City	Federal operating grants as percentage of local taxes	Percentage of federal operating grants spent on basic services	Federal operating grants for basic services as percentage of total spending on basic services
Phoenix	66.0	30.2	14.7
Cleveland	58.4	46.0	24.0
Detroit	52.4	49.0[a]	25.5
Chicago	49.6	28.7	10.9
St. Louis	44.0	49.9[a]	27.0
Los Angeles	41.6	10.3	4.5
Tulsa	40.1	18.3	11.3
Rochester	36.8	92.4	22.3
Boston	36.4	39.3	13.0
Houston	31.0	16.5	4.4
New York[b]	19.5	55.3	22.7
Average, eleven cities	43.3	39.6	16.4

Note: Basic services include public safety, public works, sanitation, and general administration. For New York and Boston, schools have also been added.

[a] Estimated on the basis of employment.

[b] Excludes AFDC and medicaid from federal funds received.

SOURCE: Case study reports.

done with federal money. The presumption that federal money is allocated more or less the same in all cities and in response to the same set of forces that drives the allocation of local funds appears unwarranted, at least for this set of cities. Politics differ, and they cause spending patterns to differ as well.

Finally, the conditions surrounding grants, particularly the uncertainty of their continuation and the amount of discretion they provide local officials, appear to have a considerable effect on how cities spend federal dollars. In spite of the large amounts of money provided to these cities under the economic stimulus package, for example, both the uncertainty of continued support and federal agency pressure to spend money in particular ways appear to have led all but the most hard pressed of these cities to avoid using these funds to support ongoing city activities. In similar fashion, different degrees of discretion stemming from CDBG regulations appear to have produced different uses of these funds across these cities.[3]

The differences in dependence and in the politics surrounding the allocation of federal funds suggest that substantial reductions in grant programs will have a very different impact on these cities. The next section suggests some of these differences.

The Consequences of Cuts

As noted earlier, the case studies focused on the local political and budgetary response to a massive build-up in the level of federal grants for cities that occurred during the mid-1970s. In particular, these studies focus on federal aid received and spent in 1978, which marked the high point of this support relative to both total federal outlays and local revenues.

Since 1978, the federal aid picture has changed sharply. The Carter administration's attempt to make the economic stimulus package programs permanent was unsuccessful, and substantial restrictions were imposed on the types of individuals who could be hired under the PSE program, their tenure once hired, and the maximum salaries they could be paid.[4] As a result of these and other changes, the amount of federal support for cities leveled off between 1978 and 1981. More recently, and more importantly, major changes have been initiated by the Reagan administration. . . .

[Fossett describes these changes as they affect cities. They consist of significant federal cutbacks (and the possibility of additional cutbacks) in numerous grant programs, consolidation of many categoricals into block grants, and an unfulfilled proposal to turn many programs back to state and local governments.—Ed.]

While a complete evaluation of the consequences of either enacted or proposed reductions is beyond the scope of this essay, it is possible to offer several general comments on the likely consequences of the budget cuts. . . .

First, the short-term consequences of the . . . budgets for cities in general, and for these cities in particular, may be limited. Most of the programs that absorbed the largest reductions in earlier budgets and were proposed to be reduced in fiscal 1984 do not provide substantial funds to city governments, although several do support services to city residents by special districts, such as transit authorities and school districts.[5] The reduction that most directly affected the city governments under consideration here in an appreciable fashion was the elimination of the public service employment program, which had different impacts in hard-pressed cities from those in the more prosperous ones.

In the more prosperous cities, the effects of eliminating PSE appear to have been negligible. Most of these cities had protected themselves against such an eventuality by subcontracting substantial numbers of PSE positions and concentrating these funds in services that could be easily terminated without establishing any claim on the city budget. As noted earlier, in 1978 Congress had imposed considerable restrictions on the types of persons who could be hired and on their maximum pay and tenure in PSE positions. Most of the prosperous places appear to have begun to reduce their involvement in the program at this point by reducing the number of PSE positions they retained in their own agencies and by moving former PSE workers they wished to retain onto the city payroll. Phoenix, for example, moved approximately 500 positions from PSE to city funding well before the program was eliminated, and Chicago shifted more than 350 slots.

Hard-pressed cities were hurt more by the PSE termination. Because of their fiscal position, these cities had been unable to reduce their participation in the program after the 1978 restrictions took effect. They were compelled either to seek waivers of program requirements or to continue participation under the more stringent regulations.

Boston, Rochester, and St. Louis were forced to reduce services after PSE ended. All three cities had come under increased fiscal pressure since 1978— Rochester as a result of a court-mandated rollback of property tax rates, and Boston and St. Louis as a result of major tax limitation measures. All were in the process of reducing city-funded work forces when PSE was terminated. As the [authors of the St. Louis case study] note:

> [The elimination of PSE], involving a loss of $21 million to St. Louis, is a severe blow because of the city's heavy reliance on PSE workers to supplement its regular civil service complement, which itself has now been significantly reduced. . . . This reduction in federal aid comes at a particularly inopportune time because of the climate produced because of the tax resistance movement. . . . Confronted with a threatened initiative referendum to abolish the 10 percent utility tax, the Board of Aldermen in 1979 passed a law phasing out the levy on residential users by 1973. When fully in effect the repeal will reduce tax revenues by about $24 million a year.[6]

Detroit and Cleveland, by contrast, were able to avoid major layoffs when PSE ended by securing large increases in local income tax rates. While the Cleveland increase passed relatively easily, the Detroit increase was the result of a long, complex, and bitterly contested campaign. State legislative approval was required to place the increase on the ballot. The legislature gave its approval, but required the city to secure substantial wage concessions from city employees and to sell city bonds to eliminate a $120 million deficit. The city was able to meet all conditions, but only after a major lobbying effort, and is confronting another sizable deficit as a result of reductions in state aid and worsening economic conditions.[7]

A second factor that may have lessened the impact of federal cuts on the cities under consideration here has been the increased flexibility in the use of Community Development Block Grant funds made available by both Congressional and administration action. The Department of Housing and Urban Development has sharply curtailed federal review of CDBG applications, has repealed the requirement that CDBG funds be "targeted" on low- and moderate-income groups, and has permitted local governments to use appreciable amounts of CDBG funds to support on-going services. While the administration's proposal to eliminate gradually restrictions on the use of CDBG funds seems unlikely to pass, the extension of the program currently being debated by Congress calls for increasing the share of funds that can be spent on services, thus allowing harder pressed cities to use enhanced amounts of CDBG funds to support basic services. While this increased flexibility does not completely offset the loss of PSE funds, it may limit the adverse effect of this loss on local services.[8]

The importance of this point should not be overstated. With the exception of Boston, the hard-pressed cities rely more heavily on cyclically sensitive revenue sources, such as city income and sales taxes, than do most other cities. This reliance makes them particularly vulnerable if the current recession continues. Further, Rochester and Boston have had to adjust to substantial losses in property tax revenues over the last three years. The loss of PSE funds has worsened these cities' fiscal burdens appreciably. . . .

The impact of the Reagan budget cuts on this set of cities, in sum, has been considerably smaller than had been previously predicted, in part because programs that supply funds to city governments have not been reduced as substantially as those that provide support to other types of governments, but more importantly because of strategies adopted by many cities to insulate themselves from the adverse results of possible reductions in federal support. While harder pressed cities have had considerably more difficulty in adjusting to these reductions than cities with fewer financial problems, the impact of reduced federal support in these places has been less catastrophic than was anticipated.

Notes

1. U.S. Bureau of the Census, *City Government Finances in 1979-80* (Washington, D.C.: U.S. Government Printing Office, 1981), table 1.
2. For descriptions of changes in the geographic allocation of federal urban aid over this period, see Richard P. Nathan and James W. Fossett, "Urban Conditions—The Future of the Federal Role," in *1978 Proceedings of the Seventy-first Annual Conference on Taxation, Philadelphia* (Columbus, Ohio: National Tax Association—Tax Institute of America, 1979); and Richard P. Nathan, "The Outlook for Federal Grants to Cities," in Roy Bahl, ed., *The Fiscal Outlook for Cities* (Syracuse: Syracuse University Press, 1978).
3. For a more developed version of these latter two arguments, see V. Lane Rawlins and Richard P. Nathan, "The Field Network Evaluation Studies of Intergovernmental Grants: A Contrast with the Conventional Neoclassical Economic Approach," paper presented at the annual meeting of the American Economic Association, 1981.
4. For a more detailed description of these changes, see Nathan *et al., Public Service Employment: A Field Evaluation* (Washington, D.C.: Brookings Institution, 1981), pp. 118-19.
5. For an evaluation of the initial effects of the 1982 budget changes including most of the

cities reported here, see Richard P. Nathan, Philip M. Dearborn, Clifford A. Goldman, and Associates, "Initial Effects of the Fiscal Year 1982 Reductions in Federal Domestic Spending," in John W. Ellwood, ed., *Reductions in U.S. Domestic Spending: How They Affect State and Local Governments* (New Brunswick, N.J.: Transaction Books, 1982).

6. Henry J. Schmandt, George D. Wendel, and E. Allan Tomey, *Federal Aid to St. Louis* (Washington, D.C.: Brookings Institution, 1983), p. 66.

7. Thomas Anton, *Federal Aid to Detroit* (Washington, D.C.: Brookings Institution, 1983), chapter 7.

8. For a more detailed description and assessment of the changes in CDBG, see Michael Rich, "Fiscal and Political Implications of the CDBG Experience in 10 Cities," paper presented at the Midwest Political Science Association Annual Meeting, April, 1983.

Part Three

Review Questions

1. What are the relative strengths and weaknesses of the different types of intergovernmental aid mechanisms—for instance, formula, project, categorical, and block grants, and revenue sharing? Be sure to include both economic and political considerations.

2. Analysts of American intergovernmental relations frequently allude to the interdependence of units in the system. How would you document this interdependence using fiscal data?

3. George Break says that fixed-amount grants for specified purposes may "conciliate appearance and reality," since they seem to support functions deemed important by the grantor while really allowing grantees to use the funds for any local purpose. Please explain this effect of the fixed-amount grant.

4. What are open- and closed-ended grants? What are their relative advantages and disadvantages?

5. The study of revenue sharing by Nathan and Adams contains findings on the issue of decentralization, specifically on citizen participation in the political processes of state and local governments. Are their conclusions consistent with those reported in the ACIR's study of citizen participation in intergovernmental programs (see the reading in Part Two)? Explain your answer.

6. Imagine that a presidential election has just taken place. The winner has campaigned on the issue of reforming the system of intergovernmental aid so that public functions would be sorted out by level of government. "Matters of national concern should be handled at the national level," the president-elect says, "and matters of more limited concern should be handled by the state and local governments. One of my first priorities is to redirect the system in this fashion." The new national chief executive calls on you, an expert in intergovernmental relations, for advice on how to carry out this program. What do you say? Be sure to consider Monypenny's analysis of the political functions of fiscal assistance, as well as Reagan and Sanzone's discussion of the functions of intergovernmental aid.

7. In an essay in Part Two of this volume, Reischauer explains how the diversity among American governmental structures and functions impedes any efforts to design rational fiscal instruments. Monypenny seems to imply that the prevalence of grants is in large measure the *result* of diversity. Are these two claims necessarily inconsistent? Discuss.

8. In today's era of cross-cutting mandates (similar or identical strings, such as nondiscrimination requirements, attached to many different grants offered in

divergent policy sectors), does Monypenny's assertion that narrow coalitions are responsible for individual programs still seem valid?

9. Some critics of the American system of intergovernmental relations claim that the current pattern of categorical grants constitutes an aberration from the fundamental features of the American political system, like governmental accountability. Is this a valid criticism? In your answer, give some attention to the forces encouraging the establishment and maintenance of categorical programs.

10. Should control over funding formulas and the expenditure of aid be placed in the hands of technical experts so that politics can be eliminated from the design of intergovernmental fiscal instruments? Why or why not? (Note Stanfield's analysis, and also consider Fossett's findings that politicians and professional administrators seem to make different decisions at the local level about how to spend discretionary money.)

11. Why might both supporters *and* opponents of increased federal aid to the nation's cities draw support from the Brookings studies on urban fiscal dependence?

12. Explain why figures for overall intergovernmental aid to a state or a city might be misleading as an indicator of fiscal stress or dependence.

13. Suppose a friend compares city officials dealing with state or federal governments to addicts hooked on narcotics (in this case, money): they can't wait to get hold of their "drug"; they try to inject it into their most vital parts; and they become, thereby, dependent on it. Does Fossett's study suggest any flaws in this analogy?

14. Would state and local officials object to parts of the analysis presented by Reagan and Sanzone? Why?

Part Four

ADMINISTRATIVE ASPECTS OF
INTERGOVERNMENTAL RELATIONS

In one policy sector after another, intergovernmental administrative arrangements are responsible for many of the most significant public decisions and the consequences of those decisions. Yet these arrangements are relatively obscured from public view. Even the most prominent bureaucratic units within individual governments, such as the cabinet-level agencies in Washington, are almost incomprehensible to the citizenry. Their byzantine procedures, obscure jargon, and large population of specialists often make them seem remote and intimidating. Complexity and misunderstanding are magnified when the administration of programs takes place in operations that span two or more government levels.

A survey of some intergovernmental administrative activities may indicate how important, if confusing, this topic is. Many of these activities are aimed at implementing some general policy idea, usually established in broad outline at the national level. Converting this general intention into specific actions while also incorporating state and local objectives may entail a set of formidable tasks. At the national level, administrative actors may be deeply involved in deciding which government units are to receive how much aid, as well as in developing program regulations, mediating and negotiating with state and local agencies, reviewing plans and operations of other levels of government, and coordinating intergovernmental programs handled by various federal agencies. At other levels, intergovernmental administration includes such activities as drafting plans (and seeking support for them within the community, the government, and higher levels of administration), negotiating with other governments, managing programs (which can involve designing, staffing, and evaluating programs), dealing with program beneficiaries and their representatives, and attempting to coordinate state and local programs with one another and with other state and local activities.

Three general comments can be made about the readings in Part Four. First, of course, the selections illustrate the links among political, fiscal, and administrative aspects of the American intergovernmental pattern. Most administrative problems and opportunities in the system are tied to aid programs, and very often administrative disputes between and among governments reflect political disagreements. Second, these articles (and, in fact, most studies of administrative aspects of intergovernmental relations) understandably focus on negative topics—

problems and dilemmas in the system. Still, it is important to recognize that in many policy areas much of the time calm, workable arrangements have developed. The fact that the system often works can be obscured by both political rhetoric and the network's very complexity.[1] Third, much of today's debate about intergovernmental relations tends to lay the blame for the weaknesses in the system, including the costliness of programs and the frequent lack of coordination, on the federal government. However, the readings in this section highlight the oversimplifications underlying this explanation. While the federal government is surely not free of blame for intergovernmental administrative difficulties, neither is it the sole culprit. Solutions to these problems do not lie with a simplistic castigation of the national bureaucracy.

Part Four begins, in fact, with an article that implies this point. Helen Ingram studied the operations of a small intergovernmental program, water resources planning grants to states authorized by Title III of the Water Resources Planning Act of 1965. Her picture of federal-state administration is a far cry from the image of a hierarchical, command-and-control implementation chain. Drawing from her field investigations, as well as the explicit models of intergovernmental politics developed by Jeffrey Pressman and Martha Derthick (excerpted in Part Two), she asserts that when federal administrative agencies deal with state units, the predominant behavior observed is bargaining. The federal government does not control the administration of programs; nor, claims Ingram, is there any substantial chance that it *could* do so, even by using stronger threats or sanctions. In this excerpt Ingram develops a set of propositions on the extent and (especially) the limits of federal administrative influence. She implies that administration in intergovernmental relations—even more than administration within a single government—involves more subtle activities than simply giving and receiving orders.

The second selection is from a study of administrators, 1,400 heads of from 65 to 70 different kinds of agencies in all 50 states across the country, conducted for the Advisory Commission on Intergovernmental Relations. The complete study examined the opinions held by state administrators about their own operations, especially their intergovernmental responsibilities. The excerpt included here discusses the sources of program management innovations in state administration. New ideas for state program management come from many sources, including other levels of government. However, within-government sources seem to be the most important; each government thus retains a distinctive perspective and a considerable degree of autonomy.

One of the most important administrative topics is regulation. Whereas governments have long used strings on grants-in-aid to attempt to control other levels of government, the quantity and perceived intrusiveness of intergovernmental regulation has accelerated in the last two decades. Today the subject is receiving a great deal of attention from politicians, administrators, and study groups concerned about the intergovernmental system. Three readings in Part Four explore various facets of this controversy over intergovernmental regulation.

The first of these is from a study by the ACIR, *Regulatory Federalism*, which focuses on the increased regulatory activity in the intergovernmental system. In this excerpt the commission distinguishes various types of regulatory mechanisms used in intergovernmental administration. Some of these varieties of regulation are associated with grants-in-aid, while others are imposed through federal laws or rules divorced from any aid program. The ACIR report also documents how recently much of the regulation has been generated.

Following this general introduction are two other selections on regulation. Both examine the impact of federal regulation at the local level, but they reach markedly different conclusions. The first, by Mayor Edward Koch of New York City, is a vivid critique of recent trends in federal regulation. Koch points out how many problems can be caused for localities by well-intended but poorly considered mandates from Washington. (In the case of one of Koch's examples, Section 504 regulations for providing access to mass transit facilities for the handicapped, federal rules have recently been altered to provide more flexibility to local governments.)[2] A particularly interesting aspect of Koch's presentation is his explanation for much of the growth in regulation: reduced funding for intergovernmental programs has encouraged national officials to try to achieve their goals by directives rather than inducements.

Although Koch portrays federal administrators as domineering and unyielding, Frederick Lazin's argument is much different. Lazin studied national-local bargaining on equal opportunity in public housing in Chicago and found that bureaucrats in the Department of Housing and Urban Development were extremely, indeed excessively, deferential toward the local power structure. Whereas Koch points to the strength of the federal presence in intergovernmental administration, Lazin emphasizes the influence exerted by local authorities. Lazin's essay shows that the frequent portrayal of state and local officials as hard-working, decent, unfairly put-upon public servants harassed by Washington is not universally accurate.

The final article in this section is Don Kettl's study of the administrative system used in Richmond, Virginia, to manage and implement two major block grant programs: the Comprehensive Employment Training Act (now replaced by the Job Training Partnership Act) and the Community Development Block Grant. He describes the interestingly complex administrative pattern Richmond used: a set of contracting arrangements with private organizations. Kettl's piece explains this new aspect of intergovernmental administration and analyzes the significant impact of block grants. Further, Kettl provides a sense of the practical administrative tasks facing local managers involved in intergovernmental programs and illustrates clearly the ever more complex and interdependent administrative patterns of today's intergovernmental relations.

Notes

1. Paul Peterson, "When Federalism Works" (Paper delivered at the annual meeting of the American Political Science Association, Washington, D.C., September 2, 1984).
2. Advisory Commission on Intergovernmental Relations, *Regulatory Federalism* (Washington, D.C.: ACIR, February 1984), pp. 229-230. For discussion of recent administrations' efforts to control intergovernmental regulation, see pp. 189-243.

28. POLICY IMPLEMENTATION THROUGH BARGAINING: THE CASE OF FEDERAL GRANTS-IN-AID

Helen Ingram

... The underlying logic of federal grants-in-aid as an implementation technique is that the federal government can hire states with money to run its errands and do its will. A large literature on the impact of grants-in-aid upon the federal system generally agrees with William H. Young, who states that grants have been the "most powerful engine in this century for reshaping national-state relations." [1] Whether federal grants-in-aid can actually achieve policy goals has, however, never been carefully tested. This paper will argue that rather than compelling states to move toward the policies that the federal government has set, federal grants simply provide guides to states which they may set aside as they pursue agendas of their own making. The result is that implementation of federal policies becomes diverted. . . .

The first task of this paper is to establish an alternative conceptual framework that centers on policy rather than institutional structure and views implementation as a process of bargaining rather than federal intervention into state jurisdiction. Once a policy perspective and a bargaining framework are established, it is possible to set forth a series of logically related propositions. These propositions will suggest that certain federal goals are more likely to be accomplished through grants-in-aid than others, and that certain conditions facilitate the realization of federal goals by grants-in-aid. . . .

A Conceptual Framework for Examining Grants-in-Aid

The usual rationale for grants-in-aid to states assumes federal dominance of an essentially hierarchical process of handing downward both federal goals and the financial resources necessary to accomplish them. States are thought of as either unwilling or unable to perform a task important to national decision

Author's Note: While the shortcomings of this article are the fault of the author, the helpful review and comments of the following persons should be gratefully acknowledged: Elizabeth Haskell, Aaron Wildavsky, Sheldon Edner, Henry Kenski, Frederick Anderson, Scott Ullery and Geoffrey Wandesforde-Smith.

From "Policy Implementation Through Bargaining: The Case of Federal Grants-in-Aid" by Helen Ingram, *Public Policy* 25 (Fall 1977): 499-526. Copyright © 1977, John Wiley & Sons, Inc., Publishers. Reprinted by permission of John Wiley & Sons, Inc.

makers. Consequently, federal funds are employed to alter state behavior. The promise of available money is expected to lure states into actions they otherwise would not take, while federal financing is intended to upgrade state capability to do what federal policy specifies. Supposedly, grants-in-aid implement federal policies indirectly by steering state agencies toward federal objectives. The reins for this process of implementation are the "strings" or conditions attached to grants which grantees must satisfy in order to qualify for funds.

A bargaining framework fits more accurately than a superior-subordinate model the complex intergovernmental relations involved in grants-in-aid. Instead of a federal master dangling a carrot in front of a state donkey, the more apt image reveals a rich merchant haggling on equal terms with a sly, bargain-hunting consumer. Bargaining is the decision-making mode used when participants share a common interest in coming to a decision but have divergent values and objectives. Both the federal agencies administering grants and the state agencies designated as the receptors of grant monies want the grant transaction to take place. While federal agencies would like the transaction to bind state recipients to federal policy, state agencies face a number of conflicting concerns. Thus the aim of state agencies in the transaction is maximum possible leeway to pursue their own separate goals with the federal money. Because each participant values settlement, neither is anxious to cause conflict if it can be avoided. For instance, federal agencies are unlikely to embark upon enforcement practices that they anticipate will bring them little support and much criticism. Similarly, when the returns to a state are substantial and certain, and the state interest sacrificed is small, the state is likely to accede to federal requirements. The result is a process of implementation that is a complex succession of bids and counterbids between the state and federal levels during which the initial aims of each are substantially modified.

Bargaining at "Arm's Length"

Much of what goes on in grants bargaining is based upon anticipated reaction; in plotting their actions, federal and state bargainers implicitly take each other into account without explicit exchange. The federal system introduces a remoteness in grant bargaining that is not at all like the close contact logrolling and compromise that occur in legislatures.[2] Most of the contexts within which federal and state officials operate are different. The states are just one part of a federal agency's political environment, which also includes departments and other agencies, OMB, congressional committees, interest groups, and the like. By the same token, individual states have their own distinctive political culture and the federal government is viewed as an outside force. Certain prevailing attitudes and prejudices that federal bureaucrats and state agency people have about one another perpetuate separation and encourage independence. The ideology of states' rights is very strong, and federal officials wish to avoid the appearance of interference. Consequently, federal administrators sometimes wait for a formal document to be submitted rather than participate in the writing of proposals. States are frequently reluctant to deal face-to-face with "Feds" because they dislike feeling dominated and outclassed.

Resources in Bargaining

What either the state or the federal government wins or is forced to concede in the grant process is determined by the distribution of resources. Federal strength is often more apparent than real. On the one hand, money is a powerful incentive, and federal administrative agencies hold the grant purse strings. One would expect the competition between localities to be intense and state officials to be highly motivated to meet both the formal requirements and informal preferences of federal officials. Only a few states are able to compete with the national government in attracting outstanding professional talent, and state counterparts are often outclassed in negotiations. On the other hand, states can offset resources by controlling the context in which the federal government acts. Furthermore, states have other important resources of their own.

Precedent and prevailing expectations often give the advantage to states. Grant bargaining between the federal agency and the states takes place in the context of previous settlements that cause each to expect certain results and to limit or expand their aspirations. Phillip Monypenny concluded that when a loose coalition is too weak to secure its program in each individual state, it turns to Congress. Congress responds with a grant-in-aid program when a wholly federal program with specific requirements engenders too much opposition to pass, but the coalition is too strong to deny altogether.[3] The resulting legislation authorizing grants-in-aid reflects the political weakness of support among the states and perpetuates it into the future. Built into the authorizing statute are explicit or implicit promises that national uniformity will not be imposed and that individual states will not be made to pursue some unshared objectives. Federal agencies are aware of these promises and are consequently reluctant to exercise supervisory powers. Furthermore, once a grant program is underway, past practice has an enormous influence upon expectations. If states have routinely been given grants on the basis of a certain level of performance, then they are likely to project past experience into the future.

States have strength in numbers. Any state has the advantage of being only one among fifty, and federal grant offices are seldom capable of giving detailed supervision of each at once. . . . There is considerable state discretion to shop around among grants and avoid some that involve quantities of federal red tape.

States control essential information for the allocation of grants and for monitoring the impacts of grants. Unless the federal agency duplicates state efforts, it must depend on the accuracy and thoroughness of documents supplied by states. Because of state representation in Congress, states have easy access to the amending process if grant negotiations go against state interest. Administrative agencies are dependent upon the ongoing support of state recipients in the congressional budgetary process. The bargaining strength of states increases in time because the more state participation increases, the more the program is likely to continue and the less likely it will be amended against state interests.[4]

The bargaining framework set out above suggests a set of rules that follow logically and that may govern the extent to which federal policies can be implemented through the grant strategy in particular programs. These rules are stated in the next section of the paper and are quite different from those one would explore if the carrot model in which the federal government is dominant actually prevailed. . . .

Propositions Concerning Implementation and Impact of Specific Grants-in-Aid Programs

Establishing a Bargaining Context

The initial bargaining position of a federal administrative agency is likely to be undercut when Congress selects grants-in-aid as a means to build support and assuage opposition in the legislative process. Congress has available a range of techniques to implement its policy objectives. These mechanisms vary in the extent to which they rely on coercion. Some, such as the provision of information, are not at all coercive. Agricultural extension programs are an example. Others, such as the provision of a subsidy, tax relief, or a grant, are gently coercive. Only rewards are distributed, and the sole penalty is failure to share in the benefits. The establishment of specific rules and regulations is more coercive because penalties are imposed for noncompliance. The coercive force of government is even greater when the federal government itself takes action by establishing management entities that become involved in issues that were formerly state and local or private.[5]

Modern legislation is often a complex composite of goals and objectives to be achieved through a variety of more or less coercive techniques. In choosing various policy strategies Congress must attend, not just to possible effectiveness, but also to the support or opposition engendered. Subsidy techniques, such as grants, are sometimes chosen less for their supposed effectiveness than for their acceptability. Because participation is in principle voluntary, state governments need not accept grants unless it is to their advantage to do so. Congressmen see to it that for state governments the ratio of benefits to cost in the grant program is high enough to be attractive.[6]

Subsidy programs are often legislatively packaged with other more coercive programs to make controversial provisions more palatable. . . .

While it is possible for Congress to make real demands on states as conditions for grants and to authorize federal agencies to apply the use of significant sanctions to states that do not comply, the use of grant programs as "sweeteners" renders congressional demands less likely. The promise of money to come serves as a *quid pro quo* for immediate legislative support. . . .

When grant programs are included to make legislation more acceptable, there follows a tendency to be vague about objectives and indefinite about the conditions under which grants can be denied to states. . . .

Another reason for the weakness of federal requirements in some grant programs is that their legislative purpose is less to impose some federal objective than to improve state programs.[7] . . .

Federal administrators who must enforce programs containing "sweetener" grants have little in terms of legal mandate, legislative history, or public expectations upon which to base a tough line on state performance. Federal bureaucrats have little legitimacy in imposing their views. . . .

Broadly Distributing Benefits

In the grant bargaining process, federal administrative agencies are likely to place highest priority upon achieving broad support, even if this means refusing to terminate funds for reasons of noncompliance or poor performance, or failing to reward states that excel in program objectives. In a bargaining situation, participants can be expected to pursue a course of least cost and maximum benefit. It serves neither the interests of the federal granting agency nor those of the states to deny grant funds. Administrators of grants are supposed to spend money for a specified purpose, and not doing so is an obvious failure. Just as Congress concentrates on grants-in-aid as a support building device, so also do federal agencies see grants as a means of building a broad state constituency. Failure to give a state its allocation is bound to elicit a complaint from its congressional delegation and evoke the sympathetic concern of other Congressmen who are made aware of potential threats to their own constituencies. Of course, states are anxious to get federal money and are willing to make some accommodation. In the process of intergovernmental bargaining, states do make concessions in order to meet some federal objectives.

It is not surprising that federal agency officials are likely to place the highest premium on maintaining support for the agency and its long-term welfare. This does not mean policy implementation is unimportant, just that there are limits to the organizational sacrifices that federal agencies will make for policy gains. As a result, the sanctions that federal agencies can impose by denying discretionary funds are exercised with caution and moderation. The threat to hold back funds is most effective as a potential resource. States cannot be completely certain that federal agencies will not, in fact, cut off the flow of funds. The leverage that comes from this potential power is most credible in the early stages of a grant program, before a routine and pattern of expectations have been established.[8] In his study of grants-in-aid for public assistance, Steiner found that, over time, states were likely to win their battles with Washington. "In the long run sense, the intensity of federal control of the public assistance program probably diminishes as the federal agency responsible for administration becomes less insecure, less of a novelty, and begins to establish quiet negotiation procedures that could serve as alternatives to noisy withdrawal of federal cooperation."[9] It is equally likely that during extended periods of intergovernmental bargaining, states have shifted somewhat toward federal objectives.

In some grant programs, even a federal agency's opportunity to apply early sanctions is foregone. Edner found that in the Southwest Region of the Environmental Protection Agency, no state has ever been denied funds. Instead, state program plans have been ranked, and marginal and poor ones have been cited, in an effort to persuade states to improve their applications.[10] Murphy found that Title V of the Elementary and Secondary Education Act has been implemented as general aid, accommodating all state applicants.[11] Of course, federal agencies have other coercive tools beyond the withholding of funds: delays are imposed, extra paper work and particular procedures are required, and so on. These strategies, too, are conflict-producing, and lose credibility if not eventually supported by imposition of financial penalties. . . .

Changing Organizations

Through the grant bargaining process, federal administrative agencies are more likely to win improvements in state organizational infrastructure than to change state action. Through the grant-in-aid system the federal government becomes a participant in the state political system. It is, however, a peripheral actor, because it has no legitimate role, no formal right to impose its decisions.[12] The federal government manipulates state actors indirectly by changing the atmosphere in which decisions are made and by increasing the benefits for acting in accord with federal objectives. In a bargaining situation states are likely to respond most positively to federal directives where the cost of compliance is small and the expected return is large. The greatest impact of federal grants is in their initial phase when it is attractive to states to establish an agency in order to be eligible for federal grants. Bitterman has noted that states acted quickly to set up organizations to receive grants from New Deal Programs. While only Wisconsin passed social security legislation before the federal government did, all states passed legislation within two years after federal funds became available.[13] In a more contemporary example, Derthick found that many local and urban organizations, especially those in urban renewal, public housing, and anti-poverty programs, have been created for the purpose of receiving and administering federal grants.[14]

State agencies established to receive federal funds are often favored by certain resources and advantages in state government. Cost sharing arrangements for programs underwritten by federal grants augment the benefits of state appropriations, and consequently grants often induce state investment. More sizable staffing naturally goes along with larger expenditures. The Kestnbaum Report found that state legislatures are less likely to investigate and supervise state agencies administering federal funds, and that federal aid "requirements" are often used as an excuse to fend off state reorganization.[15]

While states may accept or even pursue federal grants that create independent agencies with their own resources, they may not agree that these agencies, once in place, are to implement mainly federal objectives. As Ira Sharkansky has observed, grants-in-aid can be turned to states' own ends by a variety of devices.[16] For federal grants actually to affect policy outputs of state agencies, there must be common interests. The values and objectives of the designated agency must be fashioned along the lines of federal objectives. Further, these aims must carry the day in the larger political processes of the state. . . .

Imposing Administrative Rules

Through the grant bargaining process, federal administrative agencies are more likely to achieve efficient state management practices than to alter state policy-making processes. Federal agencies place a high priority upon keeping careful track of funds and avoiding scandals. Casual bookkeeping and accounting in grant programs can lead to very damaging investigations by congressional committees, the General Accounting Office, or others. Because of the stake that federal agencies have in their own institutional welfare, which goes beyond commitment to individual policies, states are likely to be held to strict financial account. These concerns produced a raft of procedural guidelines and generated a large amount of paper work in the Model Cities program, for instance.[17] Furthermore, management requirements that relate to proper and efficient operation are relatively easy to impose. Such rules are attractive because they are cast in what seem to be value-free, neutral terms.[18] So long as the federal requirements are fairly simple and reasonably related to efficiency, economy, professionalism, or other generally respected criteria, the diversity of values that exists among states is not offended. If, however, the federal rules and regulations address the way state agencies communicate with one another or favor some actors over others, then peculiar state conditions are likely to become overriding. . . .

Facilitating Policy Change

As a result of grant bargaining, federal administrative agencies can facilitate change in a willing state. But in the absence of state commitment, the federal agency cannot compel state policy change. The federal government is at best a peripheral participant in the state political process. It depends upon the existence of a state counterpart agency for implementation of its objectives. State agencies are not blind surrogates of federal agencies and are likely to have their own independent goals and objectives. Their success in implementing federal goals and/or their own goals will depend upon their own organizational characteristics, leadership, and the broader political environment within which they operate. In short, federal agencies are heavily dependent upon the initiative of the state for program innovation. In an analysis of federal water pollution control policy Sheldon Edner found that the influence of the federal program had been minimal in stimulating vigorous state counterparts. Of the two states he studied, California and Arizona, the former was much more effective in achieving federal goals because of its own initiative, not because of federal prodding. Arizona simply lacked interest in water pollution and reacted lethargically to federal incentives and sanctions.[19]. . .

Notes

1. Cited in Michael Reagan, *The New Federalism* (New York: Oxford University Press, 1972), p. 55. See also Earl M. Baker, et al., *Federal Grants, The National Interest and State Response: A Review of Theory and Research* (Philadelphia: Center for the Study of Federalism, Temple University, March 1974).
2. Lewis A. Froman, Jr., *The Congressional Process* (Boston: Little, Brown & Co., 1967), p. 22.
3. Phillip Monypenny, "Federal Grants-in-Aid to State Governments: A Political Analysis," in *National Tax Journal* 13 (March 1960), p. 15.
4. Edward W. Weidner, "Decision-Making in a Federal System," in *Federalism: Mature and Emergent,* Arthur W. Macmahon, ed. (New York: Doubleday & Co., 1955).
5. Randall B. Ripley (ed.), *Public Policies and Their Politics* (New York: W. W. Norton & Co., 1966), p. xi.

6. Martha Derthick, *The Influence of Federal Grants* (Cambridge: Harvard University Press, 1970), p. 197.
7. Reagan, *The New Federalism*, p. 67.
8. Derthick, *The Influence of Federal Grants*, p. 208.
9. Gilbert Y. Steiner, *Social Insecurity: The Politics of Welfare* (Chicago: Rand McNally, 1966), p. 84.
10. Sheldon M. Edner, "The Implementation of Federal Water Pollution Control Policy Though Grants-in-Aid" (a paper delivered at the 27th Annual Meeting of the Western Political Science Association, San Diego, Calif., 1973), p. 13.
11. Jerome T. Murphy, *Grease the Squeaky Wheel* (Cambridge: Harvard Research Center for Educational Policy, 1973), p. 33.
12. Derthick, *The Influence of Federal Grants*, p. 201.
13. Henry J. Bitterman, *State and Federal Grants-in-Aid* (New York: Mentzer, Bush, & Co., 1938), cited in Baker et al., *Federal Grants, The National Interest and State Response*, pp. 56-7.
14. Derthick, *The Influence of Federal Grants,* p. 203.
15. Commission on Intergovernmental Relations, "A Survey Report on the Impacts of Federal Grant-in-Aid on the Structures and Function of State and Local Governments" (Washington, D.C.: GPO, 1955), pp. 4, 11.
16. Ira Sharkansky, *The Maligned States: Policy, Accomplishments, Problems and Opportunities* (New York: McGraw-Hill Book Co., 1972), pp. 30-3.
17. Lawrence D. Brown and Bernard Frieden, "Guidelines and Goals for the Model Cities Program," in *Policy Sciences* (forthcoming).
18. Derthick, *The Influence of Federal Grants*, p. 198.
19. Edner, "The Implementation of Federal Water Pollution Control Policy," pp. 18-19.

29. STATE AGENCY HEADS AND ADMINISTRATIVE CHANGE: SOURCES OF PROGRAM INNOVATION

U.S. Advisory Commission on Intergovernmental Relations

Many actions taken by state agencies do not involve changes in program priorities yet they may significantly affect the character or content of agency operations. One type of action in this category is program innovation—the acquisition of new ideas that result in improved service, more equitable services, or more efficient use of resources.

Ideas for program innovation can come from a wide variety of sources. Twelve possible sources of new ideas were presented to state agency heads in the 1978 survey. The respondents were asked to *rank* the several sources according to the extent to which each source was relied upon for new ideas resulting in program improvements. Table 6 lists all 12 sources of innovative ideas grouped in three broad categories. The table also lists the scores based on the administrators' rankings of the sources. The scores are weighted frequencies, that is, they reflect both the rank and the frequency of mention made of each source. More specifically, the mention of a source is weighted by the rank given by each respondent, with 12 representing the highest rank and one the lowest. The sum of these scores for each source was then divided by the number of administrators ranking each respective source to obtain a mean score for that source—the score shown in Table 6.

Sources in State Government

Program innovation sources available to administrators from within their own governments are among the most important of the 12 sources. The four state government sources are rated higher than all intergovernmental sources and about equal to, or above, the highest ranked extra-governmental sources. Three of these—Governor, legislators, and intra-agency sources—have officially sanctioned roles in influencing agency actions, i.e., proposing ideas for program improvements. This is obvious for the Governor and legislature but it is no less true for intra-agency sources—the staff itself. All of these sources can do more than merely suggest new ideas; they can go far to encourage or mandate acceptance of

From *State Administrators' Opinions on Administrative Change, Federal Aid, Federal Partnerships* (Washington, D.C.: ACIR, December 1980), pp. 9-11. Reprinted by permission.

Table 6   Sources of New Ideas for Program Management

Source	Weighted Frequency of Rankings
Within State Government	
Within Your Agency	10.0
Legislators	5.9
Governor	5.5
Other State Agencies	5.0
Intergovernmental Sources	
Officials in Other States	4.6
National Government Officials	4.0
Local Government Officials	3.4
Joint Federal-State Agencies	3.2
Interstate Agencies	2.1
Extra-Governmental Sources	
Clientele Groups	5.8
Professional Associations	5.3
University Personnel	2.6

them. Their high level of importance here, combined with the significance of these three sources on program priority shifts, no doubt results in large measure from this official control.

A fourth source included here—other agencies—is of lesser importance. But that source still exceeds all of the intergovernmental sources. State administrators rely heavily on sources that are a part of their immediate, formal organizational world for new ideas that are pertinent to the improvement of their agency's programs.

Intergovernmental Sources

This category includes five officially constituted sources of innovation that are outside the formal structure of state government. These are, in rank order of significance, (1) officials in other states, (2) national government officials, (3) local government officials, (4) joint federal-state agencies, and (5) interstate agencies. The first two sources are rated well above the other three, yet even those two are well below the ranking for the sources imbedded in the formal structure of state government.

These results suggest that intergovernmental boundaries tend to introduce organizational distance insofar as program innovations are concerned. Those boundaries appear to place these entities on the periphery of the program or policy "space" occupied by state administrative agencies. The two intergovernmental entities that rank highest in this group—other state and national officials—are most likely to be ones whose programmatic or functional links place them more within the attention span or policy space of the respective state agency heads.

Extra-Governmental Sources

Many administrative agencies are in constant contact with elements of their environment that are outside the official structure(s) of governmental organizations. Most important, many of them contact clients who depend on the agency for service or who are regulated by the agency. These clients usually are organized to deal with the agency and often have been instrumental in the creation, structuring, and support of the agency. These groups seek to influence the agency's development and consequently may be sources of new ideas. This source—agency clientele groups—is so important that it is ranked third among the 12 presented. This source of new ideas is clearly a prominent element within the policy space of administrative agencies. It ranks only slightly below legislators as an innovation source and a little above the Governor.

Agencies, of course, are influenced by their own employees, too. This was established by the importance given "agency staff" as a power behind priority shifts and is emphasized again by the high rank administrators give to within-agency sources of new ideas. But, in many agencies, the staffs are composed of professionals who are, themselves, organized as local, state, or national associations. These associations are diverse and varied. They may engage in any or all of the following: accreditation of university programs for professionals; publication of professional journals; certification of individuals as members of the profession; lobbying for support of particular programs; representing members' economic interests; and supporting research on matters of interest to the profession. By engaging in such activities, the associations put themselves in positions of potential influence on state agencies. They may be near the center of an agency's policy space. Indeed, they may be a major source of information to some agencies and to individual agency employees. These professional associations rank fifth in importance in suggesting new ideas among the 12 sources. They trail the Governor only slightly and rank slightly above other state agencies as a source of new ideas for program improvement. It is evident that two "informal" sources of influence are noteworthy contributors to state agency program innovations.

The final extra-governmental source presented to administrators was "university personnel." (In the case of state universities, these are not really "extra-governmental" but are actually state agencies. It seems valid, however, to include them here along with private universities.) Specific sources within universities can be of a variety of types. Most obviously, many universities have government research bureaus established, in part, for the explicit purpose of providing assistance to governments in the state, although often their attention focuses on local government. But equally important, most professional schools attempt to maintain contact with practitioners of the profession in the workplace, through alumni connections or through provision of continuing education. Despite these efforts, administrators rank university personnel 11th out of the 12 groups as a source of program innovations. This does not seem surprising when one considers the high degree of applied specialization among and within state agencies contrasted with the generalist educational emphasis of most university activities.

In summary, state administrators reported that they primarily rely for new ideas on those who work for their agencies, on their professional associations, on the agencies' clients, and on the agencies' formal superiors—legislators and Governors. Other sources of ideas are of lesser importance, although none are irrelevant. In fact, even those ranked lowest were given a first place ranking by a few officials. But most dramatic is the heavy choice of within-agency sources for first place. Sixty-four percent of administrators designated it first.

30. THE TECHNIQUES OF
INTERGOVERNMENTAL REGULATION

U.S. Advisory Commission on Intergovernmental Relations

As was noted previously, an element of *compulsion* is one key feature of the new intergovernmental regulation that distinguishes it from the usual grant-in-aid conditions. The requirements traditionally attached to assistance programs may be viewed as part of a contractual agreement between two independent, coequal levels of government. In contrast, the policies which the new intergovernmental regulation imposes on state and local governments are more nearly mandatory. They cannot be side stepped, without incurring some federal sanction, by the simple expedient of refusing to participate in a single federal assistance program. In one way or another, compliance has been made difficult to avoid.

A variety of legal and fiscal techniques have been employed by the national government to encourage acceptance of its regulatory standards. Four major strategies—direct orders, crosscutting requirements, crossover sanctions, and partial preemption—are described below and are summarized in Figure 8.

Direct Orders

In a few instances, federal regulation of state and local government takes the form of direct legal orders that must be complied with under the threat of civil or criminal penalties. For example, the *Equal Employment Opportunity Act of 1972* bars job discrimination by state and local governments on the basis of race, color, religion, sex and national origin. This statute extended to state and local governments the requirements imposed on private employers since 1964. Similarly, the *Marine Protection Research and Sanctuaries Act Amendments of 1977* prohibit cities from disposing of sewage sludge through ocean dumping. Court orders based on constitutional provisions, like those banning segregated schools, are similar in nature.

For the most part, however, Washington has exempted subnational governments from many of the kinds of direct regulatory statutes that apply to businesses and individuals. Hence, although state governments may administer the *Occupational Safety and Health Act,* they (and local governments) are exempt from its provisions in their capacity as employers—as is the federal government itself. Politics often has dictated this course, but there also are some Constitutional

From *Regulatory Federalism: Policy, Process, Impact and Reform* (Washington, D.C.: ACIR, February 1984), pp. 7-10. Reprinted by permission.

Figure 8   A Typology of Intergovernmental Regulatory Programs

Program Type	Description	Major Policy Areas Employed
Direct Orders	Mandate state or local actions under the threat of criminal or civil penalties	Public employment, environmental protection
Crosscutting Requirements	Apply to all or many federal assistance programs	Nondiscrimination, environmental protection, public employment, assistance management
Crossover Sanctions	Threaten the termination or reduction of aid provided under one or more specified programs unless the requirements of another program are satisfied	Highway safety and beautification, environmental protection, health planning, handicapped education
Partial Preemptions	Establish federal standards, but delegate administration to states if they adopt standards equivalent to the national ones	Environmental protection, natural resources, occupational safety and health, meat and poultry inspection

restrictions on the ability of Congress to regulate directly. The wage and hour requirements imposed on state and local governments by the 1974 amendments to the *Fair Labor Standards Act* were greatly circumscribed by the Supreme Court in *National League of Cities v. Usery* (1976).[1] The Court's ruling held that the law interfered with their "integral operations in areas of traditional governmental functions," and thus threatened their "independent existence."

In this respect, the relationship of the federal government with the states and localities must be contrasted with that of the states and their own local subdivisions. Because local governments are creatures of state law, state "mandating" through direct orders is both legally permissible and very frequent.[2]

Much more commonly, then, Washington has utilized other regulatory techniques to work its will. These may be distinguished by their breadth of application and the nature of the sanctions which back them up.

Crosscutting Requirements

First, and most widely recognized, are the crosscutting or generally applicable requirements imposed on grants across the board to further various national social and economic policies. One of the most important of these requirements is the nondiscrimination provision included in the Title VI of the *Civil Rights Act of 1964*, which stipulates that

No person in the United States shall, on the ground of race, color, or national origin, be excluded from participation in, be denied the benefits of, or be subjected to discrimination under any program receiving Federal financial assistance.[3]

Since 1964, crosscutting requirements have been enacted for the protection of other disadvantaged groups (the handicapped, elderly, and—in education programs—women). The same approach was utilized in the environmental impact statement process created in 1969, as well as for many other environmental purposes. It also has been extended into such fields as historic preservation, animal welfare and relocation assistance.[4] A total of some 36 across-the-board requirements dealing with various socio-economic issues, as well as an additional 23 administrative and fiscal policy requirements, were identified in a 1980 OMB inventory.[5]... Of the former group, the largest number involve some aspect of environmental protection (16) and nondiscrimination (9). Two-thirds of the 59 requirements have been adopted since 1969.

Crosscutting requirements have a pervasive impact because they apply "horizontally" to all or most federal agencies and their assistance programs. In contrast, two other new forms of intergovernmental regulation are directed at only a single function, department or program. Thus, both can be described as "vertical" mandates.[6]

Crossover Sanctions

One approach relies upon the power of the purse. It imposes federal fiscal sanctions in one program area or activity to influence state and local policy in another. The distinguishing feature here is that a failure to comply with the requirements of one program can result in a reduction or termination of funds from another, separately authorized and separately entered into, program. The penalty thus "crosses over."

The history of federal efforts to secure the removal of billboards from along the nation's major highways illustrates the use of the traditional financial "carrot" along with this new financial "stick." [7] Beginning in 1958, the federal government offered a small bonus in the form of additional highway funds to states that agreed to regulate billboard advertising along new interstate highways. By 1965, however, only half of the states had taken advantage of this offer—not enough to suit the Johnson White House.

A dramatic change occurred with the adoption of the *Highway Beautification Act of 1965*. The bonus system was dropped, and Congress substituted the threat of withholding 10% of a state's highway construction funds if it did not comply with newly expanded federal billboard control requirements. Despite the bitter opposition of the outdoor advertising industry, 32 states had enacted billboard control laws by 1970, though only 18 of these were judged to be in full compliance. Nearly all of the rest of the states fell quickly into line when Congress made appropriations to compensate for part of the cost of removing nonconforming signs, and the Federal Highway Administrator stepped up his pressure on them.

A similar fiscal penalty subsequently was employed in a number of other programs. In the wake of the OPEC oil embargo, federal officials urged the states to lower their speed limits and the Senate adopted a resolution to that effect.

Twenty-nine states responded to this effort at "moral suasion." But these pleas were quickly replaced by a more authoritative measure: the *Emergency Highway Energy Conservation Act of 1974,* which prohibited the Secretary of Transportation from approving any highway construction projects in states having a speed limit in excess of 55 mph. All of the remaining states responded within two months.

Partial Preemption

The crossover sanctions, like the crosscutting requirements, are tied directly to the grant-in-aid system. Federal power in these cases derives from the Constitutional authority to spend for the general welfare. A final innovative technique, however, has another basis entirely. It rests on the authority of the federal government to preempt certain state and local activities under the supremacy clause and the commerce power.

Yet, this is preemption with a twist. Unlike traditional preemption statutes, preemption in these cases is only *partial.* Federal laws establish basic policies, but administrative responsibility may be delegated to the states or localities if they meet certain nationally determined conditions or standards.

The *Water Quality Act of 1965* was an early example of this strategy, which one analyst describes as the "if-then, if-then" approach. The statute was the first to establish a national policy for controlling pollution. Although the law allowed each state one year to set standards for its own interstate waters, the Secretary of Health, Education, and Welfare was authorized to enforce federal standards in any state that failed to do so. That is,

> ... *if* a state does not issue regulations acceptable to the U.S., *then* a federal agency or department will do so, and *if* the state does not adopt and enforce these regulations, *then* the federal level of government will assume jurisdiction over that area.[8]

This same technique—which others have called the "substitution approach" to federalism[9]—has since been extended to a variety of other areas. For example, the OSHA law asserts national control over workplace health and safety but permits states to operate their own programs if their standards are "at least as effective" as the federal ones.

The most far-reaching applications, however, are in the *Clean Air Act Amendments of 1970.* This path-breaking environmental statute set federal air quality standards throughout the nation, but required that the states devise effective plans for their implementation and enforcement. Its compass is great: for example, EPA can require states to change their own transportation policies (perhaps by giving additional support to mass transit) or to regulate private individuals (as in establishing emission-control requirements and inspection programs for automobiles).[10] Two close observers comment:

> Of all the intergovernmental mechanisms used to nationalize regulatory policy, none is more revolutionary than the approach first applied in the *Clean Air Act Amendments of 1970.* It is an approach minimizing both the voluntariness of state and local participation and the substantive policy discretion provided for officials in subnational governments. In fact, it is a mechanism which challenges the very essence of federalism as a noncentralized system of

separate legal jurisdictions and instead relies upon a unitary vision involving hierarchically related central and peripheral units.... [I]t is an approach allowing national policymakers and policy implementors to mobilize state and local resources on behalf of a national program. As preliminary measures, these resources can be mobilized using technical, financial, or other forms of assistance, but underlying this mechanism is the ability of national officials to formally and officially "draft" those resources into national service. We call this *legal conscription.*[11]

Applications and Combinations

These four techniques—direct legal orders, crosscutting requirements, crossover sanctions and partial preemption—are the major new statutory tools in the federal government's kit for the regulation of states and localities. Each has distinctive characteristics, and poses special problems of policy, law, administration, finance and politics.

... Among the major regulatory statutes examined, crosscutting requirements (18) and partial preemptions (13) clearly are relatively numerous, while crossover sanctions (6) and direct orders (6) are relatively rare.

It also should be noted that these devices have sometimes been combined. A good example is provided by the 1970 *Clean Air Act Amendments*. Basically, the law relies upon the technique of partial preemption. States must prepare State Implementation Plans (SIPs) which will control pollution to the extent necessary to achieve federal air quality standards. These must be approved by the Environmental Protection Agency. If the EPA judges a SIP to be inadequate, it must disapprove the SIP. In the event that a state fails to make necessary revisions, EPA is required to promulgate an adequate SIP.

This, however, is not the only sanction imposed by the act. More teeth are added by Section 176(a), which bars both the EPA and the Department of Transportation from making grant awards in any air quality control region which has not attained primary ambient air quality standards and for which the state has failed to devise adequate transportation control plans. This, of course, is a tough crossover sanction. Furthermore, Section 176(c) prohibits any agency of the federal government from providing financial assistance to any activity which does not conform to a state SIP. This provision uses the crosscutting requirement approach to strengthening SIP implementation.

Fund termination, as in crossover sanctions, also is used to enforce compliance with a number of the crosscutting requirements relating to nondiscrimination. Discriminatory actions can result in the cutoff of aid, not only in the program area in which discrimination was found, but to an entire institution or jurisdiction.

Notes

1. *National League of Cities v. Usery,* 426 U.S. 833 (1976).
2. For a discussion of state practices, see Advisory Commission on Intergovernmental Relations, *State Mandating of Local Expenditures,* A-67 (Washington, DC: U.S.

Government Printing Office, 1978).

3. PL 88-352, title VI, section 601, July 2, 1964.

4. See ACIR, *Categorical Grants: Their Role and Design,* A-52 (Washington, DC: U.S. Government Printing Office, 1978), chapter VII.

5. Office of Management and Budget, *Managing Federal Assistance in the 1980s, Working Papers, Volume I* (Washington, DC: U.S. Government Printing Office, 1980).

6. Catherine H. Lovell et al., *Federal and State Mandating on Local Governments: An Exploration of Issues and Impacts* (Riverside, CA: Graduate School of Administration, University of California, Riverside, 1979), p. 35.

7. See Roger A. Cunningham, "Billboard Control Under the *Highway Beautification Act of 1965,*" *Michigan Law Review* 71 (June 1973), pp. 1295-374.

8. James B. Croy, "Federal Supersession: The Road to Domination," *State Government* 48 (Winter 1975), p. 34. Emphasis added.

9. Frank J. Thompson, *Health Policy and the Bureaucracy: Politics and Administration* (Cambridge, MA: The MIT Press, 1981), p. 240.

10. Congressional Budget Office, *Federal Constraints on State and Local Government Actions* (Washington, DC: U.S. Government Printing Office, 1979), p. 7.

11. Mel Dubnick and Alan Gitelson, "Nationalizing State Policies," in *The Nationalization of State Government,* Jerome J. Hanus, ed., (Lexington, MA: D.C. Heath and Company, 1981), pp. 56-57.

31. THE MANDATE MILLSTONE

Edward I. Koch

Over the past decade, a maze of complex statutory and administrative directives has come to threaten both the initiative and the financial health of local governments throughout the country. My concern is not with the broad policy objectives that such mandates are meant to serve, but rather with what I perceive as the lack of comprehension by those who write them as to the cumulative impact on a single city, and even the nation.

I want to emphasize that my criticism is directed at the shortcomings of a system that has evolved over the course of many years. This is not the fault of particular individuals nor of today's leadership; it is rather an inheritance from the work of several administrations and Congresses, including some in which I served.

The City of New York, as an example, is driven by 47 federal and state mandates. The total cost to the city of meeting these requirements over the next four years will be $711 million in capital expenditures, $6.25 billion in expense-budget dollars, and $1.66 billion in lost revenue.

On the federal level, the current crop of mandated programs is really the second stage in the evolutionary process of activist lawmaking exhibited by the Congress. First, in the 1960's came the Great Society programs. The nation's cities could choose from a bountiful catalog of federal grants which offered to foot 80, 90, or even 100 percent of the cost of enormously ambitious programs. In a time of unprecedented prosperity, with only higher expectations ahead, local governments eagerly went after federal funds even, at times, at the expense of comprehensive planning.

Left unnoticed in the cities' rush to reallocate their budgets so as to draw down maximum categorical aid were the basic service-delivery programs taken for granted by the Great Society architects. New roads, bridges, and subway routes were an exciting commitment to the future, but they were launched at the expense of routine maintenance to the unglamorous, but essential, infrastructure of the existing systems. Further, the enticement of federal aid drew cities into new social service commitments that were soon to monopolize their budgets.

The 1960's left a bitter legacy for cities in two respects. As prosperity fell hostage to inflation, and then stagflation, the bright promises of programs so

From *The Public Interest* 61 (Fall 1980): 42-48, 55-57. Reprinted by permission of *The Public Interest*.

boldly launched with federal aid collapsed under exponential cost overruns. Projects under construction, such as New York's Second Avenue subway, had to be abandoned, and the now-concealed but still-remembered excavation serves to remind the public of how easily government can fall victim to monumental folly.

Perhaps more damaging was the shift in the 1970's in the legislative approach, particularly in Congress, to the grand commitments of the 1960's. Sweeping solutions to social ills were still in vogue, but this time the public purse had a bottom to it, and its guardians became adept at fending off the claims of local governments. The result has been an ever widening gulf separating the programmatic demands of an activist Congress from its concurrent fiscal conservatism. By the close of the 1970's, the cities found themselves under the guns of dozens of federal laws imposing increasingly draconian mandates. From the perspective of local government the mandate mandarins who write these laws appear to be guided by certain disturbing maxims, such as:

1. *Mandates solve problems, particularly those in which you are not involved.* The federal government, for example, has shown no reluctance in ordering sweeping changes, the impact of which it will never have to face since it does not hold the final service-delivery responsibilities in such areas as education, transportation, and sewage disposal.

2. *Mandates need not be tempered by the lessons of local experience.* Frequently a statutory directive will impose a single nationwide solution to a perceived problem, such as sewage treatment, that has been developed in the isolation of a consultant's office and rarely, if ever, exposed to real world conditions in the affected regions.

3. *Mandates will spontaneously generate the technology required to achieve them.* Congress has shown a disturbing penchant for prohibitions on existing approaches to problems such as ocean dumping, for which no practical replacement has been developed.

4. *The price tag of the lofty aspiration to be served by a mandate should never deter its imposition upon others.* Statutory commands are rarely accompanied by adequate financial assistance. Most extreme in this instance is the accessibility mandate for transit systems and the requirements relating to the education of the handicapped.

I do not for a moment claim immunity from the mandate fever of the 1970's. As a member of Congress I voted for many of the laws which I will discuss, and did so with every confidence that we were enacting sensible permanent solutions to critical problems. It took a plunge into the Mayor's job to drive home how misguided my congressional outlook had been. The bills I voted for in Washington came to the House floor in a form that compelled approval. After all, who can vote against clean air and water, or better access and education for the handicapped? But as I look back it is hard to believe I could have been taken in by the simplicity of what the Congress was doing and by the flimsy empirical support—often no more than a carefully orchestrated hearing record or a single consultant's report—offered to persuade the members that the proposed solution could work throughout the country. The proposals I offer address this problem by increasing the level of scrutiny applied to both the cost and feasibility of mandates directed at local governments.

Let me now turn to the case histories of some of the more onerous mandates faced by New York City. I use my city as an example because I know its problems best. The problems we face, of course, occur throughout the United States. The numbers may be larger in New York but these mandates have an equally significant impact on the budget and local autonomy of every city.

Transportation and Education for the Handicapped

An example of a mandate that may totally skew capital spending nationwide in the 1980's at all levels of government is the handicapped-access program required by regulations promulgated in response to Section 504 of the Rehabilitation Act of 1973.

No one would argue that we need not commit funds to make transit systems and buildings accessible to the handicapped. But one also has to deal with the limitations—both financial and physical—that exist in the real world beyond the printed page of the *Federal Register.*

The Departments of Transportation and Health and Human Services (the erstwhile Department of Health, Education, and Welfare) have issued regulations that set as a mandate total accessibility for the handicapped to transit *systems,* instead of dealing with the *function* of transportation: mobility. In rejecting numerous appeals for modest exemptions and waivers, these regulations impose a restrictive and inflexible interpretation of the basic mandate of Section 504. Ironically, in focusing on accessibility the regulations fail to benefit a significant portion of the severely disabled. Subways and buses may ultimately be made fully accessible, but a disabled person may not be able to get to the system to enjoy its accessibility.

In this instance, alternatives are available. New York City has a far more extensive and flexible bus system than subway system. Given the numbers of handicapped people affected—some 22,800 in wheelchairs and 110,000 semi-ambulatory for a system that carries about 5.3 million on a weekday—a more reasonable approach can be formulated to meet the transportation needs of the disabled. The City of New York has proposed making its buses accessible and providing a paratransit system for the most severely disabled. Paratransit will provide door-to-door service and can make the difference between a handicapped person being a prisoner in his or her home or a mobile member of the community. Similar paratransit services are in planning or underway in other cities.

The DOT regulations presently proposed do not accept the alternative of a bus and paratransit mix. Beyond bus accessibility, the regulations appear to demand accessibility in 53 percent of our subway stations within 30 years, at a cost in today's dollars of some $1.3 billion. Added to this will be at least $50 million in recurring annual operating expenses. And the regulations make no affirmative provision for meeting the handicapped community's myriad difficulties in getting to buses and subways.

It would be cheaper for us to provide every severely disabled person with taxi service than make 255 of our subway stations accessible. Indeed, the Congressional Budget Office, in its report of November 1979 on "Urban Transportation for Handicapped Persons: Alternative Federal Options," estimated that the cost of implementing the Section 504 regulations, when spread over the limited number of wheelchair users and severely disabled passengers, will be $38 per trip. In contrast, transit trips by the general public cost, on the average, about 85 cents.

Should we somehow achieve the prescribed level of systemwide rapid transit accessibility, I believe that even the most courageous will test it only once to satisfy themselves that they are able to ride the subways and that few will ride them on a regular basis.

The history of this mandate points up a basic fallacy in the process leading to its promulgation: unrealistic projections by federal agencies of the cost of realizing mandated goals. When the Department of Transportation issued its preliminary nationwide regulations for public review and comment in early 1978, it used a figure of $1.8 billion for the contemporary cost of making all transportation systems accessible. This was clearly an unrealistic estimate and implied an unwillingness by the Department to face up to the magnitude of the course they were proposing to require. The Congress acknowledged this credibility gap and in 1978 ordered the Department to submit by early 1980 a report on the costs of accessibility, based on a survey of all rail-transit operators.

Finally, the Section 504 regulations are crippled by the lack of available technology to achieve the mandated standard of accessibility. Bus lifts have yet to be developed that operate without frequent breakdowns; no American bus manufacturer would even bid to build the Transbus; and people are just starting to think about devices that can span the distance between a rapid-transit vehicle and the passenger-boarding platform.

The issue of transit accessibility is one that the Department of Transportation must deal with quickly. If an affirmative policy decision is not made to bring the demands of Section 504 in line with the practical limits on compliance efforts, transit subsidies in the 1980's will be severely distorted—making systems accessible to several thousand people, while forsaking improvements needed on the total system. The cost in operating reliability will very likely reduce the quality of service available to both current users and those who should benefit from improved accessibility. We may, in fact, build a system under the Section 504 mandate which most handicapped people won't be able to use because of the barriers still remaining, and which, if they do manage to board, breaks down far more frequently.

While the Congress may have been thoughtless or arbitrary in compelling universal access for the handicapped without sufficient consideration of the real world constraints on localities, it has been almost cynical in its implementation of the directive that all handicapped children be provided "a free and appropriate education." It is impossible to attack the virtues of this objective. Yet the structure of the program enacted to accomplish it not only dooms the compliance efforts of local school districts, but also jeopardizes the overall quality of education that can be offered to all children.

The federal law contains three fundamental defects. First, the formula by which accompanying federal assistance is measured looks to the national average cost of educating a non-handicapped child and thus completely overlooks the far broader scope of services that are needed to bring the promise of the mandate to the actual population it was designed to benefit. The formula contains a second fallacy in its use of a single nationwide average cost. It deprives school districts with high education costs and high concentrations of handicapped pupils of any recognition of the greater costs and special problems they face in designing compliance programs. In New York City we have had to budget $8,180 per handicapped pupil, nearly three times the cost of educating a nonhandicapped child. This compares to the national average figure of $1,400 per non-handicapped child employed by the federal government to determine the level of assistance for educational programs for the handicapped. Third, and most disturbing, has been the consistent failure by Congress even to appropriate the full measure of assistance authorized by an already restrictive formula. Here we have the Congress implicitly reneging on the delivery of an already meager federal share of the cost of meeting its own national mandates. The shortfall in appropriations has grown over the past two years to the point where less than half of the authorized amount has been distributed to affected school districts. The act authorized an appropriation in fiscal year 1980 of 20 percent of the understated federal calculation of national costs; the appropriation, however, was only 12 percent. In short, first they underestimate the costs and then they underfund the underestimate. New York City is receiving only $8.5 million in federal aid while spending an estimated $221 million in tax-levy dollars for special education in fiscal year 1980. Our commitment will grow to at least $278 million in fiscal year 1981 and we can only hope that the Congress will keep pace.

This mandate, combined with an inadequate level of federal funds for its fulfillment, has compelled the diversion of increasingly scarce local resources from the education of the rest of the school population. And as in Section 504, the absolute terms of the mandate discourage any efforts at the local level to develop alternative approaches to the statutory objective—such as the use of special facilities providing intensive attention to the needs of handicapped children—which might ease the enormous financial burden imposed by the program.

[Koch discusses other examples: programs for disposing of sewage sludge in the ocean, the federally imposed ceiling on the use of restricted public assistance payments, and mandates flowing from federal courts. Then he turns to an overall appraisal.—Ed.]

Needed Remedies

By cataloguing these arbitrary, restrictive, or counterproductive mandates I hope to have demonstrated both the complex demands confronting an urban chief executive today and the need for comprehensive revisions to the process by which such directives are formulated. A new mandate may appear to its authors to be a bold experiment in behavior modification for a worthy goal. But I do not think they view themselves as accountable for the hardship they may inflict on a particular locality. A superior level of government cannot, they would argue, be expected to anticipate every nuance in a far-reaching policy initiative. Indeed not—here lies the very reason why federal mandates must be flexible enough to accommodate local circumstances.

As the Mayor to whom those who must endure the hardship of irresponsible mandates look for relief, I can no longer accept the monotonous refrain that "it's up to Washington to correct its errors." It is long past time for the system to become responsive to the needs of those it purports to regulate, and for effective controls to be placed on the mandate machinery.

I do not claim to offer more than a rough outline for a modest measure of protection from the kinds of excesses now faced by a city like New York, but urge that prompt and careful consideration be given to the following proposals:

1. All mandates should include waiver provisions that afford an appropriate measure of recognition to a locality's efforts to address the objective through alternate means, or to integrate the required program with competing or complementary policies. New York, in several instances, commenced negotiations seeking administrative relief only to be met with an almost reflex hostility to allowing the slightest relaxation or modification of the mandate. This attitude may reflect a natural bureaucratic concern that the first variance breeds a collection of exceptions that will carve the underlying statute into an unworkable patchwork. But the administrators of these laws must be directed, by statute or Executive Order, to accommodate requests for waivers authorizing additional time or modified procedures from communities who offer reasonable evidence of an unfavorable impact.

2. Special consideration should be given to cities whose local revenue-raising and expenditure powers have come under the control of external authorities. It may be some years before we can measure the success of current efforts by all three levels of government to insulate the American metropolis from the twin cycles of declining revenues and spiraling costs. It makes absolutely no sense for the federal and state authorities to nullify their own ambitious urban assistance programs through the inflexible application of arbitrary mandates and the horrendous price tags they carry.

3. Action on any proposed mandate should be deferred until a report has been prepared on both the potential impact it would have on local government expenditures and the state of existing or proposed technology available to achieve timely compliance. Agencies such as the Congressional Budget Office and the Office of Technology Assessment are already in a position to perform an objective analysis of this nature, which could be summarized in the reports that accompany legislative proposals brought to the floors of Congress. Such a procedure would assure that the mandate makers are fully informed of the potential shock waves their action may send throughout affected communities.

4. No mandate should be imposed unless alternative methods of compliance are offered, with the final selection left to local option. In the exceptional case, in which mandates' authors are convinced that a single standard and procedure must be imposed, they should authorize variations in the timing of and approach to compliance within appropriate parameters, proportional to the degree of hardship or potential program failure among affected communities.

5. Finally, it is of overriding importance that every mandate be accompanied by financial aid sufficient to achieve compliance. The aggregate tax-levy resources which must be committed to all of the federal and state mandates presently imposed on the City amount to $938 million at a time when we must identify $299 million in net-expense budget reductions for fiscal year 1981.

Throughout its history, this nation has encouraged local independence and diversity. We cannot allow the powerful diversity of spirit that is a basic characteristic of our federal system to be crushed under the grim conformity that will be the most enduring legacy of the mandate millstone.

32. THE FAILURE OF FEDERAL ENFORCEMENT OF CIVIL RIGHTS REGULATIONS IN PUBLIC HOUSING, 1963-1971: THE CO-OPTATION OF A FEDERAL AGENCY BY ITS LOCAL CONSTITUENCY

Frederick Aaron Lazin

. . . During the 1960s both the President and Congress acted to ban racial discrimination in Public Housing. Executive Order 11063, Title VI and Title VIII of the 1964 and 1968 Civil Rights Acts, respectively, made it illegal for a local agency to operate its federally funded Public Housing program in a racially discriminatory manner. Yet these Acts did not end racial discrimination in Public Housing.[1] A recent study by this author of CHA [Chicago Housing Authority] site selection and tenant assignment policies from 1963 through June 1971 found that CHA operated its federal programs in a racially discriminatory manner. A careful examination of CHA operation of the programs, the federal role and regulations and *Gautreaux v. CHA* yielded the following findings.[2]

First, the CHA administered regular (for families), elderly and Section 23 (leasing) Public Housing to keep blacks from living in white communities of Chicago. It placed Regular Public Housing in black ghetto areas to reduce the number of black persons displaced by slum clearance and related programs being relocated in white areas. Quotas kept the number of black tenants at zero or at a minimum level in the four projects located in white neighborhoods. In Public Housing exclusively for the elderly, tenant assignment policies insured that projects in white neighborhoods had mostly white tenants. Only blacks chose to live in ghetto projects. Consequently integrated projects, that is, those with the second racial group constituting more than 10% were found only in racially changing neighborhoods. In the latter cases both the neighborhoods and the projects eventually became all black. The same pattern existed with leased housing. CHA delegated its authority to select tenants to the landlords. It gave them the right to reject tenants on the basis of "undesirability." Moreover CHA permitted landlords to choose tenants outside the almost all-black waiting list. As intended, most units in white neighborhoods were leased to white elderly tenants.

Author's Note: Prepared for delivery at the 1972 annual meeting of the American Political Science Association, Washington, D.C., September 8, 1972. Copyright, 1972, The American Political Science Association.

From *Policy Sciences* 4 (September 1973): 264-271, Elsevier Science Publishers, Amsterdam, The Netherlands.

Most blacks in the leasing program were placed in ghetto rehabilitation projects.

Second, federal civil rights laws and regulations were meaningless. HUD officials were fully aware that CHA operations violated HUD regulations designed to implement and enforce constitutional executive, legislative and judicial bans on racial discrimination.[3] In these matters HUD chose to serve rather than regulate the local constituency. The few cases of federal intervention on civil rights matters were exercises in public relations. HUD would hold up funds and investigate. Upon receipt of an official commitment from CHA that it would desist from discrimination it would release the funds. Unofficially, however, HUD would agree to let CHA continue its original discriminatory practices.[4]

Third, judicial redress proved equally ineffective. Having realized the futility of administrative redress, opponents of CHA policy filed a suit in U.S. District Court in August 1966 charging CHA with intent to discriminate against blacks.[5] In February 1969 the judge found the CHA guilty. Five months later he issued an order designed to foster integration and construction of Public Housing in white areas. But CHA refused to abide by the Court's directives and HUD refused to use its resources to enforce compliance.

How and why the civil rights legislation proved so ineffective a curb on discrimination in Public Housing is worth considering in more detail. Central to the entire case is the fact that HUD operates within a federal system: it is responsible to Congress which represents local interests. Consequently the administrative ideology of HUD holds that administrators must get local support to administer their programs successfully. Accordingly they are encouraged to serve rather than regulate. Both the Johnson and Nixon administrations reinforced this ideology.

Regardless of the attitudes of federal administrators toward Civil Rights and racial discrimination, the President and Congress forced them to confront the issue during the 1960s. President Kennedy's November 20, 1962, Executive Order 11063 and Title VI of the 1964 Civil Rights Act required federal agencies to issue regulations banning racial discrimination in site selection and tenant assignment policies.[6] While these acts provided the basis for challenges through administrative and judicial redress they did not lead to federal enforcement. Instead HUD established a system of discretionary justice in which the administrator (the "judge and jury") was already committed to the principle that in matters of race, the program would be run locally without federal interference.

The Civil Rights Orders and Acts are very general and do not define key provisions and terms.[7] Executive Order 11063 and Title VI prohibit racial discrimination in Public Housing without defining what constitutes "racial discrimination." Title VIII of the 1968 Civil Rights Act directs the Secretary of HUD to affirmatively administer his programs to foster the goals of non-discrimination on the basis of race.[8] The Act does not define "affirmative action" and "racial discrimination." While HUD regulations established to comply with these Acts might be expected to clarify the terms, they do not.

Moreover most HUD regulations issued to bring about local compliance with Executive Order 11063 and Title VI are not binding. They permit exemptions which are not explicitly defined. The revised HUD site selection regulations issued in February 1967 are a good example.[9] They were designed to provide greater choice to minority families and to prevent concentration of Public Housing in the ghetto areas. The regulation reads in part:

> Any proposal to locate housing only in areas of racial concentration will be *prima facie* unacceptable and will be returned to the local authority for further consideration and submission of either (1) alternative or additional sites in other areas, so as to provide a *more balanced* distribution of the proposed housing, or (2) a clear showing *factually substantiated*, that *no acceptable sites are available outside the areas of racial concentration*. . . (emphasis added) [10]

The regulation may make ghetto concentration of Public Housing sites *prima facie* unacceptable but it does not make it unlawful. If the local housing authority made "strenuous efforts" to build in non-ghetto areas and failed, it could concentrate sites in the ghetto.[11] All of the above emphasized words and phrases are not defined.

Therefore a federal administrator investigating a complaint against a local housing authority is not in a position to regulate even if he wants to. There is no explicit regulation or binding rule to enforce. The process of enforcement becomes arbitrary with primary responsibility placed on the individual administrator who must make a discretionary judgment. He must first determine what constitutes a violation in each particular case, and then whether the practice in question violates the newly established conditions. Most important, this system of enforcement provides the federal administrator with the legal option of non-enforcement.

In addition the Acts and subsequent regulations encourage informal bargaining rather than regulation and enforcement. In the case of a complaint or dispute the laws and regulations call for informal resolution between HUD and the local agency. Legal action where provided for is suggested only as a last resort.[12] Therefore HUD regulations instruct the administrator not to use his legal authority and power in dealing with alleged violation. A more arbitrary and discretionary arrangement is preferred.

A further element in the mechanism of civil rights enforcement was HUD's standard for compliance by the local authority. As proof of compliance HUD required that the local authority submit a resolution passed by the Board of Commissioners stating compliance. HUD's concern was with this formal evidence and not with actual CHA practices. Accordingly CHA passed appropriate resolutions stating compliance with Title VI. HUD accepted this despite its knowledge that CHA practices violated the Law, HUD and even CHA regulations.[13]

This concern for formal compliance made several cases of federal intervention in local matters ludicrous. Typical incidents were the proximity rule in elderly Public Housing and the controversy over tenant assignment—"freedom of choice versus first come—first served." In the first, CHA granted neighborhood residents a priority in tenant assignment over applicants on the waiting list. PHA held that this practice was unlawful. However, PHA wanted CHA to remove the rule from its regulations and nothing more.[14] In exchange for a promise to do so it let the CHA continue to operate the rule which it had previously argued violated HHFA regulations and Executive Order 11063. In the second example HUD carried on a two-year battle with CHA to have it adopt a "first come—first served" tenant assignment policy in the interest of integration. CHA eventually complied by formally adopting the recommended policy.[15] However it continued to operate its program in violation of the federal guidelines and its newly adopted policy. HUD knew of this but remained satisfied that the approved policy was officially adopted. Therefore the only effect of the regulations was to place CHA practices in violation of official CHA policies.

Another aspect of civil rights enforcement was the response of HUD to complaints charging the CHA with racial discrimination. HUD's commitment to support CHA and HUD's lack of concern with actual practices resulted in justification for CHA policies. There was no real investigation in response to complaints.[16] This was evident in a complaint in 1965 charging that CHA's 1965 sites violated Title VI, 11063 and HHFA regulations.[17]

PHA did not investigate the charges.[18] Instead it defended CHA's actions. It justified CHA's choice of ghetto sites by arguing that CHA complied with federal regulations implementing Executive Order 11063 ". . . affording the greatest acceptability to eligible applicants."[19] Moreover it supported the CHA position that it could find no alternative sites outside the ghetto because of City Council opposition. PHA knew that the City Council rejected other sites because of racial considerations.[20]

Finally PHA's argument that CHA did not discriminate but operated with discriminatory boundaries made Title VI ineffective.[21] Therefore the West Side Federation (WSF) complaint bolstered CHA's choice of sites in the ghetto *vis-à-vis* the 1964 Civil Rights Act and Executive Order 11063. After receipt of PHA's letter absolving it, CHA publicly announced that the federal government in two separate legal opinions had "concluded that CHA had not violated the Civil Rights Act."[22]

In summary, HUD chose to supervise CHA using its own discretion. In doing so HUD supported the local constituency whenever it deemed propitious regardless of civil rights laws and federal regulations. In the light of HUD's ideology of supporting the local constituency, this was most of the time.

This same position persisted throughout the Gautreaux case almost without exception. While HUD did not defend CHA, it sought to retain its authority to determine what constitutes a violation rather than have the court set down guidelines. It preferred to negotiate with the CHA rather than to enforce a spelled-out order.

During the negotiations over the final order from February to June 30, 1969 HUD and the U.S. Department of Justice participated.[23] The important issue at this time was whether HUD would commit itself to the judge's final order.

In late April a Washington conference was held between HUD and the Justice Department. Jerris Leonard (Justice) and [Richard C.] Van Dusen (HUD) recommended a federal commitment to an order along the lines of the plaintiff's proposals which would require CHA to build a percentage of future units in white neighborhoods. HUD General Counsel Sherman Unger opposed this position. He did not want to establish a precedent (for HUD in court) order to integrate.[24]

Several times in May and June the judge asked HUD for its comments on the proposals. HUD stalled until the judge had already reached a decision.[25]

HUD delivered its brief on the proposed order the evening before the judge issued the final binding order. It was too late to be of considerable aid and too late to make HUD a party to it. While supporting the principles of the judge's February decision, the HUD-Justice brief was critical of many of the proposed elements of the order. Many of the doubts and criticisms were of a technical nature.

One participant in the HUD-Justice negotiations said of the HUD-Justice document that it allowed all sides to read into it what they wanted. He interpreted the document as committing HUD to the order. Therefore, he suggested that HUD would comply with it and even aid in its implementation. Yet most significantly, it was not HUD's order. HUD did not write it. HUD was not an official party to it. The memorandum had put HUD on record as being critical of parts of the decree. Therefore HUD retained its powers of discretion. To have supported the order would have denied it this course of action.

The July 1969 final order in the Gautreaux case was both similar to and different from previous federal regulations banning racial discrimination in Public Housing. While it too banned discrimination, it defined and made exclusive its key terms and requirements. It was designed to prohibit the future use and to remedy the past effects of CHA's unconstitutional site selections and tenant assignment procedures. It required CHA to build 700 family units in the white areas of Chicago. The order defined white and non-white areas of the city as follows: Non-white areas (LPHA) are areas lying within "census tracts of the U.S. Bureau of the Census having 30% or more non-white population, or within a distance of one mile from any point on the outer perimeter of any such census tract" and white areas (GPHA) as all others.[26] Thereafter for each unit built or leased in the LPHA, CHA had to build and lease three in GPHA.[27] The order permitted the placement of units in the suburbs; of three units constructed and leased after the original 700 not more than one third of the regular and one third of the leased required for the white areas of the city of Chicago may "at the option of the CHA, be located in the white areas of Cook County provided that the units are available to Chicago residents who applied to CHA for housing."[28]

Several provisions were designed to win community acceptance for Public Housing to be built in white communities. One limited project size to 120 persons.[29] Another prohibited the placement of additional Public Housing in a census tract if Public Housing would constitute more than 15% of the total number of apartments and single residences on the tract. A third prohibited the placement of families with children above the third story except in the case of leasing.[30] A later court-approved tenant assignment plan gave neighborhood residents a priority over applicants on the waiting list for 50% of the new units.[31]

Despite the definition of key terms and the specific and explicit requirements, HUD had no statutory directive to enforce the order. Again the question of whether or not to enforce was an arbitrary one—one of discretion. In light of its past record, CHA critics sought in a companion suit filed against HUD to direct the courts to order HUD to desist from support of CHA's racially discriminatory policies.[32] In the spring of 1968 the judge stayed the suit pending outcome of *Gautreaux v. CHA.* In October 1969 the plaintiffs filed for summary judgment in *Gautreaux v. HUD.* They asked the judge to issue an order to involve HUD in enforcement of the Gautreaux order.[33]

HUD opposed this. It held that such an order would infringe on its legitimate constitutional right to discretionary powers. It argued that the 1968 Civil Rights Act enjoined the Secretary of HUD, not the courts, to:

> administer the programs and activities relating to housing and urban development in a manner affirmatively to further the policies of this title.[34]

The Secretary could do it best and not the court. It was clearly within his legal realm:

> The determination of which powers and programs to bring to bear upon the admittedly unsatisfactory housing situation in the City of Chicago belongs to the defendant (HUD) (and not to the court).[35]

Moreover, the objectives of the plaintiffs, HUD argued, would be "more readily achieved by the *voluntary* efforts of the defendants than by the coercion of a judicial decree." [36] Finally HUD emphasized that by congressional design "maximum responsibility for the administration of the program must be vested in the local authority." [37]

When the judge ruled on September 1, 1970 that "the government must be permitted to carry out its findings unhampered by judicial intervention" he foreclosed on possible HUD enforcement of the Gautreaux order.[38] In effect he freed HUD to practice its own system of discretionary justice designed to serve the political interests of its constituency.[39]

In June 1971 HUD released Model Cities funds for Chicago in exchange for the Mayor's commitment to provide low income housing. Significantly many of the Public Housing units involved violated the Gautreaux order. HUD had *decided not to enforce* the order.

Notes

1. National Committee Against Discrimination in Housing, *How the Federal Government Builds Ghettos* (New York: NCADH, 1968).
2. *Gautreaux v. CHA*, 296 F. Supp. 907 (N.D. Ill., 1969).
3. Throughout this paper the term "HUD officials" refers to personnel of the U.S. Department of Housing and Urban Development and its predecessor agencies before 1965—The Housing and Home Finance Agency (HHFA) and The Public Housing Administration (PHA).
4. See discussion below on the Elderly Proximity Rule.
5. *Gautreaux v. CHA*
6. Executive Order 11063 "Equal Opportunity in Housing"; Title VI (1964) Public Law 88-352, 78 Stat. 241, 42 U.S.C. 20002; Title VIII (1968) Public Law 90-284, 82 Stat. 73.
7. "Otherwise they might not have been passed," Alexander R. Polikoff, Esq., Interview, Chicago, Ill., April 1971.
8. Title VIII Sec. 808 (e) (5).
9. U.S. Department of Housing and Urban Development, Housing Assistance Adminis-

tration, *Low Rent Housing Manual*, Transmittal Number 490 (Washington, D.C.: mimeograph, February 28, 1967).

10. *Ibid.*, p. 7.

11. *Ibid.* According to the *New York Times*, the intent of this directive was to change the disposition to place sites only in the ghetto.

12. Title VI, Secs. 602, 603.

13. Chicago Housing Authority, Resolution 65 CHA 50 (April 22, 1965), and Resolution 68 CHA 232 (November 14, 1968). HUD Regional Office, Chicago, Ill.: Interviews with several staff members, 1970-1971.

14. PHA feared that other local housing authorities, especially in the South, would adopt similar policies to insure segregation. Also it charged CHA with adopting the policy, which would give white neighborhood residents priority over blacks on the waiting list in order to get City Council approval for sites. CHA policies had the effect of making tenancy in projects for the elderly in white areas all-white. Interviews with Marie McGuire, U.S. Public Housing Commissioner (Washington, D.C., January 1971); Charles Swibel, Chairman, Board of Commissioners of the CHA, 1970-1971. Letter and Supporting Brief from PHA to CHA December 11, 1963.

15. CHA Resolution 68 CHA 232 (November 14, 1968).

16. A qualified exception to this was HUD's pressuring CHA in November 1966 to drop several of its 12 ghetto sites on the grounds that they violated Title VI and they caused considerable neighborhood opposition. HUD conducted an investigation independently of CHA assistance. A compromise package was arrived at. However the compromise sites were also in violation of Title VI. HUD probably took this action because of suits filed in August 1966 (see below).

17. Letter from the West Side Federation to HHFA, August 26, 1965. The complaint was filed by the West Side Federation, an umbrella group encompassing black organizations in the West Side Ghetto of Chicago. The Chicago Urban League originally decided to appeal to HHFA. Urban League Staff wrote the letter to HHFA and had the WSF submit it.

18. Letter from PHA Commissioner McGuire to PHA Regional Administrator Bergeron, September 8, 1965.

19. Letter from PHA to WSF, October 14, 1965.

20. *Ibid.*

21. *Ibid.* PHA argued that the CHA was the sole recipient of funds and not the City Council under the terms of Title VI. Therefore *only* the actions of the CHA were subject to administrative redress under Title VI. Also see Chicago Urban League Memorandum, Harold Baron to Edwin Berry, November 5, 1965.

22. Statement by CHA, September 1965.

23. The Justice Department provided counsel for HUD and the U.S. Government.

24. The U.S. Departments of HUD and Justice, Washington, D.C., Chicago, Ill., and Cincinnati, Ohio, interviews with present (and former) staff, 1970-1972. One former Justice official claims that the Civil Rights Division of the Justice Department supported the "commitment" to improve its Civil Rights image.

25. *Ibid.* Some argue that HUD-Justice did not intentionally delay submission of their comments. They suggest that negotiations over positions and wording took until late June to satisfy all parties.

26. *Judgement Order, Gautreaux v. CHA*, 304 F. Supp. 736 (N.D. Ill., 1969). Article I (D), III (B). In the interest of de-politicizing the order, the parties agreed to refer to white and non-white areas as General Public Housing Area and Limited Public Housing Area, respectively.

27. *Ibid.*, III (C).

28. *Ibid.*, III (E).

29. *Ibid.*, IV. If impossible to comply with and if in the interest of the order, a project can contain 240 persons. This is one of the few provisions providing for discretion in enforcement.
30. *Ibid.*, III (C).
31. Order approving CHA Tenant Assignment Plan, *Gautreaux v. CHA*, No. 66C 1459 (N.D. Ill. November 27, 1969).
32. *Gautreaux v. HUD.* Filed in U.S. District Court (N.D. Ill.), August 1966.
33. *Ibid.*
34. See Frederick Aaron Lazin, "Public Housing in Chicago, 1963-1971" (unpublished Ph.D. dissertation, University of Chicago, 1972).
35. *Ibid.*
36. Emphasis added.
37. Defendant's Answering brief at 18, *Gautreaux v. HUD.*
38. *Order and Memorandum Gautreaux v. HUD.*
39. The Plaintiffs appealed. In February 1971 "The U.S. Court of Appeals found that HUD violated the Civil Rights of negroes by funding CHA construction of public housing almost entirely in the ghetto." *Chicago Sun Times*, February 2, 1971. See also *Gautreaux v. Romney*, 448F. 2 cl. 731 (1971); *Gautreaux v. Romney*, 21, 457F. 2 cl. 124 (1972).

33. THE FOURTH FACE OF FEDERALISM

Donald F. Kettl

The 1970s brought a new face to federalism, a collection of private and semi-public groups and agencies that moved into a full partnership with the national, state, and local governments in administering federal policy. This fourth face of federalism emerged from the decade's new breed of intergovernmental grant programs. Richard Nixon promised a "New Federalism" of guaranteed grants, fewer federal rules, and more discretion for state and local government on what projects could receive support. It was in general revenue sharing for all state and local governments and in manpower and community development programs, mainly for the cities, that this "new" federalism bore fruit. It was fruit, however, that the cities found difficult to pick, for the programs proved complex to administer.

Two programs—the Comprehensive Employment and Training Act, enacted in 1973 [President Reagan successfully backed the elimination of this program during his first term.—Ed.], and Community Development Block Grants, established a year later—became important sources of both revenue and services for local governments. CETA allows recipients, mostly large cities,[1] wide discretion in establishing their own manpower training and public service employment programs. CD gives cities a nearly free rein in choosing projects for housing rehabilitation, development, and public services.[2] Both programs have relatively simple application requirements and both programs leave most of the responsibility for deciding how best to administer local projects in local hands. It was as a solution to the administrative question that the fourth face of federalism emerged.

Very few—if any—cities had extensive experience in organizing and running manpower and community development programs before the 1970s.

Author's Note: Earlier versions of this article were presented at the 1980 annual meeting of the Midwest Political Science Association and appeared in the University of Virginia *News Letter*. These previous versions have benefited greatly from the comments of Clifton McCleskey, David Magleby, David O'Brien, Timothy O'Rourke, Vincent Shea, and Sandra Wiley. Work on this article has been supported by the White Burkett Miller Center of Public Affairs at the University of Virginia, whose assistance is gratefully acknowledged. Quotations in this article not otherwise cited come from interviews with Richmond city officials, whose assistance is gratefully acknowledged.

From *Public Administration Review* 41 (May/June 1981): 366-371. Reprinted with permission from *Public Administration Review* © 1981 by The American Society for Public Administration, 1120 G Street, N.W., Washington, D.C. All rights reserved.

Most of mayors' complaints during the Great Society, in fact, were that the federal government was bypassing city hall in dealing directly with clients like neighborhood groups or in providing money to quasi-municipal bureaus like redevelopment agencies that often resisted local control. CETA and CD ended that era by delivering the money directly to city hall along with the federal government's directive to go forth, plan wisely, and administer well.[3]

This was a formidable charge. In the medium-sized city of Richmond, the city government collected $9 million from CETA and $7 million from CD in fiscal year 1979, 10 cents for each dollar of the $156 million it collected from local sources. The two programs were to pay for a wide variety of services: job training, public service jobs, housing rehabilitation, downtown economic development, and many more. Moreover, the city faced a choice: Should it attempt to run directly each of the more than 100 projects? Or should it use other groups in the city? If the city ran all the programs directly, from where would the needed expertise come? If it contracted the projects out, how could it ensure that the projects were run well and were pursuing the city's goals?

For many cities, including Richmond, the choice was contracting out the direct administration of many projects to non-city agencies. As we shall see by examining the case of Richmond, that choice raised a fundamental problem of accountability for the use of the federal government's money. As the recipient, the city government had to ensure that the federal government's requirements were met. Because the city served only as the conduit for much of the money, it faced the challenge of ensuring that the non-city agencies met both federal requirements and local policy goals without interfering excessively with how those non-city agencies ran their projects. Richmond, as did many of her sister cities, solved the problem by creating new (and apparently permanent) municipal agencies to oversee the work of these non-city groups. The new city agencies in turn developed formal ties with the non-city groups. The result was a new set of bureaucratic arrangements that lifted these non-city groups into a new intergovernmental arrangement, an arrangement that added a fourth face to federalism.

Contracting Out

Richmond's city council assigned responsibility for CETA and CD to a new Department of Developmental Programs.[4] A wide collection of agencies had run earlier categorical programs, but the unified planning and reporting requirements of the new programs argued for central coordination, and the council decided to house both programs in a single agency. The department, however, runs few of the city's CETA and CD projects itself. Although other city agencies run many projects, most are contracted out to non-city agencies. In the 1978-79 fiscal year, for example, non-city agencies spent 63 percent of the CD funds and 64 percent of the CETA funds. As City Manager Manuel Deese explained, "The more you get involved and try to play the federal game, the more you have to go outside [city agencies]."

Some of the non-city agencies are neighborhood groups spurred on by the political support the neighborhoods gained during the 1970s. The Great Society's confrontation between city hall and city neighborhoods, often fueled by federal grants that bypassed city governments and were channelled directly to the neighborhoods, slowly gave way to closer (if not always pacific) ties.[5] National interest groups representing the neighborhoods struggled to win representation by an assistant secretary in the U.S. Department of Housing and Urban Development and battled their way into recognition by Jimmy Carter's domestic policy staff. "First the neighborhood organizations got the attention of City Hall and now they've got some funding," William A. Whiteside, director of the urban reinvestment task force explained. "It is a natural progression from a militant stand to get resources to a constructive role once you have the attention and the funds." [6]

Other groups are varied non-profit organizations. Some, like Opportunities Industrialization Centers from previous manpower programs and social service agencies from the Model Cities program, received funds under the categorical programs that preceded CETA and CD. Many of these agencies fully expected to continue receiving funds under the new programs. National interest groups representing some of these agencies managed, furthermore, to have provisions inserted into the CETA legislation to ensure that programs of "demonstrated effectiveness" be given "due consideration" for continued funding.[7]

Yet, other groups are quasi-city agencies like the Richmond Redevelopment and Housing Authority and the city school board, agencies responsible to the city council but not answerable to the city manager. The redevelopment agency had some old projects whose completion demanded continued funding, but Richmond went beyond past patterns of funding in giving money to non-city agencies.

Four factors shaped the choices for this strange assortment of administrative agencies. First, Richmond city officials wanted to avoid building the programs permanently into the city's bureaucracy. If the city had created, for example, a new agency to administer directly all of the city's CETA training programs and the federal government later reduced or eliminated the program, the city might face the dilemma of either laying off a large number of city employees or of funding the projects from local revenue. Cycles alternating between federal pleas for rapid spending and federal warnings of funding cuts made city officials very wary of building the programs permanently into the municipal bureaucracy. City officials were reluctant to assume direct responsibility for programs that the federal government might not later support.

Second, previous federal programs had created a large and powerful constituency for continued community-level funding. As one manpower official explained about CETA:

> First, when CETA started, there was very heavy emphasis [from the Department of Labor] on the fact that we had to do business with the people who had been doing business before with the feds. Second, the nature of city politics dictated that we had to keep these people happy.[8]

Most of these agencies, from the Community Action Program Agency to the Redevelopment and Housing Authority, depended on federal funds for their existence. Any attempt to change the pattern of funding would have stirred up loud howls from entrenched organizations.

The changing nature of Richmond politics also deeply affected these organizational decisions. As CD and CETA arrived in Richmond, the city was in the midst of a dramatic change in community power. A shift from at-large to district representation on the city council gave blacks their first city council majority, and they elected one of their number as the city's first black mayor. Before the change, the white council majority had no desire to jeopardize an already precarious position by antagonizing black community leaders with a change in funding strategy. Moreover, after the blacks gained the majority, their one-vote edge left no room for dissension. Particularly in the CETA program, the community-based organizations were enjoying support that made a dramatic reorganization unthinkable.

Finally, for some of the projects, particularly in the CD program, non-city agencies were the city's only alternative. The Richmond Redevelopment and Housing Authority, for example, had worked for years on the city's redevelopment program. For the redevelopment projects continued under the CD program, the authority was the only agency in the city with the expertise to make the projects work. Dismantling the agency would have meant destroying much needed expertise.

Federal Control of Federal Grants

The use of non-city agencies, however, complicated the city's management of the projects. As the grant recipient, the city was responsible to the federal government for ensuring that each program's requirements were met regardless of who eventually operated the projects. With more than 100 non-city agencies operating CETA and CD projects, the city (through the Department of Developmental Programs) had to devise procedures to make sure that all agencies spending federal money followed federal rules.

Despite earlier promises of few federal strings, both CETA and CD acquired a complicated collection of regulations. Some of these regulations were designed to guarantee that early charges of program abuses could not recur. Monitors of both programs in the first few years had found trouble wherever they looked: tales of CD funds used to build tennis courts and marinas (instead of housing for the poor), as well as corrupt hiring practices in CETA projects. Charges of abuse and outright fraud were legion.[9] In many cases, however, the allegations turned out to be baseless, and even where there truly was fraud or abuse, no one knew how large the problem actually was.

The very hint of abuses, however, rendered this question moot. The Department of Housing and Urban Development began taking a much closer look at CD applications and insisting that cities document the extent to which each project would benefit the poor. In the CETA program's 1978 annual renewal, Congress put limits on how long CETA participants could work and how much they could be paid. In addition to supervising local applications more closely to ensure that local governments fulfilled their federally-defined obligations to the poor, the federal government also began to conduct far more stringent monitoring. As one Richmond official explained, "They are requiring us to have a mechanism to substantiate the fact that we are benefiting low and moderate income people."

At the same time, the federal government was adding an ever-increasing number of general, crosscutting requirements to intergovernmental grant programs. These rules, totalling 59 by one U.S. Office of Management and Budget count in 1980,[10] required all grant recipients to examine the environmental impact of any projects they planned, to guarantee that they would not discriminate in the use of the funds, to keep their books in a prescribed manner, to pay workers at prevailing wages, and on, and on.

All of these actions created a complicated mix of federal controls: extensive regulations detailing what had to be done; application reviews to determine whether the cities were meeting the regulations; and monitoring procedures after program execution to see if the cities had complied with the regulations' requirements. As Richmond's assistant city manager, A. Howe Todd, explained, "Here we are five or six years down the program with HUD, and HUD is putting the screws on. I see more and more constraints being put on us, making it more and more costly for us to comply with their requirements."

The result was that the cities had to assemble an enormous mass of data to keep the federal agencies satisfied that all of the standards were being met. As Richmond Finance Director Jack Lissenden explained, "Their [the federal agencies'] monitoring is much more demanding than anything we've ever had before, even the categorical grants." The federal agencies, Lissenden said, were now sending armies of inspectors to examine the books for days, where before they might have sent one investigator to review the records for a few hours. Complicating the city's record-keeping task, furthermore, were frequent changes in those items the federal agencies wanted the cities to measure. One city official pointed to recent federal regulations in the CD program that required the city to determine the beneficiaries by income and sex for projects such as sidewalk cuts that make it easy for wheelchairs to pass over curbs. Another city official complained about HUD's requirement of keeping program records available for public inspection in a "file":

> The regulations always call for having all the information in a file. A file to me is the four drawers out there in a cabinet. But for the field man, a file means one folder. I've had to change my filing system three times. Now, I'm back to the system I used at the beginning of the program.[11]

"The diversity and complexity of the things we are doing to satisfy the federal government's demands is getting worse," one Richmond CETA official complained. He pointed out that, after quarreling with the U.S. Department of Labor for a year, he finally had to lease a word processing computer just to collect the information needed to satisfy the department's data demands. The burdens of collecting the information, the official concluded, are not all that oppressive, but they are time-consuming. "They are getting to be nit-picking," he complained. "They are capturing a lot of statistics that aren't useful. They should be asking, 'Is anything useful happening down there?' "[12]

Through all of these regulatory changes, the federal government has subtly drawn power back to Washington. This centralization has come in rules about both the substance of programs (who must be hired or what projects must be funded, for example) and about the procedures that local governments must follow (such as what public hearings must be held and what environmental effects must be examined). The federal government has required the collection of more information on more kinds of programs by more cities than was ever the case in the categorical programs.

Managing Contracts

No matter who ultimately spent the money, the federal government held the cities accountable for adherence to the regulations. The cities, thus, had to guarantee that each non-city agency receiving federal money met the federal rules and that each agency could supply the city with proof of compliance. Furthermore, the cities naturally had their own ideas of what benefits should come from the projects and the non-city agencies had goals of their own. The programs were thus encumbered with four layers of accountability: accountability to the federal government for general, crosscutting requirements; accountability to the federal government for specific program requirements; accountability to city officials for individual project goals; and accountability to those who ultimately received the fruits of the projects—usually the clients of the non-city agencies—for the quality of the services.

Richmond's contracting-out policy sought to guarantee that the city could supply the federal agencies with the answers they wanted and that the non-city agencies would provide the services the city desired. The task of extracting adequate performance from the non-city agencies, however, proved difficult. Many of the CETA and CD agencies were new to the grant business, and even for those that were not, past experience was no guarantee of present capacity. City officials charged that the federal government had not overseen community-based organizations very closely in the earlier categorical programs: "Private non-profits [non-profit organizations] can get away with a little more than governments can," one city official remarked.

Furthermore, city staff members agreed, the use of non-city agencies has often raised problems of competence. "Going to a non-city agency," one city official said, "the chances are very good that they wouldn't have the capacity to manage a project." Even basic skills like accounting for petty cash and maintaining adequate financial records, according to some city officials, are often absent. If basic operations proved troublesome, the pursuit of project goals was therefore often an elusive business. The city has faced, first, the task of factoring its general program goals into projects the non-city agencies could handle, and then the job, sometimes overwhelming, of making the agencies both productive and accountable.

To meet these needs, Richmond has relied (as have many other cities) on drafting detailed and often lengthy agreements. For city agencies conducting CD and CETA projects, these agreements take the form of countersigned memorandums; for non-city agencies, the agreements are formal contracts. These agreements spell out the administering agency's role in detail: its budget, detailed by activity such as land acquisition costs, training expenses, and administration; its responsibilities, described by the nature of the project and a "milestone chart" that indicates when each step of the project is to occur, and its reporting requirements, defined in sufficient detail to allow the city to follow the project's substantive progress and to enable the city to collect the information needed to satisfy the federal government. These agreements provide the city with its most important means of control, extracting promises from the operating agencies about exactly what is to be done in which ways. As one official explained, "We have no control over these agencies except through the contract. The only time we can dictate to them is when they are in violation of the contract."

Relations between the city government and most agencies operating CETA and CD projects, therefore, have revolved around accountability through paperwork. A written agreement details what will be done when. Periodic reports describe what has been accomplished toward the city's objectives. Other reports describe beneficiaries of the projects by income, sex, and so on, to help the city satisfy the federal government's demands. The city government, particularly its Department of Developmental Programs, serves as a contract manager, administering projects that previously would have been managed from separate field offices of separate federal agencies.

Effects on Local Administration

Department of Developmental Programs Director Aaron Knight is frank about the importance of federal grants for his agency: "The agency wouldn't exist without federal money." Of the department's 60 employees in the 1979-1980 fiscal year, only 16 (27 percent) were paid from city revenues. Federal grants—principally CETA and CD—paid the salaries of the other 44 workers. These grants, thus, have been responsible for the creation of a large—and now apparently permanent—city agency whose mission it is to service federal grants.

The federal grants, in turn, have spawned a network of *ad hoc* arrangements that have scrambled the city's traditional administrative organization. In the CD program, a multi-agency task force cuts across the city's regular departmental boundaries to deal with the problems that often occur in non-city agencies. The CETA program has a very different administrative structure. The city's CETA program is part of the Richmond Area Manpower System, a consortium formed by Richmond and four nearby counties.[13] Richmond receives most of the jobs, has half of the votes on the consortium's governing board, and administers the program for the consortium through the Manpower Bureau of the city's Department of Developmental Programs. These arrangements have tangled the lines of accountability still further, for that department serves as the staff arm for the regional CETA program at the same time it operates as the umbrella agency for administering the city's CETA projects.

The bureaucratic arrangements for the administration of CETA and CD in Richmond, thus, are intricate and convoluted. They exist to satisfy the fragmented demands of different federal programs, but they have produced unusual arrangements. The CETA projects come to Richmond's citizens through the U.S. Department of Labor, the regional consortium, the city's Department of Developmental Programs, and numerous contractors, most of which are non-city agencies. The CD funds flow from the U.S. Department of Developmental Programs (in part) and the city's Department of Planning and Community Development (in part), as well as to the task force (in part), and, finally, to the program's contractors who, again, are mostly non-city agencies.

The two programs have fostered the creation of a new agency, a new regional consortium, formal agreements among city agencies, and a network of non-city agencies officially doing the federal government's business under local direction. All of this is overlaid upon a city bureaucracy that, of course, works in different ways under different rules toward different local goals.

The result is a bureaucratization of the federal aid function in Richmond.

Large agencies have been created to manage the myriad projects and to service the federal government's demands for information. Existing ties among city agencies have been scrambled as a different, federally-oriented bureaucracy has been overlaid over locally-oriented agencies. The number and complexity of the projects, furthermore, have created formal ties between city hall and many private, quasi-public, and neighborhood-based agencies that now depend on good administrative relations with city officials to ensure the continued flow of federal aid. The federal programs have, thus, created a large network of intricate relationships that channel aid to local agencies, with the city of Richmond acting as the administrative intermediary between the federal government, with its money, goals, and requirements, and the non-city agencies, with their own disparate agendas.

Richmond city officials do not seem particularly annoyed about their new role. They grumble about conflicting or unclear demands from federal agencies, they dislike rearranging their files regularly, and they complain about the paperwork required. However, the city's administrative officials have been willing to meet nearly any requirement for the aid, provided the requirements are clear.

More important is the increase in the administrative costs. More local staff people are preparing environmental assessments, equal opportunity and fair housing plans, contracts, monitoring reports, performance reports, and financial audits; more contractors are filing reports to tell the city what they are doing and to help the city keep the federal agencies happy. There is, of course, nothing wrong with using a share of any grant for overhead costs to ensure adequate management control; but three points are significant.

First, more of these requirements are in effect now than ever before. For example, nearly all of the 59 general requirements that come with most federal grant programs are mandates established in the last 15 years; 35 of these (59 percent) were ordered during the 1970s.[14] The federal government itself pays nearly all of the costs for complying with these regulations, and, thus, they do not place a large financial burden on local governments. The regulations have, however, increased the level of "overhead costs" in the federal aid system: more money must be spent to comply with these requirements, and less money, consequently, is available for services.

Second, these requirements are more and more the responsibility of local governments rather than the federal government. Before Richard Nixon's New Federalism, for example, the federal government performed the environmental reviews now required of local governments. The programs transferred the administrative burden for complying with these "overhead" requirements into local hands. Local officials had to develop new areas of expertise: environmental reviews, planning for equal opportunity and fair housing, and so on, and they had to develop a contracting system to ensure that those who actually spent the money met the requirements.

Finally, the programs have inserted city hall as the formal intermediary between the federal government and the non-city agencies. This happened, of course, because of complaints in the late 1960s that city government officials were being excluded from important decisions that intimately affected their communities. In the 1970s, the pressures for administrative expedience and for neighborhood power gave non-city agencies a continuing but different role. City officials controlled the non-city agencies by contract, and the friction-filled days of the Great Society grew into the formal, institutionalized (but not always placid) relationships of the New Federalism.

The Changing Face of Federalism

The clear thrust of this movement is to resolve the city hall-neighborhood conflicts of the 1960s while capitalizing on the intensity of concern that first spawned the controversies. HUD's first assistant secretary for neighborhoods, Geno Baroni, explained, "There are some groups that raise hell and some groups that get involved in development. The thrust of the urban partnership is to get those latter groups and put them together with local government and the private side" to improve their own areas.[15] To a large degree, CETA and CD have succeeded. Years of experience gradually soothed the initial raw feelings between Richmond and its contractors.

These programs, however, have brought an important change to the basic function of the city. Cities, as Douglas Yates has argued, have traditionally been service providers.[16] Even as the federal government gradually relied more on outside organizations to perform its basic functions and the states struggled to define their role in a changing intergovernmental system, the cities were in the front lines providing direct services like police, fire, and sanitation. Local governments, of course, overwhelmingly still provide most of their services directly.[17] The two grant programs signal an important change in this tradition, for they have moved local government a short step from direct provision of services to management of contracted services. This not only means a change in some of what local governments do, but also a shift in who does it. Accountants, contract specialists, environmental engineers, and equal opportunity experts have moved into a key role in helping to govern urban America.

At the same time, the complicated administrative networks that manage CETA and CD have simultaneously streamlined and muddied the problem of accountability. By channeling the grants through local elected officials, the federal government has identified mayors and city councilors as those ultimately responsible for local projects. By encouraging such a complex administrative web, the programs simultaneously have made it more difficult to determine both what is going on and who is responsible for doing it. This paradox of accountability has only encouraged a basic regulatory approach to grant programs that has grown through the 1970s. Faced with confusion over program administration, federal agencies have retreated back into increasingly complex rules that seek to frame the basic administrative patterns of the programs.[18]

Perhaps most importantly, the programs have also led to formal, regular ties between city hall and a wide assortment of neighborhood, non-profit, and other non-city organizations. These ties have enabled the cities to specify with greater detail the conditions under which these agencies would receive federal funds. At the same time, these programs have led to more and more formal arrangements between the city and others, non-city local groups, arrangements that through the 1970s have strategically built the non-city groups into a fourth face of federalism.

Notes

1. Cities and counties with a population of more than 100,000 receive CETA funds as "prime sponsors." States receive grants for those areas not covered by local prime sponsors. For a description of the history and issues in the CETA program, see U.S. Advisory Commission on Intergovernmental Relations, *The Comprehensive Employment and Training Act: Early Readings from a Hybrid Block Grant* (Washington, D.C.: U.S. Government Printing Office, 1977).
2. On the CD program, see U.S. Advisory Commission on Intergovernmental Relations, *Community Development: The Workings of a Federal-Local Block Grant* (Washington, D.C.: U.S. Government Printing Office, 1977).
3. For some examples, see the author's *Managing Community Development in the New Federalism* (New York: Praeger, 1980).
4. Richmond has a council-manager form of government.
5. For a look at the tensions of the Great Society Programs, see Daniel P. Moynihan, *Maximum Feasible Misunderstanding: Community Action in the War on Poverty* (New York: Free Press, 1970).
6. Quoted by Rochelle L. Stanfield, "The Neighborhoods—Getting a Piece of the Urban Policy Pie," *National Journal*, April 22, 1978, p. 624.
7. See U.S. National Commission for Manpower Policy, *Community Based Organizations in Manpower Programs and Policy* (Washington, D.C.: U.S. Government Printing Office, 1977).
8. Interview with Richmond city official.
9. See, for example, Raymond Brown et al., *A Time for Accounting: The Housing and Community Development Act in the South* (Atlanta: Southern Regional Council, 1976); and U.S. General Accounting Office, *Administrative Weaknesses in St. Louis' Comprehensive Employment and Training Act Program* (March 2, 1979).
10. U.S. Office of Management and Budget, *Managing Federal Assistance in the 1980s* (Washington, D.C.: U.S. Government Printing Office, 1980), p. 20.
11. Interview with Richmond city official.
12. Interview with Richmond city official.
13. The four counties are New Kent, Charles City, Goochland, and Powhatan; they form an outer ring around Henrico and Chesterfield, the two counties surrounding and immediately adjacent to Richmond. Henrico and Chesterfield counties chose to form their own consortium.
14. U.S. Office of Management and Budget, *Managing Federal Assistance in the 1980s, Working Papers* (Washington, D.C.: U.S. Government Printing Office, 1980), Vol. 1, p. A-2-11.
15. Quoted by Rochelle L. Stanfield, "The Neighborhood Movement—What Price Success?" *National Journal*, November 18, 1978, p. 1863.
16. Douglas Yates, *The Ungovernable City: The Politics of Urban Problems and Policy Making* (Cambridge, Mass.: MIT Press, 1977).
17. See Donald Fisk, Herbert Kiesling, and Thomas Muller, *Private Provision of Public Services: An Overview* (Washington, D.C.: The Urban Institute, 1978).
18. See the author's "Regulating the Cities," *Publius* 11 (Winter 1981), pp. 111-125.

Review Questions

1. Ingram indicates that federal administrators, in dealing with their counterparts in the states, cannot and do not simply give orders. She claims that under some circumstances, however, federal policies are likely to be administered straightforwardly by the states. When? Why?

2. Ingram's model of intergovernmental administration suggests that, relatively speaking, the states have impressive advantages in dealing with the national bureaucracy. Apply her model (modified for federal-local relations) to the case of the Chicago Housing Authority described by Lazin. What empirical support does the case contain for Ingram's propositions?

3. Ingram claims that in intergovernmental bargaining, neither party wants to cause conflict: "Federal agencies are unlikely to embark upon enforcement practices that they anticipate will bring them little support and much criticism." Is this argument still valid in a time of federal budget cuts and strained intergovernmental fiscal relations? Would one expect even more conflict to develop with today's shrinking pie? Consider in your response the types of regulatory devices increasingly employed by the national government since the 1970s, and evaluate Koch's comments on this subject.

4. Many of the early advocates of public administrative reform argued that politics should be separated from administration; in fact, this idea is still voiced today by some advocates of good government. If one means by politics the conflict about and determination of public goals, do you think that administration and politics in intergovernmental relations can really be separated? Be specific and use examples in your response.

5. Does the ACIR survey of state administrators suggest a response to the assertion that how we structure our governments is not very important? Again based on the ACIR evidence, is there any value to establishing cooperative and coordinating structures (for instance, councils of governments) among our governments?

6. Explain why some analysts of intergovernmental administration say that federal regulation has become increasingly important because of the adoption since the 1970s of formula-based block grants.

7. Koch claims that national bureaucrats adopt and advocate regulations that extend far beyond what they might reasonably need or expect to accomplish. Does Ingram's model, when combined with other views included in this book (such as those of Pressman and Derthick), indicate that this bureaucratic behavior may have a rational basis?

8. Many observers of the American legislative process claim that lawmakers often design ambiguous, even contradictory, policies and leave tough decisions to those who implement them. What would be some reasons for such an approach? Why might this tendency be magnified on intergovernmental matters? How does the Chicago housing case support this argument?

9. Why do many American cities contract out to private organizations the provision of services funded through block grants?

Part Five

A SAMPLING OF CONTEMPORARY ISSUES

The readings presented thus far have documented the persistent salience of intergovernmental matters in American public life. A number of recent developments have raised the topic of intergovernmental relations to a very prominent position in policy discussions today.

Since the mid-1970s, for instance, the federal aid system has altered considerably, as it has both responded to and stimulated political and administrative shifts. A fiscal network of hundreds of narrow categorical programs has been broadened and made more complex by the addition of revenue sharing and the compression of numerous categoricals into block grants. Although intergovernmental regulation has increased, it has been the target of reform. Two versions of a "new federalism," under the presidencies of Richard Nixon and Ronald Reagan, have aimed at breathing vitality into the system by shifting decisions away from Washington.

As the introductory chapter in this book described, the Reagan administration in particular has proposed some dramatic changes. By suggesting a relaxation of national administrative controls in a variety of policy areas, a further shift toward the block grant method of intergovernmental finance, a clearer separation of responsibilities between the states and Washington, a turnback of many responsibilities to the states, and a major reduction in the total amount of federal financial support for states and localities, Reagan established a lengthy and controversial agenda for his administration.

During his first term, these issues were joined by many of those who have a stake in their resolution. As several of the readings in this section explain, Reagan was by no means completely successful in effecting a drastic redirection in intergovernmental matters. However, on a number of issues (especially deregulation, the creation of new block grants, and the enactment of aid cutbacks) there were major developments.

Perhaps even more importantly, Reagan's reelection and his maintenance of interest in these matters may portend further changes. Related issues may heighten the attention given to intergovernmental matters in the later 1980s and may also raise the level of conflict. The national government, for instance, currently faces imposing fiscal difficulties that are likely to produce repercussions through the intergovernmental system. The federal budget has been persistently in deficit for the last generation, and during the 1980s the deficit has hovered between $100 and $200 billion. Current projections are for shortfalls of similar magnitude or even larger. During the first Reagan term, intergovernmental aid bore more than a proportionate share of the significant budget cuts. Yet for several reasons (including a buildup in defense expenditures, economic slow-downs, and political resistance to trimming certain programs) intergovernmental aid is likely to be a carefully scrutinized budgetary item through the second half of the 1980s.

Meanwhile, of course, stern challenges face the states and localities. Following the citizens' revolts against the tax structure in many jurisdictions, a number of governments face heavy demand for public services, constrained budgets, lower levels of national assistance, increased responsibilities flowing from some of the newer block grants, and today's more complex administrative arrangements (as described, for instance, in Kettl's essay in Part Four). The pressures are especially serious in jurisdictions suffering from the regional shifts that are part of the dynamics of any interdependent and complex intergovernmental system.

Of course, earlier selections have addressed many of these contemporary issues and controversies, including the role of courts in the system, the plight of the nation's cities, the link between American race relations and the intergovernmental network, and the prominence of computer politics in policy making. Part Five provides a brief and highly selective sampling of some of the issues that have dominated the intergovernmental agenda and are likely to continue to do so at least through the 1980s.

Because of the continuing importance of the Reagan initiatives, several readings in this section focus on intergovernmental developments and issues stimulated by the Reagan presidency.

The first selection, from Reagan's 1982 State of the Union address, constitutes his most explicit statement of his intentions and proposals for the intergovernmental system. As indicated in other selections here, only a few of these proposals have been implemented as of 1985. However, the readings' emphases constitute a fairly clear summary of the Reagan approach.

The essay by Samuel Beer was written not for a scholarly audience, as were many of the readings in this book, but rather for a well-known journal of opinion, *The New Republic.* Beer explicitly challenges the viewpoint of Reagan (in general and as explained in his first inaugural address) and others who hope to "return" the American system to an era in which the United States was less con-sciously a nation, and during which there was significantly less interdependence. Beer places today's disputes in perspective against the sweep of American history and political thought, demonstrating the link between some of the most enduring concerns and the policy issues on the front pages of our newspapers.

The next two pieces focus on the impact of Reagan's new federalism in practice. Richard Nathan, Fred Doolittle, and their associates report some of their summary findings after the first phase of a multiyear study of the fiscal changes enacted in the early 1980s (especially through the monumental Omnibus Budget Reconciliation Act of 1981). Their analysis, supported by the Ford Foundation and the Commonwealth Fund, is based largely on reports from field researchers in 14 states and 40 local governments.

Although Nathan, Doolittle, and the others concentrate on financial impact,

Timothy Conlan's study of the Reagan initiatives extends to other matters. Conlan, a staff member at the Advisory Commission on Intergovernmental Relations, assesses the conflict of Reagan's intergovernmental proposals with his other policy preferences. Conlan argues that the Reagan administration has been far less consistent in and supportive of intergovernmental reform than rhetoric would suggest. His more tentative general conclusion may be even more significant: *all* recent presidents have been less than faithful in practice to the goal of a vital intergovernmental system. The complexity of the pattern, the political costs of reform, and the salience of immediate policy problems temper any efforts to make major changes from the center—that is, from Washington. (The reader may be troubled by an apparent discrepancy: Nathan's study refers to the consolidation of 54 grant programs in the early part of the Reagan administration, while Conlan counts 77. The difference arises from the complexity of the system and different counting methods used by the researchers.)

Both these studies discuss block grants in the 1980s. Part Five also contains two excerpts from a study of the important Community Development Block Grant (CDBG). While earlier excerpts in this book document various aspects of this program, Paul R. Dommel and a team of associates concentrate in detail on the effects of the shift from categoricals to this block grant. The CDBG program began in 1974 to replace several more narrowly focused programs, including model cities and urban renewal. The categoricals had allowed for or required a major federal oversight role and a targeting of resources to relatively small areas within urban centers. As did Nathan's work, this study used field observers to gather details across a number of local jurisdictions representing different regions, population levels, types of government, and degrees of need and experience. Both excerpts document the interplay of national policy factors and local variations. Block grants, according to these analysts, generate opportunities, uncertainties, and a degree of destabilization in the system at various levels. While both Dommel excerpts thus explain some of the political and administrative implications of such a change, the first piece primarily discusses the impact of CDBG prior to the Reagan years. The second selection indicates the significant effects of changing administrations in Washington on a program such as this, even if the basic authorizing legislation remains intact. In late 1984 the CDBG program was reauthorized, with a few changes; however, it is also one of the targets for Reagan's second-term budget reductions. Dommel may be quite correct: this program is likely to be an arena of increased conflict in the late 1980s.

The final readings highlight other policy issues now facing governments in the United States.

The excerpt from a study by the Northeast-Midwest Institute, a bipartisan office providing assistance to the Northeast-Midwest Congressional Coalition, is an example of how regional tensions are generated in today's intergovernmental system. Uneven distribution of energy resources is only one example of an issue that can cause regional conflict. Some analysts argue that the struggles between Sunbelt and Frostbelt are often overstated—and the authors of this selection are hardly disinterested observers; however, regionalism has often been part of intergovernmental relations, and in this era of fiscal stringency the tensions will not likely dissipate.

Finally, recent policy initiatives have led to another development that has been little studied: the "privatization" of governmental activity. Many observers (such as Kettl) have commented on how the execution of numerous intergovernmental programs has been contracted out to community groups and others. But newer policy shifts may stimulate more extensive privatization. A massive amount of the nation's basic infrastructure—bridges, roads, tunnels, subways, and water distribution and treatment systems—will be decaying and in need of replacement during the coming decades. Hard-pressed state and local governments, confronted with federal cutbacks in capital construction programs, have considered privatizing responsibility for construction, operation, and maintenance of some basic capital-intensive services. Increasingly, as well, because of changes in the law, private firms have been entering the business of providing such services. (However, certain alterations in federal tax law could make involvement by private firms less attractive, thereby modifying this trend.) The excerpt here, from a federal report on these developments in the field of wastewater treatment, points out some of the limitations of and unanswered questions concerning privatization.

In numerous policy fields, then, intergovernmental relations will likely remain a prominent item on the nation's agenda. In fact, the issues are more intractable and important now than ever.

34. THE STATE OF THE UNION

Ronald Reagan

... Now that the essentials of that program [the Reagan economic program] are in place, our next major undertaking must be a program—just as bold, just as innovative—to make government again accountable to the people, to make our system of federalism work again.

Our citizens feel they've lost control of even the most basic decisions made about the essential services of government, such as schools, welfare, roads, and even garbage collection. And they're right. A maze of interlocking jurisdictions and levels of government confronts average citizens in trying to solve even the simplest of problems. They don't know where to turn for answers, who to hold accountable, who to praise, who to blame, who to vote for or against. The main reason for this is the overpowering growth of Federal grants-in-aid programs during the past few decades.

In 1960 the Federal Government had 132 categorical grant programs, costing $7 billion. When I took office, there were approximately 500, costing nearly a hundred billion dollars—13 programs for energy, 36 for pollution control, 66 for social services, 90 for education. And here in the Congress, it takes at least 166 committees just to try to keep track of them.

You know and I know that neither the President nor the Congress can properly oversee this jungle of grants-in-aid; indeed, the growth of these grants has led to the distortion in the vital functions of government. As one Democratic Governor put it recently: The National Government should be worrying about "arms control, not potholes."

The growth in these Federal programs has—in the words of one intergovernmental commission—made the Federal Government "more pervasive, more intrusive, more unmanageable, more ineffective and costly, and above all, more unaccountable." Let's solve this problem with a single, bold stroke: the return of some $47 billion in Federal programs to State and local government, together with the means to finance them and a transition period of nearly 10 years to avoid unnecessary disruption.

I will shortly send this Congress a message describing this program. I want to emphasize, however, that its full details will have been worked out only after close consultation with congressional, State, and local officials.

Starting in fiscal 1984, the Federal Government will assume full responsibil-

From the address delivered before a joint session of Congress, January 26, 1982.

ity for the cost of the rapidly growing Medicaid program to go along with its existing responsibility for Medicare. As part of a financially equal swap, the States will simultaneously take full responsibility for Aid to Families with Dependent Children and food stamps. This will make welfare less costly and more responsive to genuine need, because it'll be designed and administered closer to the grassroots and the people it serves.

In 1984 the Federal Government will apply the full proceeds from certain excise taxes to a grassroots trust fund that will belong in fair shares to the 50 States. The total amount flowing into this fund will be $28 billion a year. Over the next 4 years the States can use this money in either of two ways. If they want to continue receiving Federal grants in such areas as transportation, education, and social services, they can use their trust fund money to pay for the grants. Or to the extent they choose to forgo the Federal grant programs, they can use their trust fund money on their own for those or other purposes. There will be a mandatory pass-through of part of these funds to local governments.

By 1988 the States will be in complete control of over 40 Federal grant programs. The trust fund will start to phase out, eventually to disappear, and the excise taxes will be turned over to the States. They can then preserve, lower, or raise taxes on their own and fund and mandate these programs as they see fit.

In a single stroke we will be accomplishing a realignment that will end cumbersome administration and spiraling costs at the Federal level while we ensure these programs will be more responsive to both the people they're meant to help and the people who pay for them.

Hand in hand with this program to strengthen the discretion and flexibility of State and local governments, we're proposing legislation for an experimental effort to improve and develop our depressed urban areas in the 1980's and '90's. This legislation will permit States and localities to apply to the Federal Government for designation as urban enterprise zones. A broad range of special economic incentives in the zones will help attract new business, new jobs, new opportunity to America's inner cities and rural towns. Some will say our mission is to save free enterprise. Well, I say we must free enterprise so that together we can save America.

Some will also say our States and local communities are not up to the challenge of a new and creative partnership. Well, that might have been true 20 years ago before reforms like reapportionment and the Voting Rights Act, the 10-year extension of which I strongly support. It's no longer true today. This administration has faith in State and local governments and the constitutional balance envisioned by the Founding Fathers. We also believe in the integrity, decency and sound good sense of grassroots Americans.

35. THE IDEA OF THE NATION

Samuel H. Beer

I have a difference of opinion with President Reagan. We have all heard of the President's new federalism and his proposals to cut back on the activities of the federal government by reducing or eliminating certain programs and transferring others to the states. He wishes to do this because he finds these activities to be inefficient and wasteful. He also claims that they are improper under the U.S. Constitution—not in the sense that the courts have found them to violate our fundamental law, but in the larger philosophical and historical sense that the present distribution of power between levels of government offends against the true meaning and intent of that document.

In justification of this conclusion, he has relied upon a certain view of the founding of the Republic. In his inaugural address he summarized its essentials when he said: "The federal government did not create the states; the states created the federal government." This allegation of historical fact did not pass without comment. Richard Morris of Columbia took issue with the President, called his view of the historical facts "a hoary myth about the origin of the Union," and went on to summarize the evidence showing that "the United States was created by the people in collectivity, not by the individual states." No less bluntly, Henry Steele Commager of Amherst said the President did not understand the Constitution, which in its own words asserts that it was ordained by "We, the People of the United States," not by the states severally.

We may smile at this exchange between the President and the professors. They are talking about something that happened a long time ago. To be sure, the conflict of ideas between them did inform the most serious crisis of our first century—the grim struggle that culminated in the Civil War. In that conflict, President Reagan's view—the compact theory of the Constitution—was championed by Jefferson Davis, the president of the seceding South. The first Republican President of the United States, on the other hand, espoused the national theory of the Constitution. "The Union," said Abraham Lincoln, "is older than any of the states and, in fact, it created them as States. . . . The Union and not the states separately produced their independence and their liberty. . . . The Union gave each of them whatever of independence and liberty it has."

As stated by President Lincoln, the national idea is a theory that ultimate

From *The New Republic,* July 19 and 26, 1982, pp. 23-29. Reprinted by permission of *The New Republic,* © 1982, The New Republic, Inc.

authority lies in the United States. It identifies the whole people of the nation as the source of the legitimate power of both the federal government and the state governments.

The national idea, however, is not only a theory of authority but also a theory of purpose, a perspective on public policy, a guide to the ends for which power should be used. It invites us to ask ourselves what sort of a people we are, and whether we are a people, and what we wish to make of ourselves as a people. In this sense the national idea is as alive and contentious today as it was when Alexander Hamilton set the course of the first Administration of George Washington.

Like the other founders, Hamilton sought to establish a regime of republican liberty, that is, a system of government which would protect the individual's rights of person and property and which would be founded upon the consent of the governed. He was by no means satisfied with the legal framework produced by the Philadelphia convention. Fearing the states, he would have preferred a much stronger central authority, and, distrusting the common people, he would have set a greater distance between them and the exercise of power. He was less concerned, however, with the legal framework than with the use that would be made of it. He saw in the Constitution not only a regime of liberty but also, and especially, the promise of nationhood.

He understood, moreover, that this promise of nationhood would have to be fulfilled if the regime of liberty itself was to endure. The scale of the country almost daunted him. At Philadelphia, as its chief diarist reported, Hamilton "confessed that he was much discouraged by the amazing extent of the Country in expecting the desired blessings from any general sovereignty that could be substituted." This fear echoed the conventional wisdom of the time. The great Montesquieu had warned that popular government was not suitable for a large and diverse country. If attempted, he predicted that its counsels would be distracted by "a thousand private views" and its extent would provide cover for ambitious men seeking despotic power.

One reply to Montesquieu turned this argument on its head by declaring that such pluralism would be a source of stability. In his famous Tenth Federalist, James Madison argued that the more extensive republic, precisely because of its diversity, would protect popular government by making oppressive combinations less likely. Hamilton did not deny Madison's reasoning, but perceived that something more than a balance of groups would be necessary if the more extensive republic was to escape the disorder that would destroy its liberty.

Hamilton summarized his views in the farewell address he drafted for Washington in 1796. Its theme is the importance of union. But this union does not consist merely in a balance of groups or a consensus of values, and certainly not merely in a strong central government or a common framework of constitutional law. It is rather a condition of the people, uniting them by both sympathy and interest, but above all in "an indissoluble community of interest as *one nation.*"

Hamilton's nationalism did not consist solely in his belief that the Americans were "one people" rather than thirteen separate peoples. The father of the compact theory himself, Thomas Jefferson, at times shared that opinion, to which he gave expression in the Declaration of Independence. The contrast with

Jefferson lay in Hamilton's activism, his belief that this American people must make vigorous use of its central government for the task of nation-building. This difference between the two members of Washington's Cabinet, the great individualist and the great nationalist, achieved classic expression in their conflict over the proposed Bank of the United States. Jefferson feared that the bank would corrupt his cherished agrarian order and discovered no authority for it in the Constitution. Hamilton, believing that a central bank was necessary to sustain public credit, promote economic development, and—in his graphic phrase— "cement the union," found in a broad construction of the "necessary and proper" clause of Article I ample constitutional authorization. Looking back today and recognizing that the words of the Constitution can be fitted into either line of reasoning, we must sigh with relief that President Washington, and in later years the Supreme Court, preferred the Hamiltonian doctrine.

Hamilton was not only a nationalist and centralizer, he was also an elitist. Along with the bank, his first steps to revive and sustain the public credit were the full funding of the federal debt and the federal assumption of the debts incurred by the states during the war of independence. These measures had their fiscal and economic purposes. Their social impact, moreover, favored the fortunes of those members of the propertied classes who had come to hold the federal and state obligations. This result, while fully understood, was incidental to Hamilton's ultimate purpose, which was political. As with the bank, that purpose was to strengthen the newly empowered central government by attracting to it the interests of these influential members of society. Hamilton promoted capitalism, but not because he was a lackey of the capitalist class—indeed, he once wrote to a close friend, "I hate moneying men." His elitism was subservient to his nationalism.

In the same cause he was not only an elitist, but also an integrationist. I use that term expressly because of its current overtones, wishing to suggest Hamilton's perception of how diversity need not always be divisive, but may lead to mutual dependence and union. Here again he broke from Jefferson, who valued homogeneity. Hamilton, on the other hand, planned for active federal intervention to diversify the economy by the development of commerce and industry. His great report on manufactures is at once visionary and far-seeing—"the embryo of modern America," a recent writer terms it.

Hamilton is renowned for his statecraft: for his methods of using the powers of government for economic, political, and social ends. But that emphasis obscures his originality, which consisted in his conceptualization of those ends. His methods were derivative, being taken from the theory and practice of statebuilders of the seventeenth and eighteenth centuries, from Colbert to Pitt. Hamilton used this familiar technology, however, to forward the unprecedented attempt to establish republican government on a continental scale. In his scheme the unities of nationhood would sustain the authority of such a regime. By contrast, those earlier craftsmen of the modern state in Bourbon France or Hohenzollern Prussia or Whig Britain could take for granted the established authority of a monarchic and aristocratic regime. They too had their techniques for enhancing the attachment of the people to the prince. But in America the people were the prince. To enhance their attachment to the ultimate governing power, therefore, meant fortifying the bonds that united them as a people. If the authority of this first nation-state was to suffice for its governance, the purpose of the state could have to become the development of the nation. This was the distinctive Hamiltonian end: to make the nation more of a nation.

The national idea, so engendered, confronted three great crises: the crisis of sectionalism, culminating in the Civil War; the crisis of industrialism, culminating in the Great Depression and the New Deal; and the crisis of racism, which continues to rack our country.

In the course of the struggle with sectionalism, John C. Calhoun defined the issue and threw down the challenge to nationalism when he said: ". . . the very idea of an *American People*, as constituting a single community, is a mere chimera. Such a community never for a single moment existed—neither before nor since the Declaration of Independence." This was a logical deduction from the compact theory, which according to Calhoun's system made of each state a "separate sovereign community."

His leading opponent, Daniel Webster, has been called the first great champion of the national theory of the union. If we are thinking of speech rather than action, that is true, since Hamilton's contribution, although earlier, was in the realm of deeds rather than words. Webster never won the high executive power that he sought, and the cause of union for which he spent himself suffered continual defeat during his lifetime. But the impact on history of words such as his is not to be underestimated. "When finally, after his death, civil war did eventuate," concludes his biographer, "it was Webster's doctrine, from the lips of Abraham Lincoln, which animated the North and made its victory inevitable." Webster gave us not only doctrine, but also imagery and myth. He was not the narrow legalist and materialistic Whig of some critical portraits. And if his oratory is too florid for our taste today, its effect on his audiences was overpowering. "I was never so excited by public speaking before in my life," exclaimed George Ticknor, an otherwise cool Bostonian, after one address. "Three or four times I thought my temples would burst with the gush of blood." Those who heard him, it has been said, "experienced the same delight which they might have received from a performance of *Hamlet* or Beethoven's Fifth Symphony." Poets have been called, "the unacknowledged legislators of the world"; this legislator was the unacknowledged poet of the young Republic.

To say this is to emphasize his style; but what was the substance of his achievement? Historians of political thought usually, and correctly, look first to his memorable debate with Senator Robert Hayne of South Carolina in January of 1830. Echoing Calhoun's deductions from the compact theory, Hayne had stated the doctrine of nullification. This doctrine would deny to the federal judiciary the right to draw the line between federal and state authority, leaving such questions of constitutionality to be decided—subject to various qualifications—by each state itself.

In reply Webster set forth with new boldness the national theory of authority. Asking what was the origin of "this general government," he concluded that the Constitution is not a compact between the states. It was not established by the government of the several states, or by the people of the several states, but by "the people of the United States in the aggregate." In Lincolnian phrases, he called it "the people's Constitution, the people's government, made for the people, made by the people and answerable to the people," and clinched his argument for the dependence of popular government on nationhood with that memorable and sonorous coda, "Liberty and union, one and inseparable, now and forever."

These later passages of his argument have almost monopolized the attention of historians of political thought. Yet it is in an earlier and longer part that he developed the Hamiltonian thrust, looking not to the origin but to the purpose of government. These initial passages of the debate had not focused on the problems of authority and nullification. The question was rather what to do with a great national resource—the public domain, already consisting of hundreds of millions of acres located in the states and territories and owned by the federal government. Large tracts had been used to finance internal improvements, such as roads, canals, and schools, as envisioned by Hamilton and ardently espoused by the previous President, John Quincy Adams.

When Webster defended such uses, citing the longstanding agreement that the public domain was for "the common benefit of all the States," Hayne made a revealing reply. If that was the rule, said he, how could one justify "voting away immense bodies of these lands—for canals in Indiana and Illinois, to the Louisville and Portland Canal, to Kenyon College in Ohio, to Schools for the Deaf and Dumb." "If grants of this character," he continued, "can fairly be considered as made for the common benefit of all the states, it can only be because all the states are interested in the welfare of each—a principle, which, carried to the full extent, destroys all distinction between local and national subjects."

Webster seized the objection and set out to answer it. His task was to show when a resource belonging to the whole country could legitimately be used to support works on "particular roads, particular canals, particular rivers, and particular institutions of education in the West." Calling this question "the real and wide difference in political opinion between the honorable gentleman and myself," he asserted that there was a "common good" distinguishable from "local goods," yet embracing such particular projects.

In these passages the rhetoric is suggestive, but one would like a more specific answer: what *is* the difference between a local and a general good? Suddenly Webster's discourse becomes quite concrete. His approach is to show what the federal government must do by demonstrating what the states cannot do. Using the development of transportation after the peace of 1815 for illustration, Webster shows why a particular project within a state, which also has substantial benefits for other states, will for that very reason probably not be undertaken by the state within which it is located.

"Take the instance of the Delaware breakwater," he said. (This was a large artificial harbor then under federal construction near the mouth of Delaware Bay.) "It will cost several millions of money. Would Pennsylvania ever have constructed it? Certainly never, . . . because it is not for her sole benefit. Would Pennsylvania, New Jersey and Delaware have united to accomplish it at their joint expenses? Certainly not, for the same reason. It could not be done, therefore, but by the general government."

Hayne was right to shrink from the logic of this argument. For its logic does mean that in a rapidly developing economy such as that of America in the eighteenth century, increasing interdependence would bring more and more matters legitimately within the province of the federal government. But logic was not the only aspect of Webster's argument that Hayne was resisting. In the spirit of Hamilton, Webster did perceive the prospect of increasing interdependence and recognized that it could fully realize its promise of wealth and power only with the assistance of the federal government. Moreover, he looked beyond the merely material benefits that such intervention would bring to individuals, classes, and regions toward his grand objective, "the consolidation of the union." This further criterion of the common good could under no circumstances be reconciled with Hayne's "system."

Like Hamilton, Webster sought to make the nation more of a nation. As he conceived this objective, however, he broke from the bleak eighteenth-century realism of Hamilton and turned his imagination toward the vistas of social possibility being opened up by the rising romantic movement of his day. By "consolidation" Webster did not mean merely attachment to the union arising from economic benefits. Indeed, he blamed Hayne for regarding the union "as a mere question of present and temporary expedience; nothing more than a mere matter of profit and loss . . . to be preserved, while it suits local and temporary purposes to preserve it; and to be sundered whenever it shall be found to thwart such purposes."

The language brings to mind the imagery of another romantic nationalist Edmund Burke; in his famous assault upon the French Revolution and social contract theory, he proclaimed that "the state ought not to be considered as nothing better than a partnership agreement in a trade of pepper and coffee, calico or tobacco, or some other such low concern, to be taken up for a little temporary interest, and to be dissolved at the fancy of the parties," but rather as "a partnership in all science; a partnership in all art; a partnership in every virtue, and in all perfection."

A later formulation echoes Burke's words and phrasing even more exactly, as Webster sets forth the organic conception of the nation: "The Union," he said, "is not a temporary partnership of states. It is an association of people, under a constitution of government, uniting their power, joining together their highest interests, cementing their present enjoyments, and blending into one indivisible mass, all their hopes for the future."

Webster articulated this conception most vividly not in Congress or before the Supreme Court, but at public gatherings on patriotic occasions. There the constraints of a professional and adversarial audience upon his imagination were relaxed and his powers as myth-maker released. Consider what some call the finest of his occasional addresses, his speech at the laying of the cornerstone of the Bunker Hill Monument on June 17, 1825. As in his advocacy and in his debates, his theme was the union. What he did, however, was not to make an argument for the union, but to tell a story about it—a story about its past with a lesson for its future.

The plot was simple: how American union foiled the British oppressors in 1775. They had thought to divide and conquer, anticipating that the other colonies would be cowed by the severity of the punishment visited on Massachusetts and that the other seaports would be seduced by the prospect of gain from trade diverted from Boston. "How miserably such reasoners deceived themselves!" exclaimed the orator. "Everywhere the unworthy boon was rejected with scorn. The fortunate occasion was seized, everywhere, to show to the whole world that the Colonies were swayed by no local interest, no partial interest, no selfish interest." In the imagery of Webster, the battle of Bunker Hill was a metaphor of that united people. As Warren, Prescott, Putnam, and Stark had fought side by side; as the four colonies of New England had on that day stood together with "one cause, one country, one heart"; so also "the feeling of resistance . . . possessed the whole American people." So much for Calhoun and his "system."

From this myth of war Webster drew a lesson for peace. "In a day of peace, let us advance the arts of peace and the works of peace. . . . Let us develop the resources of our land, call forth its powers, build up its institutions, and see whether we also, in our day and generation, may not perform something worthy to be remembered." Then he concluded with abrupt and brutal rhetoric: "Let our object be: OUR COUNTRY, OUR WHOLE COUNTRY, AND NOTHING BUT OUR COUNTRY."

With his own matchless sensibility Abraham Lincoln deployed the doctrine and imagery of Webster to animate the North during the Civil War. Lincoln's nationalism, like Webster's, had a positive message for peacetime, and it was this message that set the course of the country's development for the next several generations. Much that he did derived from the original Hamiltonian program, which, long frustrated by the dominance of the compact theory, now burst forth in legislative and executive action. During the war years, not only was slavery given the death blow, but also an integrated program of positive federal involvement was put through in the fields of banking and currency, transportation, the tariff, land grants to homesteaders, and aid to higher education. In the following decades, an enormous expansion of the economy propelled the United States into the age of industrialism, which in due course engendered its typical problems of deprivation, inequality, and class conflict.

A Republican, Theodore Roosevelt, first attempted to cope with these problems in terms of the national idea. Throughout his public career, an associate has written, Roosevelt "kept one steady purpose, the solidarity, the essential unity of our country. . . . All the details of his action, the specific policies he states, arise from his underlying purpose for the Union." Like other Progressives, Roosevelt was disturbed by the rising conflicts between groups and classes and sought to offset them by timely reform. In this sense integration was T.R.'s guiding aim, and he rightly christened his cause "The New Nationalism." Effective advocacy of this cause, however, fell to another Roosevelt a generation later, when the failings of industrialism were raising far greater dangers to the union.

None of the main points in Franklin Roosevelt's famous inaugural of March 4, 1933, can be summarized without reference to the nation. The emergency is national because of "the interdependence of the various elements in, and parts of, the United States." Our purpose must be, first, "the establishment of a sound national economy," and beyond that "the assurance of a rounded and permanent national life." The mode of action must be national, conducted by the federal government and carried out "on a national scale," helped "by national planning." No other thematic term faintly rivals the term "nation" as noun or adjective, in emphasis. Democracy is mentioned only once in Roosevelt's address; liberty, equality, or the individual not at all.

Franklin Roosevelt's nationalism was threefold. First it was a doctrine of federal centralization, and in his Administration, in peace as well as war, the balance of power in the federal system swung sharply toward Washington. Roosevelt called not only for a centralization of government, but also for a nationalization of politics. In these years a new kind of mass politics arose. The old rustic and sectional politics gave way to a new urban and class politics dividing electoral forces on a nationwide basis.

The third aspect of Roosevelt's nationalism was expressed in his policies. Those policies do not make a neat package and include many false starts and failures and ad hoc expedients. Yet in their overall impact one can detect the old purpose of "consolidation of the union."

During the very first phase of the New Deal, based on the National Industrial Recovery Act, this goal was explicit. In its declaration of policy, the act, having declared a "national emergency," called for "cooperative action among trade groups" and "united action of labor and management" under "adequate government sanctions and supervision." Engulfed in red, white, and blue propaganda, the NRA, after a first brief success, failed to achieve that coordinated effort and had virtually collapsed by the time it was declared unconstitutional in 1935. The second New Deal which followed, however, brought about fundamental and lasting changes in the structure of the American government and economy.

The paradox of the second New Deal is that although at the time it was intensely divisive, in the end it enhanced national solidarity. The divisiveness will be readily granted by anyone who remembers the campaign of 1936. The tone was set by Roosevelt's speech accepting the Democratic nomination. In swollen and abrasive hyperbole he promised that, just as 1776 had wiped out "political tyranny," so 1936 would bring "economic tyranny" to an end. The "economic royalist" metaphor that was launched into the political battle by this speech expressed the emerging purpose of the New Deal to create a new balance of power in the economy by means of a series of basic structural reforms. The Wagner Act was the most important and characteristic reform. Utilizing its protections of the right to organize and to bargain collectively, trade unions swept through industry in a massive organizing effort. Despite bitter and sometimes bloody resistance in what can only be called class war, over the years not only practices but also attitudes eventually were altered. The life of the working stiff was never again the same.

The Rooseveltian reforms had two aspects. In their material aspect they brought about a redistribution of power in favor of certain groups. No less important was their symbolic significance as recognition of the full membership of these groups in the national community. Industrial labor and recent immigrants won a degree of acceptance in the national consciousness and in everyday social intercourse that they had not previously enjoyed. In Roosevelt's appointments to the judiciary, Catholics and Jews were recognized as never before. He named the first Italo-American and the first blacks ever appointed to the federal bench. As Joseph Alsop has recently observed, "the essence of his achievement" was that he "included the excluded." And with such high spirits! He once addressed the Daughters of the American Revolution as "Fellow Immigrants!"

Recently I had a letter from a friend who asked: Did not "the new social democracy, which arose with the New Deal, make popular sacrifice, not least for foreign policy, more difficult to obtain?" Just the opposite, I replied. And I went on to recall how during the war it often occurred to me that we were lucky that those sudden, vast demands being put upon the people in the name of national defense had been preceded by a period of radical national reform. An anecdote will illustrate my point. One hot day in the late summer of 1944 while crossing France we stopped to vote by absentee ballot in the Presidential election. "Well, Guthrie," I said to one of the noncoms, "let's line up these men and vote them for Roosevelt." That light-hearted remark was entirely in keeping with the situation. Most of the GIs were from fairly poor families in the Bronx and New Jersey. Politics didn't greatly concern them, but nothing was more natural to them than to vote for the man who had brought WPA, Social Security, and other benefits to their families. Even among the battalion officers I can think of only two who did not vote for Roosevelt—the colonel and a staff officer from New York City named something or other the fourth.

None of these conflicts in nation-building is ever wholly terminated. Sectionalism still flares up from time to time, as between frost belt and sun belt. So also does class struggle. Similarly today, the cleavages among ethnic groups that boiled up with a new bitterness in the 1960s are far from being resolved.

The issue is not just ethnicity, but race. To be sure, ethnic pluralism is a fact—there are said to be ninety-two ethnic groups in the New York area alone— but this broad focus obscures the burning issue, which is the coexistence of blacks and whites in large numbers on both sides. That question of numbers is crucial. In other times and places one can find instances of a small number of one race living in relative peace in a society composed overwhelmingly of the other race. "Tokenism" is viable. But the facts rule out that solution for the United States.

Another option is the model of "separate but equal." In some circumstances this option could be carried out on a decent and democratic basis. It is, for instance, the way the French-speaking citizens of Quebec would like to live in relation to Canada as a whole. And, commonly, Canadians contrast favorably what they call their "mosaic society" with the American "melting pot." But in the present crisis Americans have rejected this option in law and in opinion as segregation. American nationalism demands that diversity be dealt with not by separation, but by integration.

For John F. Kennedy and Lyndon Johnson, the question was, first of all, civil rights. This meant securing for blacks the legal and political rights that had been won for whites in other generations. But the problem of civil rights, which was mainly a problem of the South, merged with the problem of black deprivation, which was especially a problem of northern cities. Johnson's "war on poverty" characterized the main thrust of the Great Society measures which he built on the initiatives of Kennedy. To think of these measures as concerned simply with "the poor" is to miss the point. The actual incidence of poverty meant that their main concern would be with the living conditions and opportunities of blacks, and especially those who populated the decaying areas of the great urban centers swollen by migration from the South to the North during and after World War II.

These programs were based on the recognition that membership in one ethnic group rather than another can make a great difference to your life chances. In trying to make the opportunities somewhat less unequal, they sought to bring the individuals belonging to disadvantaged groups—as was often said— "into the mainstream of American life." The rhetoric of one of Johnson's most impassioned speeches echoes this purpose. Only a few days after a civil rights march led by Martin Luther King had been broken up by state troopers in full view of national television, he introduced the Voting Rights Act of 1965 into Congress. Calling upon the myths of former wars, like other nationalist orators before him, he harked back to Lexington and Concord and to Appomattox in his summons to national effort. "What happened in Selma," he continued, "is part of a larger movement which reaches into every section and state of America. It is the effort of American Negroes to secure for themselves the full blessings of American life. . . ." Then, declaring that "their cause must be our cause too," he closed with solemn echo of the song of the marchers: "*And we shall overcome.*"

Considering where we started from some thirty years ago, our progress has been substantial. Still, few will assert that our statecraft—from poverty programs to affirmative action to busing—has been adequate to the objective. This problem still awaits its Alexander Hamilton. We may take some comfort from the fact that it is continuous with his great work. The Founders confronted the task of founding a nation-state. Our present exercise in nation-building is no less challenging. What we are attempting has never before been attempted by any country at any time. It is to create within a liberal, democratic framework a society in which vast numbers of both black and white people live in free and equal intercourse—political, economic, and social. It is a unique, a stupendous, demand, but the national idea will let us be satisfied with nothing less.

The federal system that confronts Ronald Reagan is the outcome of these three great waves of centralization: the Lincolnian, the Rooseveltian, and the Johnsonian. By means of his new federalism President Reagan seeks radically to decentralize that system. Does the history of the national idea in American politics suggest any criticism or guidance?

I hope, at least, that it does something to undermine the appeal of compact theory rhetoric. Rhetoric is important. Words are the means through which politicians reach the motivations of voters and by which leaders may shape those motivations. Both the compact theory and the national theory touch nerves of the body politic. Each conveys a very different sense of nationhood—or the lack thereof. My theme has been the national theory, which envisions one people, at once sovereign and subject, source of authority and substance of history, asserting, through conflict and in diversity, our unity of origin and of destiny.

Such an image does not yield a rule for allocating functions between levels of government. That is for practical men, assisted no doubt by the policy sciences. But the imagery of the national idea can prepare the minds of practical men to recognize in the facts of our time the call for renewed effort to consolidate the union. The vice of the compact theory is that it obscures this issue, diverts attention from the facts, and muffles the call for action.

Today this issue is real. A destructive pluralism—sectional, economic, and ethnic—disrupts our common life. It is foolish to use the rhetoric of political discourse to divert attention from that fact. I would ask the new federalists not only to give up their diversionary rhetoric, but positively to advocate the national idea. This does not mean they must give up federal reform. A nationalist need not always be a centralizer. For philosophical and for pragmatic reasons he may prefer a less active federal government. The important thing is to keep alive in our speech and our intentions the move toward the consolidation of the union.

People will differ on what and how much needs to be done. The common goal should not be denied. We may need a new federalism. We surely need a new nationalism. I plead with the new federalists: come out from behind that Jeffersonian verbiage, and take up the good old Hamiltonian cause.

36.   THE CONSEQUENCES OF CUTS

Richard P. Nathan, Fred C. Doolittle, and Associates

The most notable achievement of the Reagan administration to date in changing the policies of the U.S. national government has been in the domestic area. Although Congress did not enact all of Reagan's grand design of "swaps" and "turnbacks" for shifting responsibilities and funding sources between the federal and state governments contained in his January 1982 state of the union message, the administration nevertheless has made fundamental changes in domestic policy and in implementing a new federalism.

The most important of these changes came in the administration's first year in office. The Omnibus Budget Reconciliation Act of 1981, which brought about far-reaching budget cuts and policy shifts, stands as the major domestic policy achievement to date of the Reagan administration. In this 1981 legislation, Reagan convinced Congress to take actions that had the following effects:

- Significantly cut domestic spending and trimmed the federal government's role in domestic program areas.
- Substantially changed welfare programs.
- Increased the proportion of federal grant funds that are channeled to the states and reduced the share paid to local units of government.

Each of these three main elements of Reagan's domestic program is discussed briefly below.

Reduced Federal Role

The long period of growth in the scope and cost of the domestic programs of the federal government that began with the New Deal came to an end in Reagan's first year in office. Instead of growth and innovation, the focus of federal grant programs is now on retrenchment. New spending initiatives are out of fashion.

In relative terms, the largest cuts made under Reagan occurred in the programs of greatest interest for this research—namely, grants to states and local governments and various local nonprofit organizations. Federal grants to states and localities declined by $6.6 billion between 1981 and 1982. This is the first time in twenty-five years that there has been a year-to-year decline in the absolute

From *The Consequences of Cuts* (Princeton: Princeton Urban and Regional Research Center, Woodrow Wilson School of Public and International Affairs, Princeton University, 1983), pp. 1-8.

Table 7   Federal Outlays for Grants-in-Aid, 1981-1982 (millions of dollars)

Fiscal year	Total outlays	Grants for payments to individuals	Capital	Operating
1981	94,762	39,934	22,132	32,696
1982	88,194	40,744	20,480	26,970
Dollar change	−6,568	+810	−1,652	−5,726
Percentage change	−6.9	+2.0	−7.5	−17.5

SOURCE: Executive Office of the President, Office of Management and Budget, *Budget of the United States Government, Fiscal Year 1984, Special Analyses* (Washington, D.C.: U.S. Government Printing Office, 1983), table H-7.

level of federal grants-in-aid to state and local governments. Federal grants declined in two of the three major categories shown in Table 7.

Although the largest category in Table 7 (grants for payments to individuals) rose in 1982, this 2 percent increase was well below the increases of the previous five years, which averaged 10 percent per year. Grants for payments to individuals were relatively stable despite the sharp rise in unemployment, and the increase was less than the rate of inflation. This represents a cut in spending below what would otherwise have been expected during the recession. . . .

Welfare Changes

Although welfare programs have not been turned over to the states and localities, as Reagan proposed in 1982, existing federal welfare programs have been fundamentally altered.[1]

There are two main approaches or theories of national welfare policy. One emphasizes providing incentives for poor people to work. This approach would reward people who are trying to make it on their own by permitting them to keep a certain amount of the welfare benefits they would otherwise receive, in addition to their earnings. A second, more conservative, theory of welfare holds that because the welfare system encourages dependence, we should take steps to exclude poor people who are working, or who are able to work, from exposure to the welfare system.

In the 1970s, the first approach to welfare, the incentive approach, was ascendant. It has been embodied in changes in existing programs and in various plans for welfare reform. Both President Nixon's Family Assistance Plan and President Carter's Better Jobs and Income Plan exemplified this approach.

The Reagan administration has changed the nation's course on welfare. The administration has successfully advanced the second, work-oriented theory of welfare. Many of Reagan's ideas and proposals are based on his experience as governor of California, when he proposed reducing assistance to the working poor and requiring able-bodied adults to participate in workfare programs. These initiatives caused widespread controversy, both in the courts and in the political arena. As a result, they tended to fall short of their objectives. To a significant degree, what we are witnessing today is a much more successful effort to advance similar ideas in national policy by a president who had learned from his gubernatorial experience the problems involved in doing so.

Role of the States

A third major element of Reagan's new federalism involves the role of the states. The states are the middlemen in American federalism. At the same time that the national government is reducing its role in domestic affairs, local governments, lobbying groups, and nonprofit organizations are increasingly looking to their state capitals for help.

In addition, the states are being tested by the Reagan administration through the adoption in 1981 of new block grants combining existing grant programs—many of which previously provided federal money directly to local governments or nonprofit organizations—into new and broader programs controlled by the states. The administration consolidated fifty-four previous "categorical" grants with total budget authority of $7.2 billion into block grants in 1981. Seven new block grant programs were created, and two existing block grants were modified. This consolidation process was used to justify reductions in spending of up to 25 percent in several of the new block grants. . . .

Summary of Main Findings

We concentrate . . . on the degree to which, and the ways in which, states and localities have replaced federal funds. This subject has important implications for one of the basic aims of the Reagan presidency—to reduce the size and scope of government in the national economy, particularly in social program areas. It already appears that in these basic terms the Reagan presidency has made notable progress. While we cannot present a final analysis at this time, because changes and state and local adjustments still continue, a summary of the main findings . . . follows:

1. The most pronounced effects of the Reagan program have been on people, especially the working poor. These effects stem from cuts and changes in entitlement grants (AFDC, medicaid, food stamps, and school lunches) as well as in operating grants for such purposes as jobs and job training, compensatory education, and health and social services.

2. For state and local governments, the cuts were not as large as was expected when the 1981 budget reconciliation act was being debated. Local governments, in particular, overestimated the cuts. State and local government officials were more concerned with the deep recession and resulting fiscal problems than with the federal aid cuts in federal fiscal year 1982.

3. Few cuts were replaced with state and local funds. Most federal aid cuts were "ratified," that is, passed along to the recipients of the federally aided benefits and services.

4. Replacement was highest in three states in the sample—Oklahoma, New York, and Massachusetts. They were found to have used new revenues to replace between 10 percent and 25 percent on a new basis of the cuts in federal aid made in fiscal year 1982. Five states—Arizona, Florida, New Jersey, California, and South Dakota—replaced smaller amounts of federal aid, in their case less than 10 percent of the cuts.

5. Six state governments in the sample realized new savings of state funds as a result of the 1982 federal aid cuts. They are Illinois, Mississippi, Missouri, Ohio, Texas, and Washington. Much of the savings in state spending occurred under the AFDC program—not as a result of deliberate state action, but because, as persons were removed from the AFDC rolls, the required state matching contribution was reduced.

6. State governments on the whole were more affected than local governments by the fiscal year 1982 cuts. They have the main responsibility for federally aided entitlement programs, which tended to be the focus of the early effects.

7. The local governments of large cities in the sample that replaced the highest percentages of the cuts were those in Orlando and Los Angeles. Three other cities—Cleveland, Rochester, and Houston—replaced smaller amounts of federal aid cuts. Some cuts affecting large cities were replaced by overlying county governments, others by special districts, and others by the city itself.

8. Suburban and rural governments have been much less affected by federal grants than large cities. Some of the suburban and rural jurisdictions studied experienced increases in federal aid in certain programs in fiscal year 1982. These increases occurred primarily because the new block grants spread out funds to a larger number of jurisdictions than the previous categorical grants, which had been more concentrated on large cities and economically hard-pressed jurisdictions. Suburbs in the inner ring of metropolitan areas, which face social and economic conditions much like older and distressed cities, were much more seriously affected by the cuts than wealthier and less densely populated suburban communities.

9. Rural communities tend to receive very few federal grants. Often the aid they receive is limited to general revenue sharing funds, which were not affected by the reconciliation act. Overlying local governments in rural areas are likely to be more affected—but not greatly affected—by federal grants.

10. States and local governments used various delaying and coping tactics to put off the effects of the fiscal year 1982 cuts. Several states used carryover federal grant funds under the block grant programs established in 1981. For local governments, the changes resulting from the new block grants were smaller than at the state level in 1982, but as carryover funds are used up and states set new priorities, changes will be felt. Local officials often found that deregulation at the federal level under block grants led to new and in some cases more restrictive state regulations.

11. Although on the whole the replacement by state and local governments of the 1982 federal aid cuts was modest, it tended to occur most frequently in well-off places and on the part of governments that are generally liberal. Replacement also tended to be highest under federally aided programs that involve politically popular health and social services and for capital grants. In the case of capital grants, some jurisdictions raised new funds in anticipation of cuts that did not occur.

Many of the effects of the cuts and changes made in fiscal year 1982 are still to be felt. . . .

Notes

1. Reagan's 1982 state of the union address proposed a "swap" whereby the federal government would take over the responsibility for medicaid (the program that provides health and medical assistance to the poor) and the states would take over responsibility for the aid to families with dependent children (AFDC) program, plus the food stamp program. The 1982 address also proposed "turnbacks" of existing federal programs to the states in exchange for the elimination of certain federal excise taxes. The negotiations to draft legislation for this "swap" and "turnback" plan fell apart in late 1982, and the plan as a result was not formally transmitted to Congress.

37. FEDERALISM AND COMPETING VALUES IN THE REAGAN ADMINISTRATION

Timothy J. Conlan

To a remarkable extent, President Reagan has made federalism a central concern in his administration. He speaks frequently of his deep commitment to revitalizing the federal system and of his desire to return government responsibilities to states and localities. As he told a conference of state legislators in 1981, "My administration is committed—heart and soul—to the broad principles of American Federalism." [1] Indeed, Richard Williamson, the President's former assistant for intergovernmental affairs, has argued that federalism rests at the very top of the President's policy agenda—higher than tax or budget cuts and higher than regulatory relief:

> President Ronald Reagan has a dream. His dream is not to cut the bloated federal budget.... His dream is not about tax cuts.... His dream is not about regulatory relief.... Rather, the President's dream is to change how America is governed.... He is seeking a "quiet revolution," a new federalism which is a meaningful American partnership. [2]

The Administration has taken major strides to translate such intentions into tangible results. With the passage of the *Omnibus Reconciliation Act* in 1981, the Administration achieved the consolidation of 77 categorical programs into nine new or substantially revised block grants—almost twice the number that had been enacted in the preceding 15 years. This same legislation also produced the first absolute decline in levels of federal grants to states and localities since the 1950s, dramatically accelerating the slowdown in federal aid expenditures that began in the late 1970s. [3] Similarly, the Reagan Administration gave new impetus to the regulatory reform movement that began in the mid-1970s, becoming the first to make intergovernmental regulation—those requirements that directly or indirectly focus on state and local governments rather than the private sector—a major target of reform. By late 1982, the Administration claimed to have reduced the federal paperwork burden on states and localities by millions of hours and to

Author's Note: I wish to thank David Beam, Cynthia Colella, Robert Dilger, Donald Kettl, Lester Levine, Ann Martino, David Walker, and Margaret Wrightson for their helpful advice on earlier drafts of this article.

A paper prepared for delivery at the Annual Meeting of the American Political Science Association, Washington, D.C., August 30-September 2, 1984. Reprinted with permission of *Publius: The Journal of Federalism* 15 (1985) and the American Political Science Association.

have saved such governments billions of dollars in one-time expenses and annually recurring costs.[4] Finally, and most importantly, the President placed a sweeping New Federalism initiative at the center of his 1982 legislative agenda. Indeed, the Administration's complex proposals to sort-out governmental responsibilities and to turn back multiple programs and revenue sources to the states dominated intergovernmental debates in 1982 and attracted broad public and media attention.

The sources of the President's commitment to federalism are multiple. The small-town values of his childhood and his experiences as Governor of California both contributed to forming it. Moreover, Ronald Reagan possesses the most thoroughly developed and internally coherent political ideology of any President since Woodrow Wilson. His belief in devolution forms an integral part of this ideology and is often reinforced by other aspects of his conservative agenda: lowering federal taxes and domestic expenditures, reducing government interference in the marketplace, eliminating welfare dependency, etc.

In measuring the true depth of Reagan's commitment to strengthening federalism, however, it is instructive to examine his Administration's record on those occasions when the goal of rebalancing federalism, as the President defines it, *conflicts* with other deeply held values. How high does federalism rank on the President's scale of priorities when the truly difficult decisions must be made? When judged by this standard, federalism has not fared nearly as well under this administration. Devolutionary policies elsewhere deemed to be supportive of federalism have repeatedly lost out in the Reagan Administration when they have come in conflict with the sometimes competing goals of reducing the federal budget, deregulating the private sector, and advancing the conservative social agenda. Although a full listing would embody Administration policies and actions across the broad expanse of federal activities, from restricting local regulation of cable TV to preempting state usury laws, some of the most prominent examples include policies: urging reduced appropriations for most block grant programs; opposing the expansion of General Revenue Sharing; supporting national product liability legislation; preempting state laws regulating double-trailer trucks and establishing minimum drinking ages; overriding state objections to increased off-shore oil drilling and expanded use of nuclear power; requiring that states establish workfare programs; and regulating medical care for handicapped infants. Each of these policies is briefly described in the following three sections.

Budgetary Policy and Reagan Federalism

Domestic program budget cuts have long been an integral part of President Reagan's approach to federalism since they help to reduce the relative fiscal profile of the federal government while encouraging greater financial independence among state and local governments. All federal programs are not identical in their intergovernmental effects, however, and an intergovernmentally sensitive program of budget cuts could be expected to affect certain federal grants far more than others. In particular, narrowly prescriptive and intrusive categorical grants might be expected to bear the brunt of federal budget cuts, allowing more flexible programs such as block grants and General Revenue Sharing to be touched more lightly or not at all. Because they can be readily adapted to meet a range of diverse local needs, such programs formed the core of Richard Nixon's New

Federalism agenda, and they have remained a top priority of state and local governments. Although they were also a major policy goal of his Administration, block grants received very different budgetary treatment under Ronald Reagan.

In 1981, the President proposed enacting seven sweeping new block grants intended to consolidate 85 existing federal aid programs for state and local governments. Although most of these proposals were significantly modified by Congress, nine new or substantially revised block grants were created as part of the *Omnibus Reconciliation Act of 1981*, consolidating more federal grant programs in one stroke than all previous block grants combined.

Yet consolidation, with its attendant cuts in application, reporting, and paperwork requirements, was not the only important feature of these legislative changes. The new block grants also embodied large reductions in levels of spending. In his initial block grant proposals, the President had requested reductions averaging almost 25% below fiscal 1981 spending on the programs suggested for merger, far below the modest 10% reductions in federal aid the governors had offered to accept in exchange for broader program authority. In fact, the President recommended block grants for some of the deepest spending cuts of any segment of the federal budget—deeper than total cuts in federal aid— while entitlements and defense actually increased over 1981 spending levels (see Table 8). Although less severe, a similar pattern was evident in the actual block grants enacted in fiscal 1982 (see Table 9).

Table 8 Comparison of Reagan Budget Requests for F.Y. 1982 with Actual F.Y. 1981 Expenditures on Comparable Programs (Budget Authority, in billions)

Program category	F.Y. 1981 expenditures	Reagan F.Y. 1982 request	Percentage change F.Y. 1981-F.Y. 1982
Total Block Grants	18.7	14.8	−21%
New block grant proposals/prior categorical spending	12.8	9.7	−24%
Existing block grants[a]	5.9	5.1	−14%
Total Federal Aid	105.8	86.2	−19%
Major Entitlements[b]	311.4	335.3	+8%
Total Domestic Spending[c]	511.2	546.1	+7%
National Defense	182.4	226.3	+24%
Total Federal Spending	718.4	772.4	+8%

[a] Not including public service employment programs.
[b] Including social security.
[c] Total federal spending minus defense and international affairs.

SOURCE: *Budget of the United States, Budget Appendix,* and *Special Analyses* for appropriate years.

Table 9   Comparison of Actual F.Y. 1982 Expenditures with F.Y. 1981
Expenditures on Comparable Programs

Program category	F.Y. 1981 expenditures	F.Y. 1982 expenditures	Percentage change F.Y. 1981-F.Y. 1982
Total Block Grants	13.6	11.6	−15%
New block grants established/prior categorical programs	7.7	7.1	−8%
Existing block grants[a]	5.9	4.5	−24%
Total Federal Aid	105.8	91.9	−13%
Major Entitlements[b]	311.4	323.7	+4%
Total Domestic Spending[c]	511.2	545.9	+7%
National Defense	182.4	218.7	+20%
Total Federal Spending	718.4	779.9	+9%

[a] Not including public service employment programs.
[b] Including social security.
[c] Total federal spending minus defense and international affairs.
SOURCE: *Budget of the United States, Budget Appendix*, and *Special Analyses* for appropriate years.

This spending approach marked a dramatic shift in federalism strategy from the Nixon and Ford administrations, which demonstrated a consistent willingness to accept higher spending levels for block grant programs as a means of enhancing political support for them in Congress.[5] As a result, much of the political debate about the Reagan block grant proposals focused on their budgetary features rather than on the merits or demerits of grant consolidation. Most liberals in Congress, and even many mayors and governors, viewed the block grant proposals mainly as a Trojan horse for cutting social program budgets. As former DNC executive director Eugene Eidenberg expressed it:

> The driving force behind the Administration's decisions about federalism is primarily a concern with the federal deficit.... At the bottom of the New Federalism is, I believe, the Administration's belief that the best way to cut spending is to eliminate the substantial support that the federal government currently provides for a variety of programs administered by state and local governments.[6]

Though significant, such political concerns about the budgetary impacts of the 1981 block grants were not sufficient to prevent their enactment, principally because the normal patterns of block grant politics in Congress were temporarily overwhelmed by broader political and economic forces. Since that time, however, the Administration has made 23 additional proposals to expand existing block grants or to enact new ones. It succeeded only once, replacing the existing CETA program with the *Job Training Partnership Act* in 1982. In most cases, the Administration advocated further budget reductions in connection with its new consolidation proposals, and rarely did it subsequently signal a willingness to sacrifice these budgetary goals in order to secure block grant enactments. The message to state and local governments remained consistent and clear: The President would continue to support the general goal of grant reform, but—in contrast to alternative objectives like national defense, tuition tax credits, and urban enterprise zones—he would not adjust his fiscal priorities to advance this cause.

A similar situation existed with respect to General Revenue Sharing (GRS). General Revenue Sharing was the crown jewel of Nixon's New Federalism and the single federal program most dear to state and local governments. President Reagan has not shared this affection, however, and holds a far more skeptical view of efforts to harness the federal tax apparatus to provide funds for state and local governments. Accordingly, the President on several occasions has proposed terminating or severely modifying the program or reducing its budget. In 1975 and again in 1982, Governor and later President Reagan advocated folding the GRS program into a broad package of federal program and revenue turnbacks to the states, while in late 1981 he proposed a 12% cut in GRS spending as part of a planned across-the-board reduction in federal domestic expenditures.[7]

Such proposals stirred great concern and significant lobbying by mayors and other local government officials anxious to maintain their favorite program. Their efforts succeeded in obtaining administration agreement to retain the GRS program at existing funding levels when the program was renewed in 1983, but the Administration adamantly opposed increasing the program's funds—even to keep pace with inflation—or to reinstate funding to state governments cut from the program in 1980. Thus, the GRS program continued on uneasily, backed by a presidential commitment that, as one observer put it, "has always seemed lukewarm." [8]

Perhaps the sharpest conflict between the Administration's federalism and budget priorities occurred in the context of the President's 1982 Federalism initiative. Although the President's sweeping initiative served to underscore his extraordinary interest in intergovernmental reform, its ultimate failure to advance beyond discussions with state and local officials was due in large part to the President's unwillingness to make fiscal concessions sufficient to gain gubernatorial backing for the plan.

The structure of the Federalism initiative was complex, but in essence it had two parts: 1) a "swap" component in which the federal government would acquire full financial responsibility for the medicaid program in exchange for state assumption of the AFDC and Food Stamp programs; and 2) a "turnback" component in which the federal government would return to states full responsibility for approximately 40 federal programs, along with a variety of tax resources to pay for them. The Administration claimed that the ultimate fiscal tradeoffs between the federal government and the states would be neutral or even slightly beneficial to states, and it went to great lengths in the initial phases of its program to avoid economic winners and losers among the states. Nevertheless, this fiscal neutrality was premised on having Congress make a series of budget cuts in the affected programs prior to putting the federalism initiative into effect.

Without such cuts, the Congressional Budget Office estimated that the turned back programs would cost $34 billion to continue, rather than the $30 billion estimated by the White House or the $28 billion provided for in the trustfund.[9] Similar budget cuts were anticipated in the AFDC and Food Stamp programs. Such actions tended to reinforce earlier perceptions that the New Federalism was mainly a vehicle for shifting budget cuts to the states, an interpretation seemingly supported by some officials' attempts—most notably David Stockman's—to utilize the Federalism package to help address the federal government's growing deficit problem.[10] As Rich Williamson, the President's assistant for intergovernmental affairs, later acknowledged, such attempts to use the Federalism initiative for short term budgetary gains undercut political support for the proposal:

> In retrospect, the Administration could have taken steps that might have enhanced the prospects of reaching final agreement in sorting out. . . . First, and most importantly, we allowed ourselves as an administration to be trapped into an obsession over short-term budget considerations. The budget was allowed to dominate internal administration machinery and crowd out the Federalism initiative.[11]

Moreover, such actions heightened governors' concerns about the long-term fiscal and policy impacts of the federalism proposal. The Administration argued that, in the long run, states would benefit financially from the swap portion of the initiative because the federalized medicaid program was growing much faster than AFDC and Food Stamps, which were slated for devolution. But many state officials worried that medicaid benefits and eligibility in a nationalized program would be set so low that they would feel compelled to supplement the federal program in their states. Governors were equally concerned with establishing a viable benefit floor in the income maintenance programs. Although the Administration agreed in negotiations to retain federal funding for Food Stamps, it refused to decouple Food Stamp benefits from AFDC payments. As a result, states would confront a federal disincentive to establish higher AFDC allowances because such payments would reduce food stamp benefits to their citizens.

Despite these difficulties, negotiations on the Federalism initiative made substantial progress during early 1982, and some participants believed they came close to an agreement.[12] Agreement with the governors almost certainly could have been achieved if President Reagan had been willing to devote additional federal resources to ease their concerns, just as Nixon had done before him. This would not have guaranteed enactment by Congress, but such fiscal accommodation would have given the plan a fighting chance, securing strong gubernatorial support for the package and undercutting charges that the initiative was merely a cloak for further budget cuts. In the final analysis, however, the President was unwilling to make such adjustments for his federalism initiative. As Williamson observed, he simply could not bring himself to sacrifice his budgetary goals for the sake of federalism:

> As much as the president wanted to strike a deal with the governors, and walk in step with them to Capitol Hill, the philosophical gap proved to be too wide. To move state and local officials, the president needed a bigger carrot than in good faith he felt he could offer.[13]

Deregulation and the New Federalism

Deregulation, like federalism, has been a major policy focus of the Reagan Administration, and in many instances the two goals have tended to complement one another. Although significant regulatory reform initiatives were begun under Presidents Ford and Carter, this Administration was the first to recognize and seek to reduce the distinctive regulatory burdens imposed on state and local governments over the past twenty years. The President's Task Force on Regulatory Relief, the new regulatory review procedures established in OMB, and individual departmental paperwork reduction efforts have all been employed at various times to help redress problems stemming from intergovernmental regulation.

Yet, as in the past, most deregulation efforts in the Reagan Administration continued to focus predominantly on government regulation of the private sector, and most responsible officials continued to frame regulatory issues almost exclusively in such terms. Moreover, it readily became apparent that deregulating the private sector can easily conflict with deregulating states and localities. When it comes to regulation, business generally prefers, not only fewer requirements to more, but uniformity to diversity. Yet states—like the federal government—have become increasingly active regulators in recent years in more and more policy areas—from consumer and environmental protection to occupational and product safety. Often such activity is built upon federal regulatory foundations, as in the case of environmental programs where states are required or strongly encouraged to enforce federal minimum regulatory standards but are permitted to supplement or exceed them.[14] In other cases, states have chosen to develop their own regulatory activities independently. In either case, private industry has sought repeatedly to have the federal government restrict state regulatory activities beyond minimum national standards or to preempt state regulatory authority in a given field entirely. As one business spokesman proclaimed, when it comes to regulation the "national interest cannot be subjected to the parochial interests of localities."[15]

Such concerns have not been ignored by the Reagan Administration. As increasing conflicts have arisen between deregulation and intergovernmental deference, the Administration has sided repeatedly with business interests. According to one recent study of proposed federal preemptions, for example, the Administration "supported moves to take regulatory powers from the states" in nine out of 12 cases studied.[16] Similarly, an analysis of Reagan administration briefs to the Supreme Court concluded that:

> The Administration . . . does not hesitate to give states' rights a back seat. . . . In each instance [examined], the issue, broadly framed, concerned states' rights, and . . . the Administration argued that Federal regulation should prevail. . . . Cynics might suggest that . . . the Administration preference for big business is so strong that it will override conflicting concerns for federalism.[17]

Whatever the merits of this view, several cases involving transportation, energy, and product liability regulation illustrate the conflicts that have arisen in this area.

Product Liability

Reagan administration support for national product liability legislation has been described as a case in which "result oriented reformers [in the administration] won out over those who would have adhered to . . . the [federalist] principles of the framers."[18] Historically, manufacturers' liability for injuries resulting from defective products have been governed by state laws. In recent years, however, mounting concern has been voiced by business spokesmen about the difficulties resulting from differing and often increasingly stringent state laws in this area, and many have called for preemptive federal legislation.

Backed by the Product Liability Alliance—a coalition of over 200 trade and business organizations—legislation to this effect was introduced in Congress in 1982 by Senator Robert Kasten (R-WI). The Kasten bill would supersede state product liability laws but, in order to avoid overloading already crowded federal court dockets, would retain state court jurisdiction to try liability cases and interpret federal law. Thus, in the words of one analyst, the bill "represents a new approach to centralization that borders on state conscription."[19]

Confronted with a difficult choice between the concerns of manufacturing interests and its own federalism proclivities, the Reagan Administration "agonized" for several months over whether to support national product liability legislation. Strongest support for endorsing national legislation came from Commerce Secretary Malcolm Baldrige and from regulatory reform advocates in the Administration. As one administration supporter of preemption wrote, conflicting state liability laws have created "significant burdens on interstate commerce" and "tremendous uncertainty for manufacturers."[20] Others in the Administration, however, including Attorney General William French Smith and Labor Secretary Raymond Donovan, argued that such a position was hardly consistent with the President's recently announced federalism initiative. Moreover, opponents pointed to practical difficulties in the Kasten approach. For example, denying federal courts jurisdiction to resolve likely differences of statutory interpretation by 50 different state judicial systems was hardly a format designed to guarantee uniformity in the product liability domain. Nevertheless, when the issue was put to the President for resolution, "Reagan overrode the objections . . . that endorsement of federal legislation would run counter to the Administration's 'federalism' drive" and agreed to support the preemptive Kasten Bill.[21]

Two for the Road: Federal Regulation of Trucking and Drinking Age Standards

In the last three years, two new and highly visible federal regulations have also been enacted in the transportation field with the support and encouragement of the Reagan Administration. Like several other pioneering intergovernmental regulations enacted in the 1960s and 1970s, both requirements threaten reductions in federal highway aid as levers to force state adoption of federal uniform standards on truck size and a minimum drinking age.

Preemption of varying state restrictions on truck length, width, and weight has long been a goal of the trucking industry, which has sought by this means to expand the use of highly efficient double trailer trucks. Although such trucks were permitted in most areas of the country by 1982, they were still prohibited by

14 states and the District of Columbia because of concerns about their safety and their destructive effects on highways.[22] Against a backdrop of concerns about crumbling infrastructure and deteriorating highway conditions, the Reagan Administration launched an initiative to alter this situation in May, 1982. To help fund additional highway renovation, Secretary of Transportation Drew Lewis proposed increasing the federal gasoline tax and raising truckers' fees, but he combined these new levies with provisions to establish higher, uniform truck size and weight requirements to appease truckers unhappy about the new rates.[23] Under this proposal, states that refused to comply with the new standards would lose Federal highway funds. Shortly after it was announced, however, the President began to back away from the Lewis initiative, primarily because of his uneasiness with the sizable tax increases it contained but also because of opposition expressed by many truckers and several state governments. When the President again endorsed the need for new transportation revenues following the November 1982 elections, a lame duck session of Congress enacted legislation along the lines of Lewis' proposal in the waning days of the 97th Congress.[24]

Having helped write uniform truck standards into law, the Administration pushed preemption to its limits in its subsequent regulations. The Administration decided to permit the large new trucks not only on interstate highways, but on an additional 140,000 miles of primary and access highways—38,000 miles more than state highway departments had designated as suitable for large trucks. This action infuriated officials in many states, including some of those which had long permitted double trailer trucks on their major highways. In response to state criticism, the Federal Highway Administration eventually removed 17,000 miles of roads from its initial designation, but it added another 19,000 miles of highways to its list, and moved to quash outstanding lawsuits against its actions.[25]

In 1984, the Administration reversed an earlier position and, in the face of rapidly spreading popular pressure, endorsed a second major highway-related regulatory expansion. On July 17, 1984 President Reagan signed legislation designed to compel all states to adopt a minimum drinking age of 21 or face re- ductions by 1987 of 10% in Federal highway aid. Initially, the President had been reluctant to support such a heavy handed approach to changing state drinking laws, preferring instead to continue an existing program of incentives for state ac- tions against drunk driving. Indeed, stronger federal action on this issue appeared to be unnecessary, since 20 states had raised their drinking age since 1980 and only eight still permitted alcohol consumption at age 18.[26] Moreover, legislation in this area seemed firmly fixed within the sphere of state responsibilities—a tradition strongly reaffirmed by the wording of the 21st Amendment.

Yet, if raising the drinking age proved to be a popular cause in most state legislatures, it became almost irresistible in Congress. In the wake of emotional publicity and effective lobbying by families victimized by drunk drivers, strong support emerged in Congress for an immediate, uniform approach to the problem. Faced with the prospect that Congress might enact preemptive legislation despite his own misgivings about it, and urged to change his mind by Transportation Secretary Elizabeth Dole, the President reversed his position on June 13, 1984 and came out strongly for federal sanctions to enforce a national drinking age.[27] With this policy reversal, the legislation sailed through Congress and was signed by the President a month later. "The problem is bigger than the individual states," he proclaimed at the signing ceremony. "With the problem so clear-cut and the proven solution at hand, we have no misgiving about this judicious use of Federal power." [28]

Fueling Conflicts Over Energy

Two prominent controversies over energy policy illustrate the conflicts that have arisen when the Administration's goal of expanding domestic energy production has clashed with state environmental policies and concerns. In seeking to accelerate off-shore oil drilling and nuclear power production, the Reagan Administration has faced a series of lawsuits and Congressional action inspired by the affected states. In both cases, long running disputes have ensued as deference to state concerns has been sacrificed to other policy objectives.

Both controversies began early in the Reagan Administration's term. Indeed, one of James Watt's first actions as Secretary of Interior was to open bidding on new off-shore oil and gas drilling leases. By this action, the Administration sought to rapidly expand domestic energy production, to reduce Federal restraints on oil and gas exploration, and to utilize the proceeds from stepped-up sales to diminish federal deficits. But Interior's February 1981 sale of leases off the California coast was quickly challenged by the state in federal court. State officials were concerned about environmental impacts from the sale and successfully challenged the federal government's lack of consultation as required by the *Coastal Zone Management Act of 1972* (CZMA).

Faced with this reversal in the courts but still determined to expand the sale of off-shore leases, the Administration undertook to rewrite the regulations. According to one report, officials from Interior—with the President's support— overcame objections by the Commerce Department to altering the regulations and played a major role in rewriting the rules, even though they were legally under Commerce's jurisdiction.[29] Critics charged that the resulting regulations "virtually eliminate[d] state participation in decisions concerning their coasts" and made "a mockery of Reagan's 'new federalism.' " [30]

Having laid the necessary legal groundwork, Secretary Watt subsequently announced a massive new leasing plan. Again ignoring state objections, the Administration proposed to make a billion additional acres available for gas and oil exploration—40 times more than all the acreage leased during the previous thirty years. Once again several of the affected states went to court in an attempt to block the longterm leasing plan. They also took their case to Congress where, over administration opposition, they won legislative changes that for the first time gave coastal states a portion of the proceeds from federal off-shore lease sales.[31] Congress also limited the sale of leases off the coasts of several of the most severely affected states.[32]

A similar pattern of intergovernmental conflict emerged over administration policies supporting the construction of nuclear power plants. In 1976, the state of California enacted a moratorium on the licensing of new nuclear power plants until an adequate method for disposing of longterm nuclear wastes has been developed. Two California utilities subsequently challenged the state's moratorium in federal court, arguing that state action in this field had been preempted by federal law. Having lost the decision in circuit court in 1982, the utilities appealed the decision to the Supreme Court. Their appeal was supported by the

Reagan administration, which asserted a broad interpretation of federal powers in this field and sought to overturn the moratorium as part of a broader policy of promoting nuclear power.[33] Despite the Administration's arguments, however, the court upheld the ban as an expression of the states' historical function to regulate the economic activities of public utilities.[34]

Nationalizing Currents in Social Policy

Social policy historically has offered fertile terrain for intergovernmental conflict, and the Reagan Administration has not entirely escaped such frictions. Although most fields of social policy traditionally have come under state and local jurisdiction—thus permitting adaptations to the cultural and social diversity of the nation—issues that arise in this arena also tend to evoke fundamental principles and values. This linkage not only tends to make compromise difficult, it also creates strong temptations for policy advocates to seek a single national solution—a temptation that affects conservatives and liberals alike.

Both implicit and explicit tensions between its social policy and federal objectives have arisen in the Reagan Administration. Implicit conflicts have been most evident in education policy. President Reagan generally shares the view of many state and local advocates that the federal role in education has grown unnecessarily large and intrusive and that the federal government should focus its resources more carefully on areas of clear national responsibility, leaving most aspects of education to states and localities. Yet despite the recent flurry of state activity to reform and upgrade educational programs, the President has found it hard to resist using his office as a "bully pulpit" for advocating his own vision of educational reform, legitimizing in the process the basic concept of national strategies for educational improvement. Thus, the President has appointed and called attention to his own reform commission on education, has proposed and lobbied for the passage of tuition tax credit legislation, and, in a move that harkens back to the sputnik era, has proposed new federal legislation for enhancing math and science instruction.

There have also been explicit conflicts between the Administration's social policies and its federalism objectives. Two cases illustrate the tensions in this arena: the Administration's efforts to mandate state-implemented workfare programs for welfare recipients and its attempt to regulate medical care for handicapped infants.

Many governors, economists, and welfare reformers have long urged that funding for the nation's income maintenance programs be nationalized, in order to promote greater equity and rationality in benefit levels. Ronald Reagan has never shared this view, believing instead that welfare programs should be shaped by community standards and carefully monitored by each locality. As he remarked in one 1975 speech: "If there is one area of social policy that should be at the most local level of government possible, it is welfare. It should not be nationalized—it should be localized."[35]

Yet the President also believes that the current welfare system should be trimmed back and that anyone who is able to work should be required to do so. Hence, his administration has sought repeatedly to require that states establish "workfare" programs for able-bodied welfare recipients. It helped get workfare provisions covering AFDC and Food Stamps written into law in 1981, at which time Congress authorized—but did not require—state utilization of three workfare approaches: Community service in compensation for welfare (favored by the Administration), employment supplementation through wage subsidies, and jobs training and services through the existing work incentive program.[36] Since that time, various states have experimented with all three, usually on a small scale, in order to evaluate their costs and effectiveness.

Dissatisfied with the limited progress being made, the Administration has attempted to force faster state action in this area. In an attempt to make the community service approach mandatory, it sought to require that states involve 75% of eligible AFDC and Food Stamps recipients in such programs or face fiscal sanctions for inadequate compliance. To date, however, the states have successfully resisted the imposition of such mandates. Concerned that workfare programs may significantly raise administrative and social service costs and provide few longterm benefits for recipients, they have sought to retain the flexibility necessary to experiment with and refine alternative approaches.

Another case of social policy prescription involved administration efforts to promulgate new and intrusive regulations governing medical care to handicapped infants. Ironically, the Administration has been supportive of efforts to moderate costly regulations mandating handicapped access to local mass transportation systems. But under pressure from right-to-life groups and on the heels of a highly publicized "baby doe" case, the Administration issued interim rules on March 7, 1983 requiring all public and private hospitals receiving federal funds to prominently post information about a federal hotline for reporting suspected cases of discrimination in medical care and to permit federal investigators 24 hour access to hospital records. Failure to comply with these regulations would make hospital personnel liable for lawsuits with civil and criminal penalties and could result in funding cutoffs to the hospital.[37] These rules were promptly attacked by hospital and medical groups as unnecessary and intrusive, and the groups succeeded in blocking the new rules in federal court. Several months later, however, administration lawyers went to court in an unsuccessful attempt to obtain the records of a severely handicapped baby who was not given surgery in a state university hospital in New York.[38] In 1984, however, modified regulations dealing with this problem were issued after extensive consultations with the medical community.

Policy Dilemmas and the Future of Federalism

In all ten cases examined in this paper, the Reagan Administration has been confronted with difficult policy decisions. Forced to choose between policies supportive of its federalist objectives—devolution, enhanced state autonomy, and balanced intergovernmental relationships—and those supportive of other presidential priorities—reducing federal domestic spending, easing regulatory burdens on the private sector, and pursuing conservative social policy objectives—the Administration chose, in each case examined here, a course that was openly or implicitly contrary to its stated intergovernmental goals.

Some of these decisions were reached reluctantly. Some may have been products of bureaucratic momentum or political compromise rather than the products of a calculated strategy. Others can be defended on their merits. Moreover, there have been certain cases that have gone the other way. In 1983, the Department of Transportation declined to preempt local airport noise restrictions despite calls for uniformity from the airline industry.[39] Although it ultimately relented, the Administration long resisted legislative efforts to preempt state pesticide regulations. And, in his federalism package, the President did agree to nationalize funding of the costly Medicaid program in his effort to achieve a comprehensive sorting-out of intergovernmental roles. Nonetheless, when the truly difficult decisions were on the line, the overall thrust of policy by this administration seemed to bear little resemblance to the President's rhetoric on intergovernmental reform.

This pattern of policy making has important implications for understanding the current political status and future prospects of federalism in America. The point is not that Ronald Reagan is less supportive of strengthening federalism than other recent presidents have been. On balance, he has probably been more committed to this end. Nevertheless, President Reagan resembles his more liberal predecessors—perhaps more than either would care to admit—by his willingness to sacrifice federalism whenever it conflicts with his other deeply held policy objectives. With his administration as with others, when opportunities arise to use preemptive national action to advance desired policy goals, the temptation to do so has proven too great to resist. As former Nixon economic aide Herbert Stein has written, "Even conservative governments when in office do not want to limit their own powers." [40]

This tendency appears to be wholly consistent with popular attitudes toward intergovernmental activism. Most Americans continue to pay lip service to the ideals of federalism and decentralization, but they, like the politicians who represent them, appear to be generally unwilling to sacrifice specific policy goals to pursue this ideal. The situation is not unlike the philosophical contradiction in public attitudes discovered by Lloyd Free and Hadley Cantril in 1964. They found that in terms of abstract political values, a majority of Americans could be classified as political conservatives, voicing support for the Jeffersonian ideals of small, decentralized government and reduced public interference in the private sector and in the lives of individuals. Yet, when asked to focus on a series of specific issues of public policy, a substantial majority of the populace could be considered "operational liberals" who favored increased federal government involvement in nearly every aspect of the welfare state.[41]

In a similar way, it appears that virtually no one today—from the public at large to the public interest groups—believes that maintaining the integrity of the federal system is sufficiently important to justify sacrificing other important values to do so. This, of course, does not mean that federalism is irrelevant. Politicians and interest groups continue to use federalist arguments for tactical purposes, as a vehicle to pursue other policy ends, but fewer and fewer people view federalism as a worthwhile end in itself. Although this may be understandable, it is very different from the intellectual and emotional commitment commonly invested in other aspects of the Constitution. There are many passionate defenders of absolute adherence to the guarantees of free speech or to prohibitions on search and seizure, for example, who are willing to endure the dissemination of offensive or unpopular publications or to accept less effective law enforcement to pursue these larger goals. Once common, such tradeoffs on behalf of federalism are now increasingly rare.

Ultimately, this tendency may represent the most fundamental challenge to the federal system. It gives rise, not to a wholesale onslaught on the system or to a wellspring of support for a unitary system, but to a subtle process of erosion that eventually leaves an archaic, sterile structure bound together only by a web of mundane administrative relationships. As Laurence Tribe expressed it:

> No one expects Congress to obliterate the states, at least in one fell swoop. If there is any danger, it lies in the tyranny of small decisions—in the prospect that Congress will nibble away at state sovereignty, bit by bit, until someday essentially nothing remains but a gutted shell.[42]

Perhaps, given advances in communications, world economic integration and greater social homogeneity, this is what the public ultimately prefers. The United States can surely survive without a strong federal system just as many other countries do. But considering the prominent role that federalism was intended to play in our system of government, we ought not allow ourselves to simply slip quietly into a quasi-unitary form of government. We ought to carefully evaluate federalism's real and potential contributions to our political life and weigh the gains and losses resulting from its quiet diminution. We just might find that there is something worth an occasional sacrifice after all.

Notes

1. "First Phase in Revitalizing Federalism," *Alabama Municipal Journal,* September 1981, p. 4
2. Richard S. Williamson, "The Self-Government Balancing Act: A View from the White House," *National Civic Review* 71 (January 1982): 19.
3. ACIR, *Significant Features of Fiscal Federalism* (Washington: Government Printing Office, 1984), pp. 11, 120.
4. Presidential Task Force on Regulatory Relief, *Reagan Administration Achievements In Regulatory Relief for State and Local Government: A Progress Report* (Washington: Presidential Task Force on Regulatory Relief, August 1982), p. i.
5. See Timothy J. Conlan, "Back in Vogue: The Politics of Block Grant Legislation," *Intergovernmental Perspective* 7 (Spring 1981): 11, 12.
6. Eugene Eidenberg, "Federalism: A Democratic View," *American Federalism: A New Partnership for the Republic,* ed. Robert B. Hawkins, Jr. (San Francisco: Institute for Contemporary Studies, 1982), p. 112.
7. For more details on these proposals, see David R. Beam, "New Federalism, Old Realities: The Reagan Administration and Intergovernmental Reform," Paper prepared for the Urban Institute Conference on Governance: The Reagan Era and Beyond, Washington, D.C., 15-16 December 1983.
8. Ibid., p. 30.
9. Timothy J. Conlan and David B. Walker, "Reagan's New Federalism: Design, Debate and Discord," *Intergovernmental Perspective* 8 (Winter 1983): 9.
10. For more on this, see Laurence I. Barrett, *Gambling With History* (Garden City, N.Y.: Doubleday, 1983), pp. 342-343.
11. Richard S. Williamson, "The 1982 New Federalism Negotiations," *Publius* 13 (Spring 1983): 31.

12. "New Federalism: A Special Story," *Governors' Priorities: 1983* (Washington: National Governors' Association, 1983), p. 39.

13. Williamson, "The 1982 New Federalism Negotiations," p. 26.

14. For more details about such "partial preemption" programs, see ACIR, *Regulatory Federalism: Policy, Process, Impact, and Reform*, A-95 (Washington: Government Printing Office, 1984).

15. Quoted in Daniel Gottlieb, "Business Mobilizes as States Begin to Move into the Regulatory Vacuum," *National Journal*, 31 July 1982, p. 1342.

16. Felicity Barringer, "U.S. Preemption: Muscling in on the States," *Washington Post*, 25 October 1982, p. A11.

17. Alan B. Morrison, "N*w Fed*ral*sm Holes," *New York Times*, 20 September 1982, p. A15.

18. Alfred R. Light, "Federalism, *FERC v. Mississippi*, and Product Liability Reform," *Publius* 13 (Spring 1983): 85.

19. Ibid., p. 96.

20. C. Boyden Gray, "Regulation and Federalism," *Yale Journal on Regulation* 1 (1983): 96, 97.

21. Caroline Mayer, "Product Liability Dispute Is Settled," *Washington Post*, 16 July 1982, p. D3.

22. Tom Wicker, "Welcome, Killer Trucks," *New York Times*, 1 November 1982, p. E14.

23. Ernest Holsendolph, "Lewis Offers Plan on Trucks as Exchange for a Tax Rise," *New York Times*, 5 May 1982, p. A20.

24. *1982 Congressional Quarterly Almanac* (Washington: Congressional Quarterly, 1983), p. 317.

25. Barbara Harsha, "DOT Sets Final Routes for Large Trucks," *Nation's Cities Weekly*, 18 June 1984, p. 2.

26. Steven Weisman, "Reagan Signs Bill Tying Aid to Drinking Age," *New York Times*, 18 July 1984, p. A15.

27. Douglas Feaver, "Reagan Now Wants 21 as Drinking Age," *Washington Post*, 14 June 1984, p. A1.

28. Weisman, "Reagan Signs Bill," p. A1.

29. Michael Lerner, "Coastal Mismanagement," *The New Republic*, 14 October 1981, p. 14.

30. Ibid., p. 12.

31. *1982 Congressional Quarterly Almanac*, p. 448.

32. *1983 Congressional Quarterly Almanac*, p. 462.

33. Morrison, "N*w Fed*ral*sm Holes," p. A15.

34. *Pacific Gas and Electric Co. v. State Energy Resources Conservation and Development Commission*, 51 LW 4449.

35. Ronald Reagan, "Conservative Blueprint for the 1970s," reprinted in *Congressional Record*, 94th Cong., 1st Sess., 1975, p. 31186.

36. Linda Demkovich, "The Workfare Ethic," *National Journal*, 26 February 1983, p. 453.

37. *Federal Register* 48 (March 7, 1983), p. 9630.

38. Felicity Barringer, "Decision to Pursue Baby Doe Case Born in Confusion at HHS," *The Washington Post*, 13 December 1983, p. A19.

39. Randy Arndt, "DOT Sees Airport Noise as State, Local Problem," *Nation's Cities Weekly*, 4 April 1983, p. 4.

40. Herbert Stein, "The Reagan Revolt that Wasn't," *Harpers*, February 1984, p. 48. Similarly, William Barnes has argued that: "If the conservatives in Washington choose to govern, I think they will govern on behalf of their constituencies rather than

on behalf of an abstract idea [of deregulation] or technical efficiency. I expect then . . .
that intergovernmental mandates will continue to sprout apace." See William Barnes,
"Cities and Their Regulatory Milieu," Paper prepared for the 1982 Annual Meeting
of the American Political Science Association, Denver, 3 September 1982, p. 22.
41. Lloyd Free and Hadley Cantril, *The Political Beliefs of Americans* (New York: Simon
& Schuster, 1968).
42. Laurence Tribe, *American Constitutional Law* (Mineola, N.Y.: The Foundation
Press, 1978), p. 302.

38. THE BLOCK GRANT PROCESS AND ITS OUTCOMES

Paul R. Dommel and Associates

The Changing Federal Role

. . . Some important features of the CDBG legislation produced greater local discretion [when compared with the previous programs—Ed.]. The most significant changes in urban aid processes under the CDBG were the scrapping of discretionary funding in favor of a formula system; limiting federal review of applications to a seventy-five-day period and establishing a veto-only review procedure; eliminating virtually all federal requirements for the structure of the local decision process; and establishing a local certification process to assure local conformity with a variety of compliance requirements that cut across a wide range of federal grant programs. Substantively, local discretion was given greater scope by establishing a set of federal objectives that were sufficiently broad, ambiguous, and potentially conflicting as to permit considerable room for local as well as federal interpretation; eliminating the explicit target area approach of model cities and urban renewal; and creating a long list of eligible activities to meet physical, economic development, and supporting social service needs. Even the Senate, which took the most aggressive stand on maintaining federal controls, agreed to having the federal hand rest more gently on block grant recipients.

The administrative preference for implementing the block grant was a policy of hands-off—no federal second-guessing of local decisions. Local discretion was strengthened not only by this overarching tenet of the New Federalism but also by the fact that the first local applications had to be submitted to the Department of Housing and Urban Development (HUD) within five months of the start of the program. While this compressed application schedule might have adversely affected local development "planning," it gave local officials broad authority to act quickly on some important issues. By the second year, when the application could be prepared in a more deliberative manner, some of the most important decisions had already been made at the local level, thereby further narrowing the limits of HUD's influence over important early decisions on local processes and programs.

At the local level community development officials perceived a loosening of federal controls over community development decisions in the first year of the

From *Decentralizing Urban Policy* (Washington, D.C.: Brookings Institution, 1982), pp. 223-232, 240-242.

block grant. One official in Chicago noted that "HUD is essentially divorced from dealing with substantive issues," compared with its previous role of "aggressively raising policy issues." A similar assessment was made by a development official in Los Angeles who said: "The current program is light years away from the categorical grant program." In Sioux Falls, South Dakota, an official said: "Never in my eighteen years in the housing field has so much real decisionmaking been possible right at home." These comments, taken from the FNES [field network evaluation study; the method used to gather information for many jurisdictions over several years—Ed.], were reflected more broadly in the data for the forty-four communities of the field study sample (the sample total was sixty-one) that had had significant experience with the programs consolidated into the CDBG. In nearly all these communities, field researchers reported a reduced HUD role in making program decisions. These findings on the direction of HUD influence over program choices were also supported in the case studies. Few of HUD's interventions made a major difference in the local program; the five jurisdictions [highlighted elsewhere in this study] did largely what they chose to do. But some local officials felt that HUD's initial low level of involvement would not last and that as the program matured, the block grant would be subjected to a gradual "recategorization." [1]

Local Decision Processes

A major objective of the New Federalism [that is, Nixon's version—Ed.] in general and of the CDBG in particular was to strengthen general-purpose local governments (1) by giving them more flexibility in the use of federal funds and (2) by reducing the fragmentation of local decisionmaking that had been fostered by categorical programs that sometimes provided aid directly to semiautonomous, special-purpose agencies. The principal beneficiaries were to be elected officials or chief executives chosen by them, such as city managers. But achieving this goal required more than just a national legislative intent; local factors were certain to influence the form and dynamics of the decisionmaking processes that would emerge in the recipient communities.

Managing Conflict

The CDBG program, in ending the target area approach of urban renewal and model cities and creating a broadly defined set of eligible activities, was certain to arouse the appetites of a larger number of constituents in a community than could be readily satisfied by the funds available. It fell to local officials to manage this potential conflict. It would not be possible for local officials to simply say, "The feds want it this way," and thereby shift political costs to the federal level. Thus one of the first tasks of local elected officials was to structure the local CDBG process to maximize their political advantages or minimize political costs. The process in turn would influence the kinds of decisions made and the distribution of benefits among local constituents. Since the CDBG was established by merging several grants, there were existing processes and constituencies in many of the recipient communities. In such cases alteration of the processes and patterns of allocations was likely to create classes of "winners" and "losers," thus making the establishment of a new bargaining arena the crucial, and potentially hazardous, first step in implementing greater local discretion.

The general pattern was that the local chief executive became the principal architect of the local CDBG process. . . .[2] Local legislatures were assured a role since they had to approve an application before its submission to HUD, but their usual role was to accept decisionmaking structures proposed by the executive. A factor giving the executive an advantage was the short time, five months, provided for both organizing the CDBG process and preparing the application for the first year; executive officials were able to move more quickly.

One of the dominant features of the organization of the CDBG decision-making process was the uncertainty caused by the transition from the categorical programs to the block grant. The transition had an unsettling effect on local bureaucrats, interests, and constituencies associated with the predecessor programs. Generally the anxieties afflicted interests associated with the model cities program more than they did those clustered around the urban renewal program. Established as a five-year demonstration grant, model cities had already reached the closing phase in many places, and its future was uncertain; by contrast, urban renewal and neighborhood development programs had become routine functions in many cities. The continuity of the agencies that had been responsible for the earlier programs was at stake, and their leading officials usually became or tried to become key participants in deciding CDBG program priorities and funding. . . .[3]

. . . Urban renewal agencies did better than model cities organizations. By the end of the second year of the block grant only five of twenty-seven model cities agencies still existed, while twenty-three of thirty-seven urban renewal agencies survived as separate organizations.[4] The FNES data, however, also showed that nearly two-thirds of these agencies had little or no influence in CDBG decisions.[5]

Threats to established programs and constituencies represented only part of the turbulence and uncertainty that accompanied the changeover to the block grant. Because the CDBG could potentially operate throughout the community, new constituencies—government agencies, individuals, community groups—could be drawn in. In the case of urban counties, municipalities were likely to become contestants.

The most common type of new claimant was the neighborhood-based organization requesting particular improvements for its area. . . .[6]

The demands of newly activated interests could be expected to generate conflicts that were potentially costly for the local chief executive and other holders of local elective offices. The competition was particularly evident from neighborhoods that had been left out of the earlier programs. Even in machine-controlled Chicago the public release of the draft first-year application was delayed until after the primaries and final mayoral election had been held. In some cities, however, elected executives tended to view the CDBG more as a potential resource than a burden. . . . Whether local executives viewed the CDBG as an opportunity to reward key constituencies or as a potentially costly and unavoidable area of competing demands, it was clear from the start that the program would call for sensitive distributive decisions that needed to be coordinated and continually reviewed at the top.

Another set of new constituents and crucial participants was the established line departments of local government whose jurisdictionwide functions overlapped some of those functions that would normally be part of local CDBG implementation.[7] In many communities the block grant altered the relationship between the local chief executive and the line departments in a way that often concentrated more power in the executive. One aspect of this greater centralization was that the chief executive acquired a broadened coordinating role in order to link the flexible block grant funds with other resources used by these departments or to substitute CDBG money for local tax revenues and thereby avoid tax increases or add to local surpluses. Where the CDBG meant substantially increased federal funds or where the money now came through the chief executives rather than a semiautonomous renewal agency, executives controlled a substantial source of "new" money to be allocated through a process in which many of them were the dominant influence. . . .

Because the line departments were crucial to program execution, however, the political success of the program for local elected officials was tied to successful implementation by the line agencies. Thus a centralized, relatively conflict-free process for making allocation decisions could be unwound by serious flaws in program execution by various operating departments of local government. Local departments of planning, real estate, public works, parks, housing inspection or code enforcement, and human resources played an important role in carrying out those CDBG activities over which they maintained normal responsibility. In addition the speed with which the first-year applications had to be prepared put a premium on data and intelligence available from departmental staff. The departments also could be relied on for "off the shelf" proposals that could be readily acted upon and executed. Thus line departments were usually assured a role in the execution of the CDBG, whether the role was wanted or unwanted, and their support in the enterprise was essential to successful implementation.

Citizen Participation

Formal citizen participation was an important part of local processes, and local executives made use of their discretion to structure that participation in a way they thought would support their broader objective of having a relatively conflict-free process. . . . The CDBG required no formal structures for citizen participation. Under the law it was sufficient that residents be given an opportunity for involvement during the preparation of the CDBG application and that public hearings be held by the local government to allow citizens to express their views of the draft application. HUD's regulations did not go beyond that. The CDBG potentially opened up citizen participation to whole jurisdictions and seemed likely to enhance the leverage of more affluent residents. At the same time, many communities were left with the remnants of earlier participation structures in which lower-income residents had played a prominent part. Local executives could choose under the CDBG to continue them, or replace them with something else.

. . . The formal structures of citizen participation under the CDBG, whether new or carried over intact from the predecessor programs, were less influential than what they replaced because of greater competition from other constituencies. . . .

Communities with citizen participation structures established under the earlier programs generally chose to replace them with a more broadly representative mechanism; only a few communities maintained existing structures.[8] But the form of citizen advisory structures did not determine the degree of citizen influence. As reported in the monitoring studies, "even the most elaborate [citizen participation] structure was not necessarily indicative of substantive or influential citizen activity." [9]

The cases universally note the dominance of local government executive staff in taking the important program initiatives, with the formal citizen advisory bodies taking a subsequent "legitimizing" role. Nor did the frequent regional or neighborhood meetings at which residents could state their priorities and specific proposals turn out to be effective avenues of grass roots influence, except where the staff chose to distill the testimony and translate it into specific initiatives. . . . As a rule, the cases show that testimony was heard at the meetings but not acted upon. . . .

Generally the ability of citizen representatives and community groups to influence program decisions depended less on their formal relation to the technical staff responsible for the preparation of the plans than on their informal access to elected officials. This pattern was most evident in those instances where staff and community positions on a given issue were in conflict and elected officials, called upon to arbitrate the dispute, sided with citizen interests. . . .

This pattern of responsiveness on the part of local elected officials was found in both the cases and the field studies, and it justified to some extent the commitment of reformers at the federal level to supplanting special-purpose agencies with decisionmaking by general-purpose local governments. The success of some important interest groups in CDBG decisionmaking . . . strongly depended on their alignments with elected officials. It should be emphasized, however, that what community representatives were able to influence usually constituted a relatively small portion of an otherwise executive or staff-dominated package of program decisions.

[The authors then tackle the important matter of "Continuity and Change," that is, the extent to which the replacement of categoricals by the block grant actually contributed to different program outcomes. This section is omitted here, but its important theme is that "the new CDBG projects show a good deal of continuity in nature and in form with the categorical programs they replaced. Implicitly this also means that the block grant did not produce a wave of local strategic innovations, and the broader local discretion was applied, at least initially, to adapting familiar programs to local demands and conditions."—Ed.]

Conclusion

The new opportunities opened up by the CDBG tended to evoke a common response. Local executives, seeking to minimize conflict, accommodated new claimants. There is little evidence that development strategies rather than political concerns and distributive benefits were uppermost in their minds at the beginning. Moreover, the apparent effort to incorporate most potential constituencies into the process made the achievement of a development strategy difficult. Put another way, generally the substantive form of the program was left to take shape after process-oriented and political goals had been served.

Local programs showed considerable continuity between the consolidated programs and the block grant. Some communities were committed to continuing or completing activities started under the earlier programs, although the level of the continuing commitment varied among communities. There were also important continuities in the kinds of activities funded, continuities in the sense that, although modified in details, they were conceptually the same kinds of development approaches funded under the earlier programs, most notably neighborhood conservation consisting of housing rehabilitation and related public improvements. Such conceptual continuities and adaptations were found both in communities with prior grant experience and in some communities with no prior experience and where the block grant was new money. . . . However, in some better-off communities local discretion meant significant spending for community-wide public improvements rather than neighborhood revitalization. Usually spending spread beyond the old target neighborhoods into new areas, often needy themselves.

Several reasons appeared to underpin the adoption of neighborhood conservation as the program centerpiece of many communities. First, as already noted, it enabled local officials to expand development into new neighborhoods, making it politically attractive. Second, it was an approach heavily oriented toward the status quo; it left basically undisturbed the racial and socioeconomic mix of a community. A strategy to develop new housing would have been expensive and would have opened up some very sensitive issues concerning the relocation of lower-income groups. Third, the block grant was sufficiently flexible to enable communities to use the money to pay for the wide variety of activities that constituted neighborhood conservation, activities that might otherwise have had to be funded from local tax levies.

There were statutory development objectives, however vaguely defined, that were intended to guide local strategies. Yet at the outset federal officials gave very limited attention to those features of the law that offered the greatest opportunities for intervention, and where they did give close scrutiny to applications, they generally focused on specific activities that in most cases could only marginally influence program strategies. As a result, local discretion was maximized at the outset.

With time, HUD supervision became more feasible and opportunities for scrutinizing local performance developed as activity actually got under way and federal officials carried out the statutory requirement to review and audit local programs. Furthermore, during the second year questions about HUD's administration of the program started to be raised in Congress and the courts. . . . These factors encouraged HUD officials both in Washington and in the field to begin giving closer scrutiny to local applications. HUD field officials began to raise questions about the eligibility of individual activities included in the local application. In most instances HUD ended up going along with the activities, but to get its approval, local officials had to submit written justifications to show how the activities related to the national objectives. In most cases these justifications took the form of creative writing by local CDBG officials, but as a consequence, during the second year local officials began to sense an increasing federal role in substantive issues.[10]

Unhappiness also grew because of the amount of paperwork attached to the program.[11] Several factors accounted for this. The CDBG program gave local officials responsibility for some tasks previously carried out by HUD, such as environmental impact reviews. Local officials were also required to submit a housing assistance plan as part of their CDBG application, a requirement that most felt was a waste of time because there were not nearly enough federal housing funds to reach the housing plan goals. Another source of irritation was the performance report, required in some cases before the first year ended, which local officials found of little or no use. Sometimes, however, the grumblings about red tape came from local officials who had not worked with the earlier grants and had no real basis for comparing the CDBG with its predecessors. In any case red tape is not tantamount to control, and the general feeling among local officials in the transitional years of the CDBG was that they had more control over substantive decisions, even if the reduction of red tape had not lived up to expectations.

To summarize, when decentralized decisionmaking is implemented to maximize local discretion and minimize federal controls, the outcome takes on the character of a crap game—you roll the dice and take your chance in the arena of local politics. Of course, leaving outcomes to chance is itself a value or policy preference.

Notes

1. Quotations and other information in this paragraph are from Paul R. Dommel and others, *Decentralizing Community Development* (U.S. Department of Housing and Urban Development, June 1978), pp. 72-74.
2. Ibid., pp. 141-45; and Richard P. Nathan and others, *Block Grants for Community Development* (U.S. Department of Housing and Urban Development, January 1977), pp. 384-93.
3. Dommel and others, *Decentralizing Community Development*, pp. 128-32.
4. Ibid., pp. 128-29.
5. Nathan and others, *Block Grants for Community Development*, p. 405.
6. Ibid., pp. 455-80; and Dommel and others, *Decentralizing Community Development*, pp. 141-45.
7. Nathan and others, *Block Grants for Community Development*, pp. 398-407; and Dommel and others, *Decentralizing Community Development*, pp. 128-32.
8. Nathan and others, *Block Grants for Community Development*, pp. 432-38.
9. Dommel and others, *Decentralizing Community Development*, p. 147.
10. Ibid., pp. 74-79.
11. Ibid., pp. 79-81.

39. THE EFFECTS OF CHANGING ADMINISTRATIONS

Paul R. Dommel and Associates

Decentralization is the central conflict that has run through the CDBG program since it was first proposed in 1971. It was on this continuing issue of local discretion versus federal controls that the Nixon administration was in disagreement with Congress, that Congress was divided within itself, and that the House of Representatives and recipient communities were at intermittent odds with HUD as the program matured.

At the beginning of the program local officials expected the block grant to make a sharp break with the federal controls and complexities of the categorical system. This expectation had been encouraged generally by the philosophy of the [Nixon] New Federalism and specifically by general revenue sharing (enacted two years before the CDBG), which channeled new funds automatically to state and local governments without requiring an application and with no strings attached. But the CDBG program was different. It was not new money. It was put together by consolidating old programs and thus had left behind a programmatic, bureaucratic, and constituent legacy. Further, unlike general revenue sharing, the CDBG included several generally stated but substantive national policy goals, which if pursued with any aggressiveness at the national level, were likely to bring federal program administrators into conflict with those giving priority to decentralization.

Expectations of decentralization were certain to be disappointed, perhaps progressively as the program aged. In addition to the national objectives the legislation included a variety of compliance requirements covering such matters as environmental impacts, equal opportunity, and construction wages, which were likely to become more important as CDBG projects progressed beyond the initial planning stage. As the program matured, both HUD and Congress raised questions about how the money was being spent, and this brought HUD into matters of local management and organization. In communities that had little experience with federal programs before the CDBG, these avenues for federal influence were certain to be perceived as leading to more rather than less federal intervention.

From *Decentralizing Urban Policy* (Washington, D.C.: Brookings Institution, 1982), pp. 259-264.

The maturation process, program monitoring, and federal concern for national goals began to converge and have an effect as early as the second year of the program. HUD officials in the Ford administration, while still adhering to a hands-off policy, started to take a closer look at the programs of some communities, including in some cases the question of who was benefiting. As indicated by both the field research results and the case studies, local officials began to express concern about the direction of federal program control.

That direction became more clear in the third year of the program when new federal administrators under President Carter adopted a targeting policy to implement national objectives of the legislation. For some communities the policy had little effect, while for others it meant an important shift from communitywide public improvements to the concentration of spending in poorer neighborhoods. Significantly, the change began early in 1977, before any change in the law, through scrutiny of the grant application process, thereby demonstrating the susceptibility of CDBG policies to changes of administration in Washington.

Since the 1980 elections the political context of the CDBG has been marked by fiscal stringency at all levels of government, a new president committed to a greatly reduced federal role, and a more conservative Senate controlled by Republicans. Further, in the House of Representatives, political power is shifting from the Northeast and Midwest to the South and West. These changes have important implications for the CDBG.

Consistent with his general effort to decentralize and deregulate many areas of federal policy, President Reagan proposed and Congress adopted some major changes in the CDBG law in 1981. The most significant change was the elimination of the seventy-five-day period for review and possible veto of the local application; in effect, this made the block grant very similar to the special revenue sharing proposal of President Nixon ten years earlier. In addition, CDBG discretionary grants by HUD to small communities in metropolitan and nonmetropolitan areas were converted to block grants to state governments. The combination of greatly easing the funding requirements for entitlement jurisdictions and folding the discretionary grants into block grants to the states means greatly reduced HUD control over the entire program.

Without waiting for the legislative changes, HUD, under Secretary Samuel R. Pierce, Jr., took steps to reduce the scrutiny of local applications. On May 15, 1981, it instructed its Washington and field staffs to drop certain review procedures. Review of compliance with the benefits provisions of the law was no longer to be based on percentage standards but on a more general effort to detect any obvious failure to comply with the social targeting objective of the law. There were also new guidelines on social services that could open the way to expand the geographic area for such spending; the previous guidelines were intended to confine services primarily to neighborhoods where the CDBG activities were being concentrated. The new guidelines also sought to cut back on the number of conditions attached by HUD officials to approval of local grant applications, such as a condition stipulating the rate of expenditure to be achieved by a community.

For most communities the new guidelines were applicable to the seventh year of the program. They were unlikely to affect the substance of the seventh-year programs, however, since most plans had already cleared the local preparation process. But the changes may serve the symbolic purpose of letting both HUD and local officials know that the rules of the game are once again changing, this time back toward the hands-off policy that characterized the early years of the CDBG. Thus HUD officials of the new administration learned what their predecessors had learned four years earlier—the legislative language of the CDBG is sufficiently broad to allow a new set of policy preferences to be adopted without any change in the law itself.

In part, HUD was able to press its targeting policy under the Carter administration because it had the support of the Senate. Without that Senate support, particularly the backing of Committee Chairman Proxmire, HUD officials might have been less forceful in implementing its policy. Today there is a Republican-controlled, more conservative Senate that tends to support a Republican president who favors decentralization. It remains to be seen how the Republican administration will treat targeting. In the past, targeting under the CDBG was a liberal policy in that it was designed to redistribute resources to lower-income groups even if at the cost of greater federal intervention. Potentially, however, targeting is fiscally conservative because it may provide a rationale for a smaller, cheaper program by giving funds only to the neediest communities for use in defined neighborhoods.

A more-bang-for-the-buck targeting policy would face political difficulty. The first point at which targeting objectives can be achieved is in determining which communities receive a formula grant. The eligibility criteria of the 1974 legislation provided formula grants to a large number of growing, well-off jurisdictions, particularly in the South and the West, including central and suburban cities and urban counties. This grant spreading was partially offset by the change in 1977 to a dual formula that directed a larger share of the money to older, declining communities. In extending the program again in 1980, Congress held off making any further changes in the formula until the new census data could be analyzed, leaving open the possibility of further formula changes in 1983. But the politics that made the 1977 changes possible have been altered by congressional reapportionment. In 1977 the Northeast and the Midwest, whose cities principally benefited from the dual formula, had 225 of the 435 House seats and succeeded in getting the changes; the 1980 census shifted the balance of congressional power to the southern and western regions, which now have 227 seats. This does not offer bright prospects for either cutting out better-off jurisdictions, many of which would be in the South and the West, or further adjusting the formula to give a bigger share to the declining cities, which are concentrated in the Northeast and Midwest. Moreover, formula amendments in 1983 could reverse the direction of the changes made in 1977 since southern and western lawmakers have been unhappy about the dual formula, particularly the use of the pre-1940 housing factor.

Whatever the outcome on interjurisdictional targeting, geographic and social targeting in a community can still be pursued through administrative policy. Since it is likely that block grant money will continue to go to communities that do not really need it, the case can be made that they should be required to use the money to improve conditions in their most needy neighborhoods and for their neediest residents. The application of such clear policy standards in the CDBG, however, runs into the conflict between social and geographic targeting and those objectives not necessarily related to redistributive goals—elimination or prevention of slums and blight and meeting the needs of a particular urgent situation. Aggressive federal application of a targeting policy also runs counter to the central procedural policy of the Reagan administration—less federal control.

The Effects of Fiscal Stringency

Besides the policy preferences of national administrations, the changing fiscal fortunes of government may affect the evolution of the CDBG. The program is likely to shrink along with many other federal aid programs.

The extension of the CDBG in 1977 provided for a 4 percent growth in funds for the fifth and sixth years of the program. In 1980 the legislation was extended for an additional three years with about the same rate of growth. Because of inflation, however, there has been a continual loss in real dollars. Now the nominal dollars are going down also as part of the general reduction in federal intergovernmental aid programs.

. . . Dividing the pie is contentious when the pie is growing. It will be more so as local bureaucracies, nonprofit organizations, and citizen groups compete for fewer CDBG dollars. The more fiscally distressed a city, the greater the contentiousness is likely to be. The local resource base cannot be tapped to make up all of the lost funds. Thus for local officials generally the outlook is for operating in a more hostile bargaining arena. Assuming that there will be less HUD intervention, it will be more difficult for local officials to transfer some of the political costs to the federal level.

The likely competition for funds involves not only CDBG constituents but also constituents of other aid programs, both state and federal. State governments too are cutting spending. Fiscal retrenchment has now gained general acceptance at all levels of government, by officials as well as taxpayers. With the greater local discretion that apparently is being attached to the CDBG, the program may be perceived increasingly as a source of general funds for a variety of non-CDBG activities facing elimination or cutbacks in federal and state assistance. For example, a reduction of funds for social services might mean more pressure on the CDBG for funding such services, despite any desire local officials may have to eliminate such spending from the block grant. Conversely, demands for continued housing rehabilitation and public works spending under CDBG could force greater reductions in social services.

A political escape hatch may exist in the nature of the CDBG. Generally it is a program of small, discrete, and interchangeable activities. It may be possible to trade off these parts to reduce any additional political pressures that may accompany the reduction in funds. A smaller number of houses can be rehabilitated in a given year or fewer streets can be resurfaced; the next year some more juggling can be done among individual activities and neighborhoods. But this also means the potential diluting of the development impact of the CDBG unless the target areas can be reduced to match the shrinking resources. Since many of the neighborhoods brought into the CDBG were lower-income areas left out of the predecessor grants, any geographic shrinkage is likely to cut off some of these neighborhoods.

To conclude, the emerging combination of relaxed federal controls and reduced federal funding may require communities to relearn what the case studies showed was the earliest imperative of the CDBG—the need to manage conflict.

40. THE UNITED AMERICAN EMIRATES: STATE REVENUES FROM NON-RENEWABLE ENERGY RESOURCES

Tom Cochran and J. R. Prestidge

Introduction

National resource policy problems will continue to be among the pivotal issues facing our nation during the 1980s and 1990s. Over the past eight years the U.S. has tried to come to grips with the world liquid fuel crisis through a variety of policy responses. For example, just recently President Reagan removed all price controls on oil, ending the phased decontrol of domestic crude oil prices and producing a substantial adverse domestic economic shock. These kinds of decisions have been forced by a world energy market monopolized by a political entity, the Organization of Petroleum Exporting Countries (OPEC). The new energy economics confronting the nation requires that the market price of energy approximate the replacement value of the consumed product. This painful short-term path is necessary both to avoid a more difficult transition to world prices as domestic sources are exhausted and to encourage domestic production of energy.

The domestic economic repercussions of energy price decontrol are difficult to predict with precision, but it is apparent that the regional effects will be profound. Energy consuming regions of the nation will be faced with the negative consequences of price decontrol. Individuals and firms in these regions will pay higher costs for energy without directly receiving the benefits of production-related economic activity. In a paper published in April 1980, the Northeast-Midwest Institute introduced a second and largely unanticipated result of decontrol: the "windfall" of vastly increased revenues flowing to major oil producing states as a result of ad valorum state energy severance taxes, royalties, and other fees. These revenues will produce surpluses for the governments of energy producing states and an outflow of capital from the energy consuming regions. Energy-poor states, faced with escalating energy prices and unable to benefit directly from the production-related benefits of decontrol, also will find some of their tax revenues declining. This unanticipated result of price decontrol will increase the regional disparity in growth rates that currently is "unbalancing" our national economy.

From *The United American Emirates: State Revenues from Non-Renewable Energy Resources* (Washington, D.C.: Northeast-Midwest Institute, June 1981), pp. 1-6, 15-16.

Background

U.S. Situation

In the United States, a strong contributing factor to new energy tensions will be the extraordinary increase in severance tax and royalty revenues derived from the extraction of oil, gas, and coal during the era of domestic price decontrol.

Table 10 shows that in the U.S. nine states are major exporters of conventional energy commodities. This table ranks states by their exporting position and reveals that there is no "generally accepted" level of severance taxation. Oil is taxed at rates ranging from 12.5 percent to 1.5 percent, gas at rates ranging from 10 percent to zero, and coal at rates ranging from 30 percent to zero.

The revenues derived from the taxation of non-renewable energy resource extraction vary dramatically from state to state, as shown in Table 11.

In several of these states, energy-related royalties and other fees also are very substantial, and adding these revenues to severance tax revenues produces even higher rates of dependence on non-renewable energy for the payment of state government expenses. The reliance upon revenues from energy non-renewables by these states enables them to use other taxes less intensely or not at all (e.g., Texas has no personal or corporate income taxes). . . .

Analysis

. . . Our general concern is that the creation of a kind of "United American Emirates," a group of "superstates" with unprecedented power to beggar their neighbors in the federal system in economic and fiscal terms, will accelerate the

Table 10 Energy Surplus States by Rank[1] and Tax Rates (Percent of Value) [2]—1978

Exporting rank[1]	Oil percent	Gas percent	Coal percent
1. Louisiana	12.5	3.5[2]	0.2
2. Wyoming	4.0	4.0	10.5
3. New Mexico	7.0	5.8	8.4
4. Kentucky	1.5	n/a	4.5
5. Alaska	12.25	10.0	n/a
6. Oklahoma	7.0	7.0	0.3
7. West Virginia	4.35	8.63	3.5
8. Montana	2.1-2.65	2.65	30.5
9. Texas	4.6	7.5	n/a

[1] Chase Econometrics, cited by Richard Corrigan and Rochelle L. Stanfield, "Rising Energy Prices— What's Good for Some States Is Bad for Others," *National Journal*, March 22, 1980, p. 469.
[2] Calculated by Harley T. Duncan, Staff Associate, National Governors Association, March 6, 1980. From U.S. Department of Commerce, Bureau of the Census, *State Government Tax Collections in 1978*, January 1979.

Table 11   Severance Taxes as a Percentage of State Revenues—1978

State	Percent
Louisiana	23.55
Wyoming	22.81
New Mexico	19.16
Kentucky	6.96
Alaska	19.13
Oklahoma	17.51
West Virginia	13.99*
Montana	11.95
Texas	17.68

SOURCES: Calculated from U.S. Department of Commerce, Bureau of the Census, *State Government Tax Collections in 1978*, January 1979, and *state-supplied data.

decline of energy-poor regions and thwart efforts to revitalize the troubled economic structure of the older industrial states.

We have identified at least three separate problem areas of a more specific nature.

- First, these enormous new revenues almost inevitably will lead to powerful new location incentives for people and businesses, accelerating the massive shifts of population to these areas already taking place. In the next several years, one can expect other states to follow Alaska's lead and cut or eliminate more traditional taxes, making them even more attractive places in which to relocate. States that don't have the natural resources to tax won't be able to compete with such tactics, and will lose out.

- A second reason for concern is that several major federal funding formulas will be distorted. Under these formulas, the energy rich states actually could receive larger shares of federal funds—or continue receiving the same favorable shares they now get—even though their need for these funds will be much smaller because of the newfound wealth they can tap.

- Third, there is a strong possibility that a dangerously divisive tax warfare will break out, with each state striving to tax a precious commodity just to preserve its competitive position. In fact, this warfare may have begun already; Montana's state legislature passed its huge coal tax increase after strong debate language about the need to keep up with Texas in the severance tax business. In the mid-1970s, Pennsylvania contemplated a severance tax on electricity generated at mine-mouth plants and exported to other states. Connecticut and New York have passed special taxes on oil companies, although these taxes are under question in the courts. New Jersey, Pennsylvania, and other states are looking into a tax on oil refineries. Oregon has a tax on trees, and there is nothing to prevent the imposition of state taxes on other crops. It should not surprise us if agricultural states retaliate against other severance taxes by putting their own taxes on grains used in alcohol fuel production, or perhaps all grains.

In any such warfare, the Northeast and Midwest will be heavy losers—and so, ultimately, will the entire nation, as its states and perhaps its local governments impose heavy new tax burdens on certain sectors and become dangerously reliant on these narrow and probably regressive tax bases. . . .

41. PRIVATIZATION OF MUNICIPAL WASTEWATER TREATMENT

The Office of Water, U.S. Environmental Protection Agency

The Evolution of the Construction Grants Program

Representing one of the nation's largest Federal infrastructure development programs, for the past decade EPA's grant program for wastewater treatment plant construction has been the centerpiece of municipal efforts to meet the nation's ambitious water quality goals. In 1972, the designers of the Federal Water Pollution Control Act Amendments (P.L. 92-500) believed that to meet the stringent secondary treatment standards newly mandated by the Act, communities needed a substantial boost over the past in Federal aid. Over the next 12 years, Congress appropriated over $40 billion to assist municipalities in constructing wastewater treatment plants in a timely fashion. This large input of Federal dollars, and cooperation of State and local governments, is producing significant water quality improvements across the country.

By providing large amounts of Federal aid and an expanded Federal share (75 percent of eligible project costs), the 1972 Act spelled out a strong initial Federal role under the new municipal wastewater treatment plant construction program. However, its sponsors viewed the Federal intervention as a temporary fix. Ultimately, they underscored, construction of needed facilities was and should be a State and local responsibility. Moreover, the Act noted that significant contributions to plant construction had been made with State and local resources prior to 1972. It expressed the hope that the same level of commitment would be made under the expanded program, and that localities could continue to provide for the full costs of adequate operations and maintenance. Highlighting the short-term nature of the Federal involvement and perhaps the sponsors' optimistic estimate of the magnitude of the problem, the 1972 Act authorized $18 billion of contract authority for FY 1973-1975 for meeting an estimated "backlog" of $24 billion (at a 75% Federal share).

The 1970s saw much progress and some frustrations for the municipal wastewater treatment program. While the Federal government did not face the huge budget deficits of today and continued to fund the program at a high rate ($4.5 billion in FY 1978), municipal compliance goals were often not met.

From *Study of the Future Federal Role in Municipal Wastewater Treatment, Draft Report* (October 1984), pp. 1-1 - 1-2, 4-8 - 4-11.

Projects were sometimes delayed as grant procedures burgeoned and communities waited in line for funds, and EPA's Needs Survey continued to report large municipal demands. In an effort to devise workable alternatives, the 1977 Amendments clarified Congressional policy that States have the major responsibility to manage and implement the program. On the theory that States are more appropriate managers of the program because they are close to the problems, the Amendments provided for the creation of State program delegation and greater administrative flexibility.

By 1980, however, more far-reaching reforms in the program began to be discussed. These reforms, aimed at putting the municipal wastewater treatment construction program back on course, led to the 1981 Amendments to the Clean Water Act (P.L. 97-117). These major amendments signaled the sense of Congress and the Administration that EPA's Construction Grant Program was in a period of major transition back to the original intent of P.L. 92-500—ultimate State and local self-sufficiency in the construction, operation and maintenance, rehabilitation and replacement, and expansion of municipal wastewater treatment facilities.

The transition envisioned by the 1981 Amendments was a gradual movement from the prevailing high level of Federal financial involvement to a program focused on increased State and local independence in fulfilling the full range of obligations entailed by the Clean Water Act. The long-range implications of these Amendments were significant. Funding eligibilities were limited so as to reduce the growing level of Federal financial commitment. Specifically, there was a discontinuation of Federal grants for planning and design activities (except under certain conditions), and a reduction in the number of eligible funding categories. By focusing the grants program on existing rather than future needs, Congress limited the Federal role to completing construction of facilities needed to treat wastewater discharges as prescribed by the standards. Moreover, the 1981 Amendments specified that the Federal share of eligible projects, with some limited exceptions, would drop to 55% from 75% beginning in FY 1985. Finally, Congressional appropriations were dropped from their earlier highs to $2.4 billion per year from FY 1982-1985. . . .

Assessment/Availability of Private Sector Financing

In response to reduced Federal funding, rising interest rates, and growing difficulties in obtaining conventional financing, municipalities have become more and more interested in attracting private sector investment in wastewater treatment facilities. The private sector also is enthusiastic about investing in wastewater treatment facilities.

While as a concept wastewater privatization is new, as a financial transaction private sector financing, ownership, construction and/or operation of traditionally public utilities is well established. For decades, hundreds of communities have obtained their drinking water and other essential government services from private sector owned and operated sources. More recently, a number of resource recovery plants—totalling over $500 million in the past year alone— have been built and operated on a "turnkey" basis by the private sector.

The attractiveness of the concept lies in the use of accelerated depreciation of a facility and its equipment, the availability of investment tax credits, and the use of tax exempt industrial bonds—all of which may be used in wastewater treatment facilities if the transaction is properly structured. Although altered in some respects, the Deficit Reduction Act of 1984 reconfirmed the use of these tax benefits. Thus, privatization activity may be further stimulated on the part of both municipalities and the private sector.

While the private sector can not finance all wastewater treatment needs, any contribution can be significant and lessen the financial burden faced by municipalities. There may be substantial cost savings and programmatic efficiencies which can be realized if proper financing methods and overall transactional structure are employed. These are explored below.

Privatization Techniques and Transactions May Be Viable for Financing Wastewater Treatment Facilities

There are numerous privatization approaches and variations: with or without equity or direct ownership, industrial development revenue or pollution controls bonds, etc. While each approach has its own particular characteristics, they all have one common element—they rely on the tax-exempt revenue bond market to raise the debt necessary for construction (from 75% to 100% of project cost, depending upon whether the equity investment is part of the transaction). As experienced with solid waste and other utility operations, wastewater privatization projects can be financed on their own merits if they are economically viable and if they incorporate adequate security mechanisms. Wastewater issues could be particularly attractive to bond buyers because, in addition to the legal and financial security aspects, the systems are literally in the ground, with users dependent on continued performance for the maintenance of public health. This creates the presumption that in the event of problems, technical or financial, all necessary remedial actions will be taken to keep a system operating.

Typically, the parties to a privatization project include the owners, the operator of the facility, the engineer who plans and designs the facility, the builder who constructs the facility, the municipality which can lease the site to the owner and receives the services derived from the facility, an issuer of any tax-exempt debt, and an investment banker that raises the equity and underwrites the debt. Many of these parties will need legal, tax, and financial forecasting services.

Not every privatization transaction can be structured to capture the benefits of tax-exempt industrial development bonds, accelerated depreciation and the investment tax credit. A transaction that can provide such benefits to the private sector is a service contract agreement with a municipality, where any combination of private sector firms finance, own, and operate the treatment facility. The firms are eligible to realize all of the available tax benefits. The private sector obtains the benefits of accelerated depreciation and the investment tax credit by using a service contract under which the private owners also operate the facility. In addition, the private sector may finance up to 80% of the facility costs with tax exempt development bonds. The municipality may enter into a long-term lease agreement for the site and build in other projections.

The service contract agreement method is now being used extensively for resource recovery projects and can be readily transferable to the financing of wastewater treatment. With wastewater treatment facilities, the opportunity is present for the private sector to pass some of the lower costs of this arrangement back to the municipality through a lower service fee which would be negotiated with a municipality.

Only a few examples of privatization of municipal wastewater treatment systems currently exist. These include:

- The initiation of construction for the first stage of a plant in Chandler, AZ.
- The completion of the financial planning for a WWT plant in Norco, CA. [Since the publication of this report, the City of Norco has decided not to use privatization to construct its sewage treatment facilities—Ed.]
- The financing of a $100 million interceptor in Denver, CO.
- Bank ownership of a new interceptor in Missoula, MT.

However, there are a number of communities that are considering privatization and have published "requests for qualifications for privatization," including Salt Lake City in conjunction with Utah. Auburn, Alabama, and Orlando, Florida, and possibly other cities, have already accepted construction bids.

Privatization May Offer Some Programmatic Efficiencies

Privatization may offer many advantages to municipalities. By minimizing Federal and State involvement in local affairs, privatization allows communities greater operational flexibility, thus re-establishing local responsibility for projects and making projects more responsive to local needs specifically.

- *Reduction in User Fees.* The economics of privatization may be able to combine construction savings and tax benefits into lower user fees. A properly structured transaction may be a cost-effective alternative to local communities, as measured by the user fees necessary to establish, operate and maintain a self-sustaining facility. The user fees under an acceptable privatization should be lower than under 100% local funding for the same facility.
- *Construction Efficiencies.* Privatization proponents have argued that construction efficiencies associated with private financing transactions can lead to lowered overall costs for construction, a reduction in construction time, and greater flexibility in sizing. Such cost savings would presumably be gained by reducing delays in construction caused by Federal grant regulations for the planning, design and construction of facilities and avoiding Federal procurement laws and regulations under private financing transactions. In addition, privatization might be able to focus more closely on flow-matching the sizing of a facility to current needs, modular designs, and sequential investments to meet future needs. Proponents have argued that decreases of 20% to 40% in the capital costs of a facility can be realized.
- *Operating Efficiencies.* Contract operations by the private sector may make sense . . . if a community cannot attract and retain the necessary talents to operate a treatment facility in compliance with discharge permit standards. In other cases, through assumed economies of scale, a private operator may be able to operate a facility at a cost less than the public operating mode, even considering a profit allowance. Centralized administration, centralized maintenance, bulk ordering of chemicals and supplies, sharing key personnel among multiple facilities, etc., could contribute to these economies.

Complexity and Federal Requirements May Limit
the Use of Privatization Transactions

While privatization is a promising concept for new community development and should be considered and further explored, a note of caution is that privatization by its very nature is complex, involving numerous parties and unique relationships. It is expensive and time consuming for all parties concerned to participate in the conception or execution of a privatization project. There are numerous complex technical, financial and legal considerations that must be addressed. Considerable critical analysis is required to determine the conditions under which it is a prudent mechanism for providing the public with wastewater treatment at a reasonable cost. Communities will need to acquire expertise in reviewing financial arrangements and contracts and develop oversight provisions and flexibility.

For treatment facilities that have received Federal financial assistance, and are dependent on private funding for the expansion or upgrading of facilities, the Office of Management and Budget (OMB) Circular A-102 must be observed. This circular, in effect, prohibits the title to Federally assisted facilities from being transferred to the private sector. However, privately owned components that are distinct entities in the treatment process, such as a sludge handling unit, may be added to facilities without losing their private identity.

There are other potential hindrances to privatization transactions.

- State or local government procurement rules may effectively prohibit privatization. For example, State or local laws or ordinances may prohibit a negotiated contract and require competitive bidding. Competitive bidding may not be the most feasible way to effect the arrangement.
- Privatization may concentrate on the immediate need for sewage treatment facilities and neglect future needs since the greatest tax benefits would be realized during the initial five year period. Thus, privatization may focus on capital investment and ignore the need to adequately finance operation and maintenance costs.
- Public Utility Commissions may require approval of user fees and fee increases, increasing the complexities associated with privatization initiatives.
- The fact that equipment intensive projects are subject to the greatest financial returns may influence the design of the plant. The greater the depreciable amount, the greater the return on the investment to the private investor. For example, some technologies are more equipment intensive than others. A biological treatment plant will have a larger depreciable cost than a land-based lagoon system as the land is not subject to depreciation.
- Small communities may be less able to take advantage of privatization. Land oriented treatment projects may not make an attractive investment for the private sector. Also, the small community may not be rated credit worthy enough to be a partner in this type of joint public/private endeavor.
- Private owners need protection from price controls, changes in discharge requirements, or other forms of regulation that might force them to accept

less than a fair rate of return. This could cause negative effects on the owner's ability to provide adequate service.

- Existing labor contracts between municipalities and unions could preclude the transfer of operation and maintenance of the plant to the private sector.

Part Five

Review Questions

1. What values does Ronald Reagan seem to be pursuing in his intergovernmental reforms? Compare these values with those of the founders, as discussed in Part One. Is Reagan's effort a departure from American intergovernmental tradition, or a return to it? Can you make use of Beer's analysis in your assessment?

2. Imagine that you are Reagan's special assistant for intergovernmental relations. Advise him on the political, fiscal, and administrative implications of his early proposals.

3. Reagan asks you, his special assistant for intergovernmental relations, for an assessment of his performance in his first term. What do you say? In your answer consider using the material in Conlan's study.

4. Compare Reagan's claims for federalism with Riker's critique in Part One, and explain how the evidence in this book supports one perspective or the other. Are there data to bolster both sets of claims?

5. What are the ideas of Webster, Lincoln, the Roosevelts, and Lyndon Johnson about the concept of the American nation (see Beer's essay)? How, if at all, do they bear on today's intergovernmental issues? Explain Beer's comment that "a nationalist need not always be a centralizer."

6. Describe an imaginary discussion between Ronald Reagan and Samuel Beer. How would Reagan respond to Beer's argument about the appropriate role for the national government in American life? Include an analysis of the issues of race relations, heightened regional tensions, and the new privatization. Make use of your analysis in the preceding question in framing your response here.

7. How are the findings summarized by Nathan and others related to Beer's concerns about poverty and race relations? Do the Nathan findings support the importance of the themes of intergovernmental complexity and interdependence, or does the study imply that such themes may have been exaggerated? Explain your answer.

8. Referring to Conlan's analysis, argue that the federal government's budget problems may constitute both a stimulus and an impediment to intergovernmental reform.

9. How does Conlan's study of what happened to Reagan's efforts during his first term demonstrate the importance of complexity and interdependence in the system? If you think it does not so demonstrate, explain why not. Use examples.

10. It is sometimes said that American conservatives desire to shift power to state and local governments. Use evidence from Reagan's first term to make a case that conservatives like Reagan can find themselves resistant to such shifts precisely because of certain elements in their perspective.

11. What does the Reagan experience in intergovernmental matters thus far suggest about our ability to sort out national from state and local responsibilities?

12. How do you expect the political and administrative impacts of block grant adoption, as described by Dommel and his associates, to be affected by major cutbacks proposed by Reagan during his second term?

13. Does a shift to block grants (and therefore greater local influence) seem to mean greater citizen influence? Explain your answer.

14. Dommel's study of CDBG argues that "when decentralized decision-making is implemented to maximize local discretion and minimize federal controls, the outcome takes on the character of a crap game. . . ." What is meant by this statement? Does the statement necessarily constitute an indictment of block grants? Why or why not?

15. Given the current shifts of population and political power toward the South and West, what results do you expect from efforts to target federal aid to needy jurisdictions? Why?

16. What problems and policy issues are raised by the possibility of privatizing wastewater treatment?

17. Is privatization an option for reducing the levels of complexity and interdependence in the intergovernmental system? Why or why not?

AMERICAN INTERGOVERNMENTAL RELATIONS: CONCLUDING THOUGHTS

Today a formidable set of intergovernmental issues and problems stretches before us, yet it is important to realize that both the achievements and dilemmas of the contemporary scene are bound up with the choices made at the nation's founding two centuries ago. The framers of the American federal system made some conscious decisions about the structure and relationships within and among American governments. To protect freedom, to stimulate diversity, and to foster civic virtues like active citizen involvement in the affairs of state, the founders established a basic framework that would facilitate, indeed stimulate, dynamic, vigorous intergovernmental relations. These early Americans were under few illusions about the character of the emerging nation. They realized that structuring the basic powers and relationships of the governments would not eliminate disputes or establish some neat, orderly, static pattern. Nor, however, would an absence of central authority serve legitimate interests. Instead, the founders crafted a system designed to provide a forum for the inevitable conflict and bargaining in the large and diverse new nation.

While the intergovernmental system has changed tremendously from the earliest decades, the basic framework created by the founders continues to play a part in the perpetuation of vigorous intergovernmental relations. Historical and contemporary imperatives toward cooperation across governmental lines notwithstanding, the framework has allowed and even encouraged the rise of today's pattern, one of conflict and bargaining in a complex and interdependent system.

The enormous complexity of a system composed of over 80,000 governments suggests that it is impossible to have enough data to operate within it in a consistently rational fashion. There are too many other parties and sets of relationships, many of them highly dynamic. And in recent decades this complexity has been further increased by the addition of new elements in the makeup of the intergovernmental "mix": intergovernmental coordinating bodies, the PIGs, an active court system, regionally based lobbying groups and new regional tensions, more complicated fiscal instruments, a growing array of regulatory mechanisms, and the involvement of private parties in many intergovernmental bargains. A result of this complexity is that efforts to orchestrate dramatic change by any party, no matter how important in the pattern, are bound to fall short of expectations and may well complicate matters still further. We have seen how the efforts by one level of government to exercise control at another, the redesign of the federal government's grant structure, and the trimming of federal aid may produce unintended consequences.

A second important characteristic of the system—interdependence—is demonstrated by the sharing of power, even within functions. Action by one unit requires support or at least acquiescence on the part of others, and participants can often halt or delay action they oppose. Thus, intergovernmental politics and administration do not fit a hierarchical, command-and-control pattern. Instead, different governments need each other, and bargaining—even if not among or between equals—is the norm.

High levels of both complexity and interdependence in the system help to explain one of the most persistent dilemmas in the American network: the tension between generalists (whose responsibility is to a geographic area or general government) and specialists (who focus on specific functions that are parts of modern governments, perhaps at multiple levels). Frequently, efforts to modify the intergovernmental system are aimed at shifting the balance between these two groups or emphases. Reagan's new federalism initiatives, for instance, are motivated in part by a desire to take power from the specialists, with their influence over and preference for categoricals, and give general-purpose executives more clout (for example, by increasing the influence of governors over the use of programs like the Community Development Block Grant). Indeed, the relative influence of these two groups *can* be altered at the margin. However, the perseverance of the tension is no accident, because the conflict derives from the fundamental characteristics of the system: its complexity generates a continuing need for specialists at all levels and its interdependence drives an imperative for coordination that generalists can facilitate.

The fiscal aspects of the intergovernmental system also reflect the characteristics of complexity and interdependence. Grants emerge from as well as create bargaining contests across levels of government and between specialist and generalist. Although the politics and administration of the various fiscal instruments can differ greatly, the grant system in general appears resistant to change, as we have seen in efforts to shrink the federal role or to reassign program responsibilities. This apparent intransigence to significant redesign—as with the many other difficulties with the system—does not stem exclusively or primarily from intrusion, domination, or ill will on the part of one level of government in dealing with the others. Rather, the complexity and interdependence of the system mitigate against disentangling the several knots that hold the parts of the system together.

This observation is particularly timely today. In the past (for instance, in the 1950s), efforts to induce reform in the direction of Reagan administration policy (controlling specific programs, modifying general characteristics of the intergovernmental system, or significantly altering the balance of roles among governments) have been singularly unsuccessful. The fact of interdependence, along with the persistent sense among the American people that government should continue to be active in many fields to solve pressing and complex problems, has in the past protected the system itself from major reform. Two factors make the task of consolidating majority coalitions in favor of redirection of almost any sort nearly impossible: the multiple interconnections of participants built into the system, and the prospect of the significant dislocations—for agency functions and personnel, program recipients and other interested parties—often generated by reform.

In spite of the desire of both the citizenry and many officials to retain existing programs and the structural status quo, many observers lately have developed an acute sense of the problems of an "overloaded" system. Public enthusiasm for new intergovernmental initiatives seem to have waned. Massive federal budget problems are now a constant reminder of the apparent need to do *something* about spending and to critically scrutinize the worth and cost of each proposal. Opposition has begun to arise to some putatively "cheap" methods of dealing with problems generated by the system's interdependence and complexity. Thus, the American intergovernmental network has reached a stage of difficult decision making. Characteristics of the system render major retrenchment unlikely and, many argue, unwise. Even Ronald Reagan, at the beginning of his second term, has not been consistently able to support a wholesale reform of the network. But the status quo has become the target of nearly all participants.

The system of American intergovernmental relations is under increasing challenge. Can the basic framework continue to fulfill its essential function? The answer to this practical question will go far toward determining whether we can resolve the difficult policy problems of the modern intergovernmental world. At least one crucial aspect of the founders' design remains intact: the arrangement still clearly preserves a network for cooperation and a forum for bargaining about issue-specific disputes among governments that possess both significant autonomy and numerous ties to others.

NAME INDEX

Adams, Charles F. - 136, 147-150, 192
Adams, John Quincy - 253
Advisory Commission on Intergovernmental
  Relations - 50, 75, 245
  positions taken - 113-114, 178, 182
  studies and reports - 76-77, 85-87, 108-109,
  135-136, 139-143, 160-168, 192, 196-197,
  207-216, 241
Alsop, Joseph - 256
Anderson, William - 63-64

Baldrige, Malcolm - 272
Barnes, William - 279
Baroni, Geno - 239
Beer, Samuel H. - 244, 249-259, 302
Bitterman, Henry J. - 204
Break, George F. - 136, 144-146, 161, 167,
  192
Brooks, Jack - 176
Brown, George - 77, 110-116
Bryce, Lord James - 59
Burke, Edmund - 254
Burkhead, Jesse - 166-167

Caiden, Naomi - 122
Calhoun, John C. - 252, 255
Cannon, Joseph G. "Boss" - 165
Cantril, Hadley - 277
Cappalli, Richard B. - 112-113
Carter, Jimmy - 15-17, 176, 184, 188, 233,
  261, 271, 289
Cavanagh, Jerome P. - 97
Clark, Joseph - 61
Cleaveland, Fred - 100
Cochran, Tom - 292-295
Cohen, Wilbur J. - 163
Colbert, Jean Baptiste - 251
Commager, Henry Steele - 249
Conlan, Timothy J. - 245, 265-280, 302
Cuciti, Peggy L. - 173-174

Dahl, Robert A. - 120
Davis, Jefferson - 249
Dawson, Richard - 70
Deese, Manuel - 232

Denning, Bernardine - 173-174
Derthick, Martha - 77-78, 124-134, 137, 196
  204, 241
Diamond, Martin - 18, 20, 28-35, 73
Dillon, John F. - 58-59, 61, 66
Dole, Elizabeth - 273
Dommel, Paul R. - 245, 281-291, 303
Donovan, Raymond - 272
Doolittle, Fred C. - 244, 260-264
Dye, Thomas - 70

Edner, Sheldon M. - 203, 205
Eidenberg, Eugene - 268
Eisenhower, Dwight - 9, 45
Elazar, Daniel J. - 20-21, 36-42, 45, 52-54,
  56-57, 60, 73-74, 133
Environmental Protection Agency. *See* Office
of Water, U.S. Environmental Protection
Agency

Farber, Stephen B. - 177
Fascell, Dante B. - 174-175
Ford, Gerald - 14-15, 55, 170, 268, 271, 289
Fossett, James W. - 137-138, 184-191, 193
Fountain, L. H. - 176
Free, Lloyd - 277
Fried, Edward R. - 163-164

Gallatin, Albert - 39
Gallup, George - 79-80
Glendening, Parris N. - 76, 79-84
Goldberg, Delphis C. - 162-163, 175-176
Goldwater, Barry - 61
Graves, W. Brooke - 156-157
Grodzins, Morton - 18, 20-21, 43-54, 56, 60,
  73-74, 118, 134, 164

Haider, Donald H. - 76-77, 94-103
Hale, George H. - 77, 117-118, 133
Hamilton, Alexander - 19-20, 30, 68, 250-255,
  258-259
Harlan, John M. - 114
Harris, Louis - 80
Harsanyi, John C. - 121
Hart, Henry M., Jr. - 47